HOW TO SELL
REMODELING

by
Robert M. Gorodess

Craftsman Book Company
6058 Corte del Cedro, P.O. Box 6500, Carlsbad, California 92008

Acknowledgements

The author thanks the following for permission to use their materials in this book:

Irv Miller, National Contractors — Chicago, Illinois

Stuart-Hooper Company — Chicago, Illinois

Library of Congress Cataloging in Publication Data

Gorodess, Robert M.
  How to sell remodeling.

  Includes index.
  1. Dwellings--Remodeling. 2. Contractors' operations.
I. Title.
TH4816.G67 1985   692'.8   85-6617
ISBN 0-910460-47-7

Illustrations by Rick Geary

Second printing 1988

Contents

1 Contractors Are Salesman **5**
Why Sell Remodeling? 6
Low Bidders 6
Mr. No Sale vs. Mr. Good Sale 7
The Unqualified Lead 8
It's Always a Bad Time 8
Closing 9

2 Sales Leads **10**
House-to-House Canvassing 10
Professional Circular Distributors 15
Telephone Canvassing 15
Recommendations and Referrals 18
Mass Mailings 18
Advertising 19

3 How to Set Up Appointments **22**
The Six Rules 22

4 How to Make Sales **26**
Go to the Deal First 26
Go in Fresh 27
Enthusiasm is Essential 27

5 Sales Techniques in the Home **31**
Take Command of the Situation 31
Set the Stage to Do Business 32
Face the People You're Selling 33
Eliminate Distractions 33
Icebreakers 33
The Warmup 34

6 Sales Knowledge **36**
A Repertoire of Sales Pitches and Closes . 36
Customers - Basic Personality Types 37
Silence is a Sales Tool 38
Sell Benefits 40
Use Third-Party Selling 42
Anticipate and Overcome Objections 44

7 Financing—The Key to More Sales . . **51**
Becoming a Dealer 51
The APR 59
Co-ops 62
Employee Credit Unions 62
Farm Bureau Loans 62
Private Home Improvement Loans 62
Mortgage Financing 63
Supplement Financing 64
Consolidation 69
Co-Makers 72
FHA and VA Loans 74

8 Closing **88**
The Kitchen Table Close 88
T.O.'s 88
Team Sales 89
Assumption Close 91
Either-Or Close 91
The Story Close 91
The Price Conscious Buyer 92
Summary Close 92
Take it Away and Give it Back 93

9 Insurance Work 95
Policy Requirements 95
Getting Insurance Leads 99
Making the Sale 101
Explain the Payment Procedure 103
Try to Sell Upgrading 103
Getting the Paperwork Right 106
Avoid Collection Problems 113

10 Your Sales Force 116
Method of Compensation 116
The Par System 118
Comparing Methods of Compensation .119
Salesmen's Qualifications 122
Salesmen's Tools 126
Weekly Sales Meetings 126

**11 The Legalities—Permits
and Contracts** 128
The Building Code 128
Getting the Permit 131
Contracts 131
Cash Contracts 136
Installment Contracts 136
Standard Contract Clauses 137

12 Setting Prices 142
Markup 143
Setting Up Your Retail Price Book 143
Job Survey 144
Creating Your Own Price Book 144
Setting the Selling Price 145

13 Selling Room Additions 147
Supplying Materials 148
Avoiding the Pitfalls 150

**14 Selling Awnings, Canopies
and Carports** 151
Measuring Awnings and Canopies 152

15 Selling Bathroom Remodeling 156
Deciding on the Fixtures 157
Bathroom Finishes 159
Consider the Pitfalls 160

16 Selling Ceilings 162
Conversions .162
Fire Repairs 163

17 Selling Concrete Work 165
The Work Order 167
Survey of Pitfalls 168

18 Selling Doors 170
Selling Exterior Doors 170
Interior Doors 173
Storm Doors .175

19 Selling Attic Conversions 178
Watch Out for the Pitfalls 179
Writing the Contract 180

20 Selling New Facades 182
Checklist for Facade Remodeling 184

21 Selling Fences 185
The Fence Sketch Sheet 186

22 Selling Flooring and Tile Work 188
Ceramic Wall Tile 190
Watch for the Pitfalls 192

23 Selling Garages 193
Use a Sketch and Specifications Sheet . .194
Survey of Pitfalls 200

24 Selling Gutters and Downspouts 202
Upgrade the Sale 203
Price the Job Correctly 205

25 Selling Kitchen Remodeling 206
Kitchen Design Tips 208
Kitchen Remodeling Checklist 210
The Sales Presentation 215

26 Selling Painting and Paper Hanging .218
How to Avoid Painting 219
If You Can't Avoid the Painting 220

27 Selling Roofing and Siding 221
How to Measure for Roofing 224
Measuring for Siding 227

28 Selling Windows 228
Window Types 228
Window Glass 230
Selling Storm Windows 232

Index 236

Chapter 1

Contractors are Salesmen

To be a successful contractor, you must be a successful salesman. That's right, contractors are salesmen. Anyone who provides goods or services is a salesman. The doctor, with his engaging bedside manner, is a *salesman*. A politician, with his highly-publicized platform, is a *salesman*. Popular entertainers, such as Frank Sinatra, Barbra Streisand and Michael Jackson, are *salesmen* as well as performers. They do a selling job on the audience. A trial lawyer presenting his case in court is selling the judge or jury. He too is a salesman.

Your business card might read, *Roofer, Custom Home Builder, Kitchen Remodeler, Electrician*, or *Room Addition Expert*. Whatever your specialty, you are also — a salesman. It takes a salesman to get a signature on the bottom line of the contract. This is especially true of the contractor catering to the homeowner or small businessman. The true salesman is a professional. He works constantly to improve his technique. A successful contractor does the same. You can learn a great deal by studying sales methods of other professionals in the construction industry. No doubt, you have. But I expect that this book will provide more good selling information than most contractors learn in a lifetime.

Maybe you want to increase your income. Maybe you want to build a large organization. Maybe you're making plenty of calls, plenty of bids, but you never hear from your prospects again. You've become an expert in preparing bids, but you're not making sales. You're told that your bid was too high, or whatever pops into the mind of the person who wasted your gas, your time, and picked your brains, making a fool of you when you could have been home playing with your kids. Whatever your situation, this book will help you to improve your sales ratio and get you started down the road of successful selling.

In this chapter, I'll talk about some important subjects: why you should sell remodeling, low bidding and why not to, qualified and unqualified leads, and how to close a sale. Later on in the book, I'll take you step-by-step through subjects like how to get business, how to set up appointments, and how to set the stage for sales in the home. We'll discuss financing, pricing, insurance, and contracts, and I'll talk more about closing — proven methods which I've used successfully for my thirty years in construction contracting.

One aim of this book is to show how to get the right price by using good selling methods. My advice is to leave the low bidding to the others. Another purpose is to teach you how to exude confidence by building up a thorough knowledge of your business. This is not a book of theory. It's a practical reference manual based on my years of experience as a remodeling contractor, custom builder and speculative home builder.

Remodelers keep busy

REMODELING continues to thrive despite an otherwise depressed housing industry, according to the National Association of Home Builders.

Renovation spending ran at a seasonally adjusted annual rate of $47.4 billion during the third quarter of 1981 compared with a $38.8 billion rate three years earlier, according to the association.

The average residential remodeler grossed $297,085 on 44 jobs during 1980.

A survey of 460 remodeling firms also listed average prices nationwide for the most common renovations:

- Kitchen remodeling, $7,299.
- Bathroom additions, $5,342.
- Bathroom remodeling, $1,854.
- Room additions, $15,105.
- Finishing an attic, $6,464.
- Finishing a basement, $9,026.
- Adding a garage, $5,466.
- Adding a fireplace, $1,288.
- New siding, $3,231.
- New flooring, $1,497.
- Adding extra insulation, $804.
- Replacing a roof, $3,945.
- Total rehabilitation of a house, $46,104.

Fifty percent of the firms polled were run by the principal owner, and 41 percent by the sole owner. Only 8 percent were run by salaried executives. About 70 percent operated in suburban areas.

NINETY-ONE percent said they developed new business through customer referrals.

Remodeling is recession-proof
Figure 1-1

Why Sell Remodeling?

Remodeling is big business. Look at Figure 1-1. This article ran in the Chicago Tribune on Sunday, April 4, back in 1982. These were average costs for remodeling a home:

Kitchen remodeling, $7,299. Room additions, $15,105. Total house rehabilitation, $46,104.

That's a lot of money. But today's prices are higher still. In the sales business we call remodeling jobs "big ticket" work. And any time you're talking about that much money, there's plenty of room for good profits.

If you're a contractor, the time has never been better to go after this work. Remodeling is the most consistent sector of the construction business. High interest rates will bankrupt home builders. But remodelers go right on building because much remodeling work is financed largely out of the homeowner's bank account, and because financing is far more readily available for remodeling than for new home building. This keeps the remodeling contractor from being dependent on the whims of the home mortgage market. Chapter 7 in this book shows over a dozen ways remodeling may be financed.

Keep in mind also that remodeling contractors make better markups than nearly any other construction contractor.

Low Bidders

I'm sure you've been to auctions. The highest bidder takes all. Some contractors get into an auction every time they make a sale. They try to give the lowest bid. What they're doing is *bidding in reverse.*

We all know what eventually happens to the low bidder. A familiar cartoon that surfaces periodically expresses it best. You probably know the one I mean. A derelict is sitting on a park bench. The caption reads: "I was always the low bidder." The cartoon may be funny, but the facts aren't.

I'm told that small contractors lead the nation in business bankruptcies. I believe it. It's easy to learn the work, and it takes relatively little cash to get started. Most tradesmen think their boss makes too much money. A tradesman quits and goes into business for himself. That's the usual script. The tradesman-turned-contractor gets a few orders by under-bidding his former boss — considering only the cost of material and labor in his bid. He doesn't realize that this is just the tip of the cost iceberg. What else is there? Oh, just a few little items. Worker's Compensation and Public Liability Insurance, state and federal payroll taxes, accountant's fees, truck and vehicle operation costs (including the insurance), employee benefits and the cost of advertising. And that's just a few of them. These "miscellaneous" items come to about half the cost of construction. That's why failure in construction contracting is so common.

Now here's Mr. Low Bidder on the job. One thing goes wrong and then everything seems to go wrong. The building inspector says the job's too close to the lot line. The wiring's supposed to be thinwall instead of romex. The studs have to be on different centers. The rafters are the wrong size. If you've been in the construction trade for any length of time, you know what I'm talking about.

The low bidder can't deal with these problems. He hurts each of us by taking business away from reputable contractors and running up a big debt at the lumberyard or plumbing supply house. Then he files for bankruptcy and goes out looking for a job. He's back to square one — a tradesman again. The cycle is complete. And the damage is done.

Mr. No Sale vs. Mr. Good Sale
Here's another familiar scenario. The phone rings in your office. Mrs. Homeowner would like you to come and give her a figure for a new roof. *Sure, I'll be there at 2 o'clock.* You arrive at 2 o'clock, but the husband isn't at home. "Oh, my husband told me to get the figures and then he'll decide." So what happens? You measure the house, you figure the number of squares, you write up a proposal or you leave a price with Mrs. Homeowner. If you're the lowest bidder, you get the job.

What I've just described is how *not* to go about it. Now here's the way a professional contractor-salesman handles the situation:

"Mrs. Homeowner, I'd like to come when both you and your husband are home. Yes, I realize your husband said to get the price, but I want to discuss the method of application and the quality of the roofing materials with both of you, since you'll both be making this important decision. And, of course, I'd like to discuss the colors with both of you. When does your husband get home from work? Four-thirty? Fine, I'll come at five-thirty. That'll give you time to eat your supper."

After arriving and doing the *icebreaker* and the

warmup that I'll explain later, you figure the number of squares — but you don't give them the price just yet.

"Mr. and Mrs. Homeowner, I'm sure you know that roofing is sold by weight. The roll roofing you see on some houses is only 90-pound. The octagonal roofing you see on older houses is 135-pound. The thick butt shingles that you see on most roofs in your neighborhood are 235-pound. But we only use 240-pound fiberglass seal tab shingles. These shingles can't blow up in the wind. There are little seals under each shingle. The heat of the sun melts the seal so it is fastened permanently to the shingle below. We use fiberglass shingles because fiberglass is rotproof. You're getting a better value.

"We also use a Boston ridge and hip. Of course I'll explain. You see, ordinarily roofers use a strip of roofing along the ridges and across the top. Step over here to the window and I'll show you an example of what I mean on your neighbor's roof. Now what *we* do is use a small shingle overlapping. This is to prevent the nails from rusting and causing leaks in your roof. You see, when the nails are exposed, they'll rust and leak.

"I'd like to tell you a little story, if I may. It goes back to when I first started out in this business. When I was going to high school, I worked for a contractor during summer vacations. Whenever it rained, it was my job to be in the office and answer the flood of phone calls. My boss went to the movies every time it rained. Every call was about a leaking roof. You see, the roofs we used in those days were guaranteed to leak. We used a diamond-point roll roofing and the roofers had to nail each point. The nails rusted after a few rains, and then the roof leaked. That's why I won't use anything but a Boston ridge and hip. I do the job right, so no service calls are needed and you won't be saddled with a leaking roof. The new roof will cost you only $35 per month with no money down. Why don't we use the kitchen table to write up the order?"

You see, we haven't entered into an auction. We've compared quality of roofing, we've demonstrated confidence born of years of experience. We've offered a payment plan. And we've taken the trouble to see that everyone who will participate in the decision was there to hear our pitch. We've shown the printed guarantee of the roofing manufacturer — Johns Manville, G.A.F.,

Flintkote, or whatever brand you use. We've shown the swatch of sample colors. It takes a little bit more effort, but a sale comes in at a fair price, with a reasonable profit for you. What could be better?

The Unqualified Lead

An unqualified lead is a person who contacts you and wants to know how to lay out the job. He wants all kinds of technical information on how the job is done, down to the smallest detail. These individuals are mind-pickers. They have no intention of giving the job to you or to anyone else. They only want to know how to do the job themselves. When one of these freeloaders starts asking technical questions, the best thing to do is to ask him what improvements he's done himself. He'll proudly show you. When he does, you know it's time to bow out. Go to the next lead on your list, or go home and get acquainted with your kids. If he wants to do it himself, fine. But let him get his education somewhere else. You're not running a free school.

There's another type of unqualified lead who's looking for something for nothing — the free lunch, as they say. These guys want everything cheaper. Price is the bottom line. They're difficult to handle and can make your life miserable. You'll find these price-crazy people in every type of business. Quality means nothing to them. When they do spend money, they expect a Cadillac for the price of a Ford. Unless you want to fail in business by consistently being the low bidder, you'd better get a line on these characters. Avoid them at all costs. Let someone else write the order and suffer the losses and the headaches.

If you've traveled in foreign countries, you've had the experience of haggling in bazaars. The haggling stops when the proprietor lets the customer walk away. He doesn't call him back. The minimum profit margin was reached. The merchant has assessed the customer as an unqualified lead.

I had a friend who was in the retail business. Whenever I was in the town of Cicero, I'd stop in and say hello. Bert was constantly marveling at human nature. It was amazing, he remarked, the lengths that people would go to to save two cents. Bert was selling quarts of beer for two cents less than his competition. He catered to an elderly clientele.

Gray-haired ladies would walk out of Bert's store barely able to carry their shopping bags, which bulged with two or three quarts of beer. Although there was another store much closer to where they lived, they'd walk several blocks on icy streets. To save four or six cents, they'd exhaust themselves and risk a dangerous fall on the ice.

Price meant everything to these people.

No matter how much you talk to this type of buyer about quality, he'll say that the price is too high. He can get it cheaper someplace else. He's right. Let him. Here's another example of what I'm talking about. In Chicago, storm windows are a popular item. Department stores and low-price artists have advertised some brands as low as $25 plus installation. Believe it or not, people buy this stuff. In four or five years, they'll have to replace the windows. The aluminum is mill-finished, so it pits and mars. The screens are fiberglass. It's easy for a house cat to rip the screens with its sharp claws. The plastic latches readily snap off and the windows become inoperable.

When these price-obsessed individuals are told these facts by a legitimate salesman, they turn a deaf ear. They can only hear the price. People of this caliber I cancel out. They're unqualified leads. The only time they're qualified leads is when you're selling or building the bottom price line. For this you don't need salesmanship. The only thing that counts is the price.

It's Always a Bad Time

People come up with a million excuses not to buy. These excuses fall into a pattern. A contractor friend of mine told me he could give a reason why his customers don't buy for each month of the year:

January: Broke from Christmas.

February: Kids' college tuition is due.

March: It's been raining all month. There's no work. I don't have a red cent.

April: Had to pay income tax. No money now.

May: We spent a bundle on the kids' proms. No money now.

June: Sent the kids to camp. No money now.

July: Spent everything on our vacation. We're flat broke.

August: It's too hot to think about buying.

September: Spent everything on back-to-school clothes for the kids.

October: Had to buy fuel for the winter. Out of money.

November: Trying to pay off bills. No money now.

December: Spent everything on Christmas. We're flat broke.

To spend time, gas and energy trying to write a contract and get this sort of answer is frustrating, to say the least. Later chapters in this book will teach you how to qualify your prospect so you don't get this runaround.

Closing
The way to improve your batting average as a salesman is by constant practice. Study this book carefully, apply what you learn, and from today forward learn something on every sales call. If you miss a sale, talk it over with your partner or other estimators in your organization. Talk to the company's star salesmen. Ask them how they would handle the same situation. If you're a one-man company, or a small outfit, pump your subcontractors about their experience.

Analyze your missed sales the same way you'd analyze your bid on a losing contract. Study the chapters in this book. Apply the principles I'll explain. This should bring your closing ratio to three or four sales out of five *sits*. A sit is when you've discussed a job in full — in the house — *not* in the back yard or on the porch. To qualify as a *sit* you must have discussed financing, named the price, and asked for the client's signature.

In this chapter, we've discussed the professional approach to selling remodeling and home improvements, and touched briefly on qualified and unqualified leads and closing. In the next chapter, we'll talk about leads in more detail. We'll also cover neighborhood and telephone canvassing, marketing brochures, business cards, advertising circulars, mailings, and ads in the Yellow Pages.

Chapter 2

Sales Leads

As surely as night follows day, a contractor has to keep getting leads to stay in business. Knowing how to develop leads is as important as knowing how to frame a roof or design a kitchen. In this chapter, I'm going to explain the best way to get all the leads you need.

House-to-House Canvassing

House-to-house canvassing is the backbone of many remodeling firms. A canvasser's job is to set up appointments for the boss. In my company, we've used women, high school students, and young men to canvass. Women make good canvassers. Most housewives don't hesitate to answer the door when they see a woman. The result is a higher ratio of interviews if you use female canvassers.

I started out doing house-to-house canvassing at the age of fifteen. Most housewives I encountered thought I was a neighborhood kid. I had a fine record for setting appointments that resulted in sales.

In hiring canvassers, consider the area you want canvassed. Often, people of a particular ethnic group are more receptive to an approach by "one of their own." Obviously, don't assign canvassers to rental areas or high-crime areas.

I suggest you pay your canvassers at least the minimum wage, plus a commission on each appointment they schedule *that results in a sale*. The commission is an incentive for the canvasser to obtain qualified leads.

Match the Canvasser with the Territory

It might seem obvious, but it's absolutely essential to send your canvassers to the right territories. For example, if you're looking for remodeling business, such as kitchen and bathroom remodeling, roofing, porches, or siding, pick an older area. Older houses need this type of work. Your canvassers would be wasting their time in a new subdivision.

The same is true if you're a garage builder. You wouldn't canvass where new homes are being built with attached garages. On the other hand, your storm window and awning canvassers can hit both older neighborhoods and new subdivisions.

Canvassers for awnings, storm windows, soffits, fascia, and siding should size up the house as they approach it. An awning canvasser is wasting his time at a house that already has awnings. A storm window canvasser wouldn't canvass a house that already has storms. A canvasser for remodeling kitchens, bathrooms, dormers, recreation rooms and additions could canvass all homes in the area.

Consider Doing Some Canvassing Yourself

When you do a job on a home, take some time out to walk around the block and knock on some doors. Tell them that you're doing some remodel-

"Mr. Greene, I'm Arabella Schmilowitz from A to Z Remodelers."

ing for Mr. and Mrs. Homeowner down the street. Try to cover at least a four-block area — the four sides of the block you're working on and the four sides of the block across the street from the job site. Don't attempt to do the entire area in one day. My custom is to do a little each day when I visit the job site. It doesn't take long, and I've found it a profitable, inexpensive way to get new customers.

The Sales Talk

Each canvasser should be given a prepared sales talk as a guide. The pitch can be tailored to the canvasser's personality and to the type of remodeling being sold. He (or she) should always address the homeowner by name. Sometimes the canvasser can get the names by simply asking at each house, "By the way, could you tell me the name of the person living next door?" Often the name is on the

mailbox. And if neither of these provides the prospect's name, *just plain ask.* A person who refuses to give his name isn't a lead anyway.

Here's a sample sales talk:

"Mrs. Homeowner, I'm Bob Henry from Royal Builders. Our company's doing some remodeling work just down the street. If you've been thinking of having your kitchen or bathroom remodeled, my boss, Mr. Simpson, can save you quite a bit of money. Since we're already right here in the neighborhood, we can just keep the equipment and tools here, and pass the savings on to you. We've also got a terrific finance plan. With it, we can do the work with no money down, and with your first payment not until two or three months from now. My boss, Mr. Simpson, can explain it to you in more detail. Could I set up an appointment for him to see you and your husband this evening? What time is convenient for you? Eight o'clock? Fine. I'll check with Mr. Simpson to make sure he's free. If he's not, he'll call and arrange for an appointment that will be mutually convenient.''

Here's an example for aluminum or vinyl siding, fascia, and soffit canvassers:

"Hello, Mrs. Homeowner, I'm Frank Milton of Genesee Builders. I noticed that it's almost time for you to paint your house. This is a good time to consider siding instead of painting. You know, you can save the cost of painting simply by having your home covered with insulated aluminum or vinyl siding. Or at least you could have the soffit and fascia covered. The covering will last the lifetime of your home. You'll never have to spend money on painting again.

"Our crews are working in the neighborhood. If I could set up an appointment with you and your husband to meet my boss, Mr. Powers, he could save you a substantial amount of money by keeping the equipment here in the area. My boss is also an authorized dealer at the bank, so he can not only save you money, but he can arrange to do the work *with no money down.* And your first payment won't be till 60 or 90 days from now. In some cases, he's even postponed the first payment for longer still. I know he can work out some real satisfactory terms for you. When can I arrange for you and your husband to meet with Mr. Powers? At eight o'clock this evening? Fine. Could I have your phone number just in case he has a previous appointment and has to call you to reschedule?''

You can see how readily adaptable the basic sales pitch is. It can be tailored for awnings, storm windows, room additions, dormers, garages, roofing, or any other specialty.

When you're working in a neighborhood, people think they'll get the work for a little less money. The bargain instinct is strong. You only have to talk about how it saves money because there's no need to move equipment and materials. This hits the buying button. Everyone loves a bargain.

Forms for Canvassers
Supply your canvassers with a form, in duplicate, for the appointments they make. The original is turned in to the sales manager or business owner. It becomes the record of commissions earned. The canvasser keeps the duplicate as his record. Figure

2-1 is a sample *lead form.* If this form fits your needs, feel free to copy it, and any of the other custom forms in the book. An "instant print" shop can print up five hundred and bind them into pads for somewhere around $30.

Some companies, to keep a tighter rein on their canvassers, have them make out a *call sheet* for each unsuccessful call. See Figure 2-2. These call sheets are good material for follow-up by mailings or phone canvassing. They can be excellent sources for future leads.

Also, it's simple to add up the number of calls made. If you know the area and how far apart the houses are spaced, you can tell quickly if the canvasser is doing a full day's work or just goofing off. But remember: the canvasser's main purpose is to obtain bona fide leads. The number of calls is secondary.

A contractor who uses house-to-house canvassers to obtain leads may come under state laws on home solicitation of sales. Your library should have a copy of *Warren's Forms of Agreements,* published by Matthew Bender, which will give you this information. Or check with your attorney for the law in your state.

Sales Literature
Figure 2-3 shows a *doorhanger,* which the canvasser can leave on the doorknob if nobody's home. Consider designing and printing a supply of similar doorhangers for your canvassers to use.

Also make sure your canvassers have a supply of brochures showing the type of work you do, your company's name, address, and phone number. They should leave one with each person interviewed, whether he or she is a prospect or not. Frequently a person who's not a prospect will pass the brochure to a friend. Or the brochure may spark an interest and phone call from the spouse of the party interviewed. The smart canvasser will rubberstamp his or her name on the brochure, so that these calls will eventually result in a commission.

Marketing brochures are important. Have an attractive brochure for your particular business. If you want to save money, many material suppliers can supply inexpensive brochures printed with your company name. Talk to your storm door and window suppliers, garage door suppliers, fence manufacturers, plumbing manufacturers, or roofing material manufacturer. If brochures can't be printed with your company name, a rubber stamp will do the job nearly as well. Figure 2-4 shows a sample marketing brochure. Another essential

Lead Form

Lead date_____ Canvasser _____

Appointment date and time _____

Name_____

Address _____ Phone _____

City _____ State/Zip_____

Business Phone _____

Best time to call to verify or reschedule appointment _____

Type of work desired _____

_____

_____

_____

_____

_____

Remarks _____

_____

_____

_____

_____

_____

_____

Lead form
Figure 2-1

Call Sheet

Canvasser _____ **Date** _____

Name _____

Street _____ **City** _____ **Phone** _____

House: Brick _____ Frame _____ **Siding?** _____ Aluminum _____ Vinyl _____

Interested in: Concrete work _____ Dormer _____ Garage/carport _____ Roofing _____
Gutters _____ Room addition _____ Storm windows or doors _____
Siding: Whole house _____ Soffit and fascia _____
Remodeling: Bath _____ Kitchen _____ Basement rec. room _____ Other _____

Response: Not interested _____ Call back _____ Can't afford _____ Needs financing _____
Other _____

Name _____

Street _____ **City** _____ **Phone** _____

House: Brick _____ Frame _____ **Siding?** _____ Aluminum _____ Vinyl _____

Interested in: Concrete work _____ Dormer _____ Garage/carport _____ Roofing _____
Gutters _____ Room addition _____ Storm windows or doors _____
Siding: Whole house _____ Soffit and fascia _____
Remodeling: Bath _____ Kitchen _____ Basement rec. room _____ Other _____

Response: Not interested _____ Call back _____ Can't afford _____ Needs financing _____
Other _____

Name _____

Street _____ **City** _____ **Phone** _____

House: Brick _____ Frame _____ **Siding?** _____ Aluminum _____ Vinyl _____

Interested in: Concrete work _____ Dormer _____ Garage/carport _____ Roofing _____
Gutters _____ Room addition _____ Storm windows or doors _____
Siding: Whole house _____ Soffit and fascia _____
Remodeling: Bath _____ Kitchen _____ Basement rec. room _____ Other _____

Response: Not interested _____ Call back _____ Can't afford _____ Needs financing _____
Other _____

Sample call sheet
Figure 2-2

sales tool is the business card. One roofing company I know has an oversized business card. There's a complete sales message on it, featuring a discount price. It's a real eye-catcher. These

roofers have blanketed the city with this card. It's a very successful company.

Business cards are business getters, if you use them correctly. I know one builder who carries a pocket stapler. He staples his business card to restaurant checks and to all the bills he pays. He distributes his card all over town. The returns are not large, but a $5,000 or $10,000 contract is well worth the price of a few business cards.

Remember this: *Always bring all of your sales literature with you when you make your calls.* Make sure all of your salesmen do the same.

Professional Circular Distributors

In many cities, there are companies that will distribute circulars in any targeted area. They usually charge per thousand circulars distributed. Although it might seem that it's more expensive to use these services, it's often cheaper in the long run. Here's why. You don't have to supervise the carriers. There will be no wasted circulars, nor will any be dumped into a sewer or a convenient garbage can. Your circulars are delivered where they're supposed to go.

If your city doesn't have a distributing service, organize a crew and appoint a crew manager to see that the circulars are properly distributed. If you have teenage kids, you have a ready-made crew. This is an excellent way for teenagers to earn extra money. If you use a salesman, he can be canvassing or passing out circulars during his slack hours, when he doesn't have appointments. He should stamp his name on the circulars so he automatically gets the leads that respond. As a rule of thumb, circulars generally bring in one lead for each 100 circulars distributed.

The profit on circulars is easy to figure. Simply divide the profit from circular-generated sales into the cost of printing and distribution.

Telephone Canvassing

Telephone canvassing is also effective. There are several ways to do it. If you're a one-man company or builder, ask your wife and children to do your telephone canvassing. Or, you can do it in your spare time — if you have any.

Make calls in the neighborhood where you're working. Explain that you're doing some work at the address of your job site. Tell your prospects about saving money because you're working in the area.

Many telephone companies have a special book which lists subscribers' street addresses and phone

Door hanger
Figure 2-3

**Marketing brochure
Figure 2-4**

numbers. These books are called *cross indexes* or street address directories. You can get one from the phone company in your area.

Before you do any phone canvassing, evaluate the area to be canvassed. For example, it would be a waste of time and money to canvass apartment buildings or new subdivisions if you're a remodeler. Use the cross index phone directory to pick out streets that are residential and areas where you know there's a demand for your work. Many contractors use professional phone canvassers. Professional canvassers often work from their homes. Normally, you arrange to pay the phone bill. Some builders set up a room in their office, or provide desk space for a phone canvasser. This gives the builder, or the phone room manager, the opportunity to monitor the calls and evaluate and assist the canvassers in improving their pitch.

Phone canvassers normally receive an hourly wage, plus a commission on each lead that results in a sale.

The Phone Sales Pitch
Your phone sales approach might go like this:

"Hello, Mrs. Homeowner. I'm Janine Perry from Roberts Construction Company. The reason I called is my company's doing new siding work in your neighborhood. I thought I'd ask if you've considered having your house covered with insulated aluminum or vinyl siding. If you have a brick home, you might like to have the soffit and fascia covered. Having this work done could save you money. For one thing, you wouldn't have to hire a painter every three or four years. Pretty soon, the siding (or soffit and fascia covering) will have paid for itself.

"It will also keep your husband from balancing high up on ladders trying to do the painting himself. It can be dangerous work for someone not used to it, and it's really not worth the risk. A fall from roof height is no joke.

"Right now, we're having an off-season sale. Since our crew is already working in your neighborhood, it will save you some extra money. My boss is an F.H.A. dealer. He can do the work with no money down, and will get you low monthly payments. He can even arrange it so your first payment isn't due until about two months after the work is done.

"You have everything to gain — discounted price, easy payments at low interest rates, and top-quality work.

"What time would be most convenient to set up an appointment for you and your husband to meet with my boss? Seven-thirty Thursday night? Fine. By the way, Mr. Roberts loves coffee. I've known cases where he's taken $100 off the price when treated to a good cup of coffee."

Suppose you can't make an appointment with this sales pitch? Simply continue as follows:

"I'm sure that you know that we're remodeling experts. We do kitchen and bathroom remodeling. Are you interested in having your bath or kitchen remodeled? Oh, I see. Well, that's fine. Perhaps you'd like an extra room. Enclosing a porch or adding a dormer is an economical way to add an extra room to your house. May I set up an appointment for the boss to see you and your husband about an extra room space? No? Then maybe you can tell me what type of home improvement you and your husband would like to have. We handle electrical and plumbing repairs, concrete work, a garage . . . You name it, we do it."

If you still can't make an appointment for any type of work, close the conversation with:

"I'm happy that you don't have to spend any money for work on your house right now. Do you think any of your neighbors or friends might be interested in having some work done?"

Of course your phone solicitor can adapt the sales pitch to the situation. Be sure the tone is flexible, natural and casual. Don't ever let it sound like a canned talk. The phone canvasser should project a smile.

Tailor the sales talk to your individual specialty. It'll pay big dividends to write up a phone pitch and revise it. Then revise it again and keep on revising and polishing until it's producing maximum results. This is how professional marketing companies do it. They're very successful at phone canvassing. You will be too if you work at perfecting your sales calls.

Remember this about phone work. The longer you keep people on the phone talking about their home, what work they'd like to have done, and what kind of financing they need, the closer you are to making the sale.

Alternate Sales Talk
"Hello, Mrs. Homeowner, I'm Vickie Donahue from Roberts Construction Company. I under-

stand that you have a frame house. It's exciting to be a homeowner, isn't it? Can you tell me how many years you've been living there? Eight wonderful years. I'll tell you the reason I called, Mrs. Homeowner. All homes have to be painted every so often. The cost of painting today is very high. My boss, Mr. Roberts, can cover your house with insulated aluminum or vinyl siding so that it will never have to be painted again.

"Many homowners have told me that time seems to fly between paint jobs. Today, painting a home is so costly, what with ever-increasing wages, insurance, and everything else. I'm sure you know well enough what inflation is doing to our money. Well, one way to beat this frequent cost is to have the house covered with aluminum or vinyl siding. Then the job is done forever. No more painting costs. You know what it costs to have your house painted today. In ten years, when you'll still be having to get it painted, it's going to be double. New siding is a one-time cost — and that's it. Forever. And what's more, my boss can finance the work with F.H.A. There'll be no money down, and your first payment won't be due for several months. Sounds terrific? Well, it is!

"What time would be most convenient to set up an appointment for you and your husband to meet with Mr. Roberts? Seven-thirty Thursday night? Fine. By the way, Mr. Roberts loves coffee. I've known cases where he's taken $100 off the price when he was treated to coffee."

How people love to save money!

Before I went into business for myself, I worked for a remodeling contractor. The company had fourteen salesmen selling remodeling. Our phone-room canvassers supplied each salesman with an average of three to five solid leads a day. Their sales talk was very much like the pitch above. It included the clincher about the coffee. I never drank so much coffee in my life.

The first thing I'd hear when I'd walk into a prospect's home was, "How about a cup of coffee?" People seem to be more relaxed when they drink coffee. The sales barriers are down. The coffee-klatch creates an atmosphere of friendship and trust. The salesman is no longer an adversary. Normally, people only drink coffee with family and close friends. Drinking coffee puts the salesman in this intimate category. Believe me, a coffee lead is a first rate lead.

Recommendations and Referrals

Recommendations are the finest leads you can get. When you close your briefcase after writing up a contract, always ask: "Do you have any friends who are planning to have work done? If you'd care to pass their names along to me, I'll have a nice gift for you. Give me a ring at the office anytime."

You can also get referrals from old customers by telephone canvassing them at intervals after you've completed their job. Sometimes this will bring in new business from an old customer. Maybe your last job was a new bathroom. Now they need the kitchen remodeled, or a dormer, a garage, or a family room. What better source for new business than a former customer who's happy with your work? Repeat customers are a golden source of leads. Don't overlook them.

Referrals from Friends and Acquaintances

Have as many people as you can out looking for business for you. Your lodge brothers, former customers, and subcontractors' employees are all potential sources of referrals. Put your insurance broker to work for you. The tellers at your bank talk to a great many people every day. Clerks at the lumberyard are an excellent source of leads. They often know homeowners who are considering repair or remodeling work. Give them a reason to recommend you. Talk about your business to waitresses, clerks, your friends at the health club — anybody you meet regularly. Be friendly to everyone, and drop an occasional hint: "If you ever know of anyone needing (the type of work you do), let me know, will you? I'd sure appreciate it." Believe me, you'll get results. The business will come in if you have the numbers on your side.

Mass Mailings

Mass mailings are an excellent way to get leads. The average ratio of returns is only about 1%, which I know doesn't sound like much. But think again. You might pick up a $10,000 contract for the price of a stamp.

One effective mailing I've used is a large card telling about the type of work we do, with boxes to be checked off. The homeowner indicates what he or she needs. I use a postage-paid business reply card, so the homeowner can drop it in the mail without having to stop and look for a stamp. Be sure to mention that you'll give an estimate with no obligation and that financing is available. Ask the recipient for the best time to make an appointment.

It's a good idea to provide space for both phone numbers (home and work). Figure 2-5 shows a typical mailing piece.

One remodeling contractor I know has been using cards like this for thirty years. He tries to spend one hour each day addressing cards. When he's so loaded with work that he doesn't have time to do this chore personally, he has members of his family address the cards. Irv is very successful.

Specialized Mailings

I've used mailings to a specialized list to get leads for many years. My first specialized mailing was sent to insurance adjusters. It was a simple brochure that explained our work and quoted a few prices. Sales started out slowly. First one and then another adjuster tried us. They told other adjusters to give me a call when they needed a reliable contractor. Over the years, adjusters have switched companies and told their new associates about us. We now have an active list of adjusters, and we mail to them at least twice a year. This is a great source of leads. When an adjuster recommends you to a client, it's like walking into the sale on a red carpet.

The mailing list of your old customers is an excellent source of new leads. A good pitch usually includes an offer of a premium or gift. Offer at least $50 or $100 for any referral of a friend or neighbor that results in a sale. This type of mailing gets results. It's probably even more effective than a telephone canvass of your old customers. Figure 2-6 is a letter I've used effectively. Write a similar one yourself, and have it printed on your letterhead.

Advertising

Yellow Pages ads should be part of every lead development program. I've found this to be a steady source of business. I prefer buying a large number of small ads, rather than one large one. Place an ad wherever prospects might look in the Yellow Pages. For example, if you're a remodeling contractor, you could advertise in the following Yellow Page sections:

- Bathroom Remodeling
- Carpentry
- Concrete
- Doors

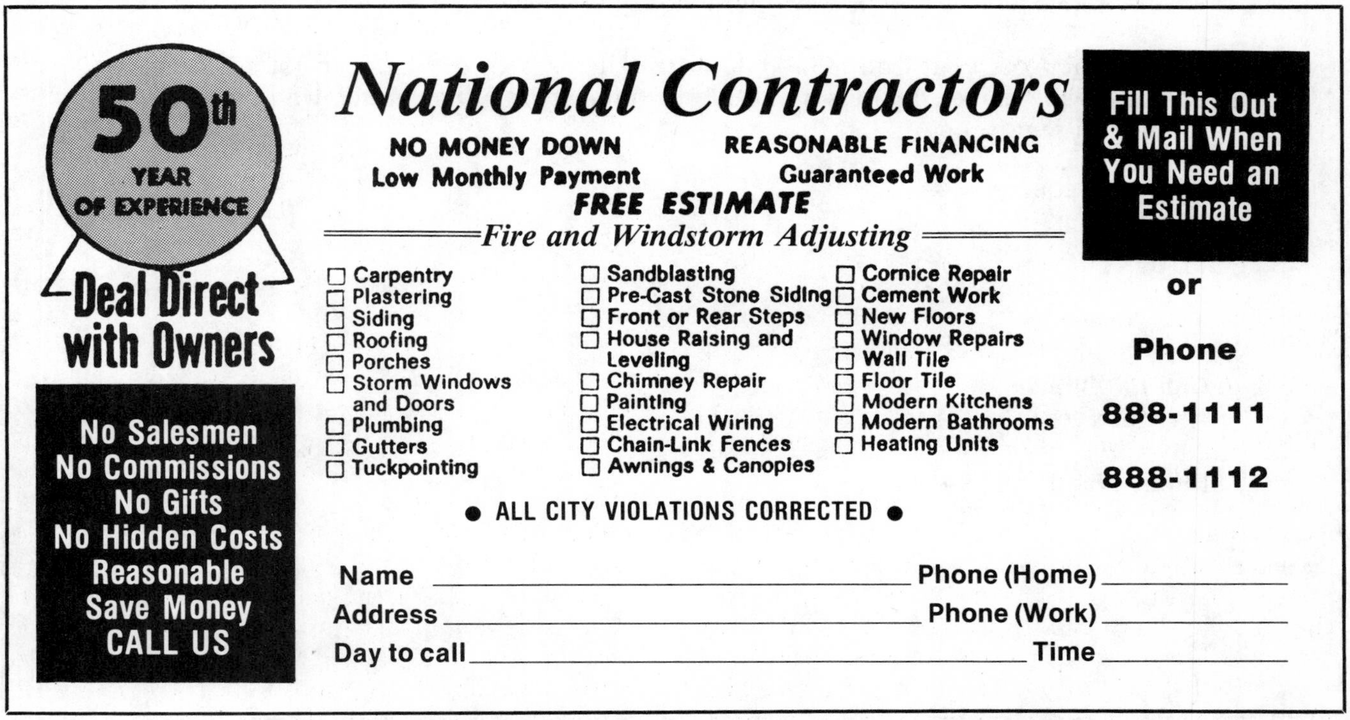

Mass mailing piece
Figure 2-5

Dear Friend:

Advertising for Business Costs Us Money!

We will pay you this cost. For each name you submit that results in a sale for us, we'll pay you the sum of $ _____.

Ask your friends what remodeling they are considering. Ask the people that you work with. Ask your lodge brothers. Ask the members of your service clubs, Elks, Moose, Kiwanis, Rotarians and other business clubs. Ask your gin rummy, mah-jongg or poker group. What kind of work do they need to have done to their homes?

The more names you submit, the more money you earn.

Let us hear from you! Call me today, or use the back of this letter to jot down your name and the names, addresses and phone numbers of your friends who may be interested in remodeling.

Cordially yours,

Bob the Builder
Any Street
Any City
Phone Number 123-4567

Mailer for previous customers
Figure 2-6

- Facade (or Front Elevation)
- Fences
- Garages
- Gutters and Downspouts
- Kitchen Remodeling
- Porches and Stoops
- Roofing
- Room Additions
- Siding

Newspaper Advertising

Of course, you can also get leads through newspaper, television, or radio advertising. These ads pull in the leads. Some will pull heavy. Contractors who use them will tell you how effective they are. But this kind of advertising takes a hefty budget. I recommend that you use a good advertising agency if you're planning to advertise in the media. The agencies do a better job of preparing copy than the media ad representatives.

Leads, leads, and more leads are the lifeblood of a contractor's business. The idea is to get the maximum number of leads at a minimum cost. Which method should you use? The answer is, all of them! Don't limit yourself by using only one or two methods. Attack the problem on all fronts. Remember, fundamentals never change. Keep promoting your business. Have as many people as you can out looking for business. You *will* get results.

In this chapter, we've talked about leads — how to find people who need your services. In the next chapter, I'll tell you how to set up appointments with the leads you've found.

Chapter 3

How to Set Up Appointments

Every contractor who's tried to make a sale has had at least one of the following experiences:

1) In the middle of your presentation the husband says, "Excuse me. It's time for me to go bowling. Please give the rest of the details to my wife, and give her the price. We'll be in touch with you."

2) As you ring the front door bell, the wife comes out and says, "My husband will be right with you. I'm due at the P.T.A. meeting in 10 minutes."

3) You arrive on time for your appointment and the wife says, "My husband had to work overtime. He won't be able to keep the appointment, but you can go ahead and give me all the details."

4) The wife stays in the kitchen and never comes out to find out what's going on. When it comes time for a decision, the husband says, "I have to talk it over with my wife."

5) "I'm the man of the house, so I do all the business for the family."

6) "My husband told me to get several estimates. Just give me the details and the price, and we'll get back to you."

7) "Everything you say is fine, but I have to discuss it with my dad (mother, mother-in-law, brother, son, etc.)"

The Six Rules

Every sales pitch should end with a decision. None of the seven sales efforts above ended in a decision. Without that essential decision, you never get a sale. Avoid the "no decision" trap by following six simple rules when making an appointment:

1) Never make an appointment unless all concerned parties will be present.

2) Be certain that all concerned parties will be home during your *entire* visit.

3) Assume that the sales pitch will take two hours.

4) Find out as much as you can about the prospects' ideas for the work they want done before the meeting begins.

5) Never make an appointment unless the work is to be done now.

6) Always ask if the prospects plan on paying cash or expect to finance the work.

Here's an example of a good call used to set up an appointment. Read it carefully. We'll discuss it for the rest of this chapter.

"Yes, Mrs. Homeowner, we'll be happy to come to your home and give you a free estimate on the work you want done. Just what sort of work did you have in mind? I see. Do you have any special ideas on layout, and so on? Oh, really? That's interesting. When would you like the job to get started? I see. Have you or your husband made plans for Wednesday night? No? That's good. What time does your husband get home from work? Five-thirty? Well, let's leave you time to have your dinner, and I'll come by sometime after six-thirty. I can't be as precise as I'd like to be about the time I can get there, as I have a lot of jobs going, but it will be between six-thirty and eight-thirty. Is that O.K. with you? Fine, I'll see you both Wednesday evening.

"By the way, will anyone else be involved in making this decision? I see. Will your mother-in-law be present when I'm there? Wonderful. If you're like most people, when it comes to a big expense like a car, a house, or this type of improvement, you'll want to have it financed. Am I correct, Mrs. Homeowner? We've been dealing with First Federal Savings & Loan for a number of years now. They provide attractive rates and offer low payment loans."

Now let's see what we've accomplished with this short phone call, and how the rules worked in our favor.

Rule Number 1: Never make an appointment unless all the key people will be present— We've determined that all decision-makers will be present. This is essential. When this fundamental rule is violated, you can be sure that you're headed for a "no decision."

Here's why:

Mrs. Homeowner, without consulting her husband, buys groceries, household items, and clothes for the kids. Mr. Homeowner, without consulting his wife, might buy a new tire, a set of golf clubs, or some gardening equipment. But when it comes to a big-ticket item, a purchase that runs into several thousand dollars, the sale will require the consent of both parties.

Here's another thing to keep in mind: If one party's missing, it's easy for a prospect to say, "We have to talk it over with Frank's mom. Don't

worry — we'll call you."

Frequently this story is merely a ploy to stall. These are people who are too meek to say no, or are afraid to tell you that they're going to get another estimate. Maybe they were only trying to get an idea of what Aunt Edna or Mr. Perkins down the street paid for a job.

If you're dealing with a widow, ask her outright on the phone, "Do you have a son? A son-in-law or a daughter, perhaps? Do they advise you?" The rule about all parties being present is especially important in this case. Make the appointment only when you know that the concerned parties will be present. This is not to say that some widows don't make up their own minds. I've sold to plenty of widows, and many were strong characters and made their own decisions. But some widows feel more comfortable if they have someone in their family help with larger decisions. I've also found that many widows prefer to pay cash.

Remember this: You can't repossess a home improvement like you can an automobile or a TV set. You need everybody's signature on the contract. The finance papers require the signatures of everyone who has an equity interest in the property. This often includes the in-laws. Maybe they put up part of the money for the original purchase of the property. Without their signatures, you don't have a sale. They can't sign the papers if they're not present. If you leave the papers for the in-laws to sign later, you could be waiting forever. Remember, they didn't hear your presentation. They may bum-rap the entire improvement or whittle it down to nothing.

It's impossible to sell to an absent party. The rule sticks. *All parties involved must be present.* That way you have an opportunity to sell all parties to the transaction, and get all the signatures. If you fail, at least you know that you weren't selling with one arm tied behind your back.

Rule Number 2: Be certain that all concerned parties will be home during your entire visit— In our sample phone call, we found out that the decision-makers had no other plans for the evening. They could stay home and listen and participate while we made the sale.

Rule Number 3: Allow two hours for your appointment— We blocked out two hours for the appointment. Promptness used to be just a virtue, but a lack of this virtue has cost many a contractor a sale.

Be certain that all concerned parties will be home during your entire visit

Suppose you have two appointments. The first took much longer than you expected. You can't leave in the middle of a sale to go to another — that's throwing away bread and butter to search for cake.

But a dozen things can happen during a business day to upset your schedule. Your tradesmen need material on the job site in a hurry. You have to drop everything and race to the lumberyard. You go to collect for a previous job, only to discover that you need lien papers. You have to run all around town picking up waivers. A customer called and wanted you to write up an extra. It took much longer than you thought it would. Your office girl called in sick and you had to take phone calls, and so on.

By allowing two hours, you cover any emergency that might occur.

What do you do when you miss an appointment? Let's face it, it *can* happen. An emergency comes up — an appointment has to give. Or maybe you're tied up closing a sale. I recommend the following steps when you have to reschedule an appointment.

When you're running late, get to the nearest phone and notify the prospects that you'll be delayed a bit. If it'll be more than a half hour, have your office call. If it's after office hours, have your wife phone the prospect and tell him or her that you've been detained due to an emergency.

If you miss an appointment entirely, and contact was not made, phone the customer the next day. Tell him or her you're sorry that you missed the appointment. Now pay close attention. Over the years, the only story I've found that the public will accept if you miss an appointment is:

"I had an accident on the freeway. It took the police an hour to get there, and another hour to get my car towed in. Then I had to make arrangements to get home. I've arranged for a car this morning, so I'd like to set up a new appointment for tonight, if possible."

Everyone accepts this story. They can relate to it. Tell them the truth — that you were held up at City Hall trying to get building permits, or had trouble with an inspector on the job, and they won't believe you. But an accident will get you not only a new solid appointment, but the sympathy of the prospect. A bad break turns into an advantage for you. Try it, it works.

Rule Number 4: Find out as much as you can about the prospects' ideas for the work they want done— Give Mrs. Homeowner all the time in the world to tell you about her ideas. (Notice that we've done this in our sample phone talk.) But keep your ears open. If she expounds at great length, you can bet a tape measure that a competitor's been there and given her a price. I'll tell you how to handle this situation later in this book.

Rule Number 5: Never make an appointment unless the work is to be done now— Is the work to be done now? Not next year, not next month, not in the spring, not the fall, but *now*. We've asked the prospect this question and received an affirmative answer. This is very important. Here's why: Too much water will pass over the dam before these prospects finally decide to buy. Prices will go up, but the prospect may try to get you to honor the price you gave last spring. That's not fair. Since you last saw them, they've had twenty different opinions. Their father-in-law has made a suggestion that changes the whole job around. More bright ideas have come from the husband's bowling buddy and from one of the guys at work. You don't even recognize the job that you laid out and priced. They want you to hold still on the price but are looking at a different job entirely.

Here's how I would handle this situation, starting at square one:

"Mrs. Homeowner, we'll be very happy to figure the job for you when you're ready to have it done. Please give us a call. Because labor and material costs are constantly changing, we've had to make it a company policy to only figure jobs that are going to be done right away."

Rule Number 6: Always ask if the prospects plan on paying cash or expect to finance the work— We've asked this question in our sample talk. By doing this, we find out more about the prospect. Cash buyers are usually shoppers. They have the cash, so they can be independent. You can expect that they'll be getting other bids. A finance customer, on the other hand, usually needs help getting the money. These are much easier sales to wrap up. Especially when you can offer a monthly payment they can handle. (I'll talk about financing in more detail in Chapter 7.)

The work must be financeable. That's the other thing we need to establish. There's not much point in setting up an appointment if the people can't pay for the work, or if they have no idea how expensive remodeling is.

Believe me, qualification will save you hours of frustration.

Ask the question, "Did you expect to pay cash, or have the work financed like most people do?" That brings the issue out into the open. "I expected to pay cash," is the reply. Your rebuttal is: "Oh? Even if the job runs between $8,000 and $10,000, as most of these jobs do?" The answer comes back: "Oh, I didn't think it would cost that much."

At this point the prospect will either cancel the appointment or opt for financing. Here's your comeback, by the way: "Most of our customers have us arrange for a loan at First Federal Savings & Loan. We've been dealing with them since 1955. Their interest rates are low and we'll get you a low monthly payment."

This type of pitch will often result in a solid appointment that will lead to a sale. The prospects weren't aware of the financing possibilities. You opened up a new vista to them. You showed them how they could have their cake and eat it too. Even though they don't have the cash, they can have the work done. That's good news for your buyers.

In this chapter, I've explained how to set up appointments to make sales. I've given you six rules to follow. I advise you to follow them religiously. They are the foundation of your sales effort. Disregard them, and you're probably talking "no sale." In the next chapter, I'll tell you *how to go out and make those sales* and discuss some methods I've used to prepare myself psychologically for successful selling.

Chapter 4

How to Make Sales

Go to the Deal First

Does this sound like one of your typical days? You look over the calls you have to make. There's a complaint to straighten out, a collection to be made, an extra to be signed, and several leads. The time on the leads is open. This happens sometimes when the prospect's going to be home all day and tells you to come by at any time.

One of the leads came from a tradesman. A prospect saw your tradesman on the job and told him to send you around. The tradesman didn't get the phone number. From the little he did tell you, you know that the prospect's shopping. However, you have another lead you know is a buyer, a solid prospect. You could smell it when you made the appointment.

Well, you decide to go and make the collection first, then go to write up the extra, take care of the mildly promising leads, and finally, do the solid lead, since you'll have worked your way across the city by that time.

Needless to say, the collection takes longer than you thought it would. The people have some friends over, and they want to talk about the job they're planning to do "in the future." Of course, you're polite. You know it's not a lead right now, but naturally you want to keep the door open.

Then it's on to the extra. This guy wants to go over every facet of the job. He insists that you stay for coffee and cake. Very pleasant, but *wow, where's the time going?*

This call was a real mistake on your part. Extras should be taken care of only during business hours. Normally, the job superintendent handles this sort of thing. If you have to take care of it personally, the best way is to run in during the day, find out what the extra is, and tell the lady of the house that you'll figure it at the office and mail the bid to them. They can sign the form right away and return it.

Your minor leads turn out sour. You can't get a building permit for the first one, and the second is unfinanceable. They simply can't qualify for a loan.

I imagine you've heard of Murphy's Law: "If anything can go wrong, it will." Most contractors know it real well.

Well, Murphy's Law hits you smack in the pocketbook when you get to that sure deal we talked about earlier. It happens like this: You finally arrive at the "solid deal" house. You're greeted warmly. Gee, they're sorry, they would have told you not to come, but they didn't know where to get hold of you on such short notice. About an hour ago they received a phone call from their brother-in-law. He'd just learned that they were going to have some new kitchen cabinets put in. It seems he has a friend who's a carpenter. He works for wages only. They'll save a bundle of money. It's just too good a deal for them to pass up. Lucky thing, too. "If you'd been here an hour earlier, we'd have signed up with you."

Strike three! You feel like you've been kicked in the face. You could almost taste that sale. The evening is a blank as far as business is concerned.

You have just violated a very important rule in selling:

Go to the deal first.

In the early 1950's, I made a number of sales calls with a Chicago remodeling salesman named Mike Dalton. The first thing out of Mike's mouth as we got into the car to make our calls was, "Let's go to the deal first." Mike lived and practiced this rule until it became like a religion with him. Mike Dalton is a highly successful remodeling salesman. He writes a lot of business by going to the deal first. That cuts his chance of getting slammed by Murphy's Law.

So, the rule is: *Go to the deal first.*

Go in Fresh

You've been up since early morning, tending to all the problems that come up during a business day. Now it's evening and you have an appointment to make a sale. You're worn out. That's not good. Because the moment you ring that front door bell, you're on the firing line. You have to be in the peak of condition. You're now a *contender.*

Back in the 1950's, I learned another useful trick from an old pro. When you arrive at the prospect's home, park at least four houses away. Turn off your lights and ignition, and take a nap for ten or fifteen minutes. You'll wake up refreshed and at peak mental alertness. For me, this mental edge gained by a ten-minute nap has been the difference in making many a sale. I'm refreshed and better able to follow the body language of the buyers — an important sales tool. I'm more alert in laying out the work, and especially in pricing the job.

When you're fresh, you have more assurance. You're more confident that you'll get the order. It's easier to have the fire, spirit and enthusiasm that make for a successful sales presentation. Believe me, the time you spend taking a nap will pay off in more sales. And you don't need to worry about losing the fifteen minutes. You've allowed yourself two hours to get to the appointment.

Enthusiasm is Essential

What is enthusiasm? It's what sells remodeling. I'm going to quote from *Funk & Wagnall's Stan-*

dard Handbook of Synonyms, Antonyms and Prepositions, by James C. Fernald:

"*Enthusiasm*" has now chiefly the meaning of an earnest and commendable devotion, an intense and eager interest, emotional zeal for a cause. Against the hindrances of the world, nothing great and good can be carried without a certain "*Fervor,*" "*Intensity*" and "*Vehemence*" (Italics mine).

Fervor, Intensity and *Vehemence.*

These joined with faith, courage and hopefulness make *enthusiasm.*

Note these descriptions:
  "Earnest and commendable devotion."
  "Intense and eager interest."
  "Emotional zeal."
  "Fervor [and] intensity."

Professional salesmen universally acclaim enthusiasm as one of their most important tools. Have you ever noticed that enthusiasm is contagious? When you're with a person who's enthusiastic about a subject, you get involved, you become interested, and you participate.

My construction company is in Chicago, but I live in a condo in Florida during the winter months. Every Saturday night during the winter there's a show in the clubhouse. I've noticed that the acts that radiate enthusiasm seem to have a charisma of their own. These acts usually get a standing ovation. Other acts without enthusiasm receive only polite applause, no matter how technically proficient. The enthusiasm of the actors is infectious.

As a young man, I was transferred to New Orleans by the company I was working for. My wife and I rented the first floor of a new duplex in Metarie Ridge. We were the first occupants. The apartment didn't come with a stove or refrigerator.

My wife and I went first to Maison Blanche, the largest department store in New Orleans. The salesman was polite. He answered all our questions and knew all the prices and features of each appliance. We told him we'd let him know, that we were shopping around. The sales pitch he gave us was brief and to the point. Later, I reflected on the incident, and I think I know what went through his head. "A couple of Yankee kids, probably tourists, with some time to kill. . ."

We went next to D.H. Holmes and Company. The salesman was very abrupt. He walked us over to the appliances. "The prices are marked," he said. "Let me know if you see something you like." I was a little annoyed. I said: "Lil, let's go

Enthusiasm is essential

back to Maison Blanche and buy the stove and refrigerator there.'' I started to walk away, and my wife followed.

The salesman heard me and interrupted our walk. ''I have to show you something,'' he broke in. In the twinkling of an eye he turned into the most inspired salesman I ever saw. He was so enthusiastic about a G.E. refrigerator and a Detroit Jewel Stove that he just carried us along with him. He knew the benefits of his products, he knew our situation, he knew the sizes we'd need. My wife found herself telling him that we had a family of six — three adults and three children. The salesman discussed space requirements with my wife, making a strong point about how, with such a large family, we needed immediate delivery. Then he asked me some questions. Who did I work for? Where did we do our banking? Did we rent or own? He gathered a few other facts, then he informed us that he'd open a credit account for us immediately.

Lo and behold, we bought from a man we were going to walk out on. My wife continued to patronized D.H. Holmes over every other depart-

ment store in New Orleans. Since that day, we've bought many other appliances, but I've never met a salesman since who knew so much about appliances — who could work up infectious enthusiasm that swept me off my feet.

Do you want to see a master salesman at work? Go to a charity fund-raising event or watch a telethon on T.V. There will usually be at least one speaker who could be described as ''dynamic.'' Sure he's dynamic. He believes in his cause, and he generates an enthusiasm that electrifies the audience. His enthusiasm generates more pledges than a dozen speakers with carefully reasoned appeals.

Fund raising is tough work. You're trying to get donations to a cause from which the donor cannot possibly derive any material benefit. Infectious enthusiasm causes people to just give their money away. Try to get a donation from these same people when they're not enthusiastic about what you're selling. You'll be lucky if all you're shown is the front door. The difference is in the *enthusiasm*, the infectious enthusiasm of the speaker, who is in reality a master salesman.

Sell the benefits of your work— Your job is simple in comparison to fund raising. You only have to work up your enthusiasm for the type of benefits you're company provides. *Be enthusiastic!* That's all you have to do. Find something of key benefit in the type of work you do and become genuinely enthusiastic about it. Here's an example of what I mean:

I can work up enthusiasm that knows no bounds when talking about traffic patterns in a room addition.

When I have a roofing customer, I get excited about how old-time roofs were really guaranteed to leak on account of the exposed nails — and how the roofs we install have no exposed nails.

When I'm selling a home, I mention the size of the eaves. Fine and good, you say. Eaves are a commodity like anything else. Everybody has them. They're all about the same. Sugar is sugar, no matter where you buy it. So why pay more? I'll tell you why. Just listen for a moment.

"Now I'd like to show you another advantage: We've made the eaves a full two feet wide. This is to shade your home in the summer months. You won't have to spend money on awnings. This will also keep your drapes from fading. Furthermore, in winter, it will keep the snow from piling up in your windows. Please note that we've boxed in the eaves. This is so that bees and wasps can't nest in your home. I know you don't want that. Right?"

You'd be surprised how many sales I've made where this latter point was the clincher. Almost automatically, the buyer will reply, "You're so right, George. I don't want to hassle with bees and wasps."

Understand this: I'm excited that this is going to be my clients' home. I want the best for them. I'm not going to sell them a house that will present problems later on. I saw a potential problem, got involved in it, and cured it. When I bring this to my clients' attention, they're happy because it's one less home-ownership problem that they'll have to face.

I stumbled on this gambit by accident. My company, like every other garage builder in the Chicago area, boxes in our eaves. One day I was making a sale to a family that had just moved to the suburbs from rural Kane County. The lady remarked, "We had a lot of trouble with wasps in

our last home. I want you to fix the roof of the garage so we don't get any." Earlier, I'd mentioned casually that we boxed the eaves. That was technical talk. It didn't penetrate. Then she mentioned her wasp problem and brought it out. Since that day I've been enthusiastic about boxed eaves. The benefit of boxed eaves is that no bees or wasps can nest in them. A minor item, you say. Not if it's what motivates the buyer to sign on the dotted line. Isn't that what it's all about?

Use your knowledge to feed your enthusiasm— How can you motivate prospects to buy if you're only going through the motions — just doing your job quoting a price. A salesman who's obviously bored is also boring his prospects. A salesman who lapses into technical talk about studs and plates might as well be talking a foreign language. There's no enthusiasm there.

On the other hand, if you enjoy your work, if you have a thorough knowledge of the work, if you know the reasons why each bit of material is used and why it's installed the way it is, you automatically have the magic ingredient — enthusiasm.

I find great satisfaction in being a builder. You probably do too. I get an inner glow whenever I drive down certain streets and say to myself, "Remember when you built that house for Mr. and Mrs. Jacoby? That house looks as good or better than the day we finished it." The Jacoby house, and others like it, are the monuments I'll leave behind. They're something I created. Not only houses, but garages, room additions and dormers. I have designed and created something for the whole world to see.

Everyone in the construction business has reason to be proud and enthusiastic about what we do. Shelter is one of man's most basic needs. It also happens to be the most expensive. Being proud and knowledgeable about your trade makes it easy to be enthusiastic when you talk to customers. Think enthusiastic and be enthusiastic. Enthusiasm is your secret weapon for making sales. Do *you* buy from bores? Don't you yourself prefer to buy from knowledgeable, enthusiastic, professional people?

Someone said, "Give me a lever long enough and I'll move the world." Enthusiasm is the lever in the gentle art of persuasion called salesmanship.

Be enthusiastic about your company, about your craftsmen, about your job layouts, about the fine material that you use, about the benefits of the job you're selling. Be enthusiastic throughout your entire presentation, and your fervor, intensity and zeal will automatically carry you into the close.

In this chapter I've hit on a few of the high points in making sales. In the next chapter I'll go deeper into specific sales techniques: setting the stage, the icebreaker, and the warmup.

Chapter 5
Sales Techniques in the Home

You've read the first four chapters of this book and applied the principles I outlined. You've qualified a prospect. He's not a "tire-kicker" — a looker never expecting to spend a dime. This prospect intends to buy *now*. He has the ability to pay. He can make a decision. You're certain that he's an excellent prospect, someone worth your best effort. He can be *sold*. The only question is, who will get the job?

Now here you are at your prospect's door. You're enthusiastic, self-assured, knowledgeable. What do you do next? Pay close attention. In this chapter, I'm going to let you in on some of the secrets of selling in the home.

Take Command of the Situation
A home builder's prospects come to his office. It's easier for a builder to discuss plans, drawings and specifications over his desk. Obviously, this is a matter of convenience. But there's an even more important reason for having the prospect come to the builder's premises: It gives the builder a psychological advantage. He's in *his* territory.

The same is true in other fields. When you need a lawyer, you go to the lawyer's office. When you get a loan, you go to the bank. The lawyer and the banker have a built-in psychological advantage when doing business from their own office.

In contrast, a contractor-salesman calling on a homeowner is on strange ground. Who has the ad-vantage now? The buyer, obviously. He's on his home turf.

The contractor-salesman — you — have to overcome this disadvantage and turn it into an advantage. You do this by taking command of the situation.

Put Yourself at Ease
It's important that you feel at ease when calling on a prospect. In the summertime, I loosen my tie. That makes me feel relaxed. During the winter, I take off my overcoat at once and lay it on the nearest chair. I've come to stay a while. I'm here to make a sale. I can't do that if I'm ill at ease, standing with my hat in my hand, like a beggar looking for scraps.

Use the Kitchen Table
Most homeowners will invite you to sit in the living room. But that's not the room where sales are closed. Suggest instead, "Why don't we go to the kitchen, where we'll all feel more comfortable? At home, my family and I spend all our time around the kitchen table, when we're not watching TV."

Using the kitchen table is extremely important. Most people are relaxed in the kitchen. Family decisions are usually made around the kitchen table. In the intimacy of the kitchen, sales barriers are lowered. By contrast, when you sit in the living room, the homeowner is the host. He's in a domi-

It's absolutely essential that you have their undivided attention

nant position and his sales defenses are likely to be up.

Most working people regard the living room as a place to entertain friends or relatives. It's the *parlor*. The family's on good behavior in the living room. They're not relaxed. People sign contracts when they're relaxed, not when they're psychologically wearing their Sunday best.

If the objection is raised that the table isn't cleaned off yet, simply tell them that you'll be happy to wait a few moments.

If your prospect offers to use the dining room table, accept. It's almost as good. But here's a note of caution: If the table top is wood, lay a pad or newspaper under your contract. Otherwise, the pressure of the pen may leave marks on the table top. If you damage their table with just a pen, they're certainly not going to let you into their home with a hammer and saw.

Remember, too, that it's also easier to make out a contract when you're sitting at a table. You start filling in the specs as you're talking. This makes writing up the contract a natural part of the sales presentation. After all, that's what you're there for.

Here's another situation to avoid. Occasionally the owner will ask you to sit on the front porch or in the back yard at a picnic table. This puts you at a big disadvantage. There are too many distractions and the atmosphere is too casual in the front or back yard. Decline the invitation. Say "Our business is confidential. Let's go into the house, shall we? There's no reason to discuss this in public."

This usually works. If it doesn't work, the best thing to do is pack up and leave, after asking for an appointment when you can talk in privacy.

Set the Stage to Do Business
Suppose your prospects *insist* on sitting in the living room? It's still possible to control the situation.

"Do you mind if we turn off the TV? Thank you. It's difficult for me to talk with the TV on."

The TV must be off, otherwise the prospects will be listening with one ear. You won't have their complete attention. You can't close a sale if your prospects are wrapped up in a football game or a quiz show.

Remember this. The sale you make could be worth up to $40,000. A television program can't possibly be more important than a decision on a big-ticket item like this. If it is, pack up your sales kit and leave with a request for a new appointment when they won't be preoccupied. You have nothing to lose by rescheduling. Continue with the TV-handicap and you're spinning your wheels.

Face the People You're Selling
Once you have undivided attention, pay attention to the seating arrangement. I'll assume that you are selling to a husband and wife. If the man's sitting on one side of the room and the wife on the other, you'll only be facing one party while making the presentation. Small matter, you say? No, it isn't. This arrangement puts you at a severe disadvantage. You can't watch the body language of a person you're not facing. You can't be sure that one party isn't passing signals to the individual you're talking to. It's absolutely essential that you face both parties when talking to them. Simply suggest, "Mr. and Mrs. Homeowner, why don't you both make yourself comfortable on the couch, if you will, please. I'll use this side chair. That way, I can talk to both of you." Take command in the seating arrangement. Be courteous, but firm.

You're on the buyer's turf, it's true. But you've eliminated the disadvantages and put yourself in the dominant position.

Eliminate Distractions
Okay. You've managed to get the TV turned off, but kids can also be a distraction. What to do? I sometimes take some paper out of my briefcase, along with a pencil and a piece of carbon paper, and show the children how to draw and make copies. They soon become engrossed.

The last distraction is pets. When a barking dog threatens to spoil my sit, I turn to the owner and say, "You know, I love dogs. Your dog probably smells my son's dog. I was petting him this morning. But I really can't talk with him barking like that. Could you please put him outside or in another room for a little while?"

Icebreakers
You're settled around the kitchen table. Distractions are at a minimum and everyone's comfortable. What do you do next? Easy. Start with a compliment and some irrelevant small talk. That starts the conversation going. It begins an exchange of information that's essential to make the sale. It begins your pitch with a friendly tone. And most important, it begins with mutual agreement — mutual agreement that ends up in a signed contract. I call this conversation starter the *icebreaker*.

Beginning with an icebreaker separates you from the class of door-to-door salesmen. It makes you socially equal with your prospect. After a successful icebreaker, the prospect will respect your knowledge. Your statements from that moment forward carry more weight. They convey powerful messages to the buyer. The buyer's anxiety and resistance are reduced.

Here are some icebreakers:

"Mrs. Homeowner, I have to say that your house is beautifully decorated and furnished. Did you plan it out yourself, or did you have it done? I wish I had your eye for color schemes."

Or:

"Mr. Homeowner, this house is beautifully kept up. Your wife must either be one super housekeeper or else she's got the rest of the family so well trained they never make any mess. My wife's still trying to train me."

One more:

"Who has the green thumb around here? I'll bet it's you, Mrs. Homeowner. You certainly have some beautiful philodendrons." Ditto for African violets, geraniums, cactus plants, or whatever. If I don't know, I ask. And of course I ask Mrs. Homeowner to tell me all about her houseplants. *How old are they? How much care do they take? How often do you water them?* People love to talk about their possessions. Incidentally, this also pushes the "pride-in-ownership" button.

In many homes, particularly in more prosperous areas, you'll spot Royal Dalton china or Hummel figurines. Your line: "Say, that's quite a collection. What beautiful craftsmanship. Did you buy them in Europe, by any chance?" Compliment the prospect's good taste. That melts ice fast.

I use the same icebreaker whenever I spot an afghan:

"What a beautiful afghan. Did you make it? You did? Well, you certainly are talented. I had an aunt who made afghans, so I know how much time and effort it takes."

The afghan icebreaker is especially effective because very few men notice such things. Try it. It works.

If you can't spot something in the house to use as an icebreaker, ask "What kind of work do you do?" You'll be astonished at how many kinds of work people do. People like to talk about their jobs — even about a job they don't like. They unwind and relax. Needless to say, a relaxed prospect is exactly what you want.

Here's another example:

Last year I called on a homeowner who turned out to be a bachelor. His home was filled with beautiful crystal figurines and antiques. I complimented him on his collection, and he informed me that he was an interior decorator. Being in the business, he was able to pick up expensive items at reasonable prices. He became more relaxed as he talked. I wound up with an order in the upper four-figure range.

Bowling trophies, photos of servicemen, and school graduation pictures are good subjects for icebreakers. Don't overlook any opportunity to compliment the prospect. Let pride-in-ownership break down sales resistance.

The Warmup

After the ice is broken, don't go right into your sales presentation. It's still too early. Allow time for the *warmup*. Here are some warmups.

A salesman friend of mine, Harvey Dinkle, is a handball enthusiast. I don't know how Harvey does it, but on every call he seems to find someone who's wild about handball. They'll go on animatedly about singles and doubles champs, tournaments and league games, and the rest of it. After they've talked handball for half an hour, you'd think these two fellows, the homeowner and Harvey, were long lost brothers. Finally, Harvey will remark, "You know, I could talk handball all night with you, but we'd better get down to business. *Tell me exactly what you have in mind on this new addition...*"

Another friend who lives in Mundelein, Illinois, is a rabid fisherman and hunter. He can talk for hours about the joys of crouching in a cold, wet duck blind, or trudging through brambles for miles to get to a secluded trout stream. When he gets into

a warmup on his favorite topics, the sales are automatic.

Still another friend played college football. He uses that for all it's worth in the warmup. I know builders who watch for Masonic, Rotary, Knights of Columbus and other lodge symbols. These are great icebreakers and warmup items.

A warmup should be some experience you've had in life, some story you can tell. Here's a warmup I've used several times.

I had a lead in Evanston, Illinois, near the Northwestern Campus. The home was large and imposing. It looked like old wealth. The lead was for a porch enclosure and new windows. I was greeted by the owner, a college professor. As he led me to the library to discuss the work, I wondered what to do for the icebreaker. I couldn't seem to find any common ground. I knew only too well that unless I could get under his skin, as the saying goes, I was only there to give him an estimate. Finally, I tried a shot in the dark:

"Professor, you certainly have some beautiful oriental rugs. Do you collect them? I notice that you have Persian, Turkish, Indian, and Chinese carpets. The Chinese rug in the living room is obviously a real *Tsien Tsin*. It must be worth a fortune."

The professor seemed surprised. "You know, you're right. But how do you know so much about oriental rugs? We've had many guests in our home, but very few realize what they're seeing."

I told the professor my story:

"My wife and I took a trip to the Far East with the Chicago Council of Foreign Relations last year. With the kids grown up and married, we decided to take the trip we've always dreamed of. Well, my daughter asked my wife to please try and buy a rug for her dining room. She gave us the dimensions of her dining room table, so we'd know the right size. In Hong Kong, my wife and I did some shopping. In the Hua Wha Department Store, my wife found a pattern she liked, but the clerk wouldn't sell it to her. He said the rug was too small. It didn't allow room for the chairs to be pulled out when dining. The clerk insisted that my wife choose another pattern, but she didn't like what he showed her. He was quite a guy. He explained to us how the rugs are made in Tsien Tsin, in China, the finest rugs in the world, how they can be cleaned with only cold water, and so on. It was a real education. We finally left the store without buying, and visited the rug shops in the Terminal Warehouse in Kowloon.

The next morning my wife said she'd made up her mind. We would buy a rug at the Hua Wha Department Store. I then called the American Consulate to find out if we could bring the rug back into the United States. The girl I talked to at the customs office in the Consulate said we could bring the rug back. She asked me what store I was buying the rug at. When I told her the Hua Wha Department Store, I received a reassuring answer. "That store has a good reputation. Whatever they tell you, you can believe. Is it a Tsien Tsin rug? If so, it's the best rug made.

"And that, Professor," I concluded, "is how I learned about oriental rugs on a shopping expedition in Hong Kong."

Well, the Professor was hooked, to put it mildly. There was only one way the sale could go, and that was my way. It was a cash sale in the mid four figures. I've never talked oriental rugs since, but on that occasion it was the perfect icebreaker and warmup.

I don't get many rural leads, being located in Chicago. But I've found them to be profitable. The following example is from a sale I made to a farmer near McHenry, Illinois.

This farm was actually owned by the farmer's mother-in-law. She was a kindly but shrewd individual. She ran the farm with an iron fist. Her son-in-law executed her orders. So much for the background. I've never lived on a farm, but I know one thing: farmers like to do business with people who speak their language and understand their problems.

Here are some of the questions I asked:

"How many acres do you have under cultivation? How many cows do you milk? How big is the herd? By the way, I was admiring that harvest store (silo) when I drove into the yard. Can you tell me how much it holds? How much does it cost to put up a building like that?"

I managed to break the ice with these questions. Next came the warmup. The warmup I used came from my experiences. It led to a sale in the upper four figures.

"Several years ago my wife and I took a trip to the Middle East. We visited several farms and noticed particularly how the milk cattle were kept. This was dry country and the cows couldn't find enough natural fodder from grazing. So the cows were kept in open pens with stanchions arranged around the perimeter. To feed the cows, they drove a tractor past the stanchions, spreading peanut cuttings, cabbages, and orange peels. Yes, that's right — orange peels. I was amazed when I saw it. They got truckloads of squeezed oranges from the juice companies and fed them to the cows. This was the staple of their diet, plus vitamin pellets. The milk was rich and creamy."

Well, these prospects were so impressed with my story that they asked all kinds of questions about farming abroad. The discussion became very animated and continued for over an hour. Now I'll ask you: what do you think happened after that? Do you think they got other bids? Do you think they said they'd have to think it over? Not on your life. They asked me how soon I could start and when we would be finished. After a sales pitch that was shorter than our discussion of farming, I said — you guessed it — *"Why don't we use the kitchen table to write up the order?"* This was a beautiful order, as I mentioned earlier. The job was done as specified, and the check came in the mail immediately.

I've used this same warmup on several other farm leads. I got a sale every time.

Remember this when it comes to the warmup: Don't tell my story — tell yours. Tell a story from your own experience to create an atmosphere that's conducive to sales. Press the pride-in-ownership button and you'll press the sales button, every time.

Chapter 6

Sales Knowledge

As everyone knows, a chameleon can change the color of its skin to blend with the surroundings. Like a chameleon, a remodeling salesman has to adapt to the situation. He has to change his sales methods as the occasion demands. He must be flexible. He has to blend his personality into that of his prospect.

For example, if you're calling on the dignified banker type, a familiar, folksy manner is more likely to cool sales prospects than create a bond between you and your client.

By contrast, when you call on a dinner-pail personality who loves a risque joke, a gentleman-of-the-old-school approach is next to useless.

A salesman's personality should be like a tree that changes from fragile spring blossoms to lush summer foliage to the brilliant colors of autumn. The tree has the same sturdy virtues all year round. But appearances change with the season. So the successful contractor-salesmen has an unchanging system of basic ethics, but handles each situation according to the customer's needs, motivation, personality and situation in life.

A Repertoire of Sales Pitches and Closes

One thing you can't do without is a complete repertoire of sales pitches and closes to fit every occasion. Adaptability, again, is the key word. You must tailor your approach to the situation.

Consider the case of a friend of mine, a West Virginia-born remodeling contractor named Speckles. Speckles received a lead from his office and called on his prospect. He was greeted with:

"Well, I suppose you're going to take up four hours of my time, without telling me a damn thing."

"You bet I am," Speckles shot back.

"I suppose you're going to tell me that your lumber's clear, and ship me lumber full of knots."

"Not only full of knots, but our company only ships lumber that's full of sap, and half of the 2 x 4's are crooked."

"Say, how much work on this room addition can I get done for $2,000?"

"Just about one corner, I'd say."

The men continued to joke back and forth. Every time the customer asked a ridiculous question, Speckles came up with something equally outrageous. Well, my friend from West Virginia eventually wrote up a remodeling job for an expensive room addition. After the papers were signed, the customer's wife told Speckles that her husband had three other contractors bid the job. He'd kidded them so unmercifully that they got flustered. The more he kidded them, the more they tried to high-pressure him into buying. He kept on kidding them, and they all wound up on the outside looking in. The point of the story is obvious. On one of my calls, I faced the opposite situation. Mrs. Olsen liked to pretend she was really tough. She greeted me with:

"How many lies are you going to tell me? I don't believe anything any salesman says!"

I just kept pitching and disregarded her tirade except to smile occasionally.

"You're a hard woman Mrs. Olsen," I said, "but I'll bet you've got a heart as big as Wrigley Field."

Her reply to this was, "Don't put me on, young man! It's a trick of the trade to flatter the customer. I'm not as dumb as I look."

When I told her that I could match the color of her roof on the garage she wanted, she came back with: "*Prove it.*"

Fair enough. I got the roofing samples from my car, and I'll be darned if Mrs. Olsen didn't get a ladder, climb up on the roof and lay the sample down to see if the colors matched.

Well, to make a long story short, I got the order. Afterwards, her husband told me, "Did you know that my wife gets a kick out of scaring off salesmen? She loves the guy that calls her bluff. She thinks a lot of you, Bob."

Speak with Authority
The professional man or woman speaks with authority. The dentist doesn't say, "Your teeth are bad, I'll fix them up for you." He talks about gingivitis, extractions and root canals. He uses words that we seldom use, but he explains their meaning and how they apply to us. The same is is true when we visit our doctor's office. He tells us we need a cystotomy, an appendectomy, a tonsilectomy. The lawyer talks about titles, deeds and encumbrances. These professionals use the nomenclature of their trade. They're full of professional knowledge. We respect them for this knowledge and pay their fees because we have confidence in them.

The contractor is also a professional. Command confidence by proper use of construction terminology. Speak with authority about soffits, ceiling joists, rafters, cripples and headers. When the subject is roofs, talk in terms of barn, gambrel, mansard, hip and gable. But don't get unnecessarily technical with a customer. Just use the right terms here and there so your customer recognizes that you know your business.

Here's an example of what I mean:

You're discussing a kitchen remodeling job, including installing some wall cabinets. Use the right word, *soffit,* to describe where the wall cabinets are hung.

"Mrs. Homeowner, we'll install a soffit over your kitchen cabinets so that dust doesn't accumulate there."

If you're installing new doors, use the correct term:

"Mr. Homeowner, your overhead garage door will have an astragal cushion so it closes tight and keeps snow and rain out. The storm door will also have an astragal to make a tight seal against the elements."

Project a professional image. Know the source of the material, how it's made, and why it's made that way. If you're an authority on your work, speak with authority. Don't parade your knowledge to make a sale. That puts buyers off. But use enough of the right terminology to assure the prospect that you know remodeling. It provides an air of assurance and generates customer confidence.

Customers — Three Basic Personality Types
I've been selling remodeling work for over 30 years. I've made thousands of sales to thousands of people. From my standpoint as a salesman, I divide the human race into three basic personality types: sanguine, nervous and phlegmatic. Some people have traces of all three types. But most prospects will fall into one of these three categories. Each type has to be handled differently.

The *sanguine* person is naturally cheerful, hopeful and confident.

The *nervous* type is intelligent but has a short attention span.

The *phlegmatic* individual is deliberate, usually laconic, and a good listener.

Develop the knack of quickly sizing up your prospects by personality type. That makes selling much easier.

A good way to learn the three personality types is to study your relatives or friends and see what categories they fall into. Then when you meet your prospect, size him up and tailor your pitch accordingly.

A phlegmatic individual is cool and calm to the point of being impassive. Phlegmatic is the opposite of nervous. To sell Mr. Phlegmatic, go slowly and deliberately over every point in your sales presentation. Mr. Phlegmatic's in no hurry. He

"Which type is he?"

needs plenty of time to digest the information you give him.

Needless to say, using the same technique on Mr. Nervous would quickly lose his attention and consequently the sale. Mr. Nervous thinks in flashes. He grasps ideas quickly and fills in the gaps himself. Because he's impatient, your sales presentation should only hit the highlights.

Mr. Sanguine is confident and optimistic. He requires still another approach. You have to get down to brass tacks quickly with him and have a straightforward pitch. Mr. Sanguine is a regular guy — practical, outgoing and convivial. He likes to be entertained after the sales pitch. And wants to keep in touch after the job's done.

I had been selling for about ten years when I first learned the theory of personality types. My company enrolled the entire sales force in a pop psychology course. I found that the course paid for itself many times over. It clarified for me what I'd been doing intuitively for years.

If you're skeptical about the value of personality typing, do this: Get a pencil and a sheet of paper.

First, write down the names of eight or ten friends and relatives. Next, list their qualities — let's say three per name. For example, "Bob: cheerful, outgoing, friendly." Now see how well the qualities listed fit under one of my three personality classes. Don't work too hard at it. Just do the best you can in a few minutes. When you finish, I bet you've been able to classify the people you know well by personality type. If these people fit nicely into one of the three categories, nearly anyone can be classified the same way.

When you meet your next prospect, classify him or her as nervous, sanguine or phlegmatic. Use the sales pitch most appropriate for that type of individual. Try it for a month and see if your closing rate doesn't improve.

Silence is a Sales Tool

Two people meet at a dinner party. One does all the talking. The other does the listening. The following day, Mr. Talker tells his wife how he met Mr. Silent yesterday, and what a terrific guy he is — charming, witty, knowledgeable and informative.

This is a typical situation. A good listener — even if he never opens his mouth — is often perceived by others as a congenial companion.

This principle is especially true in selling. Silence is an effective sales tool. Top producers frequently encourage the prospect to do the talking. That way they find out what the prospect's thinking, what his motivations are, and how serious he is about buying.

For example, last Thursday one of our younger men made an appointment for me to make a close. This man was only thinking about getting an order. He hadn't studied the lead. The individual wasn't a prospect, only a suspect, and a mighty poor one at that.

In this particular case, I opened the conversation with: "Mr. Reynolds, what did you want us to build for you, how soon do you want it built, and how do you want to pay for it?"

In three minutes I knew I'd wasted a trip.

Mr. Reynolds began to talk. I kept silent and let him ramble on. He soon revealed that what he actually wanted was for me to give him free layout ideas so he could do the job himself. Mr. Reynolds was a do-it-yourselfer. This was his fifth home in three years. In each of the previous houses he'd done improvements and wound up making a profit.

When Mr. Reynolds was interrupted by the telephone, I leaned over and whispered to our new salesman: "There's nothing here, but I'll wring it out anyway."

We could have left at that point, but I wanted to give the new man a sales lesson. I used every approach I knew, every selling pitch that had any punch to it. I hit Mr. Reynolds with the works, but he wasn't buying. Two hours later he still wasn't buying. He never was a buyer, and ordinarily I wouldn't spend five minutes with his type after I had him talking. A salesman's time is too valuable to waste on freebies.

The following day, the opposite thing happened. Another employee had made an appointment for me to see a family. As soon as the formalities were over I asked the same three questions to get the prospect talking. He talked and talked. The more he talked, the more I relaxed and devoted myself to listening. He told me he'd been married just three months. He'd inherited the house when his mother passed away. The kitchen was a terrible mess and he wanted to have it completely remodeled for his new bride. He could make the payments. He had a good job at a drug store where he'd been for 16

years. As for the layout, why didn't we just use our judgement? When he'd finished his story, we used the kitchen table to write up the order. I didn't have to say a word.

Golden silence. It frequently pays big dividends. Remember, you can't know what's on the customer's mind unless you let him open up and talk.

Don't Talk Yourself Out of the Sale

Here's another reason to use silence during your sales call. If you're not talking, you can't talk yourself out of a sale. No, I'm not joking. It happens all the time. How does a salesman talk himself out of a sale? He forgets to stop and listen, and to take action at the proper moment. He forgets to stop talking and ask for the order when he receives a buying signal. He keeps right on talking and the buyer changes his mind.

A word to the wise: Don't chatter on and on like a machine gun. Sometimes the buyer needs time to think. Give him a chance to digest what you've said. Pause, remain silent, and watch for buying signals. You can learn more by being silent. Remember, a fish would never be caught if he kept his mouth shut.

I'll never forget a large sale that I lost because I opened my big mouth at the wrong time. . .

I sold a kitchen addition and interior remodeling job to a family located in a rural area of Aurora, Illinois. I arranged for a mortgage at a Savings & Loan in Chicago to refinance their house, consolidate their bills and pay for the remodeling. They needed this work. The S&L approved the loan. On a Saturday morning I drove to Aurora, about 50 miles, picked up the customers, and drove them to the S&L. The papers were all signed. I had a terrific sale. A hefty commission check would soon be coming my way.

As we drove back to Aurora from Chicago, Mrs. Rural Homeowner asked me some questions about home financing. She was in an upbeat mood. She told me how grateful she was that her bills were being consolidated and how much easier it would be now to manage the family finances. The new kitchen was a dream come true.

She warbled happily for a few miles, then innocently asked me a question about total indebtedness.

Did I keep my mouth shut? *No.* Did I stop to think? *No.* Did I consider my reply for even one second? *No.* I just blurted out the information that every loan officer involved in consumer finances knows by heart: *You can't borrow yourself out of debt.* I didn't add that sometimes life is made easier by this maneuver, or that in this case it was certainly to their benefit.

The happy chatter stopped abruptly. I realized my mistake, but it was too late to do anything about it.

Can you guess what happened next?

Sure enough, on Monday morning, I found a telegram waiting for me at the office. The sale was cancelled. The bank also received a telegram cancelling the mortgage. It was a hard lesson, and one I haven't forgotten.

Sell Benefits

When you buy a car, the salesman sells you the *benefits* of the car, not the nuts and bolts. He sells the smooth ride, the economical transportation, the enhanced prestige.

When you buy a TV set, the salesman talks about the size and sharpness of the picture. He sells the *benefits*.

The same thing is true in the construction business. Your customers want to hear about the *benefits* they'll obtain from your work.

A big part of your job, therefore, is to know the benefits you're selling.

For example, what are the benefits that your customer receives when he buys a new roof? Well, for one thing, the roof won't leak for twenty years. It's guaranteed. For another thing, the shingles won't blow off in the wind. And since the shingles are fiberglass, the colors won't fade. A tile roof exudes beauty and strength. It makes any house look far more expensive than it is. These are benefits.

What are the benefits of buying a garage? A garage protects the customer's automobile in all types of weather. In wintertime, the car stays warm and starts easier. The garage is a place for tools and a workbench, for garden implements. It's a place to keep the kids' bikes and wagons.

What about a new kitchen? Professional layout makes it easier to store foods and prepare meals. With a double bowl sink and disposal and dishwasher, Mom's clean-up work is cut in half. She'll have fewer steps to walk, too. The kitchen will be cheery, with sunlight streaming through the windows over the sink and the breakfast table. And the roomy cabinets provide plenty of storage.

These are benefits. Sell the benefits. People buy benefits.

Study your business and make up a list of benefits for each item you install.

Here are some examples:

Storm windows and doors—
- Keep the house warmer in the winter
- Keep the house cooler in summer
- Prevent drafts
- Cut down on colds and sore throats
- Save fuel
- Keep dust and dirt from seeping in
- Windows are triple track and anodized — no pitting, scarring or rusting

Basement rumpus room—
- A place to entertain guests, play cards or other games
- A place for the children to play
- Extra closet space for storage
- Room for a sofa bed
- A place for a second TV

Dormer—
- More space for less money, because no foundation is required
- More economical to heat, because hot air rises
- No need to break a wall out of the main structure
- These advantages, plus all the benefits of a regular room addition

Brick veneering—
- Brick is made of natural materials
- It doesn't rot
- It's fire resistant
- Requires no maintenance
- Never needs to be painted

Stucco—
- Eliminates rotting siding
- Always looks clean and neat
- Is fire resistant
- Has a Mediterranean look

This is a partial list. Make up your own list. Study it, add to it, memorize it. Think benefits. Sell benefits. People buy benefits.

Paint Word Pictures

You'll be a better salesman if you learn to paint word pictures. Create dreams in the customer's mind by describing the proposed construction in vivid detail.

Here I'm selling a major addition. The family is

looking over my shoulder at a blueprint I've spread out on the kitchen table.

"The first thing you should consider is a well-designed traffic pattern. You see, it's the traffic pattern that ensures the gracious living your home can provide. Notice, for example, that when the kids come home from school, they enter through the side door or through the kitchen doorway here. They hang up ski pants, winter coats, mufflers and hats in this mud-room area. Here's where muddy galoshes go. To this side of the entry is a bathroom. That's where the kids can wash up. Opposite is the kitchen where they'll have their peanut butter and jelly sandwiches. After a snack they'll go through this hallway to their bedrooms to do their homework. Now please notice that they don't cut through the living room. The same for the dining room. This keeps heavy traffic away from your good carpeting. And of course it saves your furniture, too."

I've painted an word picture for the family, showing how they'll live in the remodeled house.

They like the picture I've painted. They're excited about it. But now they're concerned about the dimensions of one of the bedrooms.

Fine. I have a stock answer that's worked for me over the years:

"Yes, I'm sure that this bedroom is adequate. As you can see on the blueprint, it'll take an old-fashioned 9 x 12 living room rug."

I've compared the small bedroom to an old fashioned parlor. If the parlor is roomy, then the bedroom must be large enough also.

Now they want to know about the dining room.

I point out that there's plenty of room on the wall for Mrs. Homeowner's china set. The dining room is large enough for a dining room table that will seat twelve people.

I've painted a word picture. *This is how it's going to be. Here's what life will be like in your new dining room.*

You can go through room after room, painting vivid word pictures. As your prospects listen, they see themselves occupying those rooms. They see themselves entertaining friends in the graciously-appointed living room, serving a sumptuous meal in the dining room, sipping cocktails on the spacious patio. As you paint your word pictures, you're selling not a 9 x 12 room but the *quality of life* in the new home.

Dramatize Your Sales Presentation

Many building items lend themselves well to a dramatic sales presentation. This is particularly true of fiberglass awnings. I frequently take two pieces of fiberglass and rub them together to show that they don't scratch or mar. Next, I place a piece of fiberglass on the rug. I then stand on it, while mentioning my weight (170 pounds). The fiberglass doesn't crack. It's obviously very strong. This is an impressive demonstration. Then I invite the homeowner to do the same thing. Do you know of a homeowner who can resist trying it? I've never met one.

The rest of my talk goes like this:

"You know, Mr. Homeowner, a boat made of this same fiberglass may cost $50,000 or more. The awnings for your home will cost in the hundreds. While your wife selects the colors from these samples, why don't you help me measure the windows and doors?"

I've dramatized my sales presentation with a demonstration. I've stressed the relative inexpensiveness of the awnings by comparing them to a yacht. Mr. Homeowner is helping me take the measurements. At this point, how can he refuse to buy? If he helps with the measuring, he's already given his silent assent. From here on out, it's just a technical matter of pricing and writing up the order.

Top closers among the storm window salesmen use drama for all it's worth. The following is a typical sales presentation.

The salesman opens his window display case. He has made sure that the glass is free of fingerprints.

"First, I'm going to show you two pieces of aluminum. Now, this first piece I can *twist*. You see? The reason I can twist this piece of aluminum is because it's *recycled* aluminum. This second piece — as you can see — I *can't* twist. Why? Because it's *virgin* aluminum. My company uses only virgin aluminum. Here. Try it yourself.

"Now here's another feature. This is a triple-track window. See how easily I can slide the bottom pane up? Notice that when I leave it partially

The fiberglass strength test

opened, it stays there. Many people like to leave a window partly open at night. Now, please note, the window is locked into place. This is very important for your safety. Some window companies use a ratchet. The trouble with a ratchet window is that an intruder can grab the bottom of the window and slide it up. I know you don't want that.

"Now notice how easily I move the screen up and down. This screen is fiberglass. It's a terrific invention. I'd like to show you something. Could I borrow a pencil for a second?"

The salesman takes the pencil and deliberately opens up a hole in the screen. He rubs the strands together. The hole disappears.

"With this screen there's absolutely no worry about holes. Go ahead. Try it. Now rub. You see? It's foolproof.

"I'd like to show you something else about this window, if I may. This interlock on the top keeps wind, snow and rain from getting between the upper and lower sash. Here, I'll demonstrate."

The salesman takes a ten-dollar bill out of his wallet. He inserts the ten spot between the upper and lower sash.

"I'll tell you what I'll do. I'll *give* you this ten-dollar bill if you can pull it out of the window."

This of course gets the entire family into the act, trying to pull the sawbuck out of the window. But the interlock holds the bill firmly in place. The customers are impressed.

This dramatization is amazingly effective. It usually results in a sale. Only a dyed-in-the-wool price shopper can resist. Buyers like that are so cheap they wouldn't spend a quarter to see the Statue of Liberty walk across New York Harbor. Most people will be sold after watching a demonstration like this. Believe me, I've seen it happen, again and again. It's the combination of drama and emphasis on benefits that makes the sale.

Use Third-Party Selling
Pick up any magazine or newspaper and read the

ads. You'll find many manufacturers using testimonial or endorsements as sales aids. I call this *third-party selling*. It works. Why? It appeals to our universal desire to emulate the glamorous movie star, famous football hero or wealthy socialite.

Advertising is salesmanship in print. The advertising profession has developed third-party selling to a fine art because it's very persuasive. Take a lesson from the advertising professionals. Use third-party selling whenever you can. Here's how.

"In the bathroom we just remodeled for Mrs. Newman on Cumberland Avenue, we replaced the window over the tub with a glass block window with an aluminum ventilator. This insures privacy at all times. Mrs. Newman also had us install a mirrored sliding glass shower door. It's an unusual item. Her guests say they wish they had such a well-designed, functional bathroom.

"If you like, I'll contact Mrs. Newman and make an appointment for you to see her bathroom. She'd be happy to show it off."

What have we done? While describing the improvements, we've used third-party selling by referring to Mrs. Newman on Cumberland Avenue. In effect, Mrs. Newman herself was describing what a terrific job we did for her. That's an excellent way to build confidence in what we're selling.

Room additions, siding jobs, soffits and fascia jobs are naturals for third-party selling. Anyone can see and evaluate the change without ever going into the house.

If you're installing new fixtures, you can use the name of an old customer over and over again. Explain how she had you put lights in the closets that turn on when the doors open, or an exhaust fan in the attic that reduces heat in the summertime.

When I'm talking to Mr. Homeowner about the new garage he wants, one of my favorite third-party selling tools is:

"Most people in Chicago with a garage in the alley want steel doors. A steel bottom panel can't rot out when snow piles up in the winter. Our steel door offers better security. But it's so well balanced that it only takes the tips of two fingers to operate it. But Mr. Ryan on Glenlake had us go one step further. He had us install an electric door opener with a transmitter in each car. He didn't really need the electric opener because, as I said, it's fingertip-balanced. But he worries about his wife when she gets home late from shopping. Now when she drives into the alley, she doesn't have to get out of the car. She just presses a button. The door opens and a light goes on in the garage. Mr. Ryan's very pleased with his investment."

If I detect some hesitation in making a decision, I'll frequently mention names of satisfied customers that the prospect might know. Then I ask to use the phone. I call the third party and put my prospect and my satisfied customer on the line together. I let them talk it over. My old customers make the sale for me about 90% of the time — and I pick up the commission. Try it, it works.

Make a Customer List or Photo Album
I know a garage contractor who printed up a list of all his sales. The list is indexed by town and address. He gives this list to each prospect during the sales presentation. This is third-party selling. If he can't close on the first meeting, he suggests that the prospect go and take a look at a few of the garages on the list. At the same time, he sets up an appointment date for the close. The third-party list does its work before the appointment date. I'm sure you can readily see what an effective sales tool this is.

My friend Rick, who sells windows, goes a step further in third-party selling. His sales manual includes photos of completed jobs. Among them are the Wrigley Building in Chicago, the Elmhurst College Building and several Harvard University buildings. Rick presents his manual to architects, builders and owners. Prestigious photos are a powerful selling tool.

Collect Testimonial Letters
You should also put together a loose-leaf book filled with testimonial letters. Encase your letters in plastic jackets so they stay neat and clean even after years of handling. Occasionally, you'll receive an unsolicited testimonial letter, like the one in Figure 6-1. Put it in your book of letters, and use it when you make your next sales presentation.

But don't just wait and hope for unsolicited letters. Tell your prospect, "When the company's done with the job, I'd like a letter from you. I know you're going to be happy with our work." Then, when you go for the completion ticket or to make the collection, take a writing pad with you. Have the customer write the letter right there and then. Take the initiative. You have everything to gain and nothing to lose.

Ask Insurance Adjusters to Recommend You
I use testimonial selling in another way that's very

```
                              27 Eastbury Avenue
                              Highland Park, IL 60035
                              February 23, 1985


Colonial Builders, Inc.
7329 N. Broadway
Chicago, IL 60040

Dear Mr. Gorodess,

     This letter is to tell you how pleased we are
with the basement recreation room you designed and
built for us.  It was a new experience for us to
have such neat and careful workmen in our home.

     Needless to say, we will recommend you when-
ever the opportunity presents itself.


                              Yours truly,

                              Fred W. Elman

                              Fred W. Elman
```

Testimonial letter
Figure 6-1

effective. I ask insurance adjusters to recommend us to their claimants.

Insurance repair work is steady work. Fires, snow damage, vehicle damage, water damage and accidents go on, no matter how high interest rates go. I strongly recommend that you contact as many casualty adjusters in your area as you can. Explain the type of work you specialize in. Let them know that you'll cooperate with them in preparing an itemized list of the damage to be restored. Give them a list of some of your satisfied customers.

I recommend sending a mailing to the claims adjusters in your area at least twice a year. Including a copy of a testimonial letter from an insurance company also doesn't do any harm. Figure 6-2 is one that I've used. Where possible, I list my usual charges for various types of work. I suggest that

you do the same. The names of the claims departments and adjusters are listed in the Yellow Pages. The National Underwriter Company, 175 West Jackson Boulevard, Suite A2110, Chicago, Illinois 60604, prints insurance telephone directories that have all the information you need.

Remember this. There's no recommendation better than having a representative from Allstate, Aetna, or Transamerica suggest your name. That's the best testimonial you can have.

Anticipate and Overcome Objections
Every sales pitch will meet with objections — some real, some fancied, and some just a smoke screen to avoid saying yes. Most objections have no validity. But every objection must be overcome before you can close the sale.

North-American *Insurance Companies*

Home Office • P. O. Box 500 • Dallas, Texas 75221

October 17, 1984

Colonial Builders, Inc.
7329 N. Broadway
Chicago, Illinois 60040

We wish to take this opportunity to thank you most sincerely for your assistance and cooperation with our company during the adjustment of the July 21, 1984 tornado losses.

Your generosity with your time, competence, advice and submission of estimates was invaluable to us, our policyholders and the community in general.

It was a pleasure to work with you and we hope our association can continue on an equally pleasant basis mutually beneficial to everyone concerned.

Please let us know whenever we can be of assistance to you.

Sincerely,

A. B. Sweeney
General Adjuster

ABS/mk

Insurance company testimonial letter
Figure 6-2

The best way to handle objections is to be ready — ready with answers that neutralize all the objections that you're likely to hear. Better yet, rebut the most common objections in your sales pitch *even before your prospect can verbalize them.*

When you've made as many calls as I have, you'll notice that most sales jobs are about the same. Only the faces change. The standard objections come up again and again. That's the rule. New objections will be rare. When you do get one, figure out a way to overcome it. Then include the answer to the objection in each presentation. This takes away the customer's "out."

You can avoid the most common objections by careful screening of your prospects. But some prospects will let you make an entire presentation and then try to kiss you off with a statement like:

"I'm not sure."
"I have to think about it."
"I have to sleep on it."
"I never decide right away."

These people are really saying that you haven't sold them. They're not giving the real reason why they're not buying.

To uncover the real reason, you have to get them to talk. Ask *what* and *why* questions.

"What do you have in mind for the new room? Will the children use it as a playroom, or do you want to use it for entertaining? Will it be an extra bedroom? What do you think about the windows? Should they match the rest of the house, or are you thinking of awning windows? Do you want painted walls, or paneling? Why do you want a dropped ceiling?"

The more the prospects talk, the more you know about what they actually want. If you can draw out their real reasons for not buying, you can give them the answers that will result in a sale instead of a "kiss-off."

Prepare the Customer for the Price
It's vitally important during your sales presentation to prepare the customer for the price. You must establish the idea in the customer's mind that you're selling *quality*, and quality has its price. Many homeowners have done their own painting. They've bought off-brand paint on sale, only to find out later that the paint didn't hold up. Now they've learned their lesson. They buy the more expensive brand of paint because it's cheaper in the long run.

Prepare the customers to accept the price of your quality product. Your product is superior. It costs more because of its durability, practicality and quality. And, it's cheaper in the long run.

But it's no good just throwing out the word "quality." Every salesman in the world claims he's selling "quality." I can't imagine a salesman telling his customer, "Yes, I know it's junk, but as long as it holds up until your check clears, that's good enough for me." He claims he's selling quality just as fervently as you do. So you have to back it up.

The most effective way I've found of doing this is to stress that you use only the best brands and high-grade materials. In these days of "plain wrap," it's worthwhile to tell the customer that you use only name brands. Tell him what brands — Flintkote shingles, American Standard plumbing supplies, Crane, Gerber. He's more than likely heard of them, and he'll begin to see that you are indeed selling quality, not just using the word.

Explain about the grades of lumber — *clear, construction* and *utility.* Tell the customer that you use only the clear and construction grades, *never* the utility grade. Tell the customer, "But don't just take my word for it. When we do your job, I want you to examine the lumber. You'll see the grade mark stamped right on it. On every piece. Then you'll *know* you're getting quality."

If you're selling concrete work, explain about *bag mix.* The customer appreciates what you're teaching him, and he sees that you're prepared to take the time with him. Chances are, he'll figure, you'll also take the time and steps needed to see that a first-class job will be done on his house.

And support your claims to *quality* work.

"It may be true that I'm not offering the cheapest price — but is that all you're looking for? When we do your job, it's a quality job. You pay us for the extra time required and the extra skill of the craftsmen we use. We don't have any "handymen" or jack-of-all-trades on our team. Each is a specialist in what he does. They don't take any shortcuts that reduce the quality of the job. A stud gets three nails, not two. If a corner is to be mitered, it's done perfectly — you'll hardly be able to see the joint. Nails are countersunk so the heads don't protrude. Your home doesn't look like you buy cheap things. I don't think you want cheap work done in it either."

My friend Hector Rodriguez prepares his prospects for the price of his expensive specialty awnings this way:

"Mr. Homeowner, do you have money to burn? I know I don't, and I don't think you do, either. If you *do,* it doesn't matter to you what you buy, or how long it'll stand up, or what the quality is, because you can junk it whenever you like and buy a new one. But I don't think that's the case — is it, Mr. Homeowner? I think you're a working man like me. When you buy, you want quality, something that will last a long time. You need an awning that'll last thirty years, not one that's going to fall apart in two or three years. My awnings last a lifetime. I guarantee it. You pay me enough to keep me honest. I don't need to cheat on quality. It costs a little more, but it's worth it in the long run. It's like buying shoes. You wouldn't buy paper-soled shoes, no matter how cheap. No, I know you wouldn't. You'd rather pay more and buy genuine leather-soled shoes. You know that they'll last much longer. It's the same with my awnings. They cost more, and they're worth it, because they're the genuine item. In the long run, Mr. Homeowner, the price isn't as important as the value. And that's what I'm selling, value."

I've found that most people can't remember the price of an article that they're contented with several years later. Try a little test on your friends:

• Do you remember what you paid for your refrigerator?

• Do you remember what your last car cost you?

• How much did you pay for your T.V. set?

Reduce the Job to Fit the Pocketbook
Even after you've prepared the customer, one of the most common objections you'll hear is the *price objection*: "It's just too much money! I can't afford it."

Ideally, this would have been dealt with in the qualifying stages, when the lead was asked if he intended to pay cash, but if you *do* get this objection, here's how to handle it.

"Well, about how much did you expect to pay? Really? About half. You're right, it seems that everything we want to buy these days costs double what we think it should. I have an idea. Why don't I take another look at the job and see if I can figure out a way to do it that's more in line with your thinking?"

Then take a look and see if you can reduce the

job. Almost every prospect's eyes are bigger than his wallet. Everyone wants the best of everything. But few can afford it. To get the job, you cut it down to the size of the buyer's pocketbook.

Here are some examples:

"We've talked about the kitchen and we've talked about the bathroom, Mrs. Homeowner. Which is really the most important to you? I thought so, the kitchen. Why don't I figure up the cost of remodeling just your kitchen? It'll be a comfortable payment. When that's paid off, we can come in and do the bathroom for you. This way you'll have the use of a new stylish, functional and airy kitchen. If that sounds O.K. to you, I'll use the table to figure up the order."

This same type of price reduction can be tailored to every type of remodeling. For example:

• Put aluminum siding on the front of the house only.

• Room additions can be switched to basement recreation rooms sometimes, or attic dormers, saving the cost of laying a foundation.

• If the prospect's trying to keep up with the Joneses and wants a 20 x 20 room addition, point out that 20 x 20 is bigger than the whole garage. Suggest a smaller room, pointing out that an oversized room will not only cost more to heat and cool, but will cost more to furnish.

• Install storm windows in the bedrooms and the kitchen. Leave the other rooms until later.

I actually had one customer who kept ordering four storm windows at a time until she had the entire house done. That way she could afford it. I never could have sold her thirty-two storm windows and two storm doors at one time.

If reducing the size and price of the job *still* doesn't do it, then you didn't have a lead in the first place.

Sell the Benefits of Buying Before Prices Increase
Another way to overcome the price objection is to talk about rising prices:

"You've probably seen in the papers that construction wages are increasing. We don't have final figures yet, but wages are going up. If I write up the contract now, your cost is fixed, no matter what happens to wages."

"Due to forest fires on the West Coast, we're expecting an increase in the price of lumber by the first of next month. If I write up your contract now, I can protect you from this price hike."

"Roofing materials are going up by 10%. It's the oil situation. As you probably know, roofing is made of asphalt, which comes from oil. I can write up your new roof right now at today's prices. Next week I don't know what the price will be."

Sell the Increased Value of the Home

What do you do when the customer says he doesn't want to put that much money into an old house? Here's how I handle this situation:

"You admit that you need a new bathroom. You certainly could use the convenience of it. Let me ask you a question. Supposing you have an old model car and you want to put a radio in it. Well, it costs the same to put a radio in an older car as in a brand new one. Isn't that right? So, it doesn't cost any more to put a bathroom in an older home than it does in a new one. In fact a modern, easy-to-clean bathroom will add to the value of your home. If you ever decide to sell, you'll command a higher price. Doesn't it make sense, from every angle, to have this work done right away?"

"I-Have-a-Friend-Who-Can-Do-it-Cheaper"

The price objection is often followed by the "friend-who-can-do-it-cheaper" line.

Here are some tactics that will usually overcome this objection. If they don't, the only reason these people called was to pick your brains. Even then, you can sometimes turn this shopper into a buyer.

Sell Your Professionalism— When you reach the "My-friend-can-do-it-cheaper" impasse, it's your cue to sell your professionalism. Start off like this:

"Does your friend have Worker's Compensation, Public Liability Insurance or Scaffolding Insurance? Are you aware that if your friend's injured while doing this work, you are legally responsible? You could end up in court. Our company is insured, as required by state law.

"I know a homeowner who gave a similar job to a friend. This man was penny-wise and pound-foolish. His friend worked on the job only on weekends, plus a few nights a week. After all, he could hardly be expected to take off work to do it. So the job dragged on for six months. And the homeowner couldn't say a word — the guy was doing him a favor. After six months of living in builder's rubble and dirt and dust being tracked all over the house, his wife was ready for a nervous breakdown and he had aged a year. I don't call that cheap. I call that real expensive.

"We have a number of carpenters working for us. Some are trim men and some are good for rough carpentry. You have a fine home here. This friend of yours may be an excellent rough carpenter, but can he do as well on the trim?

"Using a semi-pro can be expensive. Your friend may not have the cash needed to carry the labor, material, and subcontractor burden. Have you thought about the cash required? Are you willing to make big cash advances to your friend or to suppliers? When our company does the work, whether you pay cash or finance, we handle the money problems until the job's completed."

Here are some other points you can make about the dangers of having work done by a friend:

"What about the design and layout of the job? No matter how fine the workmanship, a bad design gives you a bad job. You won't get the benefits you spent your hard-earned money for. There's a big difference between a carpenter and a designer.

"Also, when a friend's working in your house, you can't treat him as a workman. You've got to have a case of beer for him. You've got to make sure he's enjoying himself. After all, he's doing it as a favor. So how much time will be spent in socializing? When is the work going to be done? Let's face it, the work is going to take second place to the fun. How long are you prepared to have your house in turmoil? And the quality of the work is bound to suffer.

"Who'll be responsible for ordering and picking up the materials? Will your friend do it, or will you have to drop everything to run to the lumberyard for forgotten items? And can you get a load of lumber and building materials in your car? Not to mention the possible damage to your car trying to load stuff in. It may very well end up costing more because the material wasn't ordered and handled efficiently.

"Another responsibility you're taking on is the cost of wasted and damaged materials. There are always errors made in cutting lumber and ordering supplies. Even the most professional carpenter wastes a little lumber. Of course, an amateur wastes a lot more. If *we* do the job, *we* pay for any

The Price You Pay

"It's unwise to pay too much. . .
But it's worse to pay too little.
When you pay too much you lose
A little money. . .That is all.

When you pay too little. . .You sometimes
Lose everything
Because the thing you bought was
Incapable of doing the thing it was
Bought to do.

The common law of business balance
Prohibits paying a little and
Getting a lot. . .It cannot be done.
If you deal with the lowest bidder,
It is well to add something for
The risk you run, and if you do
That you will have enough to pay
For something better."

John Ruskin

Definition of quality
Figure 6-3

mistakes. Are you going to ask your friend to pay out of his own pocket for any materials that get damaged or cut wrong?''

Finally, assure the customer that he or she gets important benefits when your company does the work:

1) You get professional design and layout.

2) You get a firm time schedule, and we stick to it. You don't want the job dragged out for months, and neither do we. We come in, do the job, clean up, and we're out. You won't get that from your friend, and you won't be able to ask for it either.

3) You get all payments to suppliers and subs taken care of, as well as all Waivers of Lien.

4) You get a crew with Worker's Compensation, Public Liability and Scaffolding Insurance.

5) You get all material on the job when it's needed, so there won't be any delays.

6) You get men who are properly supervised. You won't have to worry about anybody drinking on the job, or getting rowdy, or making a mess. We use only professionals. They know how to do the work and how to behave. Now I'm not saying that your friend can't be trusted. But he's probably going to need to get someone else in to help get it done. Who's going to be responsible for *that* person?

''When you add all this up — the headaches, the aggravation, the mess, the risk of a less-than-quality job — what are you saving?''

In short, sell the professionalism and *quality* of your work. I suggest that you have the definition of quality by John Ruskin (Figure 6-3) printed up. Distribute these leaflets whenever you discuss quality with a prospect.

In this chapter, we've talked about sales knowledge — how it helps you to get the customer's signature on the dotted line. In Chapter 7, I'll talk about financing, the key to more sales.

Chapter 7

Financing – The Key to More Sales

America is the land of credit. We buy our homes, cars, televisions, refrigerators — and all big-ticket items — on credit. Home improvements are a big-ticket item. If you're a remodeling contractor, you have to offer credit. Using the credit system to your advantage can increase sales tremendously.

Becoming a Dealer

First, visit your bank or savings and loan association, and arrange to set up a home improvement dealership. As a loan dealer, you'll take loan applications from your prospects and forward the applications to the lender for approval.

This is good business for the bank or S&L. But some lenders will be more anxious to work with you than others. If your bank or S&L won't cooperate, find one that will. Small loan companies and mortgage bankers also offer home improvement loans. The lender will require an up-to-date financial statement from you to determine if you qualify for the home improvement dealership.

Many home improvement loans qualify for Federal Housing Administration (FHA) insurance. This means that your client borrows from the bank, but repayment is guaranteed by the FHA. The homeowner doesn't normally have to put up any collateral for a home improvement loan. But under certain conditions, a trust deed or mortgage on the buyer's real property, or other security, might be required.

Many clients will qualify for regular home improvement loans without FHA insurance. These home improvement loans may be issued under the *HIP Plan*. The interest rate will be slightly higher than the rate for FHA home improvement loans.

The additional interest often goes into a reserve account set up by the bank. This reserve account is audited periodically. If the loss potential is lower than the amount in reserve, the bank either issues a credit to the dealer's checking account or a check for an agreed-upon percentage of the average in the reserve account. This can add up to a substantial profit for a remodeling contractor.

The FHA Credit Application for a property improvement loan is a simple form. See Figure 7-1. A sample HIP Application is shown in Figure 7-2. *Have the customer fill out the loan application while you write up the contract.*

In this way, the customer will start looking up his loan balances and account books without you prodding him. Even more important, when the homeowner fills out the application himself, he is a *participant*, rather than just the object of the salesman's high-pressure presentation. When the application is complete, the customer has agreed to buy. You've made a firm sale.

Figure 7-3 is a Stock Retail Instalment Contract. This form includes the disclosure of terms and the APR rate required under Regulation Z of the Federal Truth-in-Lending Act.

U.S. DEPARTMENT OF HOUSING AND URBAN DEVELOPMENT
HOUSING-FEDERAL HOUSING COMMISIONER .

CREDIT APPLICATION FOR PROPERTY IMPROVEMENT LOAN

Form Approved
OMB NO. 63-R0037

This application is submitted to obtain credit under the provisions of Title I of the National Housing Act
(PLEASE ANSWER ALL QUESTIONS)

FH-1 (2-78)

TO: Lending Institution which will provide the funds:	DATE:

1. Do you have any past due obligations owed to or insured by any agency of the Federal Government? *(If the answer is "Yes", you are not eligible to apply for an FHA Title I Loan until the existing debt has been brought current.)* Check Block ☐ Yes ☐ No

2. Have you any other application for an FHA Title I Improvement Loan pending at this time? ☐ Yes ☐ No *(If "Yes", with whom - name and address.)* _____

3. I hereby apply for a loan of $ _____ (Net) to be repaid in _____ Months.

4. APPLICANT (S)

Applicant Name:	Sex	Age	Home Phone
Soc. Sec. #			Number of Dependents

Marital Status: ☐ Married ☐ Unmarried (including Single, Divorced, ☐ Separated Widowed)

(Check Applicable Box): (1)☐ American Indian or Alaska Native (2)☐ Asian or Pacific Islander (3)☐ Black, not of Hispanic origin (4)☐ Hispanic (5)☐ White, not of Hispanic origin (6)☐ Other (specify)

Co-Applicant Name (If any):	Sex	Age	Home Phone:
Soc. Sec. #			Number of Dependents

Marital Status: ☐ Married ☐ Unmarried (including Single, Divorced, ☐ Separated Widowed)

(Check Applicable Box): (1)☐ American Indian or Alaska Native (2)☐ Asian or Pacific Islander (3)☐ Black, not of Hispanic origin (4)☐ Hispanic (5)☐ White, not of Hispanic origin (6)☐ Other (specify)

The information concerning minority group categories, sex, marital status, and age is required for statistical purposes so the Department may determine the degree to which its programs are being utilized by minority families and for other evaluation studies.

Address (Street, City, State and ZIP Code):	How Long	Name and Address of nearest relative not living with you	Relationship
Previous Address (Street, City, State and ZIP Code):	How Long		

5. EMPLOYMENT AND SALARIES: *(If applicant is self-employed, submit current financial statement.)*

Employer Name and Business Address:	Type of work or Position:	No. of Years:	Business Phone	Salary (Week/Month)
				$ per
Previous Employer Name and Business Address:				
Co-Applicant's Employer Name and Business Address:	Type of work or Position:	No. of Years:	Business Phone	Salary (Week/Month)
				$ per

Other Income-Sources *(Note: Income from alimony, child support, or separate maintenance income need not be shown unless you will rely upon it as a basis for undertaking or repaying this loan.)*

Amount (Week/Month) $ per

6. BANK ACCOUNT:

☐ Yes ☐ No ☐ Checking ☐ Savings

Name and Address of Bank or Branch:

7. CREDIT ACCOUNTS: (Give name and address of finance companies or stores which have extended credit and which you have paid in full.)

a.	b.
c.	d.

8. DEBTS: List all fixed obligations, installment accounts, FHA loans, and debts to banks, finance companies, and Government agencies. *(If more space is needed, list all additional debts on attached sheets.)*

FHA Ins. Yes	No	To Whom Indebted Name & Acct. Mortgage/Contract	City and State	Date Incurred	Original Amount	Present Balance	Monthly Payments	Amount Past Due
					$	$	$	$
					$	$	$	$
					$	$	$	$
					$	$	$	$
					$	$	$	$
A U T O		Lien Holder:		Year and Make:	$	$	$	
		Lien Holder:		Year and Make:	$	$	$	

Previous Editions are Obsolete
FORM 1137 REV. 2/79

FH-1 (2-78)

FHA Credit Application
Figure 7-1

—2—

9. PROPERTY TO BE IMPROVED:

If this is a new residential structure, has it been completed and occupied for 90 days or longer? ☐ Yes   ☐ No

Address (Number, Street, City, County, State and ZIP Code):		Type - Home, Apt., Store, Farm, etc., (If Apt., Number of Units):	Date of Purchase:
Census Tract:		Year Built:	

FILL IN ONE	Is Owned By:	Name of Title Holder:	Date of Mortgage:	Price Paid: $
	Is being bought on Installment Contract By:	Name of Purchaser:	Name and Address of Title Holder:	Price Paid: $
	Is Leased By:	Name of Lessee:		Date Lease Expires:
	Name of Landlord:		Address:	Rent Per Month:

10. PROCEEDS OF THIS LOAN WILL BE USED TO IMPROVE THE DESCRIBED PROPERTY AS FOLLOWS:

Describe each improvement planned	Name and Address of Contractor/Dealer	Estimated Cost
		$
		$
		$
		$
		$

WARNING

Any person who knowingly makes a false statement or a misrepresentation in this application or causes such a false statement or misrepresentation to be made shall be subject to a fine of not more than $5000 or by imprisonment for not more than 2 years, or both, under provisions of the United States Criminal Code.

IMPORTANT - APPLICANT READ BEFORE SIGNING

The selection of a Contractor or Dealer, acceptance of materials used, and work performed is your responsibility. Neither the HUD-FHA nor the Financial Institution guarantees the material or workmanship or inspects the work performed.

I (We) certify that the above statements are true, accurate, and complete to the best of my (our) knowledge and belief. This application shall remain the property of the Lending Institution to which submitted for the purpose of obtaining a loan.

I (We) hereby consent to and authorize the Lending Institution or the HUD-FHA, after the giving of reasonable notice, to enter the improved property for the purpose of determining that the improvements specified in this application have been completed.

Name _____ (LS)   Name _____ (LS)
(Applicant)   (Co-Applicant)

NOTE TO SALESMAN: If proceeds will be disbursed to the Contractor/Dealer, the person(s) selling the above described improvements must sign the following certification.

I (We) certify that: 1) I (We) am (are) the person(s) who sold the job. 2) The Contract contains the whole agreement with the borrower 3) The borrower has not been given or promised a cash payment or rebate nor has it been represented to the borrower that he or she will receive a cash bonus or commission on future sales as an inducement for the consummation of this transaction; that the improvements have not been misrepresented; no promises impossible of attainment; no encouragement of trial purchase; no promise that the improvements will be used as a model for advertising or other demonstration purposes; and no offer of debt consolidation.

(LS) Name _____
(My true name and signature are as shown above)

If application is prepared by one other than the applicant, the person preparing the application must sign below.
I (We) certify that the statements made herein are based upon information given to me (us) by the borrower(s) and are accurate to the best of my (our) knowledge and belief.

Prepared by: _____   Address: _____

Representing: _____
(Name of Dealer/Contractor)

(Reserved for use of Lending Institution):

FH-1 (2-78) Previous Editions Obsolete FORM 1137 REV. 2/79

FHA Credit Application
Figure 7-1 (continued)

PROPERTY IMPROVEMENT LOAN APPLICATION

LOAN AMOUNT REQUESTED $	TERM REQUESTED MONTHS		DATE

BORROWER INFORMATION

NAME (PLEASE PRINT)	AGE

SOCIAL SECURITY NO. — —	MARITAL STATUS* ☐ MARRIED ☐ UNMARRIED ☐ SEPARATED

HOME PHONE	NUMBER OF DEPENDENTS:	THEIR AGES:

PRESENT STREET ADDRESS	HOW LONG? YRS.

CITY	STATE	ZIP CODE

PREVIOUS STREET ADDRESS	HOW LONG? YRS.

CITY	STATE	ZIP CODE

CO-BORROWER INFORMATION

NAME (PLEASE PRINT)	AGE

SOCIAL SECURITY NO. — —	MARITAL STATUS* ☐ MARRIED ☐ UNMARRIED ☐ SEPARATED

HOME PHONE	NUMBER OF DEPENDENTS:	THEIR AGES:

PRESENT STREET ADDRESS	HOW LONG? YRS.

CITY	STATE	ZIP CODE

PREVIOUS STREET ADDRESS	HOW LONG? YRS.

CITY	STATE	ZIP CODE

BORROWER'S EMPLOYMENT AND INCOME

PRESENT EMPLOYER NAME & ADDRESS	☐ SELF-EMPLOYED

BUSINESS PHONE	POSITION

LENGTH OF SERVICE: YEARS	GROSS SALARY $	☐ WEEKLY ☐ MONTHLY

PREVIOUS EMPLOYER NAME & ADDRESS	☐ SELF-EMPLOYED

LENGTH OF SERVICE YEARS	POSITION

OTHER INCOME SOURCE**	AMOUNT $ MONTHLY

CO-BORROWER'S EMPLOYMENT AND INCOME

PRESENT EMPLOYER NAME & ADDRESS	☐ SELF-EMPLOYED

BUSINESS PHONE	POSITION

LENGTH OF SERVICE: YEARS	GROSS SALARY $	☐ WEEKLY ☐ MONTHLY

PREVIOUS EMPLOYER NAME & ADDRESS	☐ SELF-EMPLOYED

LENGTH OF SERVICE YEARS	POSITION

OTHER INCOME SOURCE**	AMOUNT $ MONTHLY

*ANSWER ONLY IF LOAN IS TO BE SECURED BY A MORTGAGE.
**ALIMONY, CHILD SUPPORT OR SEPARATE MAINTENANCE NEED NOT BE REVEALED IF YOU DO NOT CHOOSE TO RELY ON IT AS A BASIS FOR LOAN REPAYMENT.

CREDIT INFORMATION

LIST ALL OUTSTANDING OBLIGATIONS OF BOTH BORROWER AND CO-BORROWER INCLUDING INSTALLMENT ACCOUNTS, MORTGAGES AND DEBTS TO BANKS, FINANCE COMPANIES AND OTHERS. ANY OMISSION OF ANY UNPAID DEBT IS A MATERIAL MISREPRESENTATION. IF YOU NEED MORE ROOM TO LIST CREDITORS, USE MARGIN OR SEPARATE SHEET.

MORTGAGE LOAN OWED TO (NAME & ADDRESS)	PHONE NO.	ACCOUNT NO.	DATE INCURRED
	ORIGINAL AMOUNT $	PRESENT BALANCE $	MONTHLY PAYMENT $
OBLIGATION TO (NAME & ADDRESS) ☐ IMPROVEMENT LOAN ☐ OTHER	PHONE NO.	ACCOUNT NO.	DATE INCURRED
	ORIGINAL AMOUNT $	PRESENT BALANCE $	MONTHLY PAYMENT $
OBLIGATION TO (NAME & ADDRESS) ☐ IMPROVEMENT LOAN ☐ OTHER	PHONE NO.	ACCOUNT NO.	DATE INCURRED
	ORIGINAL AMOUNT $	PRESENT BALANCE $	MONTHLY PAYMENT $
OBLIGATION TO (NAME & ADDRESS) ☐ IMPROVEMENT LOAN ☐ OTHER	PHONE NO.	ACCOUNT NO.	DATE INCURRED
	ORIGINAL AMOUNT $	PRESENT BALANCE $	MONTHLY PAYMENT $

PLEASE COMPLETE REVERSE SIDE.

HIP Application
Figure 7-2

PROPERTY IMPROVEMENT LOAN APPLICATION (REVERSE SIDE)

CREDIT REFERENCES GIVE NAMES AND ADDRESSES OF FINANCE COMPANIES AND STORES WHICH HAVE EXTENDED CREDIT AND WHICH YOU HAVE PAID IN FULL.

NAME	ADDRESS

SAVINGS ACCOUNT AT _____
INSTITUTION'S NAME   ADDRESS

CHECKING ACCOUNT AT _____
INSTITUTION'S NAME   ADDRESS

PROPERTY TO BE IMPROVED

PROPERTY STREET ADDRESS	PROPERTY TYPE (CHECK ONE)
CITY STATE ZIP CODE	☐ SINGLE FAMILY ☐ 2 TO 4 APT. ☐ 5 OR 6 APT. ☐ COMMERCIAL
DATE BUILT DATE PURCHASED PURCHASE PRICE $	☐ COMBINED BUSINESS AND APARTMENT

I (WE), THE UNDERSIGNED, AM (ARE) [CHECK ONE OF THE BELOW]

☐ TITLEHOLDER(S)   ☐ CONTRACT BUYER(S) PURCHASING FROM: _____

☐ BENEFICIARY(S) TO TRUST   _____   _____
                             TRUSTEE'S NAME   TRUST NUMBER

IMPROVEMENTS LIST REPAIRS AND IMPROVEMENTS ON WHICH THE PROCEEDS OF THIS LOAN ARE TO BE USED.

DESCRIPTION (LIST EACH IMPROVEMENT SEPARATELY)	CONTRACTOR'S NAME & ADDRESS	ESTIMATED COST
1. _____		$
2. _____		$
3. _____		$

THE SELECTION OF A CONTRACTOR OR DEALER, INSPECTION AND ACCEPTANCE OF MATERIALS USED AND WORK PERFORMED ARE THE BORROWER'S RESPONSIBILITY.

READ BEFORE SIGNING: I certify and represent that the statements on this application are true and correct; that I have included all my debts without exception; that the ownership of the property is as stated above; that the above improvement is being bought and installed on the above real estate by the undersigned as a part of said real estate. I understand that the selection of the Contractor or Dealer is my responsibility; that FIRST FEDERAL SAVINGS AND LOAN ASSOCIATION OF CHICAGO does not order the material, inspect the work performed or obtain lien waivers from any contractors or subcontractors. I authorize any one of the owners of the property to be improved to sign a Completion Certificate at any time hereafter, and the same shall be conclusive evidence of the fact that the Contract for the work to be done was satisfactorily completed by the Contractor.

I (WE) HAVE READ AND UNDERSTAND THIS APPLICATION. WARNING: A FALSE STATEMENT OR REPRESENTATION IS PUNISHABLE UNDER PROVISIONS OF UNITED STATES CRIMINAL CODE.

BORROWER: _____   WITNESSED BY _____
                                            AGENT'S OR CONTRACTOR'S OFFICER'S SIGNATURE IF
                                            APPLICATION IS SUBMITTED BY CONTRACTOR

CO-BORROWER: _____

I AM INTERESTED IN CREDIT LIFE INSURANCE.   ☐ YES   ☐ NO

INFORMATION FOR GOVERNMENT MONITORING PURPOSES

The following information is requested by the Federal Government if this loan is related to a dwelling, in order to monitor the lender's compliance with equal credit opportunity and fair housing laws. You are not required to furnish this information, but are encouraged to do so. The law provides that a lender may neither discriminate on the basis of this information, nor on whether you choose to furnish it. However, if you choose not to furnish it, under Federal regulations this lender is required to note race and sex on the basis of visual observation or surname. If you do not wish to furnish the above information, please initial below.

BORROWER:
I do not wish to furnish this information (initials)_____

| RACE/ NATIONAL ORIGIN | ☐ American Indian, Alaskan Native
☐ Asian, Pacific Islander ☐ Black
☐ Hispanic ☐ White
☐ Other (specify) _____ | SEX: | ☐ Female
☐ Male |

CO-BORROWER:
I do not wish to furnish this information (initials)_____

| RACE/ NATIONAL ORIGIN | ☐ American Indian, Alaskan Native
☐ Asian, Pacific Islander ☐ Black
☐ Hispanic ☐ White
☐ Other (specify) _____ | SEX: | ☐ Female
☐ Male |

HIP Application
Figure 7-2 (continued)

RETAIL INSTALMENT CONTRACT

[Home Improvement]

ACCOUNT NUMBER

(ASSIGNEE)

AMOUNT OF LOAN   DATE

Buyer (& Co-Buyer) - Name & Residence Address (Include: County, Zip Code, Phone & Social Security No.)   Seller and Creditor, Corporate, Firm, or Trade Name & Business Address

The undersigned Contractor (hereinafter referred to as Seller) agrees to sell and the undersigned Buyer (which means Buyer and all Co-Buyers who sign below, jointly and severally) agrees to buy the following goods and services, which are to be furnished or used in the modernization, rehabilitation, repair, alteration or improvement of the real property located at Buyer's address given below or at

Number and Street   City   County   State   Zip Code

Description of New Goods and Services: _____

TRUTH IN LENDING DISCLOSURES

ANNUAL PERCENTAGE RATE The cost of your credit as a yearly rate.	FINANCE CHARGE The dollar amount the credit will cost you.	Amount Financed The amount of credit provided to you or on your behalf.	Total of Payments The amount you will have paid after you have made all payments as scheduled.	Total Sale Price The total cost of your purchase on credit, including your downpayment of
%	$	$	$	$

Itemization of the Amount Financed:

$ _____ Cash price
$ _____ Less cash down payment
$ _____ On Date of Contract
$ _____ On Delivery of Material
$ _____ On completion
$ _____ Less trade-in
$ _____ Total Down Payment

Your payment schedule will be:

Number of Payments	Amount of Payments	When Payments Are Due

Amounts paid on your account

$ _____ Credit sale balance
$ _____ Prior balance to seller

Insurance

Credit life insurance and credit disability insurance are not required to obtain credit, and will not be provided unless you sign and agree to pay the additional cost.

Amounts paid to others on your behalf

$ _____ Pay-off prior loan
To _____
$ _____ Public officials
$ _____ Insurance companies

Type	Premium	Signature
Credit Life	$	I/we want credit life insurance _____ Signature _____ Signature
Credit Disability	$	I want credit disability insurance _____ Signature
Credit Life and Disability	$	I want credit life and disability insurance _____ Signature

$ _____ to _____
$ _____ to _____
$ _____ to _____
$ _____ to _____

You may obtain property insurance from anyone you want that is acceptable

to _____ If you get the insurance

from _____ you will pay $ _____ for the

term of _____ months

$ _____ PREPAID FINANCE CHARGE (ESTIMATE)

Security: You are giving a security interest in: ☐ the goods or property being purchased. ☒ right of set-off against any moneys, credits or other property of yours in the possession of the Holder, on deposit or otherwise. ☐ (brief description of other property).

Filing fees $ _____   **Non-filing insurance** $ _____

Late Charge: If any payment is more than 10 days late you will be charged $5.00 or 5% of the payment, whichever is less.

Prepayment: If you pay off early, you will be entitled to a refund of part of the finance charge.

See your contract terms on face and reverse side for any additional information about nonpayment, default, any required repayment in full before the scheduled date, prepayment refunds and penalties.

NOTE: If this contract is used in connection with an FHA approved loan, credit life or disability insurance may not be financed or otherwise included in the Total of Payments.

Buyer promises to pay the **TOTAL OF PAYMENTS** shown herein to Seller in _____ instalments of $ _____ each and a final instalment of $ _____, beginning _____ days after completion date as indicated on the Completion Certificate and continuing on the same day of each successive month thereafter until paid in full. Guarantor, if any, guarantees the collection of the above described "Total of Payments" and any other indebtedness due herein upon failure of the Seller to collect the above amount from the Buyer named herein. Finance Charge begins to accrue on date of completion. Buyer authorizes Seller to insert the due date of the first instalment in Seller's counterpart of this contract after Buyer signs the Completion Certificate. Due date of

the first instalment is _____.

If Buyer shall default in the payment of any instalment of the Total of Payments when due, or in the event of bankruptcy of Buyer, or the theft, substantial damage to, sale, encumbrance, removal, attachment, forfeiture or levy upon the goods, which event of default shall continue for at least **30 days**, or if Buyer shall abandon or destroy the goods, or if holder has reasonable cause to believe that Buyer is about to leave the State, holder may declare all instalments of the Total of Payments immediately due and payable, without notice or demand. In the event of acceleration, Buyer shall be credited with the same rebate of unearned Finance Charge as for voluntary prepayment.

SECURITY INTERESTS: Seller retains and shall have a purchase-money security interest in the above-described goods, together with all accessories, parts and equipment attached thereto and all accessions, until the Total of Payments and all other indebtedness of Buyer hereunder are paid in full. Buyer grants Holder the right of set-off or lien on any deposit or sums now or hereafter owed by Holder to Buyer. Seller acquires a mechanics' lien for services, material and labor furnished to repair, build upon, improve, alter or ornament Buyer's real property.

DEFAULT CHARGES: Buyer agrees to pay reasonable attorneys' fees incurred by Seller in the collection or enforcement of this contract.

REBATE FOR PREPAYMENT: Buyer may prepay this contract in full at any time before maturity of the final instalment, and if he does so, Buyer shall receive a rebate of unearned Finance Charge calculated under the "Rule of 78ths" less an acquisition cost of $12.00. No rebate of less than $1.00 will be made. Prepayment in full will reduce the insurance charge (if any) for this contract.

IDENTIFICATION OF A SECURITY INTEREST:
☐ Trust Deed or Mortgage on Real Property of Buyer at Above Address
☐ Other

NOTICE OF PROPOSED GROUP CREDIT LIFE INSURANCE

If a charge is made above for credit life insurance and if such insurance is to be procured by Assignee, the undersigned takes notice that decreasing term insurance written under a Group Credit Life Insurance Policy is to be purchased on the life of the Buyer(s) whose signature(s) appear above, subject to acceptance by the insurer and insurance of a certificate by

_____ (Insurer) _____ (Home Office Address)

The amount of premium is shown above. The term of insurance will commence on the date of this contract and expire on the originally scheduled maturity date of the indebtedness. The initial amount of insurance will be equal to the initial indebtedness and will decrease as any payment is made on the indebtedness in an amount computed by multiplying the amount of the payment by the ratio of initial insurance over the initial indebtedness. The proceeds of any insurance paid will be applied to reduce or extinguish the indebtedness. If insurance is terminated prior to the scheduled maturity date of the indebtedness, any premium refund will be paid or credited promptly to the person entitled thereto. Refund formula is on file with the Director of Insurance and with creditor. All of the foregoing is subject to the provisions of the certificate of insurance to be issued.

NOTICE

ANY HOLDER OF THIS CONSUMER CREDIT CONTRACT IS SUBJECT TO ALL CLAIMS AND DEFENSES WHICH THE DEBTOR COULD ASSERT AGAINST THE SELLER OF GOODS OR SERVICES OBTAINED PURSUANT HERETO OR WITH THE PROCEEDS HEREOF. RECOVERY HEREUNDER BY THE DEBTOR SHALL NOT EXCEED AMOUNTS PAID BY THE DEBTOR HEREUNDER.

NOTICE TO THE BUYER: (1) Do not sign this agreement before you read it or if it contains any blank spaces. (2) You are entitled to an exact copy of the agreement you sign. (3) Under the law you have the right, among others, to pay in advance the full amount due and to obtain under certain conditions a partial refund of the Finance Charge.

Executed this _____ day of _____, 19 _____   RETAIL INSTALMENT CONTRACT

Buyer _____

SELLER

By _____ Title _____   Buyer _____

Guarantor _____

I, hereby guarantee the collection of the above described amount upon failure of the seller named herein to collect said amount from the buyer named herein.

©COPYRIGHT 1982   FORM 114 4/82   151393 - STUART-HOOPER CO., CHICAGO

ORIGINAL

Stock retail instalment contract
Figure 7-3

Figure 7-4 is the Notice of Right to Cancel, or Rescission Form. I buy these forms and Instalment Contracts from the Stuart-Hooper Company, 8757 S. Greenwood Avenue, Chicago, IL 60619.

Don't let a rescission form scare you. It actually protects the legitimate contractor. The right to rescind has run many of the suede shoe boys out of the home improvement field. That helps every legitimate home improvement contractor.

The right of rescission gives every homeowner the right to cancel (within three working days) any purchase made inside the home, provided the purchase cost $25 or more. The law was made to protect people who buy on impulse from high-pressure, house-to-house salespeople. These homeowners often find themselves locked into contracts they don't understand, can't afford and can't back out of unless they pay a high penalty.

The right of rescission is the most difficult paper to get signed. People will sign a note, a mortgage on their home or a contract for thousands of dollars. But they'll balk at the right of rescission. It's something they've never heard of, and they're leary of it. Here's how to present the right of rescission.

"I need your signatures on this form, Mr. and Mrs. Homeowner. This form, under the government law, gives you the right to cancel this order in three working days. Now, I know you aren't going to cancel this order, because you wouldn't have spent an hour and a half with me, right? So, if you want to cancel, tell me now, and I'll tear the contract up, and I'll leave. We'll still be good friends. But I think you want the work done. O.K. Mr. Homeowner your signature goes here. Mrs. Homeowner your signature goes here."

If there are any problems in the contract, now's when they'll come out. And you'll have a chance to clear them up. You can see how important it is to explain the right of rescission clearly. After the customer signs, your sale is complete. A cancellation isn't likely. If the homeowner *does* cancel after three working days, your lawyer has a good case for collecting damages for you. Make sure you get a signature on this important form.

The Promissory Note has to be signed by all owners and a co-signer. See Figure 7-5.

Most home improvement loans set the first payment date at 60 days after completion. The first payment date has to be specified in the note. (The *note* is the promise to pay that the borrower signs.)

Usually you won't know in advance exactly when the job will be done. The loan officer at the lending institution where you discount the paper (note) should help you with this problem.

Until you've worked with a lending institution for several months, let the lender fill out the note. The lender fills it out and you get the client's signature on it when you pick up the completion ticket after the job is done. Otherwise you have to make an extra trip to the client's house.

Under lending regulations, the bank or S&L must send either a letter of approval or rejection to the borrower. The letter of approval states the amount of the note, the interest rate, length of the term of the note and the dollar amount of the total interest. There are several ways for you to become a dealer. Banks and S&L's blow hot and cold on home improvement loans. But some lending institution in your community will almost certainly be anxious to cooperate with you. Finance companies are looking for the "home improvement paper," as these notes are called. Mortgage bankers make home improvement loans to their existing borrowers.

Sell Easy Payments

You've been appointed a dealer. Now you're ready to do business. What you're going to sell is payments. When the payments are within the buyer's budget, it's easy to sell construction work. The buyer's favorite "out" has been eliminated. He can't tell you that he can't afford it. With easy terms, nearly everyone can afford what you're proposing.

During the sales pitch, recap the work you're planning to do for your customer. Do this before you give him the total price. This recap should emphasize each sales point and paint a glowing picture of the completed job. This makes the buyer more receptive to your price.

"In your garage, Mr. Homeowner, we'll install a 22 x 20 concrete floor with wire mesh (to meet code), a 3-foot concrete apron, studs 24 inches on center, and double top plates and corners, with sway braces in each corner. And so on.

"We can do this job for *no money down* under the FHA plan at First Federal Savings for only $120.37 per month for 60 months. The first payment will be due 60 days after completion. You're comfortable with that? Good. The total price is $5,000, at an APR rate of 15%. That's cheaper than your bank credit cards or your oil company

H-8 RESCISSION MODEL FORM (General)

NOTICE OF RIGHT TO CANCEL

Consumer Name _____

Address _____

| |
| ACCOUNT NUMBER |

Identification of Transaction _____

NOTICE OF RIGHT TO CANCEL

1. Your Right to Cancel.

You are entering into a transaction that will result in a [mortgage/lien/security interest] [on/in] your home. You have a legal right under federal law to cancel this transaction, without cost, within three business days from whichever of the following events occurs last:

(1) the date of the transaction, which is

_____ ; or

(2) the date you received your Truth in Lending disclosures; or

(3) the date you received this notice of your right to cancel.

If you cancel the transaction, the [mortgage/lien/security interest] is also cancelled. Within 20 calendar days after we receive your notice, we must take the steps necessary to reflect the fact that the [mortgage/lien/security interest] [on/in] your home has been cancelled, and we must return to you any money or property you have given to us or to anyone else in connection with this transaction.

You may keep any money or property we have given you until we have done the things mentioned above, but you must then offer to return the money or property. If it is impractical or unfair for you to return the property, you must offer its reasonable value. You may offer to return the property at your home or at the location of the property. Money must be returned to the address shown below. If we do not take possession of the money or property within 20 calendar days of your offer, you may keep it without further obligation.

2. How to Cancel.

If you decide to cancel this transaction, you may do so by notifying us, in writing, at

_____
(Name of Creditor)

_____
(Creditor's Business Address)

You may use any written statement that is signed and dated by you and states your intention to cancel, and or you may use this notice by dating and signing below. Keep one copy of this notice because it contains important information about your rights.

If you cancel by mail or telegram, you must send the notice no

later than midnight of _____ (date). (or midnight of the third business day following the latest of the three events listed above). If you send or deliver your written notice to cancel some other way, it must be delivered to the above address no later than that time.

I WISH TO CANCEL.

_____
Consumer's Signature   Date

Each Signer Acknowledges Receipt of TWO (2) Copies of this
NOTICE OF RIGHT TO CANCEL

_____   _____
Date   (Consumer)

_____   _____
Date   (Consumer)

H150922

ORIGINAL

Rescission form
Figure 7-4

PROMISSORY NOTE

$ _____ Chicago, Illinois _____ , 19 _____

For value received, I, we, or either of us, promise to pay to _____

_____ or order the

sum of _____ Dollars

in _____ successive monthly installments each $ _____ except the final installment which shall be the balance due on this note, commencing on the _____ day of _____ , 19 _____ , and on the same day of each month thereafter until paid, with interest on principal, after maturing of entire balance as herein provided, at the highest lawful rate, and at the option of the holder, a reasonable sum as attorney's fee, if placed in the hands of an attorney for collection after default, and all collection and title costs incurred thereunder. On non-payment of any installment when due, all remaining installments, at the option of the holder, shall become immediately due and payable. A "late charge" of 5% of the monthly installment (maximum $5.00) may be made on any installment paid more than 10 days after due date. And to secure the payment of said amount, I, we, or either of us, hereby authorize, irrevocably, any attorney of any Court of Record to appear for me, or us, in such Court, in term time or vacation, at any time after default in payment of any installment, and confess a judgment without process in favor of the holder of this Note for such amount as may appear to be unpaid thereon, together with costs, and all collection and title costs, and reasonable attorney's fees and to waive and release all errors which may intervene in any such proceedings, and consent to immediate execution upon such judgment, hereby ratifying and confirming all that my, or our, said attorney may do by virtue hereof. Protest and notice of dishonor are waived by all parties hereto including endorsers. Upon sale of the property improved with the proceeds of this loan, at the option of the holder of this Note, the unpaid balance of this Note shall become immediately due and payable. In the event of prepayment, from any source, a minimum charge of $5.00 shall be imposed for the insurance premium if insurance has been written in connection with this debt.

NOTICE

ANY HOLDER OF THIS CONSUMER CREDIT CONTRACT IS SUBJECT TO ALL CLAIMS AND DEFENSES WHICH THE DEBTOR COULD ASSERT AGAINST THE SELLER OF GOODS OR SERVICES OBTAINED WITH THE PROCEEDS HEREOF, RECOVERY HEREUNDER BY THE DEBTOR SHALL NOT EXCEED AMOUNTS PAID BY THE DEBTOR HEREUNDER.

NEGOTIABLE and PAYABLE at the

_____ (SEAL)
(Signature)

_____ (SEAL)
(Signature)

Promissory Note
Figure 7-5

charge cards. And I'm sure you know how much more your car loan cost — probably 21%! By the way, although I quoted to you the APR rate, as the law requires, you'll be paying a lot less in actual dollars. I'll take a moment to explain the APR to you, if I may.''

If your customer balks or sits in silence when you suggest payments of $120.37 for 60 months, your sale is hanging by a thread. Here's how to handle it.

''Maybe you'd like a shorter term? We can give you 48 months (36 months, 30 months, 24 months, whatever the customer desires). Shall I figure out the payments on 30 months, for example?''

Get the customer to tell you how long a term he needs. Everyone is different. Each client has different financial assets or income. They all have their own ideas about how many payments they want to make. If they're *still* sitting in silence even

after you offer a variety of terms, then they may be looking for a smaller payment. Here's how to suggest it.

''Maybe you'd like a smaller payment? We can arrange whatever payment is comfortable for you. The rate book goes up to ten years. What size payment would you like to make?''

The APR

Here's how to explain the APR rate to your customer.

''Let's say you borrow $1,000 for one year. Now, if you're paying 6% interest, your total interest on $1,000 is $60. Right? So for one year, your total loan will be $1,060. However, the government insists under Regulation Z that we give you the APR rate. The APR rate is 11%. Here's how interest rates are figured into your payments.

''Let's look again at our $1,000 loan at 6%. Take $1,060 and divide it by 12 months. The monthly payment is $88.33, rounded out. So at the end of the first month you make a payment of $88.33. You now have a loan balance of $911.67. Let's carry it on another month. At the end of the second month you make another payment of $88.33. Now you only owe $833.34. It continues in the same manner until the entire loan is paid off. Your payments include interest on the entire $1,000. The total amount of that interest was $60.''

It's extremely important to explain the interest rates and how they work. People make their monthly payments in dollars. Consumers know how many dollars they have to spend each month. The consumer wants to know and should know the rate of interest he's paying. He should know the discount rate in addition to the APR rate. Knowing all the facts takes the sting out of the APR rate.

Suppose a competitor has already called on your client. His bid might be higher or lower than yours. He probably also offered financing, but you can bet he didn't explain how financing really works. When you explain to the customer exactly what he's paying for, he knows that you appreciate his hard-earned dollars. You're acting as his financial advisor, and he'll put his trust in you. Naturally, he'd rather buy from someone he can trust.

This is the easiest close in the building industry. It's what the public wants to hear: *EASY MONTHLY PAYMENTS.*

"I'll start writing up the credit application now if that's okay with you, Mr. Homeowner. I've been a dealer at First Federal Savings since 1982. In effect, I'm an agent of theirs. I can take your application right here on the kitchen table. You won't have to take time off from work to go to the bank and file an application.''

Invariably, the buyer's impressed and relieved, because he doesn't have to apply in person at the bank and try to fill out unfamiliar papers and answer unfamiliar questions.

Having the application in your briefcase is like having the bank endorse your services. The bank wouldn't provide you with forms unless they knew you were running a reputable operation. Thus the name of the bank or S&L adds stature to you and to your company. A word of caution, however. Never, never say that the bank or S&L recommends you. It isn't so. You are a dealer of theirs.

The bank or S&L will give you a rate book, similar to the one shown in Figure 7-6. I usually open the rate book and explain the figures to the buyer as I pencil them out.

"This is the APR rate. And this is the amount needed to pay for your work. This is the total monthly payment of principal and interest. This is the total loan amount. By deducting the amount borrowed, you can see the amount of interest you're paying for 60 months.''

Point to these figures in the rate book so that the buyer can see them. This convinces the buyer that you're not hiding anything from him. Many customers are quoted one payment figure by the salesman, then when the payment book arrives, they discover that the figure was wrong, and their monthly payments are going to be higher. Protect yourself and your customers. Be honest with them at all times.

"Most families take the 60-month plan. On a longer loan the interest rate is higher. Even families who don't think they need 60 months to pay take the 60-month plan. That provides an extra cash cushion for a rainy day.''

This is also the time to stress prepayment privileges. Explain that under federal law the customer only pays interest for the time the money's used. This is the Rule of 78, which is the lender's way of calculating unused interest. It's all spelled out in the contract. Following is a typical paragraph:

Rebate For Prepayment: Buyer may prepay this contract in full at any time before maturity of the final instalment, and if he does so Buyer shall receive a statutory rebate of unearned Finance Charge equal to that proportion of the original Finance Charge, less an acquisition cost of $12.00, as the sum of the periodical time balances beginning with the next payment period bears to the sum of all the periodical time balances under the schedule of instalment payments in this contract.

This statutory computation follows the "sum of the digits" method, also known as the Rule of 78ths. No rebate of less than $1.00 will be made. Use of the statutory method of computation will result in a rebate that is less than a proration of the Finance Charge for the period after date of prepayment. The difference may be constructed as a penalty for prepayment.

By explaining this procedure, you remove one more doubt from the customer's mind, thus firming up your deal and promoting customer confidence. In selling the prepayment feature, I often tell a customer:

"When you receive your income tax rebate, Christmas bonus, or hit the big winner in the lottery, pay off the loan. Or prepay as much as you can. Remember, you only pay interest for the amount you use under the rule of 78.''

6% DISCOUNT RATE — PAGE 55

BAL.	48 MONTHS NOTE	PAYT.	54 MONTHS NOTE	PAYT.	60 MONTHS NOTE	PAYT.
1	1.24	.03	1.27	.03	1.30	.03
2	2.48	.06	2.54	.05	2.60	.05
3	3.72	.08	3.81	.08	3.90	.07
4	4.96	.11	5.08	.10	5.20	.09
825	1023.49	21.33	1047.79	19.41	1072.09	17.87
830	1029.69	21.46	1054.14	19.53	1078.59	17.98
835	1035.89	21.59	1060.49	19.64	1085.09	18.09
840	1042.09	21.72	1066.84	19.76	1091.59	18.20
845	1048.30	21.84	1073.19	19.88	1098.09	18.31
850	1054.50	21.97	1079.54	20.00	1104.58	18.41
855	1060.70	22.10	1085.89	20.11	1111.08	18.52
860	1066.91	22.23	1092.24	20.23	1117.58	18.63
865	1073.11	22.36	1098.59	20.35	1124.08	18.74
870	1079.31	22.49	1104.94	20.47	1130.57	18.85
875	1085.52	22.62	1111.29	20.58	1137.07	18.96
880	1091.72	22.75	1117.64	20.70	1143.57	19.06
885	1097.92	22.88	1123.99	20.82	1150.07	19.17
890	1104.12	23.01	1130.34	20.94	1156.56	19.28
895	1110.33	23.14	1136.69	21.05	1163.06	19.39
900	1116.53	23.27	1143.04	21.17	1169.56	19.50
905	1122.73	23.40	1149.39	21.29	1176.06	19.61
910	1128.94	23.52	1155.74	21.41	1182.55	19.71
915	1135.14	23.65	1162.09	21.53	1189.05	19.82
920	1141.34	23.78	1168.45	21.64	1195.55	19.93
925	1147.55	23.91	1174.80	21.76	1202.05	20.04
930	1153.75	24.04	1181.15	21.88	1208.54	20.15
935	1159.95	24.17	1187.50	22.00	1215.04	20.26
940	1166.15	24.30	1193.85	22.11	1221.54	20.36
945	1172.36	24.43	1200.20	22.23	1228.04	20.47
950	1178.56	24.56	1206.55	22.35	1234.53	20.58
955	1184.76	24.69	1212.90	22.47	1241.03	20.69
960	1190.97	24.82	1219.25	22.58	1247.53	20.80
965	1197.17	24.95	1225.60	22.70	1254.03	20.91
970	1203.37	25.08	1231.95	22.82	1260.52	21.01
975	1209.57	25.20	1238.30	22.94	1267.02	21.12
980	1215.78	25.33	1244.65	23.05	1273.52	21.23
985	1221.98	25.46	1251.00	23.17	1280.02	21.34
990	1228.18	25.59	1257.35	23.29	1286.51	21.45
995	1234.39	25.72	1263.70	23.41	1293.01	21.56
1000	1240.59	25.85	1270.05	23.52	1299.51	21.66
1005	1246.79	25.98	1276.40	23.64	1306.01	21.77
1010	1253.00	26.11	1282.75	23.76	1312.50	21.88
1015	1259.20	26.24	1289.10	23.88	1319.00	21.99
1020	1265.40	26.37	1295.45	23.99	1325.50	22.10
1025	1271.60	26.50	1301.80	24.11	1332.00	22.20
A.P.R.	11.00%		10.91%		10.83%	

PAGE 55

6% DISCOUNT RATE — PAGE 56

BAL.	48 MONTHS NOTE	PAYT.	54 MONTHS NOTE	PAYT.	60 MONTHS NOTE	PAYT.
1	1.24	.03	1.27	.03	1.30	.03
2	2.48	.06	2.54	.05	2.60	.05
3	3.72	.08	3.81	.08	3.90	.07
4	4.96	.11	5.08	.10	5.20	.09
1030	1277.81	26.63	1308.15	24.23	1338.49	22.31
1035	1284.01	26.76	1314.50	24.35	1344.99	22.42
1040	1290.21	26.88	1320.85	24.47	1351.49	22.53
1045	1296.42	27.01	1327.20	24.58	1357.99	22.64
1050	1302.62	27.14	1333.55	24.70	1364.48	22.75
1055	1308.82	27.27	1339.90	24.82	1370.98	22.85
1060	1315.02	27.40	1346.25	24.94	1377.48	22.96
1065	1321.23	27.53	1352.60	25.05	1383.98	23.07
1070	1327.43	27.66	1358.95	25.17	1390.47	23.18
1075	1333.63	27.79	1365.30	25.29	1396.97	23.29
1080	1339.84	27.92	1371.65	25.41	1403.47	23.40
1085	1346.04	28.05	1378.00	25.52	1409.97	23.50
1090	1352.24	28.18	1384.35	25.64	1416.46	23.61
1095	1358.45	28.31	1390.70	25.76	1422.96	23.72
1100	1364.65	28.44	1397.05	25.88	1429.46	23.83
1105	1370.85	28.56	1403.40	25.99	1435.96	23.94
1110	1377.05	28.69	1409.75	26.11	1442.45	24.05
1115	1383.26	28.82	1416.10	26.23	1448.95	24.15
1120	1389.46	28.95	1422.45	26.35	1455.45	24.26
1125	1395.66	29.08	1428.81	26.46	1461.95	24.37
1130	1401.87	29.21	1435.16	26.58	1468.45	24.48
1135	1408.07	29.34	1441.51	26.70	1474.94	24.59
1140	1414.27	29.47	1447.86	26.82	1481.44	24.70
1145	1420.47	29.60	1454.21	26.93	1487.94	24.80
1150	1426.68	29.73	1460.56	27.05	1494.44	24.91
1155	1432.88	29.86	1466.91	27.17	1500.93	25.02
1160	1439.08	29.99	1473.26	27.29	1507.43	25.13
1165	1445.29	30.12	1479.61	27.41	1513.93	25.24
1170	1451.49	30.24	1485.96	27.52	1520.43	25.35
1175	1457.69	30.37	1492.31	27.64	1526.92	25.45
1180	1463.90	30.50	1498.66	27.76	1533.42	25.56
1185	1470.10	30.63	1505.01	27.88	1539.92	25.67
1190	1476.30	30.76	1511.36	27.99	1546.42	25.78
1195	1482.50	30.89	1517.71	28.11	1552.91	25.89
1200	1488.71	31.02	1524.06	28.23	1559.41	26.00
1205	1494.91	31.15	1530.41	28.35	1565.91	26.10
1210	1501.11	31.28	1536.76	28.46	1572.41	26.21
1215	1507.32	31.41	1543.11	28.58	1578.90	26.32
1220	1513.52	31.54	1549.46	28.70	1585.40	26.43
1225	1519.72	31.67	1555.81	28.82	1591.90	26.54
1230	1525.92	31.79	1562.16	28.93	1598.40	26.64
A.P.R.	11.00%		10.91%		10.83%	

PAGE 56

Rate book
Figure 7-6

The Rule of the Three C's

The more you know about customer financing, the more tools you have for closing the sale. It's important to understand how credit is granted when you're making sales to homeowners. Credit managers may express it differently, but the underlying idea is the Rule of the Three C's: *Character, Collateral* and *Capacity to pay.*

Character is the reputation of the buyer and his record for meeting his obligations. It's the absence of criminal convictions, bankruptcy or civil judgements (although there might be mitigating circumstances, which are taken into consideration). Good character goes along with well-maintained property and clean housekeeping.

Collateral is the property that backs the loan. The property should provide plenty of equity to pay off previous mortgages and loan expenses. It should also cover the remodeling loan and any existing home improvement loans or other obligations that the buyer wishes to consolidate.

Capacity to pay is having a steady income big enough to meet all expected obligations. There should be enough money left after all expenses are met to cover the mortgage, taxes and insurance payments.

A client who rates high in all three areas will have no trouble qualifying for a home improvement or mortgage loan. Understanding the Three C's, you can make a quick decision about the financial ability of a customer.

Types of Financing

Direct Lenders

Many lending institutions don't have a dealer setup, yet they do make home improvement loans. Some follow only their own lending plans, and others make only FHA loans. Occasionally you'll find a lender that has both plans.

Surprisingly enough, lenders who have their own plans and make loans only to existing customers frequently have lower interest rates.

If you decide to use the services of a direct lender, here's how:

Phone the loan officer, and give him a rundown on the loan you're seeking for his banking or savings customer. Arrange an appointment that coincides with your *customer's time off.* This is important. When trying to arrange financing for a customer, the most common objection will be that he can't take time off from work. Missed work means lost income and possibly trouble with the

boss. Keep this in the back of your mind. Be considerate of your prospect. Make appointments that don't conflict with his work schedule.

Pick up your customers and drive them to the lending institution. Be sure to remind them to bring whatever documents the loan officer has requested. Sit with your clients while the loan officer makes out the application.

Give the loan officer your copy of the improvement contract. Explain the type of job that you'll be doing. Ask him if he wants you to supply a contractor's statement and waivers of lien. This will impress the loan officer and expedite approval.

Ask that you be notified when the loan is approved. Make arrangements to pick up Mr. and Mrs. Homeowner and take them to the bank or S&L to sign the final documents.

Co-ops

Co-ops are popular in some areas. Usually the co-op runs a credit union with liberal lending terms for members. Co-op members may get a better deal on home improvement money from the co-op credit union. But in some cases the interest rate is actually higher than what banks and S&L's are offering. Even so, a dyed-in-the-wool co-op member would rather do business with the co-op than with a bank.

Employee Credit Unions

The same holds true for employee credit unions. When qualifying the customer, if you suspect he works for a company that has an employee credit union, discuss credit union financing. Interest rates may be lower, and there may be another advantage: Borrowing the money from his own company may provide job security for him. The firm may be less likely to lay off someone who owes them money.

Farm Bureau Loans

Farm co-ops are another source of financing. The Farm Bureau offers excellent terms and will handle all the mechanics of the loan. To become a member of the Farm Bureau, a farmer must have a minimum number of acres under cultivation. In the state of Illinois, for example, he must have five or more acres under cultivation.

Private Home Improvement Loans

You've written up an order to be financed by a home improvement loan. The property's free and clear. There's no mortgage. This is an opportunity

In the remodeling business, it takes financing to make the sale

to make an additional profit, if you have some cash reserves. How? Carry the paper yourself.

The returns are much better than you can get in any savings account or money market fund, or practically any other investment that you could make. It's very close to a risk-free investment. To calculate the yield, go back to the section in this chapter on APR's. You take a trust deed on the property to secure the loan. In the rare case of a default, you could wind up owning the property for the net balance due on the loan.

But before doing your own financing on free and clear houses, get some experience in passing regular FHA or HIP paper so that you're thoroughly familiar with the procedures. Discuss with your lawyer the state requirements for loans on real property.

Remember, the more ways you know to finance a customer, the better chance you have of closing the sale.

Mortgage Financing

We've seen four important sources of dealerships for home improvement loans: banks, S&L's, small loan companies and mortgage bankers. We can also use direct lenders, co-ops, employee credit unions, farm bureaus, or carry the paper ourselves. Now let's take a look at mortgage financing.

Use mortgage financing only when you cannot obtain a home improvement loan. Home improvement loans are simple. There's a minimum of red tape, and you get your money fast. Mortgage financing is complicated, time-consuming and expensive. Make sure the sale warrants all this extra work and expense.

Open-end Mortgages

"Do you have an open-end mortgage on this house?"

Ask this question and many homeowners won't know what you're talking about.

Here's how I give a customer the lowdown on the open-end mortgage:

"I'm glad to hear that you have your mortgage with First Federal Savings. They have open-end mortgages. Chances are that you have one. If so, I can build your addition with no money down and finance it at First Federal by adding it to the balance on your present mortgage.

"This will give you excellent terms. If you'll tell me the balance you owe on your present mortgage and the amount of your original mortgage, we'll see if you have enough equity in your open end. Let's see, your original mortgage was $30,000. You now owe $18,000. That means you have $12,000 in your open end. Our contract is only $9,300. You have plenty of room in your loan.

"I suggest that we write up the contract now, with instructions that the contract is to be paid from the proceeds of a mortgage loan. I'll take the contract over to First Federal and get the ball rolling for you. When the papers are ready, I'll pick you up and take you to the S&L. The loan officer will take care of your paperwork and make arrangements for me to deliver the waivers of lien and the contractor's statement, which means that all the bills will be paid. This is for your protection."

Note that I've been very assertive. Until the mortgage application's signed, along with the note and the mortgage, I don't have a deal. I'm only on the way. To get past the first hurdle, many S&L's will give you a supply of their mortgage application blanks. You fill in the application blank at the customer's home. You could also use a stock application blank. See Figure 7-7.

Payouts
Figure 7-8 is a sample form that many savings and loan associations use for direct payouts. The direct payout can conserve your capital and make it easier for you to do larger jobs. The lender pays your subs directly. This keeps you from being squeezed for capital. When you hire a sub, tell him up front that he'll be on direct payout with the lender. Many subs like this form of payment, because they know exactly when and how they're going to be paid.

Supplement Financing
Now let's look at this job from another angle. Suppose our homeowner qualifies for financing under the Rule of the Three C's. He wants a job that runs $16,000. But he only has a spread of $12,000 in his open end. What do we do?

Here's the solution. We break the job down into two parts — one part for $12,000 and the other for $4,000. Notice that we're talking about *two separate jobs*, not two contracts for the same work. The latter would be a false application to the lender, which the lender might well consider fraud.

For example, the room addition component prices out at $12,000. The kitchen remodeling component comes to $4,000. These are two separate and distinct jobs. They can both be financed. Next

we write a contract for the $12,000 part and submit it to the mortgage lender. After it's approved and the documents are recorded, we write up the $4,000 job and submit it to the home improvement lender. The home improvement credit application shows the new mortgage balance, which is made up of the old balance plus the new $12,000 for remodeling work.

Balance on previous mortgage	$13,200.00
Remodeling contract	12,000.00
Estimated closing costs, taxes, insurance esrow	800.00
Declaration of 1st mortgage:	$26,000.00

We've laid all the facts out in the open. The improvement loan can be approved since it's not based on a first mortgage. This type of financing works well with open-end mortgages. Keep in mind that federal regulations prohibit supplemental financing with FHA or VA mortgage applications.

Now let's pencil out the monthly payments for our customer. Interest rates fluctuate, but we'll assume a rate of 15¼%. Our customer might have a higher or lower interest rate.

The homeowner has 18 years left to pay on the mortgage. Payments are $407.92 per month including principal and interest. This will pay off the house and the $12,000 remodeling contract. Based on 15¼% interest, the $4,000 contract will pay off in 60 months. That's 5 years at the rate of approximately $103 per month, or an APR of 17%.

18-year mortgage	$407.92
5-year home improvement loan	103.00
Total monthly payments for 5 years	$510.92
Monthly payments for balance of term	$407.92

Earlier in the chapter I explained the APR rate. To find how much the homeowners will be paying per month on the total construction improvements, subtract the old mortgage payment from the new monthly payment. This gives you the differential for the improvement. Now add on the home improvement figure. This will give you the total for the first 60 months.

LOAN APPLICATION

DATE _____ SALES PRICE _____ LOAN AMOUNT _____ TERM YEARS _____ ☐ FHA ☐ VA ☐ OTHER

PROPERTY ADDRESS _____ No. _____ Street _____ City _____ State _____ Zip _____ GAMC REP. _____

PERSONAL	APPLICANT A	APPLICANT B
	NAME	NAME
	BIRTH DATE SOC. SEC.	BIRTH DATE SOC. SEC.
	MARITAL STATUS ☐ MARRIED ☐ UNMARRIED	MARITAL STATUS ☐ MARRIED ☐ UNMARRIED
	FINAL DIVORCE DECREE (SEE ECOA NOTICE) DATE COUNTY STATE	FINAL DIVORCE DECREE (SEE ECOA NOTICE) DATE COUNTY STATE
	AGES OF DEPENDENTS	AGES OF DEPENDENTS
	YRS. SCHOOLING HOME PHONE	YRS. SCHOOLING HOME PHONE

EMPLOYMENT 2 YEARS REQUIRED		
	EMPLOYER'S NAME	EMPLOYER'S NAME
	ADDRESS ZIP	ADDRESS ZIP
	OCCUPATION	OCCUPATION
	EMPLOYEE NO. EMPLOYER'S PHONE	EMPLOYEE NO. EMPLOYER'S PHONE
	YRS. EMPLOYED FROM TO	YRS. EMPLOYED FROM TO
	BASE PAY HR./WK./MO. HRS. WORKED WK./MO.	BASE PAY HR./WK./MO. HRS. WORKED WK./MO.
	REGULAR OVERTIME PER MO. REGULAR INCENTIVE PER MO.	REGULAR OVERTIME PER MO. REGULAR INCENTIVE PER MO.
	EMPLOYER/PREVIOUS/PART TIME	EMPLOYER/PREVIOUS/PART TIME
	ADDRESS ZIP	ADDRESS ZIP
	OCCUPATION	OCCUPATION
	YRS. EMPLOYED FROM TO	YRS. EMPLOYED FROM TO
	EMPLOYER/PREVIOUS/PART TIME	EMPLOYER/PREVIOUS/PART TIME
	ADDRESS ZIP	ADDRESS ZIP
	OCCUPATION	OCCUPATION
	YRS. EMPLOYED FROM TO	YRS. EMPLOYED FROM TO

OTHER INCOME	A—APPLICANT A	B—APPLICANT B	A OR B
	PENSION, RETIREMENT, DISABILITY, SOCIAL SECURITY, ALIMONY, CHILD SUPPORT (SEE ECOA NOTICE) OTHER INCOME		
EXPLAIN			
INCLUDE CLAIM NO.			

MILITARY	SERVICE DATES	BRANCH	OCCUPATION	SERIAL NO.

RESIDENCE 5 YEARS REQUIRED						
PRESENT ADDRESS						
NO.	STREET	CITY	STATE	ZIP	HOW LONG	
PREVIOUS ADDRESS						
NO.	STREET	CITY	STATE	ZIP	HOW LONG	
PREVIOUS ADDRESS						
NO.	STREET	CITY	STATE	ZIP	HOW LONG	
PREVIOUS ADDRESS						
NO.	STREET	CITY	STATE	ZIP	HOW LONG	

LANDLORDS 2 YEARS						
PRESENT LANDLORD						
NO.	STREET	CITY	STATE	LANDLORD	HOW LONG	
PREVIOUS LANDLORD						
NO.	STREET	CITY	STATE	LANDLORD	HOW LONG	
PREVIOUS LANDLORD						
NO.	STREET	CITY	STATE	LANDLORD	HOW LONG	

MONTHLY HOUSING EXPENSE	MORTGAGE PMT. OR RENT	HEAT & UTILITIES	TAXES, SPEC. ASSESS.	MAINTENANCE
	OTHER			

Stock mortgage application blank
Figure 7-7

NAME AND ADDRESS OF CREDITOR (INCLUDE PAYMENTS FOR ALIMONY, CHILD SUPPORT, CHILD CARE AND LIABILITY AS CO-MAKER OR ENDORSER ON ANY NOTES—Explanation needed.	ACCOUNT NO.	MONTHLY PAYMENT	BALANCE	A OR B

LIABILITIES (GIVE EXPLANATION UNDER WHICH ACCOUNT(S) CARRIED)

NAME AND ADDRESS		ACCOUNT NO.	$ (CHECKING)	$ (SAVINGS)

DEPOSITS

DEPOSIT PAID ON CURRENT PURCHASE   TO WHOM PAID

ASSETS

BONDS, STOCKS, ETC.	LIFE INS. AMOUNT	MONTHLY PREMIUM	CASH OR LOAN VALUE
AUTO. MAKE	YEAR	VALUE $	HOUSEHOLD PERSONAL ITEMS—
MAKE	YEAR	VALUE $	OTHER ITEMS OF VALUE
MAKE	YEAR	VALUE $	

NOTE—ALL ASSETS REQUIRED FOR CLOSING MUST BE VERIFIED

OTHER REAL ESTATE OWNED

ADDRESS	MKT. VAL.	MONTHLY PAYMENT
MORTGAGE HELD BY	ORIGINAL MORTGAGE AMT.	UNPAID BALANCE
LENDERS ADDRESS	LENDER'S LOAN NO.	
ADDRESS	MKT. VAL.	MONTHLY PAYMENT
MORTGAGE HELD BY	ORIGINAL MORTGAGE AMT.	UNPAID BALANCE
LENDER'S ADDRESS	LENDER'S LOAN NO.	

IS ABOVE REAL ESTATE TO BE SOLD ☐ RENTED ☐ $ PER MO. (VERIFICATION REQUIRED)
NOTE: EXPLANATION AND VERIFICATION IS REQUIRED E.G.:
PURCHASE AGREEMENT/ESCROW ESTIMATIONS/ESTIMATED NET PROCEEDS/DISPOSITION OF REAL ESTATE/VERIFICATION OF CREDIT

LEGAL

HAS ANY APPLICANT EVER FILED BANKRUPTCY? (DISCHARGE PAPERS/EXPLANATION LETTERS)	YEAR	COUNTY & STATE	TYPE

HAS ANY APPLICANT EVER HAD ANY SUITS, JUDGMENTS, LIENS, REPOSSESSIONS OR COLLECTIONS (EXPLANATIONS LETTERS NEEDED)   WHEN

HAS ANY APPLICANT EVER HAD A HOME LOAN THAT RESULTED IN FORECLOSURE OR DEED IN LIEU OF FORECLOSURE? (EXPLANATION LETTERS NEEDED)   DATE   PROPERTY ADDRESS
LENDER NAME   ADDRESS

HAS ANY APPLICANT SOLD PROPERTY WITHIN PAST 2 YEARS WHICH HAD AN FHA MORTGAGE?   IF YES, GIVE ADDRESS OF PROPERTY

IF YES, GIVE DATE

Have you owned a home before? _____ $ (Market Value) _____   Do you have major medical coverage? _____

Do you intend to occupy property? _____

Do you have health and accident insurance? _____   Will this property be your primary residence? _____

AGREEMENT

The undersigned mortgage loan applicants certify that all information in this application is true, correct and complete to the best of their knowledge and belief. Permission is hereby granted to GAMC or GREAT AMERICAN MORTGAGE CORPORATION and/or the FHA and VA to verify any information from any source named herein, and to transfer this information to other forms and transmit it to the FHA, VA, Private Mortgage Insuror, and any Lender that may fund this loan. We fully understand that it is a federal crime punishable by fine or imprisonment to knowingly make false statements concerning any of the above facts, as applicable under the provision of Title 18, United States Code, Section 1014.

We acknowledge receipt of the HUD Booklet explaining settlement costs.

It is understood that this does not constitute approval of my loan application. Any approval of the loan will be by written commitment issued contemporaneously with the instructions to close the loan given to the attorney. No other indication either written or oral may be construed as an approval of or commitment to make a loan. SHOULD THIS LOAN BE CANCELLED, WE AGREE TO REIMBURSE GAMC ANY EXPENSES INCURRED.

I understand that if my loan is not approved, I will be notified. I hereby authorize_____ to notify my Real Estate Agency in the event I cannot be contacted by phone within a reasonable time.

_____ _____ _____ _____
(Applicant's Signature)   (Date)   (Co-Applicant's Signature)   (Date)

SELLING BROKER	PHONE	LISTING BROKER	PHONE

ADDRESS

SALESMAN	PHONE	SALESMAN	PHONE

TITLE COMPANY   CLOSING COSTS PAID BY   ☐ BUYER   ☐ SELLER

ESCROW COMPANY   ESCROW NO

CONDITIONAL OR CRV.   ☐ ORDER   ☐ REQUEST FROM

Stock mortgage application blank
Figure 7-7 (continued)

PAYMENT REQUEST

TO _____ Date _____

THIS IS TO CERTIFY, That _____ , Contractor
                                                    (Name of Contractor)

for the _____
                                    (Type of work or material)

whose address is _____ , and telephone No. _____ ,

is entitled to a payment of _____ DOLLARS ($_____)

for labor, services, fixtures and material, or either, furnished to, or installed in, the building located at _____
                                                                                                        (Address)

_____ , which amount is to be paid and charged to the loan account of the undersigned in connection with said premises.
   (City and State)

Contract Price . . $_____   Previously Paid . $_____   OWNER _____
Extra Work . . . $_____   This Payment . . $_____   The aforesaid payment is authorized and accepted
Deductions . . . $_____   Balance Due . . $_____   as a charge against the general contract.
                                                                      Gen'l. Contractor
   TOTAL . . . $_____   TOTAL . . . $_____   By _____ Title _____
APPROVED FOR PAYMENT _____   Payment Rec'd. _____
                              (Architect - Builder)   (Contractor)

....

WAIVER OF LIEN
(This waiver, and all supporting material waivers, must be in exact amount of payment)

STATE OF

COUNTY OF _____ }SS.   Date _____

   WHEREAS, the undersigned, _____.ha ____ been employed
                                          (Name of Contractor)

by _____
                              (Name of party by whom employed)

to furnish _____
                              (Type of work or material)

for the building located at _____ in _____ , Illinois,
                              (Street address or location)   (City)

   NOW, THEREFORE, KNOW YE, that the undersigned, for and in consideration of $_____ , and other good and valuable

considerations, the receipt whereof is hereby acknowledged, do ____ hereby waive and release any and all lien, or claim or right of lien

as to the above described building and premises, and also with respect to, or upon, monies which may be due from the Owner, under the

Statutes of the State of Illinois, relating to Mechanics' Liens, on account of labor, services, fixtures and materials, or either, furnished (1)

_____ (2) or which may be furnished, by the undersigned to or an account of the said _____

for said building or premises.   (Name of party by whom employed)

   By the execution of this waiver the undersigned _____ do ____ also agree and
                                                          (Name of Contractor)

covenant that the entire remaining balance which will be due and payable to the undersigned upon completion of the furnishing and instal-

lation of all the labor, services, fixtures and materials, or either, by the undersigned, **after this payment**, will be $_____

and no more.   (Insert balance due, or word "None")

   GIVEN under the hand and seal of the undersigned this _____ day of _____ , A. D. 19____ .

                              (3) _____ (SEAL)

                                  _____ (SEAL)

Direct payout form
Figure 7-8

"PARTIAL" OR "FINAL" WAIVERS OF LIEN, IN THE EXACT AMOUNT OF PAYMENT REQUESTED IN
"DUE & BEING APPLIED FOR" COLUMN BELOW, MUST BE FURNISHED
BY EACH TRADE OR MATERIAL SUPPLIER WITH EACH PAYMENT REQUEST

ALL PREVIOUS PAYMENTS RECEIVED MUST BE LISTED IN "AMOUNT PAID TO DATE" COLUMN

"ONE DOLLAR" WAIVERS WILL NOT BE ACCEPTED.

THE "CONTRACTOR'S AFFIDAVIT" BELOW, MUST BE ACKNOWLEDGED BEFORE A NOTARY PUBLIC,
AND HIS SEAL AFFIXED.

CONTRACTOR'S AFFIDAVIT

(This affidavit must be executed in support of the within waiver)

STATE OF _____ } SS.
COUNTY OF _____

THE AFFIANT, _____, being first duly sworn, says that he is
(Name of person signing affidavit)

(1)_____, of (2)_____,
the contractor for the_____ for or in the building located
(Type of work, service or material)

at _____ owned by _____
(Address, City and State) (Name of Owner)

in connection with which an agreement was entered into for the furnishing of labor, services, fixtures and materials, or either, in the total
sum of $_____, and on which premises the_____ of_____,
(Name of Loan Ass'n. - Mortgagee)

Illinois, has made a mortgage loan; that in connection with said work the following are the names of all persons, firms or corporations, who
or which furnished, or are to furnish, labor, services, fixtures and materials, or either, in performance of the work herein referred to; that
there are no other contracts for work, labor, services, fixtures or materials outstanding; that there is nothing due or to become due to any
person, firm or corporation for labor, services, fixtures and materials, or either, other than as follows: (See note 3).

KIND OF WORK OR MATERIAL	SUPPLIERS' NAMES	Amount of Contract	Amount Paid to Date	Due & Being Applied For	Balance Remaining Due or to Become Due After This Payment
TOTAL AMOUNT OF LABOR, OVERHEAD AND PROFIT OF THIS CONTRACTOR					
	TOTALS (4)				

THAT AFFIANT makes this affidavit for the purpose of inducing_____
(Name of party by whom employed)

and _____ and _____ to make a
(Name of Owner) (Name of Loan Ass'n. - Mortgagee)

_____ payment of (5) $_____ on account of said work, labor, services, fixtures and material, or either, out of the loan
(Partial or Final)

account on said premises. That each of the waivers of lien submitted herewith in support of this payment request is genuine and the representations therein contained are true and correct; that each of said waivers was unconditionally delivered and that none of said waivers
was obtained by or through mistake, fraud, or duress; that no claim exists, either in law or in equity, to defeat the validity of any of said
waivers of lien.

_____ (SEAL)

Direct payout form
Figure 7-8 (continued)

It's usually easiest to add a home improvement loan to a regular first mortgage, providing there's sufficient equity and the Rule of the Three C's is met. Remember, the Three C's control all mortgage financing.

When you're considering supplemental financing for a customer, discuss it with the loan officer who's going to make the first mortgage. Be sure that he has no objection to supplemental financing. To do otherwise is to court disaster. If the loan officer objects to supplemental financing, try to overcome the objection by showing that the borrower has the capacity to pay. Review the borrower's income versus expenses. The buyer's character has already been approved, and the collateral is a first mortgage.

If the loan officer still objects to supplemental financing, ask what he considers a reasonable length of time for the loan to be seasoned. At that time, you can go back and sell the balance of the job. You get a legitimate sale for now and a layaway sale coming up when the mortgage is seasoned.

I recommend that you either get a free rate book from your mortgage lender or buy a copy from Financial Publishing Company, 82 Brookline Avenue, Boston, MA 02215. The rate book is essential for figuring monthly payments. Figure 7-9 shows a simplified chart for monthly payments on a conventional mortgage.

Recasting the Loan

Many homeowners prefer to have the new loan with the present mortgage lender. This is fine. The lender will recast the loan. This means he'll pay off the old loan, plus the loan expenses and escrow, and add the amount required for the remodeling. This is called recasting the loan, but it also means charging the current rate of interest. The old loan may be at a much lower rate. The new loan will be charged at the going rate. Thus the lender upgrades his profit margin. He's usually delighted to retain an old customer at a higher profit.

Let's say your customer borrowed $50,000 to buy his home ten years ago. Purchase price was $60,000. The work he wants done comes to $20,000. On the face of it, he doesn't qualify under the Collateral section of the Rule of the Three C's. He's probably paid off less than $10,000 of the original loan. But the house is probably worth $100,000 on the present market. Thus, the homeowner has enough equity. The lender can make the loan and you can do the work.

If the present mortgage lender doesn't want to recast the loan, shop elsewhere. His reasons for not wanting to recast aren't necessarily a reflection on you or your customer. Usually it means that the lender has loaned all that can be loaned under banking regulations. Banks and S&L's must maintain certain reserves. Also, your client may have a history of slow payments. If so, the lender may be glad to get rid of the loan. This isn't the end of the road, however. Another lender may look at the homeowner differently. My advice: shop the loan.

Consolidation

Let's try another approach. Your prospect is a divorced mother with a weekly income of $375. Based on a 4⅓-week month, that's $1,625 per month. The prospect makes monthly payments of:

House payment	$210.00
Car payment	140.00
Small loan	65.00
Furniture and T.V. payments	130.00
Total monthly payments	$545.00

Do we have a sale? The answer is yes, if we can finance it. The customer has laid out her personal finances for us. That makes designing a package for her much easier.

We're trying to sell a remodeling job for $8,450. At first this looks like an unfinanceable lead. The problem is a small monthly income combined with a large debt load.

Here's how this customer measures up under the Rule of the Three C's:

Character - O.K.
Collateral - Very good
Capacity to pay - Limited

To find the equity in the property, use the Equity Analysis Chart, Figure 7-10.

Our finance chart tells us that there's enough equity to cover the debts, the closing costs and the proposed remodeling job. This owner has profited by inflation. She has a large equity. But if we take the original purchase price and deduct the present balance and debts, the client can't qualify. Therefore we use the current market value.

Conventional Loan Rate Per Thousand Dollars (30-year Loan)

Interest Rate	Dollar Amount
10%	$ 8.78
10½%	9.15
11%	9.53
11½%	9.91
12%	10.29
12½%	10.68
13%	11.07
13½%	11.46
14%	11.85
14½%	12.25
15%	12.65
15½%	13.05
16%	13.45
16½%	13.86
17%	14.26
17½%	14.67
18%	15.08
18½%	15.48
19%	15.89
19½%	16.30
20%	16.72

Example:
A $10,000 loan at 12% for 30 years:
Multiply $ 10,000.00
x   10.29
$102,900.00 ÷ 1,000 = $102.90

is the monthly payment on the principal and interest.

Note: If the current rate of interest is 12% then memorize the rate $10.29 per thousand.

If the rate is 15% then memorize $12.65 per thousand dollars.

Remember: There may be a slight variance in the final figure due to the number of decimal places used.

Memorize the current rate.

Simplified rate chart for conventional mortgage
Figure 7-9

Equity Analysis

Present market value of house	$47,000.00
Balance due on present mortgage	-9,160.00
Owner's gross equity in property	$37,840.00

Indebtedness:

Balance due on the mortgage	$ 9,160.00
Balance due on the car payments	840.00
Balance due to the small loan company	585.00
Balance due to the furniture store and for T.V.	+ 1,365.00
Total indebtedness	$11,950.00

Equity Available For Remodeling:

Present market value of house	$47,000.00
Total indebtedness	-11,950.00
Owner's net equity in property	$35,050.00
Estimated closing costs for new loan	- 600.00
Equity available for remodeling	$34,450.00

Equity analysis chart
Figure 7-10

This customer could have as much as $34,450 worth of remodeling work done if we we went solely on the basis of equity, but the capacity to pay won't carry this debt load.

Here's a good rule of thumb to use: A mortgage should not exceed 2½ times the annual income. Another rule of thumb used to be that mortgage payments shouldn't exceed 1/4 of the monthly income. Nowadays, 1/3 is acceptable.

In recent years, mortgage lenders have broadened their rules of thumb. When you contact mortgage lenders, make sure you find out their current rules. FHA and VA lenders have a more complicated formula that includes taxes and other items. Ask them to explain it to you in detail.

Our next step is to do some more analysis of the customer's capacity to pay. Check the Payment Analysis Chart, Figure 7-11.

Consolidation is clearly the answer to this customer's problem. If the customer has high monthly payments, simply consolidate them into one payment, including the remodeling job. The customer will have a single payment that she can handle and you can do the remodeling job she wants. That's progress!

On a sale like this you have no competition because the competition doesn't know how to put this type of deal together.

Converting to Articles of Agreement

Suppose a loan officer says to you, "I think the collateral is O.K., but the loan's borderline. I'll make the loan to *you*."

Here's how you handle this situation:

Explain to your client that you're having a problem in getting the loan approved. Many states give you an alternative called *articles of agreement*. This arrangement requires the cooperation of your prospect.

"The loan company's willing to make the loan to me because of my top credit rating. Then I could make the loan, but you'll have to deed the property to a trust at the abstract, title company or bank. I'll enter into articles of agreement with you. You'll make your monthly payments of principal and interest plus the escrow fee directly to the loan company."

The mechanics of articles of agreement are simple, but I suggest you use a lawyer the first time you do it. That's what I did, and after that it was a matter of routine to copy the original papers and make the necessary adjustments.

If you don't feel comfortable doing the paperwork, or if the laws of your state require an attorney, have your attorney bill the client for his services directly.

Here's a step-by-step outline of the procedure:

1) Set up a land trust at your abstract, title company or bank, with yourself as beneficiary. Use this instrument as a model for succeeding transactions.

2) Get a warranty deed from the owner to the land trust.

3) The direction to the land trust by the beneficiary is issued at this time, authorizing the land trust to do the following:

Payment Analysis

A Find net amount allowable for monthly mortgage expense:

Monthly income	$1,625.00
Allowable housing expense (not to exceed ⅓ of the monthly income)	542.00
Deduct estimated monthly escrow for real estate taxes and fire insurance premiums	100.00
Net amount available for monthly mortgage expense	$442.00

B Translate amount available for monthly mortgage expense into total dollar amount of mortgage. Use the rate chart shown in Figure 7-9.

Present mortgage rate	17%
Dollar amount per $1,000.00 @ 17% for 30 years	$14.26
Net amount available for monthly mortgage expense	$442.00
Divide $442.00 by 14.26 and multiply by 1,000 to get total allowable mortgage	$30,996.00

C Summary:

Present indebtedness	$11,950.00
Closing costs	600.00
Remodeling contract	8,450.00
Total mortgage required	$21,000.00
Dollar amount per $1,000.00 @17% for 30 years	$ 14.26
Multiply $21,000.00 x 14.26 and divide by 1,000 to get new mortgage payment	$ 299.46
Escrow for taxes and insurance	100.00
Total new monthly payment	$ 399.46
Previous monthly indebtedness	$ 545.00
Monthly payments reduced by	$ 145.54

**Payment analysis
Figure 7-11**

a) Execute the mortgage as per the agreed terms.

b) Execute the assignment of rents, when required.

c) Execute any documents required for stamp tax.

d) Execute the note for the mortgage.

e) Execute the articles of agreement.

4) Depending on your state's laws and your attorney's advice, you can have your customer also sign the remodeling contract and specifications as the contract buyer. There are other alternatives, but *it's best to have the contract buyer sign the contract and specs.* In this way, he'll be fully aware of the specs and terms. And it will eliminate any suspicion that the specs have been altered in any way. He'll have the signed copy with his own signature on it.

Co-Makers

Here's another way to go if the loan is borderline. But it requires a good working relationship with the loan officer. Suppose the loan officer tells you, "I'd like to approve the loan for you, but it's a little weak. If you'll co-sign it, I'll approve the loan." I've never hesitated in these instances. Nor have I ever been called upon to make the loan good or bring the payments current. The papers were drawn so that in case of default or foreclosure by the lender, I have the right of redemption.

Note, however, that the law may be different in your state. Before entering into this type of arrangement, check out the right of redemption with your attorney. If the deal goes sour, you could have a nice profit if you redeem and then sell the property.

Compensating Deposits

Suppose the loan officer at the bank or S&L tells you: "You have a good loan application. I'd like to make this loan. But right now my hands are tied. We're up to our limit. We can't make any loans until our portfolio's back in balance with our cash position."

You may still be able to get a loan through this lender. Here's how: Ask the loan officer if they accept *compensating deposits*. If the answer is yes, you're on your way.

Many lenders will make a loan equal to a deposit made to a savings account. Let's say you need a $35,000.00 loan to finance your job and pay off the previous mortgage. You arrange a savings deposit for that amount. The lender can then make the loan.

But, you ask, where does that $35,000 come from?

It may be easier to find that money than you think. In most large cities you'll find money brokers that have the authority to direct funds to any insured account. Many represent school boards, park districts, municipalities, churches, synagogues, fraternal organizations, or unions. You probably have some connection with an organization that holds funds in a savings account. Some funds may be available for transfer. The interest and the passbook belong to the organization that has advanced the funds, of course. But the lender may reward you by making the loan to your client.

The money brokers usually have discretion on where funds are deposited. Expect to pay a nominal fee for making the transfer to the insured account of your choice. The lending officer at your bank or S&L may be able to supply the name of a fund broker.

A compensating deposit helps the lender, homeowner and the builder. The lender makes a profitable loan from new cash coming into the institution. The homeowner gets his financing. You, the builder, make a profit on the job.

Keep in mind though, that the compensating deposit is not security for the loan. The lender grants a mortgage just as in any loan. The deposit is just the source of funds. Some lenders are reluctant to make loans like this because they're afraid the deposit will be drawn out before the loan is repaid. There's no way for the lender to prevent this.

Pledges

Here's another situation: The lender recognizes that the borrower qualifies for the loan. But he insists that the loan requested would be larger than his appraised value. He can't make the full loan requested.

Here's how to solve this one. Ask the lender if he'll consider a pledge. A pledge is used when the difference between the loan amount that can be granted and the mortgage request is less than the profit on your job. For example:

Mortgage request	$34,000.00
Loan approval	32,000.00
Discrepancy	$ 2,000.00

Here are the mechanics of a pledge:

First, the lender makes a $34,000 loan to the borrower. Next, the lender disburses only $32,000 of that amount to pay for the current project and clean up any other loans or expenses. The lender opens a passbook savings account in your name and deposits the $2,000 balance of the loan proceeds in that account. This is your money, but it can't be withdrawn until the loan outstanding is reduced to the $32,000 maximum. This account pays the current interest rate, of course.

Since you know the details of the mortgage, you know when the mortgage will be reduced to $32,000. Thus you know how long your money will be tied up.

If you can afford to tie up $2,000 for a year or two, pledge financing can be very useful. In some cities, there are brokers that buy pledges at a discount. If you feel that you've made a good profit without the pledge, you can sell the pledge and be cashed out on the job in full.

MGIC stands for Mortgage Guarantee Insurance Company. MGIC is a private insurance company that insures mortgages. It works like FHA. But there's a difference: MGIC is a private company and operates with a minimum of red tape. MGIC works through savings and loan associations. It insures a portion of the lender's exposure.

MGIC should be used when equity is thin. If the equity left in the home will be small after the remodeling project is complete and the new loan is made, consider MGIC. The average S&L requires the owner to have at least a 25% or 30% equity. Remodeling can eat this up. With MGIC, the owner only needs a 5% equity. He could get a loan of up to 95% of the appraisal value of the house.

Here's an example:

Balance due on present mortgage	$25,000.00
Remodeling contract	20,000.00
Total loan needed	$45,000.00

To secure a loan of $45,000, the house must appraise out at $47,500.00. The average S&L wouldn't touch this loan. There isn't enough equity. This is where MGIC comes in. MGIC reduces chance of loss by the lender. For example, in Illinois on a 30% coverage, the exposure is reduced to about 67% on a 95% loan. The exposure varies according to the amount of coverage.

For a fee, MGIC insures a portion of the loan. The S&L handles all the paperwork, and the red tape is minimal. Approvals are fast. Furthermore, the premium doesn't extend for the entire length of the mortgage as it does under the FHA. The premium covers a shorter period. The loan is with a local S&L, so your client can go in and discuss any problem with a loan officer.

Insurance coverage is limited to loans secured by first liens on improved one- to four-family residential property. Owner-occupied property as a primary residence (1-4) family dwelling can be insured up to 95% of value. Using MGIC can dramatically increase your sales volume. Your S&L will fill you in on the requirements for your state.

When discussing business with a savings and loan, ask if they use MGIC insurance or a similar service. It's another tool for getting business.

FHA and VA Loans
FHA and VA mortgage financing usually offers better terms than conventional loans. These packages are more difficult to put together, however. There's more paperwork and more time is needed for processing. Under FHA, loans can't exceed 85% of the appraised value. On VA it's 100% of appraised value.

V.A. Form 26-1880 is the request for determination of eligibility for the veteran. See Figure 7-12.

As in a conventional loan, a mortgage application is required. See Figure 7-13.

In both FHA and VA loans, the deposit has to be verified. See Verification of Deposit, Figure 7-14. This form is sent to the banks to verify that the applicant's funds are as stated.

The next form is the Verification of Employment. This form verifies the length of employment and the income. See Figure 7-15.

The Buyer's Statement is a very simple form. The buyer states that none of the money used as a down payment came from the proceeds of an unsecured loan. It also says that the buyer is not indebted to the seller and further will not have any unpaid obligations contracted with the purchase or construction of the property. See Figure 7-16.

The next form (Figure 7-17) is the Occupancy Form and Freedom to Choose Title Underwriter.

The maximum interest rate is set by the FHA or VA. See Figure 7-18.

Figure 7-19 is the Equal Credit Opportunity Act form. It prohibits discrimination of credit applicants on the basis of age, color, religion, national origin, sex, or marital status.

See Figure 7-20 for Notice to Borrowers required by Federal Law and Federal Reserve Regulation.

Figure 7-21 is a letter to be presented to the mortgage holder for verification of terms and payment experience. The signature of the applicant is required before release of this information.

Figure 7-22 shows the Good Faith Estimate required by the VA. At first this may seem like a lot of paperwork. But after a few sales it becomes routine. FHA and VA financing are good for the small contractor. Don't overlook this opportunity.

FHA loans require less equity than conventional mortgages. FHA is an excellent source of refinancing when equity is a problem. But FHA loans do require close cooperation with the mortgage banker that processes the loan. Figure 7-23 is a finance chart for figuring monthly payments of principal and interest and FHA insurance.

Figure 7-24 is the Anti-Coercion Statement re: The Purchase of Insurance.

The Cash Buyer
The cash buyer can be a difficult customer when the amount of the sale is large in proportion to your cash flow. The cash buyer may become a perfectionist when it's time to pay the bill. He develops a penchant for discovering flaws. He doesn't like the color of the paint and you'll have to do it over before he pays up. Or you have to install an extra rafter (not in the specs) before he'll consider the job done. Or he wants smooth instead of textured siding (or the reverse), and it must be changed before he'll write a check. Or: "I have to wait until it rains to make sure the roof doesn't leak." This sort of malarkey can go on and on. The list is endless.

I've found that the best way to handle cash buyers is have them deposit the entire contract price into an escrow at the title or abstract company. Payouts to each sub, as well as the general overhead and profit, are listed as separate items. (For a typical contractor's statement, see Figure 9-6 in Chapter 9. Figure 7-8 in this chapter is a payout request to the lender.)

The escrow method prevents or eliminates most alibis when it comes time to collect. The general and the subs submit their payment requests and authorizations to the title company for payment with the requisite waivers of lien.

The expense of the escrow should be carried 50-50 between the contractor and the buyer. This cost will be acceptable to the buyer when you explain that the escrow is for his protection. A

Form Approved
OMB No. 2900-0086

VA Veterans Administration	VETERANS ADMINISTRATION ATTN: LOAN GUARANTY DIVISION

REQUEST FOR DETERMINATION OF ELIGIBILITY AND AVAILABLE LOAN GUARANTY ENTITLEMENT

TO

NOTE: Please read instructions on reverse before completing this form. If additional space is required attach separate sheet.

1. FIRST - MIDDLE - LAST NAME OF VETERAN	2A. ADDRESS OF VETERAN *(No., Street or rural route, City or P.O., State and ZIP Code)*
2B. VETERAN'S DAYTIME TELEPHONE NO. *(Include Area Code)* **3. DATE OF BIRTH**	

4. MILITARY SERVICE DATA *(ATTACH PROOF OF SERVICE – SEE INSTRUCTIONS ON REVERSE (Paragraphs F and G.1))*

PERIOD OF ACTIVE SERVICE		NAME *(Show your name exactly as it appears on your separation papers (DD214) or Statement of Service)*	SERVICE NUMBER *(Enter Social Security No., if appropriate)*	BRANCH OF SERVICE
DATE FROM	DATE TO			
A.				
B.				
C.				
D.				

5A. WERE YOU DISCHARGED, RETIRED OR SEPARATED FROM SERVICE BECAUSE OF DISABILITY OR DO YOU NOW HAVE ANY SERVICE-CONNECTED DISABILITIES? ☐ YES ☐ NO *(If "Yes," Complete Item 5B)*	5B. VA FILE NUMBER C-	6. IS A CERTIFICATE OF ELIGIBILITY FOR LOAN GUARANTY PURPOSES ENCLOSED? ☐ YES ☐ NO *(If "No," Complete Items 7A and 7B)*
7A. HAVE YOU PREVIOUSLY APPLIED FOR A CERTIFICATE OF ELIGIBILITY FOR VA LOAN PURPOSES? ☐ YES ☐ NO *(If "Yes," give location of VA office(s))*	7B. HAVE YOU PREVIOUSLY RECEIVED SUCH A CERTIFICATE? ☐ YES ☐ NO *(If "Yes," give location of VA office(s))*	7C. THE CERTIFICATE OF ELIGIBILITY PREVIOUSLY ISSUED TO ME HAS BEEN LOST OR STOLEN. IF RECOVERED IT WILL BE RETURNED TO THE VA *(Check if applicable)* ☐

8. HAVE YOU PREVIOUSLY ACQUIRED PROPERTY WITH THE ASSISTANCE OF A GI LOAN? ☐ YES ☐ NO *(If "Yes," complete Items 9 through 18. Please attach a separate sheet if more than one loan is involved. If "No," skip to Items 19 through 21.)*	9. ADDRESS OF REGIONAL OFFICE(S) WHERE LOAN WAS OBTAINED *(City and State)*

10. STATE TYPE(S) AND NUMBER OF LOAN(S) *(Home, Mobile home, Condominium, Direct, Farm, Business, etc.)*	11. ADDRESS(ES) OF PROPERTY PREVIOUSLY PURCHASED WITH GUARANTY ENTITLEMENT	12. DATE YOU PURCHASED THE PROPERTY(IES)
13. DO YOU NOW OWN THE PROPERTY DESCRIBED IN ITEM 11? ☐ YES ☐ NO *(If "Yes," do not complete Items 14 through 18)*	14. DATE(S) THE PROPERTY WAS SOLD	15. IS THERE ANY UNDERSTANDING OR AGREEMENT WRITTEN OR ORAL, BETWEEN YOU AND THE PURCHASERS THAT THEY WILL RECONVEY THE PROPERTY TO YOU? ☐ YES ☐ NO

NOTE: It will speed processing if you can complete Items 16, 17, and 18.

16. NAME AND ADDRESS OF LENDER(S) TO WHOM LOAN PAYMENTS WERE MADE	17. LENDER'S LOAN OR ACCOUNT NUMBER
	18. VA LOAN NUMBER(S)

I certify that the statements herein are true to the best of my knowledge and belief.

19. SIGNATURE OF VETERAN	20. DATE SIGNED

FEDERAL STATUTES PROVIDE SEVERE PENALTIES FOR FRAUD, INTENTIONAL MISREPRESENTATION, CRIMINAL CONNIVANCE OR CONSPIRACY PURPOSED TO INFLUENCE THE ISSUANCE OF ANY GUARANTY OR INSURANCE BY THE ADMINISTRATOR.

THIS SECTION FOR VA USE ONLY

DATE CERTIFICATE ISSUED AND DISCHARGE OR SEPARATION PAPERS AND VA PAMPHLETS GIVEN TO VETERAN OR MAILED TO ADDRESS SHOWN BELOW	TYPE OF DISCHARGE OR SEPARATION PAPERS RETURNED	INITIALS OF VA AGENT	STATION NUMBER

VA FORM 26-1880, JUN 1982   DO NOT DETACH

IMPORTANT - You must complete Item 21 since the Certificate of Eligibility along with all discharge and separation papers will be mailed to the address shown in Item 21 below. If they are to be sent to you, your current mailing address should be indicated, or if they are to be sent elsewhere, the name and address of such person or firm should be shown in Item 21.

The amount of loan guaranty entitlement available for use is endorsed on the reverse of the enclosed Certificate of Eligibility. This certificate must be returned to the VA at the time a loan application or loan report is submitted.

NOTE - PLEASE DELIVER THE ENCLOSED PAMPHLETS AND DISCHARGE OR SEPARATION PAPERS TO THE VETERAN PROMPTLY.

VA FORM JUN 1982 **26-1880**	SUPERSEDES VA FORM 26-1880, JUN 1981, WHICH WILL NOT BE USED.	627735

Determination of Eligibility
Figure 7-12

RESIDENTIAL LOAN APPLICATION

MORTGAGE APPLIED FOR	☐ Conventional ☐ VA	☐ FHA ☐ ____	Amount $	Interest Rate %	No. of Months	Monthly Payment Principal & Interest $	Escrow/Impounds (to be collected monthly) ☐ Taxes ☐ Hazard Ins. ☐ Mtg. Ins. ☐ ____

Prepayment Option

SUBJECT PROPERTY

Property Street Address	City	County	State	Zip	No. Units

Legal Description (Attach description if necessary)	Year Built

Purpose of Loan: ☐ Purchase ☐ Construction-Permanent ☐ Construction ☐ Refinance ☐ Other (Explain)

Complete this line if Construction-Permanent or Construction Loan ☛	Lot Value Data Year Acquired ____ $	Original Cost $	Present Value (a) $	Cost of Imps. (b) $	Total (a + b) $	ENTER TOTAL AS PURCHASE PRICE IN DETAILS OF PURCHASE.

Complete this line if a Refinance Loan		Purpose of Refinance	Describe Improvements [ ] made [ ] to be made
Year Acquired	Original Cost	Amt. Existing Liens	
$	$	$	Cost: $

Title Will Be Held In What Name(s)	Manner In Which Title Will Be Held

Source of Down Payment and Settlement Charges

This application is designed to be completed by the borrower(s) with the lender's assistance. The Co-Borrower Section and all other Co-Borrower questions must be completed and the appropriate box(es) checked if ☐ another person will be jointly obligated with the Borrower on the loan, or ☐ the Borrower is relying on income from alimony, child support or separate maintenance or on the income or assets of another person as a basis for repayment of the loan, or ☐ the Borrower is married and resides, or the property is located, in a community property state.

BORROWER			CO-BORROWER		
Name	Age	School Yrs	Name	Age	School Yrs
Present Address No. Years ____ ☐ Own ☐ Rent			Present Address No. Years ____ ☐ Own ☐ Rent		
Street			Street		
City/State/Zip			City/State/Zip		
Former address if less than 2 years at present address			Former address if less than 2 years at present address		
Street			Street		
City/State/Zip			City/State/Zip		
Years at former address ☐ Own ☐ Rent			Years at former address ☐ Own ☐ Rent		

Marital Status ☐ Married ☐ Separated ☐ Unmarried (incl. single, divorced, widowed)	DEPENDENTS OTHER THAN LISTED BY CO BORROWER NO. AGES	Marital Status ☐ Married ☐ Separated ☐ Unmarried (incl. single, divorced, widowed)	DEPENDENTS OTHER THAN LISTED BY BORROWER NO. AGES

Name and Address of Employer	Years employed in this line of work or profession? ____ years Years on this job ____ ☐ Self Employed*	Name and Address of Employer	Years employed in this line of work or profession? ____ years Years on this job ____ ☐ Self Employed*

Position/Title	Type of Business	Position/Title	Type of Business

Social Security Number***	Home Phone	Business Phone	Social Security Number***	Home Phone	Business Phone

GROSS MONTHLY INCOME				MONTHLY HOUSING EXPENSE**			DETAILS OF PURCHASE	
Item	Borrower	Co-Borrower	Total	Rent	PRESENT	PROPOSED	Do Not Complete If Refinance	
Base Empl. Income	$	$	$	First Mortgage (P&I)	$	$	a. Purchase Price	$
Overtime				Other Financing (P&I)			b. Total Closing Costs (Est.)	
Bonuses				Hazard Insurance			c. Prepaid Escrows (Est.)	
Commissions				Real Estate Taxes			d. Total (a + b + c)	$
Dividends/Interest				Mortgage Insurance			e. Amount This Mortgage	( )
Net Rental Income				Homeowner Assn. Dues			f. Other Financing	( )
Other† (Before completing, see notice under Describe Other Income below.)				Other:			g. Other Equity	( )
				Total Monthly Pmt.	$	$	h. Amount of Cash Deposit	( )
				Utilities			i. Closing Costs Paid by Seller	( )
Total	$	$	$	Total	$	$	j. Cash Reqd. For Closing (Est.)	$

DESCRIBE OTHER INCOME		
▷ B—Borrower C—Co-Borrower	NOTICE:† Alimony, child support, or separate maintenance income need not be revealed if the Borrower or Co-Borrower does not choose to have it considered as a basis for repaying this loan.	Monthly Amount $

IF EMPLOYED IN CURRENT POSITION FOR LESS THAN TWO YEARS COMPLETE THE FOLLOWING

B/C	Previous Employer/School	City/State	Type of Business	Position/Title	Dates From/To	Monthly Income
						$

THESE QUESTIONS APPLY TO BOTH BORROWER AND CO-BORROWER

If a "yes" answer is given to a question in this column, explain on an attached sheet.	Borrower Yes or No	Co-Borrower Yes or No	If applicable, explain Other Financing or Other Equity (provide addendum if more space is needed).
Have you any outstanding judgments? In the last 7 years, have you been declared bankrupt?			
Have you had property foreclosed upon or given title or deed in lieu thereof?			
Are you a co-maker or endorser on a note?			
Are you a party in a law suit?			
Are you obligated to pay alimony, child support, or separate maintenance?			
Is any part of the down payment borrowed?			

*FHLMC/FNMA require business credit report, signed Federal Income Tax returns for last two years, and, if available, audited Profit and Loss Statements plus balance sheet for same period.

**All Present Monthly Housing Expenses of Borrower and Co-Borrower should be listed on a combined basis.

***Neither FHLMC nor FNMA requires this information.

FHLMC 65 Rev. 8/78   **FOR LENDERS SUBJECT ONLY TO FEDERAL RESERVE SYSTEM REGULATION B**   FNMA 1003 Rev. 8/78

FHA and VA mortgage application
Figure 7-13

This Statement and any applicable supporting schedules may be completed jointly by both married and unmarried co-borrowers if their assets and liabilities are sufficiently joined so that the Statement can be meaningfully and fairly presented on a combined basis; otherwise separate Statements and Schedules are required (FHLMC 65A/FNMA 1003A). If the co-borrower section was completed about a spouse, this statement and supporting schedules must be completed about that spouse also.

☐ Completed Jointly   ☐ Not Completed Jointly

ASSETS		LIABILITIES AND PLEDGED ASSETS			

Indicate by (*) those liabilities or pledged assets which will be satisfied upon sale of real estate owned or upon refinancing of subject property

Description	Cash or Market Value	Creditors' Name, Address and Account Number	Acct. Name if Not Borrower's	Mo. Pmt. and Mos. left to pay	Unpaid Balance
Cash Deposit Toward Purchase Held By	$	Installment Debts (include "revolving" charge accts)		$ Pmt./Mos.	$
Checking and Savings Accounts (Show Names of Institutions/Acct. Nos.)				/	
				/	
Stocks and Bonds (No./Description)				/	
				/	
Life Insurance Net Cash Value Face Amount ($)		Other Debts Including Stock Pledges		/	
SUBTOTAL LIQUID ASSETS	$				
Real Estate Owned (Enter Market Value from Schedule of Real Estate Owned)		Real Estate Loans			
Vested Interest in Retirement Fund					
Net Worth of Business Owned (ATTACH FINANCIAL STATEMENT)					
Automobiles (Make and Year)		Automobile Loans		/	
Furniture and Personal Property		Alimony, Child Support and Separate Maintenance Payments Owed To			
Other Assets (Itemize)					
		TOTAL MONTHLY PAYMENTS		$	
TOTAL ASSETS	A $	NET WORTH (A minus B) $		TOTAL LIABILITIES	B $

SCHEDULE OF REAL ESTATE OWNED (If Additional Properties Owned Attach Separate Schedule)

Address of Property (Indicate S if Sold, PS if Pending Sale or R if Rental being held for income)	Type of Property	Present Market Value	Amount of Mortgages & Liens	Gross Rental Income	Mortgage Payments	Taxes, Ins. Maintenance and Misc.	Net Rental Income
		$	$	$	$	$	$
TOTALS →		$	$	$	$	$	$

LIST PREVIOUS CREDIT REFERENCES

B—Borrower C—Co-Borrower	Creditor's Name and Address	Account Number	Purpose	Highest Balance	Date Paid
				$	

List any additional names under which credit has previously been received _____

AGREEMENT: The undersigned applies for the loan indicated in this application to be secured by a first mortgage or deed of trust on the property described herein, and represents that the property will not be used for any illegal or restricted purpose, and that all statements made in this application are true and are made for the purpose of obtaining the loan. Verification may be obtained from any source named in this application. The original or a copy of this application will be retained by the lender, even if the loan is not granted. The undersigned ☐ intend or ☐ do not intend to occupy the property as their primary residence.

I/we fully understand that it is a federal crime punishable by fine or imprisonment, or both, to knowingly make any false statements concerning any of the above facts as applicable under the provisions of Title 18, United States Code, Section 1014.

_____ Borrower's Signature   Date _____   _____ Co-Borrower's Signature   Date _____

INFORMATION FOR GOVERNMENT MONITORING PURPOSES

If this loan is for purchase or construction of a home, the following information is requested by the Federal Government to monitor this lender's compliance with Equal Credit Opportunity and Fair Housing Laws. The law provides that a lender may neither discriminate on the basis of this information nor on whether or not it is furnished. Furnishing this information is optional. If you do not wish to furnish the following information, please initial below.

BORROWER: I do not wish to furnish this information (Initials) _____   CO-BORROWER: I do not wish to furnish this information (Initials) _____

RACE / ☐American Indian, Alaskan Native ☐Asian, Pacific Islander   RACE / ☐American Indian, Alaskan Native ☐Asian, Pacific Islander
NATIONAL ORIGIN ☐Black ☐Hispanic ☐White ☐Other (specify)___ SEX: ☐Female ☐Male
NATIONAL ORIGIN ☐Black ☐Hispanic ☐White ☐Other (specify)___ SEX: ☐Female ☐Male

FOR LENDER'S USE ONLY

(FNMA REQUIREMENT ONLY) This application was taken by ☐ face to face interview ☐ by mail ☐ by telephone

_____ (Interviewer)   _____ Name of Employer of Interviewer

FHLMC 65 Rev. 8/78   REVERSE   FNMA 1003 Rev. 8/78

FHA and VA mortgage application
Figure 7-13 (continued)

Replaces Form FHA-2004-F, which is Obsolete

Form Approved OMB No. 63R-1062

VETERANS ADMINISTRATION AND U.S. DEPARTMENT OF HOUSING AND URBAN DEVELOPMENT
HUD COMMUNITY PLANNING AND DEVELOPMENT
HUD HOUSING - FEDERAL HOUSING COMMISSIONER
REQUEST FOR VERIFICATION OF DEPOSIT

PRIVACY ACT NOTICE STATEMENT - This information is to be used by the agency collecting it in determining whether you qualify as a prospective mortgagor for mortgage insurance or guaranty or as a borrower for a rehabilitation loan under the agency's program. It will not be disclosed outside the agency without your consent except to financial institutions for verification of your deposits and as required and permitted by law. You do not have to give us this information, but, if you do not, your application for approval as a prospective mortgagor for mortgage insurance or guaranty or as a borrower for a rehabilitation loan may be delayed or rejected. This information request is authorized by Title 38, U.S.C., Chapter 37 *(if VA);* by 12 U.S.C., Section 1701 et seq., *(if HUD/FHA);* and by 42 U.S.C., Section 1452b *(if HUD/CPD).*

INSTRUCTIONS

LENDER OR LOCAL PROCESSING AGENCY: Complete Items 1 through 8. Have applicant(s) complete Item 9. Forward directly to the Depository named in Item 1. DEPOSITORY: Please complete Items 10 through 15 and return DIRECTLY to Lender or Local Processing agency named in Item 2.

PART I - REQUEST

1. TO *(Name and Address of Depository)*	2. FROM *(Name and Address of Lender or Local Processing Agency)*

I certify that this verification has been sent directly to the bank or depository and has not passed through the hands of the applicant or any other party.

3. Signature of Lender or Official of Local Processing Agency	4. Title	5. Date	6. Lender's Number *(Optional)*

7. INFORMATION TO BE VERIFIED:

Type of Account and/or Loan	Account/Loan in Name of	Account/Loan Number	Balance
			$
			$
			$
			$

TO DEPOSITORY: I have applied for mortgage insurance or guaranty or for a rehabilitation loan and stated that the balance on deposit and/or outstanding loans with you are as shown above. You are authorized to verify this information and to supply the lender or the local processing agency identified above with the information requested in Items 10 through 12. Your response is solely a matter of courtesy for which no responsibility is attached to your institution or any of your officers.

8. NAME AND ADDRESS OF APPLICANT(S)	9. SIGNATURE OF APPLICANT(S)

TO BE COMPLETED BY DEPOSITORY
PART II - VERIFICATION OF DEPOSITORY
10. DEPOSIT ACCOUNTS OF APPLICANT(S)

Type of Account	Account Number	Current Balance	Average Balance for Previous Two Months	Date Opened
		$	$	
		$	$	
		$	$	
		$	$	

11. LOANS OUTSTANDING TO APPLICANT(S)

Loan Number	Date of Loan	Original Amount	Current Balance	Installments (Monthly/Quarterly)	Secured by	Number of Late Payments within Last 12 Months
		$	$	$ per		
		$	$	$ per		
		$	$	$ per		

12. ADDITIONAL INFORMATION WHICH MAY BE OF ASSISTANCE IN DETERMINATION OF CREDIT WORTHINESS: *Please include information on loans paid-in-full as in Item 11 above)*

13. Signature of Depository Official	14. Title	15. Date

The confidentiality of the information you have furnished will be preserved except where disclosure of this information is required by applicable law. The completed form is to be transmitted directly to the lender or local processing agency and is not to be transmitted through the applicant or any other party.

DEPOSITORY—RETURN BOTH COPIES TO LENDER

VA 26-8497a/HUD-92004-F-6234 (7-80)

Verification of Deposit
Figure 7-14

Previous Editions are Obsolete   Form Approved OMB No. 63R-1062

PRIVACY ACT NOTICE: This information is to be used by the agency collecting it in determining whether you qualify as a prospective mortgagor under its program. It will not be disclosed outside the agency without your consent except to your employer(s) for verification of employment and as required and permitted by law. You do not have to give us this information, but if you do not your application for approval as a prospective mortgagor may be delayed or rejected. The information requested in this form is authorized by Title 38, U.S.C., Chapter 37 (If VA); by 12 U.S.C.,Section 1701 et.seq. (If HUD/FHA) and Title 42 U.S.C., 1471 et.seq., or U.S.C., 1921 et.seq. (If U.S.D.A. FmHA).	VETERANS ADMINISTRATION, U.S.D.A. FARMERS HOME ADMINISTRATION, AND U.S.DEPARTMENT OF HOUSING AND URBAN DEVELOPMENT HOUSING - FEDERAL HOUSING COMMISSIONER **REQUEST FOR VERIFICATION OF EMPLOYMENT**

INSTRUCTIONS	LENDER: *Complete Items 1 through 7. Have the applicant complete item 8. Forward the completed form directly to the employer named in Item 1.*	EMPLOYER: *Complete either Parts II and IV or Parts III and IV. Return form directly to Lender named in Item 2 of Part I.*

PART I - REQUEST

1. TO: *(Name and Address of Employer)*	2. FROM: *(Name and Address of Lender)*

3. *I certify that this verification has been sent directly to the employer and has not passed through the hands of the applicant or any other interested party.* _____ *(Signature of Lender)*	4. TITLE OF LENDER	5. DATE
		6. FHA,VA, or FmHA NUMBER
	I have applied for a mortgage loan and stated that I am/was employed by you. My signature in the block below authorizes verification of my employment information.	

7. NAME AND ADDRESS OF APPLICANT	8. EMPLOYEE'S IDENTIFICATION SIGNATURE OF APPLICANT

PART II - VERIFICATION OF PRESENT EMPLOYMENT

EMPLOYMENT DATA	PAY DATA		
9. APPLICANT'S DATE OF EMPLOYMENT	12A. BASE PAY $_____ ☐ ANNUAL ☐ HOURLY ☐ MONTHLY ☐ WEEKLY ☐ OTHER *(Specify)* ☐ COLA $_____ PAID PER_____	FOR MILITARY PERSONNEL ONLY	
10. PRESENT POSITION		Type	Monthly Amount
		BASE PAY	$
11. PROBABILITY OF CONTINUED EMPLOYMENT		RATIONS	$

12B. EARNINGS			FLIGHT OR HAZARD	$
Type	Year to Date	Past Year		
BASE PAY	$	$	CLOTHING	$
OVERTIME	$	$	QUARTERS	$
COMMISSIONS	$	$	PRO PAY	$
BONUS	$	$	OVERSEAS OR COMBAT	$

13. IF OVERTIME OR BONUS IS APPLICABLE, IS ITS CONTINUANCE LIKELY?

OVERTIME   ☐ Yes   ☐ No
BONUS   ☐ Yes   ☐ No

14. REMARKS *(If paid hourly, please indicate average hours worked each week during current and past year)* AVERAGE HOURS WORKED PER WEEK:____HOURS

GROSS EARNINGS 19___, $_____: GROSS EARNINGS 19___, $_____: GROSS EARNINGS YTD 19___, _____. *(◄ Indicate per Year, Month, Week, Hour)*

INDICATE FUTURE RAISES DUE: DATE_____ AMOUNT_____ PER_____

IF THIS EMPLOYEE WAS OFF FOR ANY LENGTH OF TIME, PLEASE INDICATE DATES: FROM_____TO_____

REASON:

PART III - VERIFICATION OF PREVIOUS EMPLOYMENT

15. DATES OF EMPLOYMENT	16.SALARY/WAGE AT TERMINATION PER (YEAR) (MONTH) (WEEK)			
	BASE	OVERTIME	COMMISSIONS	BONUS
17. REASONS FOR LEAVING	18. POSITION HELD			

PART IV - CERTIFICATION

"Federal statutes provide severe penalties for any fraud, intentional misrepresentation, or criminal connivance or conspiracy purposed to influence the issuance of any guaranty or insurance by the VA Administrator, the HUD/FHA Commissioner, or the USDA Farmers Home Administrator."

19. SIGNATURE	20. TITLE OF EMPLOYER	21. DATE

EMPLOYER—RETURN BOTH COMPLETED COPIES DIRECTLY TO LENDER   HUD-92004-g; VA-26-8497; FmHA-410-5 (12-79)

Verification of Employment
Figure 7-15

First Mortgage Company
3061 Money Street
Anytown, Vermont 00000
Phone (123) 456-7890

Buyer's Statement

Case No. _____

Gentlemen:

The undersigned hereby certifies that the down payment of $ _____
and the balance of $ _____ required for the completion of this transaction
came, or will come, from the source or sources indicated below:

1) Bank account (name of bank) _____

2) Sale of stocks or bonds _____

3) Proceeds from sale of real estate _____

4) Gift (submit gift affidavit) _____

5) Loan on, or cash value of, life insurance_____

6) Other _____

All of the above money as well as funds reported on the application were accumulated
from income, and none of it represents the proceeds of an unsecured loan.

I/We, the prospective owners of said property, am/are in no way indebted to the seller
and will not have outstanding any unpaid obligations contracted with the purchase or construction of said property other than the prospective insured mortgage.

Warning

Section 1010 of Title 18, U.S.C., Federal Housing Administration Transactions provides: "Whoever, for the
purpose of . . . influencing in any way the action of such Administration . . . makes, passes, utters, or publishes
any statement knowing the same to be false . . . shall be fined not more than $5,000 or imprisoned not more than
two years, or both."

Buyer_____

_____

Buyer's Statement
Figure 7-16

First Mortgage Company
3061 Money Street
Anytown, Vermont 00000
Phone (123) 456-7890

Re: Loan No: _____
Property Address: _____

    I/We hereby certify that we intend to occupy the subject property, which we are purchasing as our home. Said purchase is being financed through _____.

    I/We further acknowledge that we have been advised that we are free to choose that title underwriter of the mortgagee's title insurance policy and the Private Mortgage Insurer, however, we agree to use the Title Underwriter and Private Mortgage Insurer selected by the lender.

_____
Purchaser/Mortgagor

_____
Purchaser/Mortgagor

**Statement of occupancy and freedom
to choose title underwriter
Figure 7-17**

First Mortgage Company
3061 Money Street
Anytown, Vermont 00000
Phone: (123) 456-7890

Re: Loan No. _____

Property Address: _____

Gentlemen:

The undersigned who have applied for a mortgage loan on the above property agree that the loan will bear the maximum interest rate authorized by FHA/VA at the time of disbursement of the loan, but in no event less than the minimum rate of _____%. If the maximum authorized FHA/VA rate is less than such minimum rate and FHA/VA does not permit the closing of the loan at such minimum rate, you will have no obligation to disburse the loan even though the mortgage documents have been executed or recorded. If the maximum authorized FHA/VA rate is increased before the loan is disbursed, we agree to execute such new loan documents as may be appropriate to give effect to such increase.

_____

Date: _____   _____

**Maximum interest rate form
Figure 7-18**

First Mortgage Company
3061 Money Street
Anytown, Vermont 00000
Phone: (123) 456-7890

E.C.O.A. Notice

The Federal Equal Credit Opportunity Act prohibits creditors from discriminating against credit applicants on the basis of race, color, religion, national origin, sex, marital status, age (provided that the applicant has the capacity to enter into a binding contract); because all or part of the applicant's income derives from any public assistance program; or because the applicant has in good faith exercised any right under the Consumer Credit Protection Act. The Federal Agency that administers compliance with this law concerning this creditor is:

Federal Trade Commission
730 Peachtree Street, N.E.
Room #800
Atlanta, Georgia 30308

Copy received by:

_____

_____

Date: _____

I hereby acknowledge receipt of the following:

_____ Settlement Costs Booklet   _____ Advance Disclosure of Costs

Buyer:_____

Buyer:_____

Equal Credit Opportunity Act Notice
Figure 7-19

NOTICE TO BORROWER(S) REQUIRED BY FEDERAL LAW AND FEDERAL RESERVE REGULATION Z
REAL PROPERTY TRANSACTION SECURED BY A FIRST LIEN ON DWELLING

LENDER:

DATE
LOAN NO.
TYPE

BORROWERS
ADDRESS
CITY STATE/ZIP
PROPERTY

ANNUAL PERCENTAGE RATE The cost of your credit as a yearly rate. %	FINANCE CHARGE The dollar amount the credit will cost you. $	AMOUNT FINANCED The amount of credit pro-vided to you or on your behalf. $	TOTAL OF PAYMENTS The amount you will have paid after you have made all payments as scheduled. $

ITEMIZATION: You have a right at this time to an ITEMIZATION of AMOUNT FINANCED.
☐ I do not want an itemization_____ (Initials)   ☐ I want an itemization_____ (Initials)

PAYMENT SCHEDULE:

NUMBER OF PAYMENTS	AMOUNT OF PAYMENTS	WHEN PAYMENTS ARE DUE	NUMBER OF PAYMENTS	AMOUNT OF PAYMENTS	WHEN PAYMENTS ARE DUE

DEMAND FEATURE: ☐ This loan does not have a Demand Feature.   ☐ This loan has a Demand Feature as follows:

VARIABLE RATE FEATURE: ☐ This loan does not have a Variable Rate Feature.
☐ This is an Adjustable Rate Loan. The ANNUAL PERCENTAGE RATE may increase during the term of this loan if the applicable interest rate index increases. Applicable interest rate index governing this loan is:

☐ This is a Renegotiable Rate Loan. The lender may increase the ANNUAL PERCENTAGE RATE during the term of this loan as follows:

Any increase in ANNUAL PERCENTAGE RATE will: ☐ Increase the principal balance due.   ☐ Increase the dollar amount of payments.

EXAMPLE: If the ANNUAL PERCENTAGE RATE of interest is increased by _____ % after _____ , your payment would increase by $ _____ to $ _____ per _____

SECURITY: ☐ You are giving a security interest in the property located at:

ASSUMPTION: ☐ Someone buying this property   ☐ cannot assume the remaining balance due under original mortgage terms.
☐ may assume subject to lenders conditions the remaining balance due under original mortgage terms.

FILING / RECORDING FEES: $
PROPERTY INSURANCE: ☐ Property hazard insurance in the amount of $ _____ with a loss payable clause to the lender is a required condition of this loan. Borrower can purchase this insurance from any insurance company acceptable to the lender, but may be purchased through the lender at an estimated cost of _____ for a _____ year term.

LATE CHARGES: If your payment is not received when due, a late charge of _____ % of the overdue payment amount will be added.

PREPAYMENT PENALTY: ☐ You may be charged a penalty to prepay this loan in full or in part.
See your contract documents for any additional information regarding non-payment, default, required re-payment in full before scheduled date, and payment refunds and penalties.

CREDIT LIFE AND DISABILITY INSURANCE: LIFE AND DISABILITY INSURANCE IS NOT REQUIRED TO OBTAIN CREDIT.
Credit Life Disability and Life / Disability insurance is available through the lender at additional cost.

I/We want to apply for:	TERM	PREMIUM	BORROWER - APPLICANT SIGNATURE
Credit Life insurance			☐
Credit Disability insurance			☐
Credit Life and Disability insurance			☐

E = ESTIMATED
I/We hereby acknowledge reading and receiving a complete copy of this disclosure along with copies of documents referred to in this disclosure.

_____ BORROWER / DATE   _____ BORROWER / DATE

VMP-15 B   **LENDER COPY**
CONSOLIDATED BUSINESS FORMS, INC. - MT. CLEMENS, MI 48043 313/792-4700

Notice to Borrowers
Figure 7-20

First Mortgage Company
3061 Money Street
Anytown, Vermont 00000
Phone: (123) 456-7890

Date: _____

Re: Our Loan No. _____/ Your Loan No. _____
    Name: _____
    Property Address: _____
    _____

Gentlemen:

We have received a loan application from the above referenced that shows you as the holder of the mortgage on his property. Your cooperation in furnishing us with the following information will be appreciated.

1) FHA, VA, Conventional Loan_____
2) Original sales price _____
3) Date of mortgage _____
4) Original mortgage amount _____
5) Present unpaid balance _____
6) Monthly payment _____
7) Due for _____
8) Payment experience _____
9) Legal description _____
    _____

By: _____

Thank you.

Very truly yours,

I hereby authorize you to release the information on my mortgage account.

Mortgagor: _____

Mortgagor: _____

Verification of terms and payment experience
Figure 7-21

First Mortgage Company
3061 Money Street
Anytown, Vermont 00000
Phone: (123) 456-7890

Good Faith Estimates

This list gives an estimate of most of the charges you will have to pay at the settlement of your loan. The figures shown, as *estimates,* are subject to change. The figures shown are computed based on a sales price of _____ and proposed mortgage amount of _____ as stated on your loan application.

Estimated Settlement Charges

Discount on Conventional Loans	_____
801 Loan Origination Fee 1%	_____
805 Lenders Inspection Fee	_____
806 Mortgage Insurance Application Fee	_____
*901 Interest (Estimated for ____ days)	_____
902 Mortgage Insurance Premium	_____
1107 Attorney's Fees	_____
1108 Title Insurance (Mtgee. & Owners)	_____
1201 Recording Fees	_____
1202 Intangible Tax	_____
1203 State Stamps (Documentary Stamps)	_____
1301 Survey	_____
809 Warehouse Fee	_____

*This interest calculation represents a portion of interest you could be required to pay at settlement. The actual amount will be determined by which day of the month your settlement is conducted. To determine the amount you will have to pay, multiply the number of days remaining in the month in which you settle times $_____, which is the daily interest charge for your loan.

On Conventional loans interest is from date of closing until date of first payment.

Prepayments are not included in the figures above.

This form does not cover all items you will be required to pay in cash at settlement, for example, deposit in escrow for real estate taxes and insurance. You may wish to inquire as to the amounts of such other items. You may be required to pay other additional amounts at settlement.

In addition to the above costs, you will be required to pay for a Hazard Insurance or Homeowner Insurance and/or Floor Insurance Policy for a full year in advance at closing.

I/We hereby acknowledge the receipt of the above estimated costs.

_____

_____

Good faith estimates
Figure 7-22

F.H.A. Loan Rate Per Thousand Dollars (30-year Loan)

Interest Rate	Dollar Amount
10%	$ 9.20
10½%	9.57
11%	9.95
11½%	10.33
12%	10.71
12½%	11.10
13%	11.49
13½%	11.88
14%	12.27
14½%	12.67
15%	13.07
15½%	13.47
16%	13.87
16½%	14.28
17%	14.68
17½%	15.09
18%	15.50
18½%	15.90
19%	16.31
19½%	16.72
20%	17.14

Example:
A $15,000.00 loan for
30 years at 14%:
Multiply $ 15,000.00
$\underline{\text{x} \qquad 12.27}$
$184,050.00 ÷ 1,000 = $184.05

is the monthly payment on
principal and interest
including 1st year mortgage
insurance.

Note: If the current
rate of interest is
14%, then memorize the
$12.27 rate per thousand
dollars.

If the rate is 16% per
thousand dollars, then
memorize the rate $13.87
per thousand.

Memorize the current
rate.

Remember: There may be a
slight variance in the final
figure due to the number of
decimal places used.

Rate chart for F.H.A. mortgage
Figure 7-23

First Mortgage Company
3061 Money Street
Anytown, Vermont 00000
Phone: (123) 456-7890

Anti - Coercion Statement

The Insurance Laws of this State provide that the lender may not require the borrower to take insurance through any particular insurance agent or company to protect the mortgaged property.

The borrower, subject to the rules adopted by the Insurance Commissioner, has the right to have the insurance placed with an insurance agent or company of his choice, provided the company meets the requirements of the lender. The lender has the right to designate reasonable financial requirements as to the company and the adequacy of the coverage.

I have read the foregoing statement, or the rules of the Insurance Commissioner relative thereto, and understand my rights and privileges and those of the lender relative to the placing of such insurance.

I have elected the _____ Insurance Agency, or the
_____ Insurance Company to write the hazard insurance covering property
located at _____
_____

_____

_____

_____
Date

Anti-coercion statement
Figure 7-24

general contractor might skip paying one or more subcontractors or suppliers, resulting in a lien against the home.

In this chapter we've discussed various methods of financing. The difference between the men and the boys in the remodeling business is that the men know that *it takes financing to make the sale*.

Remember, the following methods of financing can make your business more profitable:

- Cash jobs
- Co-ops
- Compensating deposits
- Credit unions
- Conventional mortgages

- Farm financing
- FHA loans
- Finance company loans
- HIP, home improvement, private bank or S&L loans
- Life insurance companies
- Mortgage financing (include debt consolidation)
- Open-end mortgages
- Pledges
- Private parties
- Recasting an existing mortgage
- Supplemental financing

In the next chapter we'll take a look at some proven professional methods of closing the sale.

Chapter 8

Closing

While the tomcat may say, "You have to make calls to get results," getting results in the construction business takes more than just making calls. It takes qualifying the buyer. It takes a professional sales presentation. Above all, it takes a good strong close.

Salesmen who come home with signed contracts are called *closers*. This means that they have the ability to convert qualified prospects into paying customers.

The essential part of the close is asking for the order. If you don't ask for the order, you've wasted your time in qualifying the lead, going through the demonstration presentation, and financing the prospect.

You must ask for the order. It's as simple as that. The worst that can happen is that your prospect will say, "No." And no isn't the end of the world. A little persistence can turn a no into a yes!

The Kitchen Table Close
My favorite close is one that I've used for years. You probably know the one I mean. I've mentioned it several times. I say, "Do you mind if I use your kitchen table to write up the order?" If I get a no, I ask, "Would you prefer that we use the dining room table?"

If there's a dog in the kitchen (or dining room), watch out. A dog can distract the customer enough that he'll lose track of your line of reasoning. Your carefully planned and executed presentation can lose its entire impact as the customer turns his attention to the dog instead of to the line you want him to sign on. Simply ask, "Can you please put the dog in the bathroom or basement so we can use the table to write up your order?"

Remember this: In home improvement sales, if you don't get the order when you've finished making the pitch, you'll probably never get it. Why? Because the next salesman will either undercut your price, change the job, offer a premium, or confuse the buyer. If that doesn't happen, your prospect will decide he needs a new car or a condo in Florida more than he needs his home remodeled. Two days later he can't even remember what you were selling.

T.O.'s
If you can't close a sale, consider making a hand off, or turn over (T.O.). You turn the sale over to another salesman, preferably another strong closer.

Here's how I handle a T.O.:

"I can see that there's still some doubt in your mind. Let me make an appointment for you with our sales manager, Mr. Browning. He knows everything there is to know about home improvements. I'm sure he can cover the questions that I wasn't able to answer for you. He may see

If you can't close a sale, consider making a T.O. to another salesman

some way to improve on what I've suggested. He might even find a way to save you some cash.''

You need a strong hook to make a T.O. The strongest hook is money.

You've probably had a T.O. when shopping for a car. As you're about to walk off the lot, the car salesman says, ''Let's go talk to the sales manager and see if he can give you a better deal.'' The car salesman does this only when he's given up trying to write the order himself.

The T.O. system works. Sometimes a new face can close a sale quickly once some other salesman has done the preparation. There may be better communication between the T.O. salesman and the buyer. Or the T.O. salesman may find an opening that the first salesman missed. Be sure the T.O. salesman is introduced with an impressive title such as Sales Manager, Associate General Manager, Construction Engineer, Superintendent, or Treasurer. That's probably why the T.O. system works. Your prospect's flattered to know that he's dealing with the boss.

Team Sales

Some very aggressive sales firms use a team on every close. For many years I.B.M. used two-man sales teams regularly. Most sales teams consist of a front man and a closer. Team salesmen use several methods to get signed contracts.

Method A — The front man visits all the leads first. He informs them that he's from the company's advertising department. His boss, Mr. Superintendent, was tied up so he came in his place. He wants to get an idea of the work to see if they can use it for ''before'' and ''after'' pictures. He then qualifies the lead:

Is the work to be done now?
Is it the kind of work the company does?
Is the job financeable?
Will all parties to the contract be present at the close?

Next, he sets up an appointment for the closer,

Mr. Superintendent. Before he leaves, he tells the customer what a great guy Mr. Superintendent is, how many terrific jobs he's designed, how he financed people that were unfinanceable, and so on.

Mr. Superintendent arrives for the appointment. He's been *fronted in.* He's received with respect. His word is pure gold. It's a cinch for Mr. Superintendent to close the sale.

Method B— The team arrives together. The front man qualifies the prospect and makes a complete presentation. He does all the talking, simultaneously building up his boss, Mr. Sales Manager. Mr. Sales Manager sits quietly, taking everything in, until the front man asks him to chime in. Then, Mr. Sales Manager comes up with a deal which is just a little bit better than anything Mr. Front Man has been able to put together.

Method C— This system takes some coordination. The front man is the Sales Engineer. The closer is the Treasurer of the company.

After the icebreaker and warm-up, the front man says:

"You can see how attractive this design will be and how much it will add to the enjoyment and value of your home. The only thing I haven't covered is financing. If the job can't be financed, what we're talking about is impossible. We're very lucky, tonight, to have the Treasurer of the company with us. He processes loan packages for our company. Mr. Treasurer, what can we do for Mr. and Mrs. Homeowner?"

The closer, Mr. Treasurer, takes over. He qualifies the lead as to income, equity and debts. He quickly arrives at the dollar amount that can be financed. Turning to the prospects, he announces:

"I can qualify you for a loan of X dollars. If that figure will carry this job, Mr. Sales Engineer, the only thing left to decide is when to get started. I'll process the loan papers for you first thing tomorrow morning."

The customers are relieved to know that they can borrow the money needed to do the job. All people like to hear that they have good credit.

The cost of the job will usually be close to the maximum amount that can be financed. That shouldn't be a surprise. Most home buyers buy the most expensive home they can qualify for. And most homeowners will never make a better investment!

Hooks

When you go fishing, you use bait on a hook to catch a fish. In advertising, there's often some type of bait in the ad that will cause the prospective buyer to hurry up and buy the item or service being offered. Advertising people have a name for this bait: *hooks.* Here are some examples of hooks taken from a local newspaper:

- Sale Ends Saturday

- Sale Prices While Quantities Last

- Easy Credit

- Free Gift Certificate

- Sale 20% to 35% Off

When you're trying to close a sale, it's often necessary to use a hook. A hook can be a premium you give in return for a prompt affirmative decision. Here's an example of a hook an aluminum siding contractor might use:

"We need work for our men next week. So as a gift, I can give you a new storm door."

The garage builder can use an electric door opener as a hook. If you're remodeling a bathroom, an electric wall or ceiling heater makes a good hook. If it's a kitchen, offer a free range hood or garbage disposal. If the job's big enough, use a trash compactor as bait. When selling a rec room, offer a wet bar. A bar is a terrific hook.

Here are the important points to remember about a hook. The gift must be in exchange for an immediate "yes." A decision tomorrow or next week is too late. Don't worry about losing the sale tomorrow or next week. If you don't close now, you never will.

To make sense to your prospect, there should be a logical reason for the hook. Your company made a volume purchase at a discount, so you're passing the savings along. It's off-season and you can offer a discount because you want to keep your crews busy. You already have a job in the neighborhood and can save money if the men and equipment don't have to start working on the other side of town.

Remember: A premium should never be given away unless the customer gives you a prompt affirmative decision in return. Otherwise, you're just cutting your price. Here's the proper way to handle premiums:

"If you can come to a decision right now, Mr. Homeowner, and let me write up the order, it'll save me the time and expense of making another trip. I'll give you a portable T.V. set (waffle iron, coffee maker, other small appliance)."

Make it clear you want an affirmative decision in return. That's why you're willing to part with a valuable gift. The transaction must be *quid pro quo*. The gift is *only* in exchange for an immediate yes.

Assumption Close

I learned the assumption close when I was a teenager working for a garage builder. The salesman in an assumption close just *assumes* that he's taking an order. It goes like this:

The salesman uses his order blank to list the important facts: square feet of floor, wall height, materials and the other specifications. He writes in the price and the monthly payments. Then he turns the contract so it faces the buyer, hands the buyer a pen and says:

"Just write your name and we'll get started. I'll call the bank first thing in the morning to get your loan approved."

Sometimes the buyer signs and the sale is closed just like that — especially if it's something simple like a garage, some siding or cabinets. If the buyer won't sign, the salesman says:

"Oh. I thought you were placing the order. Well, I've got everything down on paper. Let me explain what the price covers." He continues his sales pitch, noting specifications, price and payments, just as before. Then he tries again for the close. Some prospects will sign the contract on the second pass.

But there are some dyed-in-the-wool shoppers who'll want to continue to shop. Try a hook on them, or appeal to their vanity. Tell them how the remodeling job is going to make their home the most beautiful, luxurious and practical home in the neighborhood. Or try the scare appeal:

"Our workmen are getting a raise, and material prices are going up. I won't be able to offer you this price next week. Take it now before prices go up."

If the buyer still doesn't yield, don't give up. Most people cannot resist a salesman who's persistent and who knows his business. Even if all seems hopeless, try again. This attempt may be the straw that breaks the camel's back and gets you the order.

Great musicians practice continually to improve their technique. Making sale after sale, your technique will improve too — especially if you analyze what you did right and wrong in each sale.

Either-Or Close

Another good close is to have the customer make a decision on a secondary item. For example:

"Do you want textured or smooth siding?"
"Do you want the stainless steel sink or the porcelain?"
"Do you want bifold closet doors or sliding doors?"
"Do you want casement windows or sliders?"
"Would you rather have us start next week or after the holiday?"

These questions demand answers. The buyer must make a choice. Each choice made makes consent to the order more likely.

In closing a sale, another key question that demands an answer is:

"Do you want us to arrange financing for this job, or are you paying cash?"

Whichever way the customer answers, he's given you the okay to write the order.

The Story Close

"You know, Mr. Homeowner, this job reminds me of a job we did for Mr. and Mrs. Novak, over on Chestnut Street. They have a lovely home — built in 1910! We took out the two old-fashioned narrow windows in the living room and installed a triple picture window. At the side we installed new removable sash windows that you just snap out to wash. We built an eyebrow canopy clear across the picture window and front entry door. We hung a modern hand-carved entry door with three staggered glass lites. That's a beautiful door. The

Novaks just love it! Then we covered the front of the house with insulated aluminum siding. The Novaks' home looks terrific now. It's a credit to the neighborhood. When they decide to sell, they'll get a lot more out of that project than they put into it. In the meantime, they take a lot of pride in their home. If you have a few minutes, Mrs. Homeowner, I can drive you over to Chestnut Street to take a look at the job. I'm sure Mr. and Mrs. Novak would love to show you around. You don't have time? Well, O.K., maybe some other time. Just sign here and we'll get started with your project."

Story telling is testimonial selling. It's especially effective if you've done jobs for prominent people in the community and can mention their names.

An indispensable aid to story telling is an album of "before" and "after" pictures. Have a freelance photographer do the work. You can probably get pictures taken very cheaply if you guarantee a freelancer several jobs a month. A professional photographer will put your work in the best possible light.

When you display your pictures, don't just thumb through the album. Mention each owner's name, address and city. Explain how the house looked before, pointing out the features that had to be corrected. Then turn to the "after" pictures. Point out what you did. Explain how the job was done, not in technical language but in terms of the benefits received by the owner. Do this with a number of sets. The more you show, the more you impress the buyer.

The Price-Conscious Buyer

For some buyers, price is the bottom line. You can talk quality and service until you're blue in the face. But if you can't offer them the lowest price, you won't get the order. Here's how to handle this type of customer.

When a prospect is shopping for price, he usually ends up comparing apples to oranges, instead of apples to apples. He gets bids from different contractors who are offering different jobs. Your competitor can offer a lower price, because he's not offering the same remodeling job.

This confuses the prospect. And it's unfortunate for you, because most buyers only remember the price. They don't think about what they're getting for their money. If your prospect tells you another builder has put in a lower bid, ask him what the price was and what, exactly, the other builder was

going to do. If you can beat the price, you'll get the order. Or here's another tactic you can try:

"Mr. Homeowner, I can give you two other bids. The bid I gave you was for our highest quality materials and labor. I can give you another bid for the same job only using average materials, construction grade, not No. 1 grade. And I'll use a different crew of carpenters than I was planning on using. I was going to give you our best trim crew. This other crew works a little slower, but they'd get you plenty of compliments from friends and relatives who come to visit you. I can give you still another bid if I change the job description a little. It'll just take a few minutes to refigure the job. Perhaps we can make a few changes so that the work comes within your budget."

The price-conscious buyer may also tell you that he can't give you the order now, because he has to arrange his own financing. You can follow this line with:

"That's fine. I'll go ahead and write up the order now, and make it subject to obtaining financing. You'll probably need a firm contract to present to your lender. We can write up the contract with all of the specifications. The specs are an aid to the lender — they'll help expedite approval. If it'd be helpful to you, I can go with you to meet your loan officer and explain the specifications to him."

If the buyer agrees, you have the order locked up.

Summary Close

Here's how I handle the summary close:

"Now let me check this contract over one more time. This wall comes out, Mrs. Homeowner, to give you 50% more room in the kitchen. The new window over the sink complements the new built-in planter by the sill. Your plants will get plenty of sunlight, and your kitchen will be bright and cheerful. The porcelain double-bowl sink goes right here under the window. When you're at the sink, you'll have a full view of the garden. This layout cuts wasted steps to a minimum. From the refrigerator to the sink is only two steps. To the range is only three steps. The new wall and base cabinets keep dishes, pots and pans at your fingertips. The knick-knack shelves dress up the window arrangement and are highlighted by the recessed light fixture over the sink. In front of the light goes the scalloped valance. The new appliance plugs go here, here and here above the 4-inch backsplash on the new countertop. It will be self-edged, of course, for cleanliness. There! That looks right to me. Please write your name right down here."

During your summary, remember to stress all the benefits the buyer will receive:

- Kitchen sink area becomes a scenic greenhouse

- Easy storage of perishables

- Groceries stored next to the refrigerator

- Walk only two steps in any direction to reach what you need

- All food preparation essentials located together

- Plenty of electrical outlets for kitchen appliances

Stressing the benefits *doesn't* mean describing the construction or the technical way you're going to build the new kitchen. Don't tell the buyer how you're going to anchor the cabinets to the wall. Paint a verbal picture of how the dream kitchen will look when it's finished. Paint a picture of the customer's own desires.

When the storm window salesman makes his summary, he'll be sure to stress the following benefits:

- Having screens in the summer to keep the bugs, flies, mosquitoes out

- Saving on fuel bills in the winter

- Eliminating drafts that cause colds

- Reducing heat loss

- Having windows that can be removed from the interior for easy cleaning

- Having triple tracks for storage of screens in winter and storm panes in summer

- Having virgin, not recycled, aluminum, which won't pit or mar

- Having marine glazing and mitered corners

- Having easy payments handled through the company's dealership

Then he'll summarize the job, and ask for the order. It's important to summarize when you close. Here's why. You'll never close until everything is clear in the mind of your prospects. You can't get consent from a prospect who's uncertain about something in the contract. And of course, if you don't ask for the order, you won't get it.

"As I explained, Mrs. Homeowner, we can do this job for no money down. The first payment — $69.36 — will be due 60 days from now. How does that sound? Let's use the kitchen table to write up the order."

I have a friend who closes sales like this: He does all the figuring on 3 x 5 cards that he carries in his pocket. He always leaves his briefcase in the car until the close. When he's ready to close, he says:

"I'll have to get my briefcase out of the car to write up the order."

If there are no objections, he knows the sale is closed. If the prospects won't let him go to the car, they still have some objections. They have to state those objections now to keep him from going to the car. He answers those questions, goes over his summary again, and explains the benefits. Then he tries the briefcase gambit again. When he finally goes to the car, the sale's closed. This has been extremely effective for him over the years.

Take It Away and Give It Back
If you have kids, you know how this one works. Deny your kids a treat, an activity, or the privilege of staying up late, and the result is a clamor. The thing denied becomes the focus of all their attention. Observant salesmen have noticed that adults behave the same way. Tell them they don't qualify and suddenly qualifying becomes the most important issue — ahead of both the job and the price.

Tell the prospects there's a reason why they can't have the work done and they'll beg for it. That's when you agree to give it to them. Sound farfetched? Maybe, but it's true and it works.

The best place to use the Take It Away and Give It Back close is with financing:

"This job's going to be almost impossible to finance. The problem is your . . . ." You supply the reason — either not enough income, not enough equity, too many debts, irregular employment, or bankruptcy.

Dwell on these difficulties. "I'm sorry, but there's not much I can do." Pack up, put on your coat and start to leave. Then:

"Say! There might be one way to work it! If you really want us to do this job, I could take it to the loan officer personally. I'll need a copy of the signed contract though. Let me write up the order now as though there were no problem. I'll call tomorrow when I've talked with the loan officer. Maybe I'll have some good news!"

Nine times out of ten, the customer will sign the order.

You may be able to use zoning problems in the Take It Away and Give It Back close. Suggest there may be a zoning regulation that holds up the job. But use this approach only when you are familiar with the local building code and have taken the time to get a copy of the regulations. And be on the lookout for the building inspector who makes off-hand decisions that really don't comply with the law. Know your building code. Study it, and interpret it correctly.

In this chapter we've talked about the most important part of the sale, the close. True, there are probably as many ways to close a sale as there are sales in the home improvement business. But what I've recommended here has worked for me — over a thousand times. I suspect it will work for you, too.

In the next chapter, we'll go on to an important market many salesmen overlook — insurance referrals.

Chapter 9

Insurance Work

Insured losses caused by fire, tornadoes, floods, snow collapse, gas explosions, accidents, earthquakes or lightning can provide profitable, steady work for home improvement contractors. Everyone who sells home improvement work should know how to develop this market.

Policy Requirements
Misconceptions about insurance repairs keep many contractors from going after insurance work. The biggest misconception is the belief that insurance companies always need three bids. An insurance broker may ask the customer to get three bids. But insurance brokers seldom settle claims. In most cases, they just sell insurance. The broker wants to keep his loss ratio as low as possible. The lower the claims, the better his record. Insurance companies use adjusters to settle losses. They are also trying to buy the claim as cheaply as possible. This, too, is only human nature. Insurance companies want to make money, just like every other business.

The policy paragraph titled "Requirements in Case of Loss" establishes the procedure for settlement. This paragraph is essentially the same in all insurance policies:

The insured shall give immediate written notice to this company of any loss, protect the property from further damage, forthwith separate the damaged and undamaged personal property, put it in the best possible order, furnish a complete inventory of the destroyed, damaged and undamaged property, showing in detail quantities, costs, actual cash value and amount of loss claimed; and within sixty days after the loss, unless such time is extended in writing by this company, the insured shall render to this company a proof of loss.

The policyholder or his contractor should submit a detailed list of what was lost or destroyed and the replacement cost. To meet this requirement, prepare a schedule like Figure 9-1. The schedule lists each item in each room separately, with footage, cost per unit and total cost of replacement of each item.

Phone the adjuster, and set up a time to go over the loss schedule in person. When you meet with the adjuster, it's a simple matter for the adjuster to go over each item and agree or disagree on each unit cost. When you've settled the amount to be paid, prepare your contract and job specs based on what the insurance company has agreed to pay. Have the customer sign it and you're ready to go!

Bear in mind that you're not submitting a job proposal. You're just meeting policy requirements. This cost breakdown will normally get you a higher price for the work than preparing an estimate for a competitive bid.

The Adjustment or Assignment Form
If it's legal in your state, have the customer sign a form naming you as the adjuster representing the

National Construction Co.
General Remodeling - Fire Repairs
P. O. Box 45
Chicago, IL 60645

Schedule for Hutchins Title & Trust Company
Under Trust No. 4314
280 Maple Avenue   Gibraltar Insurance Co.
West Chicago, Illinois   #h 77 21 96
Sunside Subd.   Fire 7/17/84

Kitchen 14 x 13 x 8

Wash and paint walls and ceiling	614	.40	$245.60
Wall cabinet 30 x 18	--	--	116.00
Corner wall cabinet 34 x 30	--	--	140.00
Wall cabinet 36 x 30	--	--	182.00
Wall cabinet 42 x 18	--	--	156.00
Underlayment	182	.60	109.20
Vinyl tile floor	182	1.50	273.00
Nail pops ceiling	182	.60	109.20
Paint two openings	2	20.00	40.00
Rewire duplex outlets	3	40.00	120.00
Rewire wall switch	1	40.00	40.00
Rewire ceiling outlet	1	40.00	40.00
R & R ceiling fixture	--	--	70.00

Bathroom 6 x 9 x 8

Nail pops ceiling and walls	179	.60	107.40
Wash and paint walls and ceiling	179	.40	71.60
Paint one opening	--	--	20.00
Clean tile and regrout	125	2.00	250.00
Accessories	--	--	70.00
Refinish door	--	--	30.00
Underlayment	54	.60	32.40
Medicine cabinet	--	--	70.00
Flooring	54	1.50	81.00
Rewire switch	--	--	40.00
Rewire hookup medicine cabinet	--	--	40.00

Loss schedule
Figure 9-1

Insurance leads can provide profitable work

claim against the insurance company. Figure 9-2 shows a typical adjustment form. If you plan to use a form like this, have your attorney go over it with you to make sure it meets your state's requirements.

Some states now have laws that require adjusters to be licensed. That makes it illegal for a contractor to represent the homeowner in his claim against the insurance company — unless the contractor is a licensed adjuster. It's still legal, of course, to prepare an estimate and have the customer sign both the estimate and a contract to do the repairs. The nearest office of your state insurance department will explain what your state requires.

If you have to be licensed, the adjustment form won't work. Instead, use an assignment form like the one in Figure 9-3. This form is an authorization by the policyholder to have the insurance company put your name on the check or draft. This protects you. It guarantees that you'll be paid the full amount of the agreed loss. Prepare this form in triplicate. One copy goes to the claim department of the insurance company. The second goes to your

customer. Keep the third for your records.

It's important that you mail the insurance company's copy out promptly. Some contractors use certified mail. That way they have a record of receipt by the insurance company. I send the assignment form to the insurance company with a cover letter headed "Important Notice" (Figure 9-4).

Use Insurance Terminology

Make it easier for adjusters to work with you. Learn and use insurance terminology. *R and R* is the shorthand expression for remove and replace. Most insurance work is R and R: studs, rafters, interior and exterior doors, and drywall. When you estimate R and R, the cost has to include both the new work and ripping out damaged material. A partial R and R price list might look like this:

R and R studs per BF	$_____
R and R rafters 2 x 8's per BF	$_____
R and R joists 2 x 10's per BF	$_____
R and R window glass, per UI	$_____
R and R 1/2'' drywall, per SF	$_____

Adjustment Of Insurance Claim
Assignment Of Insurance Claim
Power of Attorney

WHEREAS, the following undersigned _____ Grantor(s)
Whose address is _____
City of _____ County of _____ State of _____
Hereby makes, constitutes and appoints _____
Whose address is_____
City of _____ County of _____ State of _____
as (his) (her) (their) true and lawful attorney in fact for (his) (her) (their) name, place and
stead: Represent _____
in a claim against _____ Insurance Company whose Policy Number is
_____ Claim Number is _____ resulting from loss or
damage by _____ to the premises commonly known as _____
_____
City of _____ County of _____ State of _____
which occurred on or about _____ 19_____.

This authorizes the making of a claim under said policy, adjustment of the claim and
receipt from said insurance company of drafts or checks in payment of said loss. The adjustment fee of 10% of the adjusted loss, is to be waived if repair contract is awarded to:
_____.

Granting to said attorney in fact the full authority and power to do and perform any
and all other acts which may be necessary or incidental to the performance and execution of
the powers hereinabove authorized, as fully to all intents and purposes as the grantor might
or could do if personally present, with full power of substitution.

I do hereby ratify and confirm whatsoever said attorney may lawfully do pursuant to
the power of attorney herein granted.

Given under my hand and seal this _____ day of _____, 19_____.

_____

_____

State of _____) SS
County of _____)

I, _____, a Notary Public in and for, and residing in said County and State
aforesaid to hereby certify that _____
personally known to me to be the same person whose name subscribed to the foregoing instrument appeared before me this day in person and acknowledged that he signed and
delivered the aforesaid instrument as a free and voluntary act for the uses and purposes
therein set forth.

Given under my hand and notarial seal this _____ day of _____, 19_____.

My commission expires: _____

_____
Notary Public

Typical adjustment form
Figure 9-2

Assignment

Insurance Company_____

Policy No._____

Claim No. _____

Date of Loss _____

I, or we, hereby authorize_____insurance company

to name _____

on the loss payable draft for the loss or damage by _____

which occurred on or about _____, 19_____,

to the premises commonly known as _____

Given under my hand and seal this _____ day of _____, 19_____.

_____ (Seal)

_____ (Seal)

_____
Witness

Assignment form
Figure 9-3

Other important insurance terms include: scrape and paint, sand and seal.

Getting Insurance Leads

Before we go into the mechanics of selling insurance work, let's discuss how you find leads in this specialty.

First, write to the National Underwriter Company, 420 East Fourth Street, Cincinnati, OH 45202. Ask for an *insurance telephone directory* that lists insurance adjusters in your area. If they don't publish a directory for your community, they'll probably have a mailing list of adjusters (independent, public, and staff) and claims managers for your area. Contact some of these adjusters. Let them know you're in the loss repair business and are anxious to work with them.

Some public adjusters will work with a contractor, passing along leads on a fee basis. It's common for the insured to ask an adjuster for the names of contractors who specialize in fire work. In many cases, a staff or independent adjuster will suggest three names. The more adjusters you have mentioning your name, the more leads you'll get. Remember, too, that when an adjuster gives your name to an insured, you're getting a red-carpet testimonial.

Second order of business: Look in the Yellow Pages under the heading *Adjusters* for a list of local adjusters. Many of these adjusters will be in the directory published by the National Underwriter Company. But others will not. And some names on the National Underwriter list won't be in the Yellow Pages.

Important Notice

Attention:

Re: Claim No.

Your Insured:

Date of Loss:

Enclosed please find an assignment of proceeds from your insured to guarantee payment to us upon completion of the work. Our contract to complete this job is in the amount of $_____, less a deductible of $_____.

The assignment is hereby sent you so as to protect our interest when payment is due our firm. Therefore, **any and all drafts or checks to your insured are to include the name of _____ as per the assignment.**

If you have any questions, please do not hesitate to call.

Assignment form cover letter
Figure 9-4

Third, contact the "board up" contractor in your community. Most larger cities have at least one contractor who specializes in covering up the exterior of a building after a fire. This contractor is usually the first on the scene after the firemen have left. He finds out about the loss even before the insurance company does. Some "board up" companies pass leads to contractors for a fee. They usually aren't in the construction contracting business. Many are glass companies that do this work as a service.

Fourth: Place at least two ads in the Yellow Pages, stating that you do fire insurance repairs. Run these ads under *Insurance Repairs* and *General Contracting* in the Yellow Pages.

Fifth: If you have any friends or family members who are firemen in your area, mention to them that you'd sure appreciate it if they'd just give you a call when a loss occurs.

Getting Adjusters to Recommend You
Once you're sure that local adjusters know of you,

how do you get them to recommend you? Here's how. Provide a service that can make their work easier. Supply them with a price list of the components of a loss. Adjusters for many companies have price schedules that list how much the adjuster can settle for. If you can supply a price list that can be compared with the adjuster's list (or the loss manual), the adjuster's job is much easier. Adjusters appreciate a fixed price list. Think about it. When you go into a store, you see set prices everywhere. It would be a waste of time if you had to take each item to the checkout counter and wait while the clerk gave you a quote. We don't like to shop where we have to haggle over prices and never really know if we got the best deal. Insurance companies also want the actual cost without having to do any haggling.

My company has sent out a fixed price list for garages for many years. The price list includes enough items so adjusters can figure the major cost items. But most jobs require some additional work.

That means the adjuster has to phone us and discuss the loss. During the discussion, we ask for the address of the loss, the insured's name and the claim number. That's what we need to visit the site and make a pitch for the job. Figure 9-5 shows a price list form we've used in the past.

I suggest that you make up a price list that covers the major loss items. Use prices that reflect what adjusters are authorized to pay for these items. Your prices don't have to be lower. The idea is that adjusters can depend on you to charge fixed prices submitted as a loss schedule. There are estimating manuals that have prices generally accepted by insurance adjusters. Several are listed in the order form at the back of this book.

Personalize your price list. Put your name and phone number on it. Make it easy for adjusters to call you to discuss a loss or to refer a loss (lead) to you. Naturally, prices have to change from time to time. When you publish a new list, put the new date on it and have the printer use a different color paper. Color-coding the price list alerts adjusters to the changes.

The price list should go out to all adjusters in your work area. That means you'll have to maintain a mailing list of active adjusters. Keep it on 3 x 5 cards. In fact, I recommend that you keep two lists. One set of cards is kept in alphabetical order by company name — listing the names of adjusters, their addresses, and phone numbers. The second set of cards is in alphabetical order by the adjuster's name. It should list the company he represents, the address, and the phone number. The price list is the hook that will catch the adjuster. He'll feed leads, sales and profits directly to you.

Making the Sale

Selling an insurance job is like selling any job. At your first meeting with the homeowner, go through the icebreaker and warmups. That's automatic. But in insurance work, add one more step: assure the customer that you know the intricacies of insurance claims processing.

At this first meeting, clear up any misconception about needing three bids. Here's what my sales pitch might sound like:

"When you submit several estimates to an insurance company, they're going to pay only the lowest bid. They take out the deductible and the depreciation if the policy calls for it. There could also be a co-insurance clause. That cuts your

recovery even lower. Look at it this way, Mr. Homeowner: You're cutting your own throat — and wasting time — with all those bids. An itemized list showing each loss item is the right way to go. If the list covers every item, you've protected yourself."

I often use an example that almost everyone can relate to. I ask the customer if he's ever had a car accident. It seems like everyone has. I follow through with:

"If your adjuster is like mine, he used a pad to list each item; the right fender, the strip molding, the headlight. Right? He didn't tell you to get three bids. He figured out a fair cost for repairing your car. It's the same way with the fire loss on your home. Start by working up a schedule for the adjuster. That's what I can do for you. It'll take several hours, but there's no charge. And we'll do all the repair work for the agreed-upon sum that we arrive at with the insurance adjuster."

Deductible as a Selling Tool

This is a good one, so pay close attention. Consider telling the customer that *you'll absorb the deductible.* Most people want something for nothing. So give it to them! Absorbing the deductible is an appeal that can clinch the sale.

"Don't worry about the deductible. We'll pick it up for you. What that means, Mr. Homeowner, is that you'll get the work you need done, properly, and without spending one red cent. How does that sound, Mr. Homeowner?"

Believe me, this is a powerful hook. $100 is the most common deductible. On a fire loss running into many thousands of dollars, the $100 you give up is peanuts.

There's another way to use the deductible as a premium:

"We'll do all the repair work. All it's going to cost you is the $100 deductible in your insurance policy. You don't have to make a downpayment or lay out any of your own money. The deductible, $100, is due on completion. And that's absolutely *all* you have to pay."

Advantages of Doing the Work Now

Explain the advantages of doing the work now:

2017 Butler Avenue
Chicago, IL 60645

355-0407

Nolan, Inc.
Garage Builder
One Price To Everyone

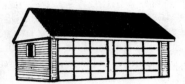

Owners Concrete

Size	Hip Roof	Gable Roof	Aluminum Siding
14 x 20 x 7'-6''	$2,660.00	$2,795.00	$2,825.00
18 x 20 x 7'-6''	$3,130.00	$3,230.00	$3,795.00
18 x 22 x 7'-6''	$3,300.00	$3,445.00	$4,010.00
20 x 20 x 7'-6''	$3,400.00	$3,545.00	$4,110.00
20 x 22 x 7'-6''	$3,500.00	$3,640.00	$4,220.00

Construction based on city of Chicago codes

Prices include:
16' x 6'-6'' steel overhead sectional garage door with astragal and key lock
Wood flush or panel door, torsion spring - $100.00 extra
One service door with key lock

One picture window, choice of jalousie or slider with aluminum frame

#240 seal tab shingles .. choice of stock colors (if roll roofing deduct $50.00 from listed price)

8'' boxed eaves

12'' primed hardboard siding with vapor barrier

Contact us for prices on following as per job
Wrecking and hauling of debris
Prefinished hardboard siding
Electrical installation
Painting
Odd sizes of garages or higher wall height
Suburban building codes
Removal of concrete
Concrete installation
Building permit service
Repairs or replacement of overhead doors

Price list - May 1984 - prices subject to change without notice

Insurance work our specialty
Specialists in fire loss - tornado - explosion - windstorm and hail -
auto or vandalism damage to garages.

Price list
Figure 9-5

"The policy calls for *replacing the damage* within a limited number of months. Mrs. Homeowner, the clock is running. If you don't do the work, the insurance company *only* pays the ACV — *the actual cash value.* That may be only 30 or 40% of your loss. You see, depreciation cuts down your ACV. By not doing the work, you forfeit the rest of the money. You can't take the money and run. I wouldn't be surprised if no one's told you about this. Your insurance adjuster won't volunteer it.

"Not too long ago, I did a job for a widow who lived in an old mansion. Her three-car garage had burned down. She didn't need a garage any more and didn't plan to rebuild. I explained why she should. She doubted what I told her at first. But when the adjuster finally informed her that she'd receive a very small amount for the ACV, due to depreciation, she had me build a new garage for her. She knew the property was worth more with a garage. So she figured, why not let the insurance company pay for a new one.

"You may not be aware that the bank or S&L that holds the note on your home can insist that the work be done. Their mortgage covers the whole property. That's why they want you to have coverage and why their name is on the policy and on the loss draft — so the value of their security isn't diminished."

Explain the Payment Procedure

"I'll tell you something else which I doubt that anyone's taken the trouble to explain to you. The draft you get as a settlement, which is really like a check, has the lender's name on it. The lender won't endorse it, as a rule, unless they receive the contractor's statement and the waivers of lien. This is for your protection, Mrs. Homeowner, to make sure that no liens are placed on your home. Both of your names will be placed on the draft, plus my name as the contractor.

"When the work's completed and the bank or S&L has endorsed the draft, both of you will sign the check. That's my payment. On this job, the settlement will probably be for more than I have coming. You have a contents claim. Many insurance companies combine the contents and property damage settlement into one final draft. We'll settle up at the bank or S&L when they endorse the draft. The check will be cashed there. You get your contents money and my company gets its payment.

"In most cases, Mrs. Homeowner, the insurance company sends two checks. The first is the ACV check. The second won't be mailed until my work is done. The ACV check will be mailed shortly after you sign the proof of loss and send it to the insurance company. Has the adjuster told you what to expect as a settlement? Good. When you get the check, we'll apply it as payment for the work. It's like a downpayment to us, except that your job will already be well under way."

We've given the insured valuable information. She's grateful because we've taken time to explain the mechanics of the loss settlement. The insurance broker or adjuster she's dealt with didn't have the knowledge or interest to supply this information. The insured realizes that not only is she going through a traumatic period, but learning what will occur is a frustrating surprise. The result? We get the order.

You've told the customer about the Contractor's Verified Statement (Figure 9-6) and the Waiver of Lien (Figure 9-7) required by the lender before the check will be endorsed. You can get these important forms at almost any office supply store.

Preparing the Contents Claim

There's one more bit of knowledge that you can offer. It's gratuitous on your part. I usually do it to cement relations even further.

First, I suggest to the customer that she prepare the contents claim as soon as possible. I take a large sheet of paper, such as a legal pad, and make up a sample:

Item	Year purchased	Amount paid	(Leave this space blank for adjuster)
T.V. set	1980	$475.00	
Kitchen table	1975	$300.00	
Power mower	1978	$280.00	

I then tell the customer: "The adjuster will reduce the price you paid to present value by taking off depreciation. I suggest that you try to locate as many bills as possible to present to the adjuster. This will substantiate the prices you paid. When you've completed your list, I'll turn it over to the adjuster for you if you like."

Try to Sell Upgrading

Every so often, you'll come across an insured loss where the family had considered some remodeling even before the loss. Point out that now is the ideal time to do the work. The house is torn apart anyway. It'll be cheaper. Your men and tools are on the property. Tell them that you have excellent financing available (with no money down) to do the additional remodeling. That suggestion should add about 50% to the value of about one insurance job in ten.

SWORN STATEMENT FOR CONTRACTOR AND SUBCONTRACTOR TO OWNER

𝔖tate of _____ } ss.

ℭounty of _____

𝔗he affiant, _____ being first duly sworn, on oath deposes

and says that he is (1) _____

_____

contractor___with (2) _____ owner___ for

(3) _____

on the following described premises in said County, to-wit: _____

_____

That, for the purpose of said contract, the following persons have been contracted with, and have furnished, or are furnishing and preparing materials for, and have done or are doing labor on said improvement. That there is due and to become due them, respectively, the amounts set opposite their names for materials or labor as stated. That this statement is made to said owner ...... for the purpose of procuring from said owner...... (4) Partial—Final Payment on said contract, and is a full, true and complete statement of all such persons, and of the amounts paid, due and to become due them.

(1) A member of the firm of, or officer of the corporation of, naming same. If a subcontractor so state and name the contractor. (2) Name of the owner or owners. (3) What the contract or subcontract is for. (4) Partial or Final Payment.

NAME AND ADDRESS	CONTRACT FOR	AMOUNT OF CONTRACT	AMOUNT PAID TO DATE	AMOUNT OF THIS REQUEST	BALANCE TO COMPLETE

AMOUNT OF ORIGINAL CONTRACT	$	AMOUNT OF THIS REQUEST	$
EXTRAS TO CONTRACT	$	LESS % RETAINED	$
TOTAL CONTRACT AND EXTRAS	$	NET AMOUNT OF THIS PAYMENT	$
CREDITS TO CONTRACT	$	AMOUNT OF PREVIOUS PAYMENTS	$
NET AMOUNT OF CONTRACT	$	BALANCE TO COMPLETE	$
		TOTAL AMOUNT OF CONTRACT	$

Signed _____

_____

Subscribed and sworn to before me this _____ day of _____ 19___

_____
Notary Public

Contractor's Verified Statement
Figure 9-6

STATE OF _____ } SS
COUNTY OF _____ }

𝕎𝕒𝕚𝕧𝕖𝕣 𝕠𝕗 𝕃𝕚𝕖𝕟

Know All Men By These Presents: *that* _____

Date _____

WHEREAS, the undersigned, _____ ha _____

(Name of Contractor)

been employed by _____

(Name of party by whom employed)

to furnish _____

(Type of work or material)

for the building located at _____ in _____

(Street address or location)   (City)

NOW, THEREFORE, KNOW YE, that the undersigned, for and in consideration of $ _____ and other good and valuable considerations, the receipt whereof is hereby acknowledged, do _____ hereby waive and release any and all lien, or claim or right of lien as to the above described building and premises, and also with respect to, or upon, monies which may be due from the Owner, under the Statutes of the State of _____ relating to Mechanics' Liens, on account of labor, services, fixtures and materials, or either, furnished _____ by the undersigned to or an account of the said _____ for said building or premises.

(Name of party by whom employed)

Dated this _____ *day of* _____ 19 _____

at _____

_____ (SEAL)

_____ (SEAL)

signed, sealed and delivered in the presence of:

_____

_____

ALWAYS MAKE AND RETAIN A COPY FOR YOUR FILES

Waiver of Lien
Figure 9-7

COLONIAL BUILDERS, INC.
29 Stewart Road
Albany, North Dakota
725-7309

_____ 19 ____

NOTICE

You are hereby authorized to repair the fire damage of _____ to my building situated _____

It being understood that such repairs will be made in accordance with agreed specifications. You are to receive for said work an amount equal to the agreed loss under the fire insurance claim.

For service rendered and/or to be rendered, I hereby assign COLONIAL BUILDERS, INC. all sums which may become due me by the

_____

_____

Signed _____

Approved
_____   _____

Authorization form
Figure 9-8

Getting the Paperwork Right

The paperwork in fire insurance repairs is fairly simple. But don't neglect it. Do the paperwork to be sure your name is on the loss check. When your name's on the check, neither the insured nor the mortgage company can cash it without your endorsement. Your payment is guaranteed.

This allows you to do business without being dependent on customer financing. And the customer is under his own pressure to get the job done. He's not going to go out and get five bids for a "maybe" job. This is work he needs done now.

If the customer has sufficient insurance and you handle the paperwork properly, the job will only cost the customer his $100 or so deductible — no matter how large the job!

Authorization form: I recommend that you use either of the following forms to get a commitment from your customer. My favorite is the small authorization form (Figure 9-8). Mine is printed as a sales check and numbered in triplicate. It's small enough to carry in your pocket. You keep the first copy. Promptly mail the second copy to the insurance company along with the Important Notice form. The third copy is for your customer.

Of course, if you have already obtained a signature on the adjustment form, you don't need the authorization form. The adjustment form (Figure 9-2) includes a power of attorney. If you use it, be sure to have your attorney review it for compliance with the laws of your state. This form should also be executed in triplicate, so you, the customer, and the insurance company (or the adjustment company) all get copies.

Rescission form: When your customer has signed the assignment or authorization form, you should explain the right of rescission and have the Notice of Right to Cancel signed. See Figure 9-9.

Insurance information form: This is for your protection. It's a great aid in collecting. Have it filled out promptly. Make up an information form like my sample in Figure 9-10.

G-9 RESCISSION FORM (When Increasing the Security)

NOTICE OF RIGHT TO CANCEL

Consumer Name _____

Address _____

Identification of Transaction _____

NOTICE OF RIGHT TO CANCEL

1. Your Right to Cancel.
You have agreed to increase the amount of the [mortgage/lien/security interest] [on/in] your home that we hold as security for your open-end credit account. You have a legal right under federal law to cancel the increase, without cost, within three business days after the latest of the following events:

(1) the date of the increase in the security which is

_____ ; or

(2) the date you received your Truth-In-Lending disclosures; or
(3) the date you received this notice of your right to cancel the increase in the security.

If you cancel the increase in the security, your cancellation will apply only to the increase in the amount of the [mortgage/lien/security interest]. It will not affect the amount you presently owe on your account, and it will not affect the [mortgage/lien/security interest] we already have [on/in] your home. Within 20 calendar days after we receive your notice of cancellation, we must take the necessary steps to reflect that any increase in the [mortgage, lien/security interest] [on/in] your home has been cancelled. We must also return to you any money or property you have given to us or to anyone else in connection with this increase.

You may keep any money or property we have given you until we have done the things mentioned above, but you must then offer to return the money or property. If it is impractical or unfair for you to return the property, you must offer its reasonable value. You may offer to return the property at your home or at the location of the property. Money must be returned to the address shown below. If we do not take possession of the money or property within 20 calendar days of your offer, you may keep it without further obligation.

2. How to Cancel.
If you decide to cancel the increase in security, you may do so by notifying us, in writing, at

_____
(Name of Creditor)

_____
(Creditor's Business Address)

You may use any written statement that is/signed and dated by you and states your intention to cancel, or you may use this notice by dating and signing below. Keep one copy of this notice no matter how you notify us because it contains important information about your rights.

If you cancel by mail or telegram, you must send the notice no

later than midnight of _____ (date).
(or midnight of the third business day following the latest of the three events listed above). If you send or deliver your written notice to cancel some other way, it must be delivered to the above address no later than that time.

I WISH TO CANCEL.

_____   _____
Consumer's Signature   Date

Each Signer Acknowledges Receipt of TWO (2) Copies of this
NOTICE OF RIGHT TO CANCEL

_____   _____
Date   (Consumer)

_____   _____
Date   (Consumer)

H150923

ORIGINAL

Rescission form
Figure 9-9

Information Sheet

Jobs cannot be processed without this information

Customer's Name _____   Address _____

Job Address _____   Phone No. _____

Adjuster's Name _____   Adjuster's Phone No. _____

Adjusting Company _____   Address _____

"Claim No." _____

Insurance Company _____   Policy No. _____

Insurance Company _____   Claim No. _____

Broker's Name _____   Address _____

Broker's Phone No. _____

Savings & Loan or

Mortgage Co. _____   Loan No. _____

Address _____   Phone No. _____

Insurance information form
Figure 9-10

Take-off form: Figure 9-11 will help you prepare the estimate. Use it as your working checklist. Then take one room at a time. Make a thorough survey of the loss. Then go on to the next room and the next until all rooms have been surveyed. Make your computations and add the totals to get the grand total.

Notification to mortgage holder: Don't forget to send a notification to the bank or S&L that has the mortgage. See Figure 9-12. The lender's security is protected by the insurance policy. Any checks the insurance company issues will be payable to the lender as well as you and the insured. Every mortgage company has different check endorsement policies. So notify them in advance that you have funds coming due, and ask what they will require. If there's a problem with the lender, this should flush it out before work begins.

Completion form: When the job's complete, have your customer sign the completion, satisfaction and authorization form, Figure 9-13. Mail one copy as quickly as possible to the insurance company (or adjusting company) so they can issue a check or draft.

Homeowners insurance may limit the initial recovery to the ACV, actual cash value. That's probably about 40% of the cost of repairs. When this amount is determined, write it into your contract as a progress payment due at a certain stage of the work or as a downpayment. The balance isn't payable by the insurance company until the loss has been replaced. The final payment is due only after completion. That's why you want to get the completion form signed and mailed to the insurance company as quickly as possible.

Have your customer sign an extra copy of Figure 9-13 for the mortgage holder. Many lenders won't endorse the draft or check until the homeowner has authorized them to do so.

Estimate Take-off

Insured's Name _____   Policy No.: _____

Address _____   Loss Date: _____

Phone No. _____   Kind of Loss _____

Can be reached at: _____

Quantity	Item	Per Quantity	Unit Cost	Total
	Room size X			
	Paint walls and ceiling			
	Clean walls and ceiling			
	Wallpaper			
	Dry wall (repair cracks and nail pops)			
	Window glass/storm window glass			
	Storm door glass			
	Prime windows complete			
	Alum. comb. storm windows			
	Drywall replacement (tape, bed, texture)			
	Front grade door (jamb, threshold)			
	Foyer door			
	Front entry door .			
	Front alum. comb. storm door			
	Window trim			
	Base trim (Vinyl—Wood—)			
	Cove moulding			
	Floor - Hardwood/sub			
	Sand and seal			
	Floor tile/linoleum/V.A.T.			
	Wall tile - ceramic/plastic			
	Paneling			
	Interior door			
	Interior door (jamb, trim)			
	Subflooring			

Take-off checklist
Figure 9-11

Quantity	Item	Per Quantity	Unit Cost	Total
	Rear grade door			
	Rear alum. comb. storm door			
	Interior door			
	Interior door (jamb, trim)			
	Interior door			
	Closet door			
	Shades			
	Venetian blinds			
	Carpet			
	Cabinets, upper			
	Cabinets, lower			
	Formica, repair/replace			
	Stove, repair/replace			
	Vent-a-hood			
	Exhaust fan			
	Sink			
	Mirror			
	Accessories			
	Mirror/medicine cabinet			
	Bathtub			
	Water closet			
	Lavatory or vanity			
	Shower doors			
	Rewire outlets			
	Rewire wall switches			
	Supply and install fixtures			
	Thermostat			
	Doorbell/chimes with transformer			
	Ceiling tile			
	Insulation, walls			

Take-off checklist
Figure 9-11 (continued)

Quantity	Item	Per Quantity	Unit Cost	Total
	Insulation, ceiling			
	Openings			
	Shelves			

Building Exterior

	Item			
	Paint openings and trim			
	Paint complete exterior (inc. trim)			
	Paint siding only			
	Replacement			
	Replace siding partial/repair			
	Remove damaged siding			
	Gable louver vent			
	Replace gutters			
	Replace downspout			
	Roof and shingles, repair			
	Roof and Shingles, replacement			
	Remove shingles			
	Electric mast, box			
	T.V. antenna			
	Repair insulation/sheathing			
	Rebuild wall-framing			
	Repair wall-framing			
	Repair roof sheathing boards			
	Replace/repair chimney			
	Fence, repair			
	Fence, replacement			
	Shutters			
	Awnings, repair			
	Awnings, replace			
	Cornice, rake, fascia board			

Take-off checklist
Figure 9-11 (continued)

Quantity	Item	Per Quantity	Unit Cost	Total
	Outside lights			
	Rebuild wall structure			
	Patio doors			
	Glass block windows			
	Attic structure			
	Brick/masonry			
	Foundation repairs			

General

	Electric			
	220 feed			
	Wrecking			
	Hauling and clean up, debris removal			
	Plumbing			
	Heating			
	Board up service			
	Temporary repairs			
	Building permit			
	Temp. electric			

Take-off checklist
Figure 9-11 (continued)

Important Notice

        Re: Your Mortgage_____

              Loan Number _____

              Address_____

              Insurance Company_____

              Policy No._____

              Date of Loss _____

This is to advise you that we have the contract to replace the damage done by _____ to the captioned address.

Please acknowledge this notice and notify us at once of your requirements as to the endorsement of the draft or check. This can be done by checking off the items on the duplicate sheet and returning it to us in the self-addressed envelope, which we have enclosed.

Inspection_____Waiver of Lien_____Cont. Statement_____

Authorization to release funds by mortgagee _____

Your prompt reply will be appreciated.

Yours truly,

Notification to mortgage holder
Figure 9-12

Avoid Collection Problems

The best way to prevent collection problems is to get an assignment (Figure 9-2 or 9-3) signed and forwarded to the adjuster or the claim office of the insurance company right at the outset. (Include the Important Notice form.) That way your name will be on the check, making your bargaining position much stronger. The check can't be cashed without your endorsement.

Sometimes a homeowner who's had a fire will be seriously delinquent on his loan. The mortgage holder may want to apply the entire check against the delinquency rather than have the damage repaired. What then? You've got a contract to do all the work, but the lender wants to pocket part of the cash.

One thing is certain, you don't want to be left holding the bag when it comes time to collect. The owner doesn't have the money. The bank or S&L wants the check endorsed over to them and applied against the delinquency. By notifying the mortgagor and asking for an acknowledgement, you should be alerted to any problem.

Here's my pitch when the lender wants the proceeds applied against the delinquency:

"I appreciate your position. But it's in your interest to make the building habitable again. I sug-

Nolan, Inc.
Garage Builder
(312) 355-0407
7448 Claire Avenue
Chicago, IL 60659

Insurance Company_____

Policy No. _____

Claim No. _____

Date of Loss _____

Attention:

Dear Sir:

This is to inform you that the loss, damage or construction has been completed to my satisfaction by the Nolan, Inc. Garage Builders. You are authorized to release to them the amount of their contract.

Date _____

Yours truly,

_____   _____
Witness   Homeowner

Completion form
Figure 9-13

gest that you agree that we go ahead and remove the debris and do whatever wrecking and repairs are necessary to put the building in a safe condition. I'll only charge . . . (I quote a figure, high enough to compensate for the loss of the job). You, Mr. Mortgagee, can keep the rest of the claim to apply against your loan. That way, you're in a better cash position than you were before, you won't be cited for building violations, and the building won't become a derelict.''

In every case, this has worked for me. Sure, I could have insisted on my right to proceed with the contract. But that's just buying trouble. When it comes time for the mortgagee to endorse the draft, he can put all kinds of stumbling blocks in your path. He can stall indefinitely by delaying inspections or refusing to process the contractor's statement and waivers. My advice: Do only as much as the lender will tolerate and agree to pay for. Make a clean profit on that work, take the money and run. Better a smaller profit than none at all.

Broker notification form: It's a custom in the insurance world that the companies selling through brokers mail the draft or check to the broker first. The broker then delivers the money to the insured. That shows what a great job he's doing. But some brokers are too busy looking for new business to mail the drafts out to their customers. I've found that a broker notification form (Figure 9-14)

Re: Your Client _____

Address _____

Insurance Company _____

Policy No. _____

Gentlemen:

This is to notify you that we have the contract to replace the damage done by _____ which occurred on or about _____ to the captioned premises.

When you receive the draft or check from the insurance company please notify us at once. A phone call would be appreciated. We can then pick up the draft and deliver it to your insured for his or her endorsement and also obtain the endorsement of the mortgage holder.

If you have any questions, please do not hesitate to call.

Yours truly,

Broker notification form
Figure 9-14

speeds forwarding of the check. When you're through with a job, mail the notification form to the broker immediately. The broker will mail the draft directly to you or phone you when the check arrives. You can then take the draft or check to your customer for endorsement.

In this chapter we've covered some pretty specialized material. But if you've absorbed the information presented here and use the forms in this chapter, you're set up to handle this profitable specialty. In the next chapter we'll get back to the mainstream of selling remodeling work. We'll talk about the salesmen in your organization — how to screen them, how to hire them, what to pay them.

Chapter 10

Your Sales Force

Making sales is an important part of every home improvement business. I've never seen a thriving, prosperous home improvement company that didn't have at least one good salesman — someone who could develop prospects, meet customers, quote prices and close sales. In many cases, that sales expert was the boss, the owner, or a co-owner who founded the company and really made it grow.

But the more successful the boss is at selling, the less time he has to make sales. The manager of a growing business is forced to spend more time dealing with lenders, lawyers and accountants and handling business problems. That leaves less time for making sales calls. Many owners are forced to decide between making sales and running the business. Running the business usually wins.

That's one reason why many home improvement contractors hire salesmen. But it isn't the only reason. Sometimes there are just too many sales leads to follow up — too many opportunities to pursue. If more sales calls will bring in more business, it pays to find someone who can make those calls.

Each salesman hired should magnify the amount of total sales. In other words, if the owner could make a certain number of sales per month, two salesmen should be able to sell about two and one-half times that number. Since they're concentrating on sales full time, they can cover leads the owner would miss.

Method of Compensation

Once you've made the decision to use salesmen, you have to decide whether to put them on the payroll or have salesmen who are independent contractors. The most common practice is to make each salesman a home improvement dealer — a subcontractor. A dealer is free to come and go as he pleases. He doesn't have to account for his time. The only thing that's expected of him is that he bring in profitable contracts from qualified customers.

If you're going to make your salesmen independent dealers, you'll need a written agreement that spells out the understanding between the company and the salesman. Figure 10-1 is the agreement I use. If you plan to use it, have your attorney revise it to meet the requirements of your state.

Just putting salesmen on the payroll seldom works. I've never seen good home improvement salesmen on the payroll on straight salary. Salary both destroys incentive and makes close supervision essential. Underproductive salesmen prefer working for salary alone. Highly productive salesmen hate it. You want as few of the former and as many of the latter as possible. For best results, find good sales people, provide an incentive compensation system like I'll describe in this chapter, and then let them do their thing.

Sales Agreement

This Agreement, made and entered into this _____ day of _____, 19 ____, by and between _____ an Illinois Corporation hereinafter referred to as the Company, and _____, hereinafter referred to as the Dealer.

WHEREAS, the company is in the business of _____ and desires to retain Dealer's services to sell such _____ as an independent merchant.

WHEREAS, Dealer desires to associate with the Company as an independent merchant for the purposes of selling such products. THEREFORE, it is agreed as follows:

1) **Services:** The Dealer agrees to work diligently and with his best efforts to sell the Company's products at such prices and upon such terms as the Company may dictate from time to time. The Dealer agrees to solicit customers and conduct his business so as to maintain and increase the goodwill and reputation of the Company.

2) **Commissions:** The Company shall pay to the Dealer commissions on the basis of the attached commission schedule, computed on the amount of net business completed each month.

3) **Facilities:** In the performance of his services under this agreement, the Dealer may share with other Dealers the facilities of the Company's office at _____, City of _____, State of _____, including the sales room, necessary stationery, promotional materials and product information.

4) **Promotional Programs:** The Company agrees to furnish, and the Dealer agrees to utilize, during the term of this agreement, special training and assistance pertaining to the promotion and sales of the Company's products.

5) **Terms:** This agreement shall be for a term of _____ from the date hereof and may be extended for such additional periods of time as the parties shall in writing agree.

6) **Relationship:** The relationship hereby established between the Company and the Dealer is solely that of builder and independent sales representative, and the Dealer is neither an employee nor a legal representative of the Company and may not assume any obligation of any kind, implied or expressed, on behalf of the Company.

7) **Employment:** Upon the expiration of the term of this agreement and any extensions thereof, the parties may enter into an agreement whereby the Dealer is employed as a salesman of the Company, and participates as an employee in the Compensation plan in accordance with the Company's policies.

8) **Termination:** Either party may terminate this agreement at any time by written notice of the termination delivered to the other party.

9) **Assignment:** Dealer shall not transfer or assign nor attempt to transfer or assign this Agreement or any right or obligation hereunder without the prior written consent of the Company.

IN WITNESS WHEREOF, the parties have executed this Agreement the day and year first written above.

COMPANY

In the presence of:

President _____

_____

Dealer _____

_____

Sales agreement
Figure 10-1

Addendum To Sales Agreement

Dated:_____, 198_____.

By and between Company and Dealer

Re: Paragraph No. 2.

Commission shall be figured as follows:

To the actual cost of the job shall be added 20% for overhead, plus 5% lead cost. The total shall be deducted from the net sale price. The profit shall then be split, 50% of the profit to the Company and 50% of the profit to the Dealer. In the event the Dealer supplies his own leads, the 5% charge will be waived.

Signed this _____ day of _____, 198_____.

COMPANY

_____   _____
President   Dealer

Sales agreement
Figure 10-1 (continued)

The simplest method of compensation is straight commission — a fixed percentage of the total sale. Commissions in home improvement work run from 5% to 10%. The most common commission is 8%. Consider adding a 2% bonus if the sale price exceeds the par price and deducting 2% if the job is sold short. In the next section, I explain what I mean by a par price. Many home improvement companies use salesmen on straight commission. If you're successful with straight commission salesmen, I won't argue. But there's a major flaw in commission selling where the price has to be negotiated on every sale. The salesman is willing to sell at a big discount if necessary to get the sale — even if the discount produces a loss on the job. The salesman gets his commission even if his company takes a beating. It works the other way too. The company pushes for high prices even if it means turning down lots of sales. That's an arrangement apt to produce resentment and hostility.

Of course, the flaw in commission selling disappears if the salesman has no control over prices. But that's a mistake too, in my opinion. *Every salesman needs some authority to negotiate prices.* You understand why if you've ever sold home improvement work. A salesman who can't quote prices has to get home office approval for every pricing decision. Your customers will resist buying from anyone who doesn't have authority to deal. That's part of the reason why the boss usually makes a good salesman. He can tailor the price to the circumstances.

The Par System
But prices determine profits. Setting the price too low may get sales, but it also puts you out of business. How can the salesman quote prices and offer discounts without putting the company's profit margin in jeopardy? The answer is the *Par System.* It's the most common method of compensation for home improvement contractors and a significant improvement over straight commission selling. Here's how it works. The company sets a minimum price for its work and then splits whatever the salesmen gets over par. The split can be 50-50, 60-40 or 70-30.

Here's an example. Suppose an anodized aluminum triple-track storm window carries a par of $60.00 installed. Sixty dollars covers all labor, materials, taxes, insurance, supervision, overhead and provides a profit on this window. The salesman sells this window for $79.00. That's $19.00 over par. On a 50-50 split, the salesman makes $9.50 per window. The company makes a packed profit in the par price, plus $9.50.

The salesman's retail price book shows par prices on all the common items he sells. When he can sell for above par, he's well rewarded for his effort. If he has to discount heavily to get the job, there's little incentive for him (or the company) to get the contract. That's why the par system works. It makes every salesman a profit partner with the company he's selling for. The salesman's and the company's interests run parallel. If one makes money, both make money.

There's a refinement on the Par System that I call *Par Plus*. The prime defect in the par system is that the burden to produce leads is on the home improvement company, not the salesman. Under Par Plus, about 5% is added to the par price to cover the cost of getting leads. In effect, the company generates leads and charges the salesman a portion of that cost. Where the initial contact was the result of company promotion, par prices go up 5%. If a salesman finds his own prospect, the par price is not modified.

Par Plus creates a strong incentive for the salesman to bring in his own leads. A salesman who has to pay for his leads will mine his customers for referrals. He's more apt to canvass neighborhoods where jobs are in progress and to send out his own mailers. For most home improvement work, 5% of the par cost is a fair price to pay for leads.

To find your actual cost of leads, divide annual sales by the annual cost of producing leads. That's the percentage of lead cost per sale, the "plus" in Par Plus. To find the average lead cost per sale, divide the annual advertising cost by the number of sales.

Figuring Your Par Prices

The Par System won't work if you can't anticipate what the job will cost. That makes accurate job costing essential. Figure 10-2 shows a ledger form any contractor can use to record actual job costs. Make sure every cost item gets included in your cost record. And remember to charge each job for all insurance and taxes: state unemployment insurance, worker's compensation insurance, public liability insurance, FICA, Medicare and FUTA. This information is vital in setting up the retail price book I describe in Chapter 12.

Payroll taxes and insurance currently add from 20% to 25% to your labor cost on every job. For every $100 you pay tradesmen, you'll have to pay an additional $20 to $25 in taxes and insurance: $4 for state unemployment insurance, $7 for F.I.C.A. (Social Security), $.70 for F.U.T.A. (unemployment), $2.50 for liability insurance, and $5 to $10 for worker's compensation insurance.

There's no legal way to avoid paying these taxes and buying insurance to cover employees. Calling your employees "subcontractors" doesn't help. Both the states and the federal government have active enforcement programs that impose heavy penalties on employers who don't buy the insurance required or who fail to pay quarterly taxes when due.

Taxes, worker's compensation insurance and public liability insurance — including scaffolding insurance in those states where it's required — should be charged against each job. The best way to do this is to include the cost of insurance in your hourly labor cost for each tradesman. Your accountant can suggest how much taxes and insurance to add to the hourly labor cost for each trade. Liability and worker's comp rates are higher for some trades, in some states, and for contractors with poor safety records.

Taxes and insurance are major costs for all contractors. But they're sometimes overlooked. Don't forget to include taxes and insurance in every job. And here's a hint to keep your insurance costs down. In many states the general contractor is liable for a subcontractor's losses if the subcontractor doesn't have insurance coverage. That increases your insurance cost. Protect yourself and keep your cost of insurance down. Demand a Certificate of Insurance from every sub.

Comparing Methods of Compensation

Let's look at five possible ways to compensate a salesman who's sold a small siding job for $3,800. Figure 10-3 shows earnings on a straight commission basis. If you use straight commission, the only decision is finding the percentage that provides enough incentive for salesmen without cutting too deep into profits.

Job Cost Ledger

	Date	Amount billed	Credits	Net	Rec'ts	Balance
Job No. _____						
Job Name _____						
Address _____						
_____						

Date	Name	Subcontract	Labor	Materials	Insurance & Taxes	Other Account	Other Amount

Job Cost Ledger
Figure 10-2

Selling price	$3,800.
5% commission	190.
6% commission	222.
7% commission	266.
8% commission	304.
9% commission	342.
10% commission	380.

Straight commission system
Figure 10-3

Straight commission is the easiest and simplest way to pay salesmen. My experience, and the experience of many home improvement contractors, is that flat-rate salesmen sell too cheap if they have any discretion at all in pricing. The 2% bonus for above par sales and 2% penalty for short sales is one solution to this problem.

Figure 10-4 shows the same job under the Par System with a 50-50 split. The job cost (including all taxes and insurance) is $2,300. Markup is 20% to cover overhead and a slim profit. Par is $2,760. Everything over that is split evenly between the company and the salesman. For every dollar of discount the salesman has to offer, fifty cents comes out of his pocket.

Figure 10-5 shows the Par System again with the

Job sells for		$3,800.
Job cost	$2,300.	
20% markup (overhead and profit)	460.	
Par price	$2,760.	
Gross profit		$1,040.
50% to salesman		520.
50% to house		520.
Recap		
House profit	$520.	
20% markup	460.	
Total profit	$980.	
Salesman earned	$520.	

Par system with 50-50 split
Figure 10-4

same facts except that the split is 60-40, with 40% going to the salesman. Notice that this cuts the salesman's share by more than $100.

Job sells for		$3,800.
Job cost including taxes	$2,300.	
20% markup (overhead and profit)	460.	
Par price	$2,760.	
Gross profit		$1,040.
40% to salesman		416.
60% to house		624.
Recap		
House profit	$624.	
20% markup	460.	
Total profit	$1,084.	
Salesman earned	$416.	

Par system with 60-40 split
Figure 10-5

The form of compensation that seems to work best year after year with many companies is shown in Figure 10-6. Here the split is 50-50 again, but the lead cost has been added to par. The lead cost ($115) is 5% of the job cost before overhead and profit are added. Compare Figures 10-6 and 10-4. Notice that adding the lead cost of $115 into the calculation has reduced the salesman's cut by only $53. The company still carries most of the cost of generating leads.

Figure 10-7 shows the same calculation as in Figure 10-6 except that the split is 60-40, with the salesman getting 40%. Notice that the salesman's earnings in Figure 10-7 are nearly 10% of the selling price, even though this compensation schedule is the least favorable of the four par arrangements shown. Why is that? It's because this was a profitable sale. The salesman did a good job of selling the benefits and providing high perceived value to his customers. He's entitled to a substantial part of the proceeds. If the job had come in much closer to par, that wouldn't be the case.

There are hundreds of possible variations on these formulas. The key is making salesmen profit partners with your company. "Par" is short for partnership. Give salesmen the incentive to do the

Job sells for		$3,800.
Job cost including taxes	$2,300.	
20% markup (overhead and profit)	460.	
5% lead cost	115.	
Total cost	$2,875.	
Gross profit		$925.
50% to salesman		467.
50% to house		467.

Recap

House profit	$467.
20% markup	460.
5% lead cost	115.
Total profit	$1,042.
Salesman earned	$467.

**Par plus with 50-50 split
Figure 10-6**

Job sells for		$3,800.
Job cost including taxes	$2,300.	
20% markup (overhead and profit)	460.	
5% lead cost	115.	
Total cost	$2,875.	
Gross		$925.
40% to salesman		370.
60% to house		555.

Recap

House profit	$555.
20% markup	460.
5% lead cost	115.
Total profit	$1,130.
Salesman earned	$370.

**Par plus with 60-40 split
Figure 10-7**

job and an interest parallel with your interest. Then watch the profitable sales come rolling in.

One final point. My salesmen aren't paid in full until the job is completed. But everyone has to live. It's customary to provide a draw against compensation as work is going on. That gives a new salesman some income while his jobs are being completed. I give my salesmen a settlement monthly, and a statement showing the compensation after costs when the job is completed.

Salesmen's Qualifications

To this point you've decided that you need a salesman and how you're going to pay him. The next step is to find the right man for the job. Here are some suggestions on interviewing and hiring the salesman who'll do the best job for you.

Any time you have to fire an employee, it's because *you* made a mistake — a hiring mistake. If he was a poor employee, he shouldn't have been hired in the first place. The decision to fire was probably right. But if you had evaluated the candidate more carefully, he would never have joined your sales team. Then the firing wouldn't have been necessary. From that standpoint, evaluating each job candidate carefully is very important. Putting an incompetent on staff is an expensive mistake.

All people have aptitudes and weaknesses. Salesmen are no different. Some do well with intangibles. Others don't. What we're looking for are *closers*. They get the signature on the dotted line on the first call, and rarely have to go back a second time.

Here's a sample interview with an applicant:

Q: "What's your sales background?"

A: "I've sold awnings, storm windows, garages and remodeling. I also worked for a pharmaceutical company, calling on doctors' offices. I have a degree in marketing."

Comment: Since the candidate has sold home improvements, he's a natural. But be sure his previous employer gives a favorable recommendation. Having a college degree and having called on professional people is also good. But it could pose a problem. Can the candidate sell to wage-earners and blue-collar families? Will his leads feel that he's putting on an air of superiority? That would lose sales.

Q: "How long did you work at your last job and the job before that?"

A: "Two years. Before that, five years."

Comment: Is the candidate a job skipper? The

Find the right man for the job

answer he gave is a good one. A series of jobs lasting less than a year would be bad.

Q: *"Why did you quit? Or were you fired?"*

A: *"I left because of a personality conflict with the sales manager."*

Comment: Phone the sales manager to get another version of the candidate's reasons for leaving.

Q: *"How many leads did you cover per day?"*

A: *"Three or four."*

Comment: To sell a quality lead takes about two hours. From this answer you can judge whether the applicant was a closer or just an order taker.

Q: *"What was your selling ratio per lead?"*

A: *"Three out of five, I'd say."*

Comment: This may be good or bad, depending on the type of selling. In home improvement work, a top salesman will close on three to four out of five prime leads.

Q: *"Are you on the FHA black list?"*

A: *"No sir, I'm not."*

Comment: Salesmen who violate FHA regulations are black listed. They are prohibited from making sales where the loans will be processed through the FHA.

Q: *"Can you work nights and weekends?"*

A: *"Yes. I'm married to a nurse. She works nights and weekends by choice. Working then is no problem for me."*

Comment: Home improvement is a family decision. Families decide at night and on weekends when the decision-makers are together. A salesman who doesn't like working nights and weekends isn't

---

Lopez Construction, Inc.
1293 Rampart Street
Chicago, Illinois 60659

Date

Dear _____:

It's been quite some time since we finished your kitchen. But that doesn't mean that we've forgotten you.

I have a $35 gift certificate good for any merchandise of your choice at Jensen's Department Store if you refer a friend to us.

I'm sure that you know either a friend, neighbor, club member, someone at church or work that's talking about remodeling.

I've enclosed ten business cards for your use. Just write your name on the reverse side. Tell your friends to show it to me when I prepare their estimate. If they have us do the work, I'll send your gift certificate and give your friend a $35 discount to boot!

Cordially,

Sample letter offering a bonus
Figure 10-8

much good to you.

Q: "Do you have any health problems that might interfere with your work?"

A: "No sir."

Comment: Leads must be covered promptly. Salesmen with health or other problems will leave leads uncovered. That costs you money.

Q: "Do you speak any language other than English?"

A: "I can get along in Spanish."

Comment: America is an ethnic hodgepodge. You'll sell to anyone willing to pay your price. A salesman that speaks a second language can open up an entirely new market for your company.

During the interview make it clear that your company doesn't tolerate side agreements or promises not written into the contract. You don't want any surprises. Only ill-will can come from a customer who discovers that the company is unaware of a promise made by an overeager salesman.

What about the candidate who has no previous selling experience? My advice is to ask yourself the following questions. *Do I have the time to train a green recruit? Can I afford to gamble precious leads on a novice? If the candidate doesn't make it, am I prepared to spend additional time training someone else?*

If the answer to these questions is "no," hire only a professional salesman, a known quantity. But if you can afford to train someone, don't rule out an inexperienced applicant who seems exceptionally well qualified. One advantage of hiring an inexperienced person is that he learns the business

Lopez Construction Inc.
1293 Rampart Street
Chicago, Illinois 60659

Date

Dear Homeowner:

N e e d   m o r e   l i v i n g   s p a c e?
Your house too cramped? It's TOO expensive to buy a new home!

Call us, the House S t r e t c h e r s !!!!!

- **Additions on houses**
- **Dormers**
- **Rumpus rooms in basement or cellar**

We do the complete job. No money down.
Act now. Phone **561-5000** for a free estimate.

Yours truly,

P.S. We expect a price increase on lumber May 1st.

Sample letter to new prospects
Figure 10-9

your way. If you come across an applicant who is highly motivated, the time it takes to train him can pay big dividends.

There's a fundamental axiom about salesmen: *No salesman was ever fired for doing business.*

A salesman might get fired for not doing his paperwork, for being a troublemaker, for neglecting collections, and especially for making promises that aren't written into the contract. But no salesman was ever fired for doing business.

Sowing What You Intend to Reap
For their own good, your salesmen should send out at least ten letters a day to new prospects and old customers. One proven lead generator is offering a bonus for new leads. See Figure 10-8.

Ten letters a day times five days a week equals fifty letters a week. Multiply this by fifty-two weeks, and you have twenty-six hundred letters per year. If only 3% respond and you do $3200 worth of work for each, that's a quarter of a million dollars in sales. At 8% commission, that comes to $20,000 a year. Not bad for three or four nights a week and a few weekends each month.

It only takes a few minutes to address ten envelopes. Make printed letters available to your salesmen so they only have to type in the address, date and salutation. It pays to contact customers every three or four months.

Figure 10-9 shows a sample letter to homeowners who are new prospects. Encourage your sales staff to send out ten letters like Figure 10-8 or 10-9 every day.

Salesmen's Tools
Every type of business has its specialized tools. The doctor has his stethoscope, the lawyer his briefcase, the plumber his wrench and the carpenter his saw. Professionals can't do business without the right tools. Similarly, a home improvement salesman needs a ruler, graph paper, a 50 foot tape, contracts, credit applications, finance rate charts, samples, calculator, price book, and a pen for writing the contracts. It's also extremely important for the salesman to carry and use his portfolio of before and after pictures. A salesman without this equipment is like a preacher without his Bible. When a customer's ready to buy, or even at a point of indecision, you need to make an irresistible offer immediately. If you're unprepared, poorly equipped or lack a key sales document, the battle's lost.

Some of the old pros who should know better violate this rule most often. They're the cocky guys who've gone stale on the job, the ones who've been calling on leads so long they think they know it all. Pretty soon, the only thing they know is that their sales have slipped. Believe me, I've seen it happen. The alibis are terrific. But closing sales requires being prepared with all the essential tools and information.

Weekly Sales Meetings
If your company has more than three or four salesmen, hold sales meetings weekly at a regular time. An informative sales meeting can be time well spent. But even more, a good sales meeting is a confidence and enthusiasm builder. Selling can be a lonely, discouraging job. A good sales meeting can leave everyone who attended refreshed and charged up, realizing that he's an important part of a successful sales team. If your meetings don't do that, they may be a waste of time.

Here are some of the activities I have included at sales meetings:

Recognize the salesman who has generated the most business for the week or month. Remember, a pat on the back goes a long way.

Present prizes for:

1) The salesman who brought in the most business from his own leads.

2) The salesman with the greatest dollar volume.

3) The salesman with the greatest profit-to-volume ratio.

Gift certificates and tickets to the theater or ballgame make good prizes. For long-term sales contests, dangle junkets to conventions in resort cities.

At the meeting, the construction superintendent should point out problems that salesmen didn't anticipate in their contracts. He should explain what to watch out for, and suggest steps to prevent recurrence of the problems. These explanations will make the salesmen more knowledgeable and more effective in selling remodeling. The sales meeting should be stimulating and enthusiastic. This is the kind of feedback that helps keep your sales force on its toes. And it helps prevent future problems in pricing work and writing specs.

You'll also want to talk about leads. Which method is best at producing qualified leads? What leads are getting the most closings? Get some feedback from your salesmen on the quality of your advertising. Ask for their recommendations. What pitch might create more leads? Note how many referrals produced jobs so far in the current month. Remind everyone that referrals are the backbone of the business.

Encourage your salesmen keep a file of leads gathered from canvassing the neighborhoods, referrals, and talking to carpenters on the job. Tradesmen on the job are a good source of inquiries. Remind salesmen to stop by jobs they sold to find out if any inquiries have been made. Encourage each salesman to pass out business cards at his racquetball club, fraternal organization, church, or civic association meeting.

Conduct a workshop on closing. Give each salesman an opportunity to explain how he overcame objections in a sales presentation.

Invite supplier representatives to the sales meeting to explain and demonstrate new products. It's a feather in the cap of a salesman to be current on some new building product or technique.

Invite a loan officer to the sales meeting. Ask him to discuss the credit approval process. He may be able to suggest better ways to get loans approved. What helps a prospective buyer qualify? What disqualifies an applicant? This will help your sales force avoid lost causes and concentrate on hot prospects.

Mortgage brokers and S&L officers are experts on appraising property by the square foot or cubic foot method, using comparables, and figuring equity. This is information your salesmen can use.

Other topics for a sales meeting are changes in the building code or zoning ordinances, collection procedures and business trends.

Role playing can help less-experienced salesmen. Try it at a sales meeting sometime. Here's how it works: One salesman takes the role of a prospect. Another tries to make the sale. The audience should kibitz and then comment on the salesman's performance.

Sales meeting are also a good time to practice demonstrating products. For example, the storm window salesman can challenge his colleagues to pull a ten-dollar bill out of the sash. The awning salesman stands on a piece of fiberglass to show that his fiberglass awnings are unbreakable. It's a good idea to offer a prize to the salesman with the most dramatic presentation. Demonstrations sell. Dramatic demonstrations help to close more sales.

Make your sales meeting informative, enthusiastic, stimulating and as short as possible. It can be time well spent.

In this chapter we've discussed salesmen: when and how to hire them, how to pay them, and finally, how to get the most from them. In the next chapter we're going to get down to some paperwork. We'll discuss building permits first. Then I'll take you through the mechanics of writing a contract.

Chapter 11

The Legalities – Permits and Contracts

Now let's get down to the fine print, as they say. We're going to do some paperwork.

Building permits are a necessary evil in the remodeling business. There's a right way and a wrong way to follow the building code. I'm going to suggest a few steps that make code compliance easier and less expensive.

After we've hit the high spots on the code and building permits, we'll move on to contract documents — how to write them, what clauses to include, what loopholes to watch out for, and how to protect yourself from the most common contract problems. Using verbal understandings or haphazard written documents is neither prudent nor professional. Fortunately, it's easy to develop a good basic contract. Then all you have to do is fill in the blanks on future jobs.

The Building Code

First, understand this. The building code is a regulation (like a law) adopted by a government agency to control how construction is done in that city or county. Your city or county can adopt any kind of building code it wants to. But because it takes a lot of time and study to write a complete and effective building code, your city probably adopts one of the three widely-recognized "model" codes. The *Uniform Building Code* is used in most states in the western U.S. and Canada.

It's published by the I.C.B.O. in Whittier, California. The Southern Building Code Congress publishes a code that's used in most of the southeastern U.S. The B.O.C.A. in Chicago publishes a third standard code. Differences among these three major model codes are less significant now than they once were.

Most cities have adopted one of these three codes and re-adopt the code every time a new version is published by either the I.C.B.O., B.O.C.A. or S.B.C.C. But it's not unusual for a city to make minor (and sometimes major) changes in the code they adopt. The result is a crazy-quilt maze for any contractor who does business in several cities or counties.

Just having a copy of the code that applies can be a big step forward. You can't comply with the law if you don't know what the law is. Before you have a code compliance problem, get a copy of the building code that's enforced in each area where you solicit business.

Understanding the code isn't easy. It's a complex law, written to be enforced rather than read and understood. Information on some subjects is scattered in several parts of the book. Just finding all the paragraphs that apply to a particular question may be difficult. The index is little help. It's common to find exceptions within exceptions within exceptions. Many tables require an understanding of

Every contractor is assumed to know the code

engineering principles. If you're not a tax lawyer, the building code can be a seamless web of obfuscation. Some books are available that put the code in contractor language. One of them, *Contractor's Guide to the Building Code*, written by a building inspector and published by Craftsman Book Company, Box 6500, Carlsbad, California 92008, may be ordered using the order form at the end of this manual.

Having the code book on file in the office isn't good enough. You must know the basics of the code and the cost of permits when you make your sales calls. Charge for the permit in the contract. Don't just try to collect later — the homeowner may find a way to squeeze out of paying for it. The best way to guarantee reimbursement is to include the permit cost in the contract.

Make sure all salesmen have the code and permit information they need. Set up a section in the price book for this information. Figure 11-1 is a sample permit page. If your business covers many cities,

you'll need a separate building permit book. Each salesman should have his own copy of the section or book, with each page in a plastic cover for protection and neatness. Have each salesman sign a note for $100 as a bond for the permit book. This will ensure that the book is returned when the salesman leaves your company. The information it contains is invaluable and takes time and effort to prepare.

Someone in your office should be assigned to write to each community during January every year to update the code information. Make the permit books loose-leaf, with communities listed in alphabetical order. Many communities have preprinted requirements for garages and remodeling work. They distribute these free on request or charge a nominal fee. Insert these requirements in plastic covers and put them in your permit book.

When setting up your price book, be sure the charges include travel time and parking fees if free public parking isn't available. Charge for getting

COMMUNITY OF _____ PHONE _____

ADDRESS _____ ZIP CODE _____

SEC'Y _____ HOURS _____

BLDG. COMM. _____ INSP. REQ. _____

BLDG. INSP. _____ ELECTRICAL INSP. _____ PLUMBING INSP. _____

| MIN. INFO. REQUIRED TO OBTAIN PERMIT: | CONCRETE REQUIREMENTS |

PLOT OF SURVEY _____ LEGAL TAX# _____

PLOT SKETCH & COMPLETE MEAS. TO LINES _____

SEPTIC LAYOUT _____ DRIVE LAYOUT _____

TOWNSHIP _____ VOL. # _____ ITEM # _____

OTHER _____ WELL LAYOUT _____

BOND AMT.	TYPE	BY

CROSS SECTION REQUIRED _____

PLANS REQUIRED _____

PLANS WITH ARCHITECT SEAL REQ. _____

LAND USE _____

PERMIT FEES: _____
Min. Fee _____
Plan Exam _____
Cert. of Occ. _____
Grading _____
Electric _____
Patio _____
Break Curb _____
Sidewalk _____
Wrecking _____
License Fee _____
Variance _____
Zoning _____

OFFICE USE:
Permit by: Office _____ Owner _____ Salesman _____
Mail _____ Bring in _____ Ret. env. _____ Pick-up _____
Salesman _____ W/Check _____ No Check _____
Appl _____ Survey _____ Our Form _____ Form _____
Plot Sketch _____ Spotted Plot _____ Elec. Appl. _____
Contract _____ Work Order _____ Bond _____
_____
_____
_____
_____

CONCRETE REQUIREMENTS

GARAGE LOCATION: To wall _____ To eaves _____

HOUSE: FRAME _____

w/FIRE WALL _____

REAR: ALLEY _____

NO ALLEY _____

SIDE: CORNER LOT _____

FRONT DRIVE _____

ALLEY DRIVE _____

ATTACHED _____

MIN. SET-BACK/FRONT LINE _____

CONCRETE	MIX	MESH	THICKNESS	
GARAGE & APRON				
DRIVEWAY				
PARKWAY				
SIDEWALK				
FTG. REQ.	WIDTH	DEPTH	SIDES	B/G
FRAME				
BRICK				
ATTACHED				
FOUNDATION				

DEBRIS: _____ SOD: _____

ANCHOR BOLTS: _____

EXPANSION JOINTS:	
FILL	
WATER LEDGE	
DAMPPROOFING	

CARPENTRY REQUIREMENTS

STUDS   2x4 - _____ o.c. _____
         2x4 - _____ o.c. _____
RAFTERS 2x - _____ o.c. _____
X-TIES   2x - _____ o.c. _____ - Width

SIDING REQUIREMENTS _____

DOUBLE WALL _____

SHINGLES _____ FELT _____

CORNERS 2x4 - _____ VENTS _____

COLLAR TIES _____ EAVES _____

MAX. SIZE: PATIO _____

FRAME _____

Sq. Ft. _____ Ht. _____

BRICK _____

HEADER REQ. _____

Permit page for price book
Figure 11-1

the permit, the permit fee, the license fee and the insurance or cash bond if that's required. The fees vary from community to community. Some have fixed fees, some have graduated fees.

Every contractor is assumed to know the code. Every contract you sign is based on construction that complies with code requirements. That's bad enough when you're working new construction. But it can create a nearly impossible burden when you're remodeling an older home. Before the 1920's, there were many areas in which home builders didn't have to comply with any code. But today, the building inspector can require you to bring the wiring, plumbing, framing, exits, venting, fire resistance, stairs, roof and flashing up to current standards throughout the house — even if you're only remodeling a bathroom! That's a can of worms no builder or owner wants to open.

Fortunately, your contract can exclude most of the risk of code compliance, as I'll explain later in this chapter. For now, just be aware that code compliance is a potential source of trouble on every home improvement job.

Avoiding Problems

The key to living with the code (and the inspector) is to anticipate problems. You're seldom going to win the argument when an inspector says something is wrong and has to be done over. Having a copy of the code available is the first step. The second is talking it over with the inspector when you can't find an answer in the code or don't understand what the code says. Ask the inspector what he'll approve. And ask before you've signed the contract.

Getting the Permit

If you're doing anything more drastic than hanging a few kitchen cabinets, you're going to need a permit. The code requires a permit for nearly all construction, no matter how trivial. And every professional construction contractor should take out a permit on every job where a permit is required. Your reputation and your right to do business as a professional in the construction business depend on it. Note also that in some jurisdictions the fee is doubled if you fail to get a permit before beginning work. So get the permit first. *Then* begin work.

The building department charges for the privilege of hassling you about the code. The fee is seldom less than $35 and will be about 1% of the construction cost on many jobs. If you aren't

licensed to do business in the city, you'll probably have to pay a license fee and maybe post a cash or insurance bond before leaving city hall. The building permit fee covers the cost of inspections and paperwork in the building department.

In addition to the permit fee, you'll probably have to pay a plan check fee. Typically the plan check fee is set at 50% of the building permit fee. The plan check fee covers the cost of reviewing the plans you submit with your application.

Here's something else to watch for. A contractor who's only doing carpentry work may have to buy an electrical permit if the owner's doing some electrical work himself. This can also happen with other trades in which you're not involved. Note also that some cities have a mandatory 10-day waiting period for permits. This usually means two trips to the building department office.

Many cities require that plans be signed by a state-licensed architect. If you plan to remove any walls or do any structural work, the building department may also require a certificate by a licensed engineer. The engineer's or architect's fee may be steep. And the architectural or engineering work may take several weeks. Use Figure 11-2 to add up the total permit fees for each job.

When you need approval by a licensed professional engineer or architect, have the customer advance the fees to you. Give the client a credit against the job for this advance payment. The architect becomes your subcontractor. That prevents any delay in closing the sale. Collecting in advance has another advantage. If the client doesn't like the plans and refuses to accept them, that's O.K. The fee has already been paid.

Figure 11-3 is an agreement form I use when architectural services are needed before the construction contract is signed.

Contracts

The purpose of a contract is to identify the obligations of each party. Unfortunately, contracts don't prevent all problems. They don't discourage the chiseler who thinks he's found a loophole and insists on getting more work than the contract calls for. Neither do they prevent an honest misunderstanding. Finally, even the most complete and airtight contract takes a back seat to the building code.

Let's look at some of the more common legal pitfalls. Most experienced home improvement contractors have had problems like these.

Extras Required by Code— The contract calls for a new dishwasher in the kitchen. There isn't an electrical outlet available, so the plans show a new appliance outlet under the sink. No problem so far. But now the electrical inspector arrives at the job. He says the present wiring doesn't conform to the code. You'll need a new service, he says. Now the job's half done and you're stuck! The inspector won't let work go forward until the electric system is overhauled. The owner refuses to pay for that. He says it's your tough luck. After all, you're a contractor. Contractors are expected to know the building code! You should have known what was happening when you signed the contract.

Unless you anticipate problems like this, you'll

Architectural fees	$ _____
Minimum or graduated fees	$ _____
Bond amount $ _____	
Premium cost	$ _____
Cash bond	$ _____
License requirement	$ _____
Plan examination fees	$ _____
Certificate of occupancy fees	$ _____
Electrical fees	$ _____
Plumbing fees	$ _____
Driveway and curb breaking fees	$ _____
Patio or sidewalk and/or concrete fees	$ _____
Wrecking fees	$ _____
Debris removal and use of chute fees	$ _____
Sidewalk scaffolding fees	$ _____
Subtotal of fees	$ _____
Total charge for building permit service	$ _____

Total permit charges
Figure 11-2

wind up playing Santa Claus while the job profit goes down the drain.

There are two steps to avoiding this problem. Make sure you take both. First, be alert for code compliance problems when selling the job. If the house has been modified or remodeled without taking out a building permit, or if the house was built more than 40 years ago, expect problems with the inspector. Warn the owner that an inspector will be on the job and may insist that some part of the house be brought up to current standards. Point out that there's no way for you to predict or control what the inspector demands. That's just a risk in every remodeling project. Any improvements beyond what the contract requires will cost extra. But those improvements add to the resale value of the home and the owner's equity. That's step one.

Step two is to put this clause in the contract:

Contractor is not responsible for existing building code violations and assumes no responsibility for making code-mandated changes to the existing structure or its mechanical or electrical systems except as identified in this agreement.

Code-mandated changes, when done by Contractor, will be done at owner's expense. Contractor will charge cost plus _____%.

In older homes, neither the plumbing nor the electrical system will be up to current code standards. This can present problems. The house may be improperly vented or completely unvented. Fixtures may lack shutoff valves. The house may have a septic tank or a well. If sewer and water systems are available, the building department may require sewer and water hookup. Protect yourself by warning the owner and drafting a contract that shifts the risk to the owner.

Avoid Exact Dimensions— Here's another contract trap. Let's say you're adding an 18' x 20' room to the rear of a house. The contract should read "*approximately* 18' x 20'." Why? Well, suppose the cement man's off an inch or two on his foundation. You have to build the addition two inches smaller to fit on the foundation. Now you go to collect and your perfectionist client says, "I want a $1,000 discount." Why? The contract called for an 18' x 20' room. You built an 17'10" x 19'10" room.

In point of fact, you didn't comply with the contract. The client refuses to pay. Result: you give the $1,000 discount or spend months trying to collect. Inconsequential as it may seem, your client has a legally sufficient ground to hang his hat on.

Agreement for Professional Services

This agreement made this _____ day of _____ , between

(Names) _____

(Address) _____ Phone: Bus. _____ Res. _____

of the City of _____ County of _____ State _____ Zip _____

hereinafter called Owner(s) and the _____
                                                    (Contractor)

Address _____ Phone _____

The Contractor is authorized by the Owner(s) to engage the services of a licensed architect

of the State of _____ to prepare drawings and specifications for the

following proposed work: _____

_____

_____

_____

to be done on the premises located at _____

City _____ State _____ Zip Code _____

The architect is to provide sufficient prints and specifications for the requirements of the
building and zoning departments, various sub-contractors, a copy for the contractor's office
plus one for field work and a copy for the Owner(s).

The Owner(s) agree to pay for the above plans and prints the sum of $ _____

_____ as follows:

$ _____ as of the date of this contract.

$ _____ upon delivery of the plans.

Upon the execution of a construction contract between the Owner(s) and the
Contractor for the proposed work, the Contractor shall issue a credit to the Owner(s)
for the sums of money the Contractor has received under this agreement.

Dated _____ at _____(city) _____ (state) _____

Accepted for _____   _____
                          (Contractor)   (Owner)

By _____   _____
                                                                          (Owner)

Agreement for professional services
Figure 11-3

The simple way to avoid this problem is to include in every contract you draft the words, *"All dimensions are approximate."*

Specify Brand Name or Equal— When you write up a contract, always include the words "or equal brand" whenever mentioning a brand name. Why? In your sales presentation to the customer, you discussed brand names. But the wholesaler or lumberyard might be out of the brand you need when the materials are needed. Maybe they've discontinued stocking the item. You might be able to pick up a close-out at a substantial savings. The factory or distributor might be on strike. There are a thousand reasons why some particular item may not be available. Be smart. Add "or equal brand" every time you mention any brand name in a contract.

Use the Phrase "Stock Colors"— Always write "owner's choice of stock colors," or if a particular color is desired, add the words "stock color" after mentioning the color. For example, if the owner wants mist green, the contract should say, "mist green, stock color" or "ceramic tile in stock color mist green."

If the customer doesn't like the stock color the supplier delivers, you can say: "No problem! We can get any color you want. But this is the stock color. Custom colors will cost more."

An even better safeguard is to have the customer sign the back of a color sample. Then write into the contract: *Color to be a stock color per the signed sample which is made a part of this agreement.*

Buyer's Allowance for Fixtures— Using the term "allowance" in contracts has saved many home improvement contractors a bundle of money. Use it any time you're having difficulty picking out a material that will satisfy the customer.

An allowance is like a budget. The actual cost may be more or less than the allowance. But the risk is on the owner — he pays extra if costs exceed the allowance. The allowance is just the amount included in the contract price.

It's common practice when building custom homes to bid electrical fixtures on an allowance basis. The owner picks out the fixtures he likes when it comes time for installation. The allowance is credited against purchase price, and the owner pays any extra charge. Follow the same procedure with kitchen cabinets, wall paneling, carpeting or anything where the owner will select the actual item

to be installed after the contract is signed.

Knowing that your customer bears the risk of cost overruns makes bidding easier. The customer knows that if he exceeds the allowance, he'll pay the difference.

Be Careful with Concrete Work— With concrete work, specify the bags of concrete per cubic yard and whether rod or mesh reinforcing will be used.

Make it clear that you're not responsible for any damage to the driveway or shrubs done by a ready-mix truck. A concrete truck is probably the heaviest load your client's driveway will ever support. Many driveways have cracked under weight like that. There's no way of telling what will happen when the truck rolls up on a driveway. All the ready-mix companies I've dealt with deliver at the contractor's risk. They won't repair a damaged driveway. You shouldn't have to either. Protect yourself by inserting this clause in the contract: *Contractor is not responsible for any damage to the driveway caused by the concrete truck.*

Here's another common problem. You're adding a wing or garage to the house. The ground where the addition goes is covered with grass, bushes and debris. There's no obvious pitch to the grade. When the cement man starts the job, he discovers that the site slopes or that one corner of the foundation is going to be on filled soil.

The cement man phones your office with the news that the job needs a retaining wall or a deeper foundation. It's going to cost you extra. You didn't charge the customer for it. The customer won't pay the extra charge. He has a contract with a set price. You're the expert. You should have known about the problem.

The cure for this dilemma is a little foresight. Here's what your contract might say about foundations and retaining walls:

The contract price is based on a maximum foundation wall height of 24" measured vertically from the bottom of the foundation to the top, and includes no retaining walls or other support other than the foundation and footing for that foundation. If, for any reason, the foundation wall height must exceed 24", or if a regular or reverse retaining wall is required, the additional concrete and excavation work will be priced as follows:

Then add the additional cost per cubic yard of concrete needed or per inch of additional depth.

This is fair. The customer is on notice that a retaining wall is a possibility and knows what the charge will be if the wall must be built.

Specify What You're Doing and Not Doing— It goes without saying that your agreement has to identify everything that's included in the job. Being specific is very important. For example, don't just say that you'll provide an electrical connection for the new dishwasher. Spell it out as "23' of Romex cable, a 4" outlet box with 125 volt duplex receptacle and cover, connected to the existing service panel." No one would interpret that as requiring you to furnish new electrical service.

Spelling it out in detail with a complete list of materials is the best way to protect yourself. True, that makes your contracts longer. But it also eliminates a financial loss if you forgot something when pricing the estimate. Here's an example:

You're remodeling a bathroom. As part of the job, the owner wants a new low-profile quiet-flush water closet. You discussed it when making the sales pitch. But the estimate and your contract price omitted the cost of the fixture. The contract includes a complete list of materials and omits any mention of the water closet. The plans show a water closet, but it could be either the existing W.C. or the new one the owner wants. True, omitting the W.C. was your fault — admittedly an oversight on your part. But does that mean you have to buy and install a $500 W.C. at your own expense? Not at all. The owner missed it too. The contract identifies all work to be done and the W.C. isn't included! You're off the hook. The W.C. is an extra charge.

Describing every item to be installed is important. But it may be just as important to exclude everything that isn't in your estimate. Always give yourself an out by specifying what you're *not* doing. That way, you're sure the customer doesn't expect it. Some contracts say, "There are no trades not specified in this contract." I prefer to spell it out in greater detail:

There is no painting or decorating in this contract.
There is no sheet metal or electrical work in this contract.
There is no plumbing or heating work in this contract.
There is no gutter work in this contract.
There is no hauling of dirt from the premises in this contract.

There's another way to limit and define the scope of the work:

This contract is for carpentry work only.
This contract is for cement work only.
This contract is for masonry work only.

It's easy to add a sentence or two like this. Do it. They prevent misunderstandings, reduce the chance of collection problems and help avoid lawsuits. When it comes to contracts, an ounce of prevention is well worth a pound of cure.

Owner's Labor— Where the owner is to do his own finishing, specify as follows:

This contract is for a shell, room addition, dormer, shell porch (or as is appropriate). *Contractor is to do the rough carpentry work only* (or as is appropriate).

Owner is to supply and install his own electric, plumbing, drywall, painting and seaming, flooring (carpeting or tile).
Owner to do his own floor sanding or finishing.
Owner to supply and install his own storm windows and doors or screens.
Owner is to do his own concrete work.

List Items Owner will Supply and Install— Some later chapters have sample work orders. It's important that they be filled out completely, *signed* by the owner and made a part of the contract. This prevents the owner from claiming that there's a discrepancy in style, size or specifications between what he ordered and what he received.

Spell Out the Finance Clauses— When the contract is to be paid out of a mortgage loan, insert the following clause:

This contract to be paid from the proceeds of a mortgage loan to be obtained by Owner at Owner's expense. Contractor will cooperate with Owner to obtain financing. However, it is Owner's responsibility to obtain financing. Contractor need not proceed until satisfied that the proceeds are in a sufficient amount to finance the project and are available. Contractor, at his option, may require a deposit to be placed into an escrow account.

Explain this clause to the customer as follows:

"You're the owner of the property, so you have to sign the loan documents. Mortgage expenses will include the usual closing costs, as you know. We'll help by preparing your loan application. It's easy for us to do the legwork. We do it all the time and have good contacts with lenders and loan officers.

But we can't sign the papers for you or guarantee payment of the loan.''

If the owner has given you an assignment on the insurance claim, use the following clause in the contract:

This contract will be paid from the proceeds of a claim number 00000 against Blank Insurance Company on policy number 00000.

When the owner's handling his own adjustment, either by himself or through an adjuster, insert the following clause in the contract:

Work under this agreement will commence when Contractor receives notice in writing that a proof of loss has been filed with XXXXX Insurance Company, and that the amount of the settlement is sufficient to cover the cost of this contract.

This is a very important clause. When an owner handles his own adjustment, it's easy to make a mistake. The result might be a reduced or delayed settlement. You could end up holding the bag.

Here's an example: The owner and the adjuster agreed that the loss was $4,750. The owner passes this information along to you. You begin work. Two weeks later the draft comes from the insurance company. It's only for $2,612. The owner has no other cash available and may not be able to borrow enough to cover the difference. What happened?

Several things could have gone wrong. The owner may not have had a homeowner's policy. If the insurance is a straight fire policy, the insurance company will reduce the settlement by the amount of depreciation.

Another possibility: Maybe the owner rented out part of the home — an attic apartment. Consequently his policy is a straight fire policy, not a homeowner's. That reduces his settlement proportionately. Or maybe the owner was underinsured. The principle of co-insurance reduces the settlement if the home is insured for less than the full value.

Whatever the reason, you need some protection against an inadequate settlement. A contract clause like the one above gives you the option of either reducing the job or financing the balance.

Discuss these clauses with your attorney. Have him adapt them to your local requirements, if necessary.

Cash Contracts

Federal regulations make it necessary for every contractor to have two contracts, one for cash sales and one for sales that are financed. For your protection, have your attorney draw up a contract for cash sales that includes a payment clause and the other protective clauses we've discussed. Here's a sample payment clause:

The owners agree to pay for the above work, the sum of _____Dollars ($___) as follows:

(a) _____*Dollars ($___) On the date of this contract*

(b) _____*Dollars ($___) On completion of concrete work*

(c) _____*Dollars ($___) When work is ___% completed*

(d) _____*Dollars ($___) Upon completion*

Installment Contracts

Any time a loan is involved in the sale, federal law prescribes certain disclosures that have to be made and procedures that have to be followed. Any bank or S&L will be up-to-date on these rules.

If you have to provide your own installment contract, I can recommend the installment contract for home improvements sold by Stuart-Hooper Company, 8757 S. Greenwood Avenue, Chicago, Illinois 60619. Ask for their form 114.

Larger libraries will have two other references that I've found to be useful. The first is *Jones Legal Forms*, published by Bobbs-Merrill. Check the sample documents in the section "Building and Construction Contracts." Another source is *Warren's Forms of Agreement*, published by Matthew Bender. Have your lawyer review these forms before you print up your contracts.

Completion Clauses

Some contracts include a penalty for late completion. There's no advantage in that, from your standpoint. Avoid setting any completion date in the contract. If you have to set a date, the word "approximately" can be a lifesaver. Write the sentence this way, "This contract to be completed approximately 5 weeks after work begins." That takes you off the hook for a delayed start date. Most delays occur before work begins, not during construction.

What if the customer insists on a firm date and won't accept the word "approximately?" What if he insists on a penalty of $50 for every day completion is delayed beyond a certain date. My advice is to walk away. Better yet, run. This kind of work you don't need. If you feel you *must* go ahead with the contract, be smart. Make it a two-way street. If you're going to be penalized $50 a day for being late, provide the same bonus for early completion.

Any time you mention a completion date, include the following in the contract:

All completion times set by this contract shall be extended for the duration of delays caused by acts of God, inclement weather, strikes, lockouts, material shortages, lack of utility services, fire, storm, theft, vandalism or other causes beyond the contractor's control.

Standard Contract Clauses

There are several standard clauses that should be in every construction contract you write. The remainder of this chapter covers the more common clauses that protect you, the contractor. Since you're preparing the contract for the owner's signature, make sure these clauses are included in the agreement.

Insurance Clauses

Losses during construction are common. The owners should provide coverage during the period of construction. If they don't, you may have to furnish coverage and recover the cost from the owners. Here's the language that lets you do that:

The Owners further agree to keep all buildings and all building appurtenances at the construction site adequately insured against loss by fire, theft, vandalism and malicious mischief or other cause. Owners will purchase insurance coverage from one or more reliable insurance companies on behalf of the Contractor and the secured lenders on the property. If the Owners do not insure the premises, the Contractor is hereby authorized to insure the premises at Owners' expense for an amount sufficient to protect the interest of the Contractor, its assigns and all secured lenders. In the event of loss, the Owners will pay to the Contractor as much of the proceeds of the settlement as the Contractor or its assigns are entitled to under the terms of this contract.

All employees will be covered in full by Worker's Compensation and Public Liability Insurance.

Change of Ownership or Title Clause

You don't want your collection of the contract placed in jeopardy because of a change of ownership or title. Always file a mechanic's lien to protect your interest if the property is sold or changes title for any reason. This clause covers it:

The contractor will file a mechanic's lien under the laws of the State of _____ immediately. This is to protect the interest of the contractor from any hazard of a change in title or ownership, or encumbrances placed on the property.

Governing Laws Clause

Notice to the Buyer:

1) Do not sign this agreement before you read it or if it contains any blank spaces.

2) You are entitled to an exact copy of the agreement you sign.

3) Under the law you have the right, among others, to pay in advance the full amount due and to obtain under certain conditions a partial refund of the time price differential.

4) You have the right to give the assignee named (or if no assignee is named, to give the seller) written notice of any defense or right of action which you may have against the seller within five (5) days of delivery of the merchandise described herein. If a notice is not received within that time, you may not assert such defense or right of action against the assignee. (This paragraph does not apply where the merchandise is a motor vehicle, or where any negotiable instrument is made in accordance with the provisions of Subchapter I of the National Housing Act.)

Contractor's Notice

The law requires that Seller, in its capacity as a contractor, shall submit to Buyer a sworn statement of persons furnishing materials and labor before any payments are required to be made to Seller, in its capacity as a contractor.

Your contract must also include this notice:

Any provision herein found to conflict with the provisions of the Retail Installment Sales Act of (your state) effective _____, 19___, Title 1 of the National Housing Act, or the Uniform Commercial Code of (your state) shall be void and of no effect and shall not affect in any way the remaining provisions of this contract. No provision hereof shall be interpreted so as to conflict with the provisions of said Acts or Code, and where more than one interpretation is possible, that interpretation shall be adopted which is consistent with the provisions of said Acts or Code.

There are two more notices your contract must include. Both should be printed in bold type.

You, the owner(s), may cancel this transaction at any time prior to midnight of the third business day after the date of this transaction. See the attached notice of cancellation form for an explanation of this right.

Owner(s) and each cosigner acknowledge that a completely filled-in copy of this signed contract has been delivered to and retained by owner(s) and such cosigner.

Check with your attorney as to the requirements of your state concerning the contractor's sworn statement on materials and labor and the other notices quoted above.

Permit Clauses

Get the owners to agree to pay the building permit and plan check fee, no matter what that fee may be.

The Owners agree to secure all required permits and fees which may be imposed by any agency of government before the construction agreed to under this contract can be completed.

Owners warrant that all necessary surveys and permits for the work can be secured, and authorizes Contractor, on their behalf, to obtain same. Owners warrant that the existing structure conforms with all codes and ordinances and agree to assume full legal responsibility for any existing improvements which do not comply with local building codes, local zoning ordinances or are constructed beyond the boundaries of the property. Owners authorize all necessary changes in the existing structure or to the plans and specifications for the improvement to be completed under this agreement so that the building and proposed improvements comply with all codes, zoning ordinances and government regulations. All such changes shall be paid for by Owners. Contractor to charge cost plus _____%.

Acceptance Clause

This agreement shall not be binding on the Contractor unless accepted in writing by an officer of the Contractor, and when so accepted, this contract and all the provisions thereof shall inure to and be binding upon the parties hereto and their respective heirs, executors, administrators, successors and assigns.

Agreement and Completion Clause

An acknowledgement of completion of the work signed by any one of the Owners or the failure of the Owners within seven days after notice by the Contractor of the completion of the work to deliver to the contractor a written notice specifying any defects or deficiencies in the work or materials, shall be conclusive evidence that this contract was satisfactorily completed by the Contractor in accord with the terms of this contract and in a good, substantial and workmanlike manner.

Assignment Clause

In the event of the assignment of Contractor's right under this contract, any assignee of such rights shall thereupon, and so long as such assignment is in effect, be vested with and entitled to all the rights and powers of Contractor under this contract; but, except as expressly otherwise provided, such assignee shall not be subject to any obligations or liabilities of Owners, and no waiver or modification of the terms and conditions of this contract shall be binding upon such assignee except as expressly set forth in a writing signed by a duly authorized officer or such assignee.

No Side Agreements Clause

This contract contains all of the agreements of the parties hereto, and no agreements, representations, promises or statements have been made by or on behalf of Contractor, except as expressly set forth or incorporated herein; nor will any waivers or modifications of the terms and conditions of this contract, or any other agreements, representations, promises or statements relating to this contract hereafter purportedly made by or on behalf of Contractor, be binding upon Contractor or any assignee of Contractor's rights under this contract, except as expressly set forth in a notation, signed by a duly authorized officer of Contractor.

Owners hereby further agree and acknowledge that, except as otherwise expressly specified herein: (a) Contractor shall not be liable or responsible for any delay or damages caused by strikes, weather conditions, materials, shortages or causes beyond Contractor's control; (b) Contractor assumes no liability for any damage to the premises or to materials located on the premises resulting from the work herein contracted for; (c) in the event Owners shall assert a claim against Contractor, it shall be a complete defense thereto, that Owners have been compensated for such claim by insurance or otherwise.

Cancellation Clause

Should this contract be terminated for any reason whatsoever before the completion of the work as specified herein, Owners agree to pay in full for all labor and materials furnished up to date of such termination at the Contractor's usual selling price, and in addition thereto, if terminated by Owners, 25% of the total contract price as liquidated damages and not as a penalty. This contract shall, at the election of the Contractor, terminate upon the loss or damage of any of said work or materials by fire, theft or other cause whatsoever.

Default and Collection Clauses

The occurrence of any of the following events shall constitute a Default (as such term is used herein): (a) Non-payment, when due, of any amount payable by Owners hereunder or Owners' breach of any agreement, warranty or obligation contained herein; (b) Any statement, representation or warranty of Owners herein or in any application or other writing at any time furnished by or on behalf of Owners to Contractor in connection with the transaction evidenced by this contract to be untrue in any material respect; (c) Owners become insolvent or unable to pay debts as they mature or make an assignment for the benefit of creditors, or any proceeding is instituted by or against Owners alleging that Owners are insolvent or unable to pay debts as they mature; (d) Contractor for any other reason whatsoever has reasonable cause to deem itself insecure. Subject to any restrictions imposed by applicable law, whenever a Default shall be existing: all obligations of Owners hereunder may, notwithstanding any other provision of this contract, at the option of Contractor, and without demand or notice of any kind, be declared and thereupon immediately shall be due and payable.

The Owners hereby waive trial by jury in any litigation arising out of this contract. The Owners hereby voluntarily and expressly agree that venue may be had in the county of execution of this agreement, at Contractor's election.

No delay on the part of Contractor in the exercise of any right or remedy shall operate as a waiver thereof, and no single or partial exercise by Contractor of any right or remedy shall preclude other or further exercise thereof or the exercise of any other right or remedy.

Warranty

Except as expressly set forth or incorporated herein, Contractor makes no warranties, express or implied, with respect to the work. If Contractor has given to Owners a written warranty of Contractor covering the work, all of the terms, conditions, exclusions and limitations contained in such written warranty are hereby incorporated in this contract. Contractor makes no warranties, express or implied, of either merchantability or of fitness for a particular purpose with respect to the work which are not covered by such a written warranty of Contractor. Contractor shall in no event be liable for consequential damages except only to the extent that Contractor's liability for such damages arises under and is not disclaimed in any such written warranty of Contractor.

Extra Charges

Extra charges can be a problem for any contractor. Construction is complex. Even on a simple garage job, it's hard to anticipate everything that should be done. And construction is too expensive and permanent to omit making an improvement when it becomes obvious that an improvement is needed. There will be changes, no matter how complete and careful your planning may be.

Given those facts, every contractor has to deal with changes. But here's the point: the owner should pay for all changes. The cost of changes shouldn't come out of your pocket. Comply with the specs exactly. When the owner suggests making a change, no matter how minor, whip out a change order form and offer to figure the cost of the change right on the spot. That will do one of two things: Either the owner will agree to make the change at his expense, or stop making suggestions for improvements.

No work will be done or material furnished except as specified herein or agreed to in writing. All changes requested by Owners or required hereunder shall be paid for by Owners in addition to the contract price. All of Contractor's rights and remedies will extend to changes. Unless otherwise agreed to in writing, and except as otherwise provided herein, all changes will be at Contractor's regular price.

Contractor may make minor variations in work or substitute material of equal or better quality without consent of Owners.

Figure 11-4 is the change order form I use. If you don't want to print a change order form, use your regular contract and write in this phrase:

This extra is made a part of the original contract between _____Owner _____Owner and _____Contractor dated _____, 19_____

Site Problem Clauses

All material incorporated in said premises or stored at or by the site thereof and all labor performed under this contract shall be for the account of and at the risk of the Owners, and the Owners shall not be relieved of the obligation of payment therefore by reason of loss or damage by fire, theft, or any other cause whatsoever.

On all work performed at or on the Owners' site, Owners agree to provide what contractor considers ample space for his work. It is agreed that all salvage removed from the premises is contractor's property and Owners will receive no compensation whatsoever. Contractor is not responsible for damage to shrubbery, grass, trees or landscaping.

If unusual subsoil conditions, obstructions above or below grade or facts known to Owners and not disclosed to Contractor require change in work, any increase in the contract price by reason thereof shall be paid for by Owners. The Owners agree to pay the Contractor's cost of labor, materials, supervision and overhead plus 25% for overcoming unusual soil conditions.

Miscellaneous Clause

The term Seller wherever used in this contract shall mean the contractor, and includes any assignee of contractor's rights hereunder; and the term Buyer(s) wherever used in this contract shall mean the owners, and include any cosigner of this contract.

Additions/Changes/Extras

Order for Labor and Material

The undersigned homeowner _____ whose street address

is _____ city of _____ county of _____

State of _____ zip code _____

Hereby orders from _____ contractor, street address

is _____ city of _____ county of _____

State of_____ zip code _____

the following additions, changes and/or extras desired by the owner. All in addition to

other labor and material heretofore contracted for. This is in addition to the work called

for on the contract dated _____ , 19 ____ and previously signed, and

this agreement incorporates all the terms and regulations of said signed contract.

_____

_____

_____

_____

Owner therefore agrees to pay the additional sum of $ _____

Owner(s) _____(Seal)

Accepted for the   Owner(s) _____(Seal)

_____
          Contractor's Name

By_____

Title_____

Date_____

Change order form
Figure 11-4

The clauses I've recommended in this chapter are examples. Your standard contract has to comply with the laws of your state and Federal Regulation Z, and should be tailored to the type of work you handle. Discuss each clause with your attorney when preparing your contract. He can advise you of the adaptability of the clauses to your situation and your state. He'll also let you know what has to be printed in bold type under current regulations.

It's a little extra work to develop a complete contract. But the judge will read the contract very carefully if a dispute winds up in court. Your client is expected to abide by the agreement, even if he signed without reading it. Take the time to use a good contract that protects you and anticipates as many problems as possible.

Chapter 12

Setting Prices

Every year many remodeling and home improvement contractors leave the business. Some leave voluntarily because they see better opportunities elsewhere. Others are forced out of business because suppliers aren't willing to advance more credit. Many just give up because they aren't making enough money to cover expenses.

There's no single reason why some make it in the home improvement business and others don't. But if I had to identify the most common cause of failure, it would be poor estimating and pricing. Far too many inexperienced home improvement contractors consistently underprice or overprice the jobs they're writing up. This chapter is intended to help you avoid pricing mistakes.

First, understand this. You can't price home improvement work the same way you price new construction. The proportion of labor expense is greater and there's far more risk of cost overruns in remodeling. Let's look at an example.

Hanging doors in new construction is a 1-2-3 affair. You know ahead of time exactly what's required. There won't be any surprises. You built the wall, installed the frames and know the doors will fit right the first time. You can estimate the cost of material and labor with a high degree of accuracy.

Now let's look at the same task on a remodeling project. First, notice that your tradesman may be working with only one door. There's no chance to improve the production rate on second and later

doors on this job.

Work starts with removing the old door. Next, the tradesman installs a blind dutchman where the original hinges were. If the frame's badly chewed up from years of neglect and abuse, he'll have to remove and replace the whole frame. Don't forget that the building has settled over the years and everything's out of plumb. That means more problems and more time spent in getting the work lined up and leveled out. Finally the door's installed, but still the job's not finished. You have to haul away the old door and the debris.

All remodeling has similar problems: no chance for mass production, difficulty in removing just enough of the old, adding new materials to deteriorated or nonstandard existing materials, matching designs, colors and textures, covering up for another contractor's mistakes, struggling with inadequate access to the point where work has to be done, and the surprises that seem to be inevitable in home improvement work. Estimating new construction is a snap by comparison.

And notice who's called on to price home improvement work. It's seldom a full-time, professional estimator/specialist, as on larger, new construction projects. As often as not, the same person that made the home improvement sale has to figure the price.

Maybe you understand now why pricing is the area where most home improvement contractors are weakest. It's difficult work, with lots of opportunities for a major error. And even though pricing is crucial to your financial survival, you probably have less experience in pricing than in any other part of the business.

In this chapter I'll cover markups and setting up a retail price book. In the following chapters I'll explain how pricing differs in each type of home improvement work. Emphasis will be on avoiding the pricing pitfalls most salesmen make.

Markup

There are hundreds of ways to figure the "right" markup on a job. In truth, there is no single right price for either new construction or remodeling. And there is certainly no single correct way to arrive at that price. Every builder has his own method and sets his own goals. If your method is working, no one will claim it's wrong.

But there's a general guideline that I can recommend. Over the years I've found that many successful remodelers work with about a 70% markup. This is usually enough to cover selling expense, overhead, supervision and contingencies, and leave a modest profit. The method I've seen work consistently is to multiply your *hard costs* by 1.70. The result is the contract price. Hard costs are material expense, subcontract costs, and labor (including taxes and insurance). Of course, some jobs warrant more markup and others can get by on less. A smaller job with more risk and done for a demanding client should be worth more. A larger job that's done mostly by subcontractors will probably carry a smaller markup.

Home improvement contractors have all the overhead of any business: office rent, telephone, owner's salary, office salaries, legal and accounting expense, insurance, auto and truck expense, and more. But unlike other contractors, home improvement includes the cost of removal of the existing, disposal of removals, patching, repairing, revamping, adjusting, and altering. There's risk in work like that. Surprises are seldom pleasant in the repair and remodeling business. Most of what you didn't anticipate will end up costing more, not less. That's a remodeler's risk. And it's the reason why markups have to be higher in the home improvement business.

Naturally, competition dictates markups. If you're not getting enough work at 70% markup, maybe 70% is too much for your area. But remember that bidding remodeling work is seldom done from a level field. New construction usually goes to the lowest responsible bidder. But a creative salesman who follows the procedures I've laid out in this book has an advantage over lowball bidders who rely on price alone to sell their services.

Setting Up Your Retail Price Book

Every home improvement salesman should be able to quote prices out of a price book as he sells the job. The price book lists selling prices for all common items. It doesn't show any costs to the contractor, just the contractor's selling prices. A good price book will eliminate most major pricing errors.

If you're selling from cost, it's easy to overlook an item or fail to take into account some hidden cost. My book is a three-ring vinyl binder with 6″ by 9½″ pages. Each page covers the most common items in a single category. For example, on a single page I can list selling prices (including labor and markup) for all common interior doors. I don't have to list every size for every type of door. The cost difference between a 2'8″ and a 3'0″ door is peanuts. All prices listed in my book include hanging, hinges and lockset. All the salesman has to do is find the one price that fits the description of what's needed.

I keep a master copy of my company's price book with just material descriptions — no prices. From time to time I add new items and change existing items. Then my secretary retypes the page, but only with material descriptions — still no prices. To enter the prices, I make a copy of each master page with our copying machine. Prices are written in by hand on the copies. When all items have been priced on the copies, any salesman can make up his own current price book by copying each page of my book. When prices change, I make a new copy of the page from the master, enter new prices on the copy and distribute copies of my copy to all salesmen. It's quick, easy and foolproof.

To price any job, the salesman just makes up a list of the work to be done and applies a price from the book to each item. Of course, you'll probably want to review estimates on all jobs prepared by the salesmen. And, as I've explained, your salesman needs some flexibility when presenting his proposal to his prospect. Allow him to modify the proposal to meet objections, changes that are suggested, or the competitive situation. Of course, he should have blanket approval to use any price that's in the price book.

A price book doesn't solve all problems, of

course. You can still make mistakes in addition. But using selling prices eliminates adding the markup. The biggest problem will be forgetting some important item. There's no way to avoid that risk entirely. But each item in your book should be a complete installed cost. An exterior door, for example, would include hinges, lockset and weatherstripping. Your contract offers protection if something is accidentally left out of the cost estimate. But your client will resent extra charges later for what he (and you) assumed was included. So make sure costs in your price book include *all* the work needed to complete the installation.

The first thing to do in pricing any job is to write down the cost of the building permit and the estimated cost of debris removal. This ensures that these important costs aren't forgotten.

Job Survey
Get in the habit of completing a job survey before pricing any job. My price book includes a job survey form for each type of home improvement work. These survey forms are included in many of the chapters that follow. The job survey will help you anticipate problems and unusual conditions before the contract is signed. That way you can charge for this extra work and make a profit on it.

I recommend that salesmen be required to turn in a completed job survey form with each contract. The survey helps the job superintendent learn exactly what's expected. A completed job survey form guarantees that the salesman has covered every item that the customer wants to buy or must assume responsibility for.

Creating Your Own Price Book
Setting up a retail price book for remodeling is a new concept to most contractors. Here's how to do it.

First, contact each sub you use regularly. Get a list of prices he quotes for most typical installations. You don't need a promise that the subs will stick to these prices. All you're collecting is information.

From your cement man, for example, get prices for the following:

Flatwork — 5 bag mix poured 4" thick over 4" fill, at least 5 yards of material.
Extra charge when job is under 5 yards.
Break out and remove old concrete slab.
12" x 12" grade beam in garage floor.
Water ledge in garage floor.
Retaining walls, cost per inch over 8".

When you have these prices, add your markup to find the selling price.

From your electrician, get costs for:

A new service.
Moving one, two or three meters to the outside.
Adding one, two or three meters to an existing building.
New outlets installed in open walls, per outlet.
Fishing wire, per outlet.
How much per circuit added for two, three or four circuits.
Furnace controls, thermostat wiring.
Medicine cabinet and switch.

From your heating sub, get costs for hot and cold ducts per linear foot, furnace cost based on 100,000 or 120,000 Btu units or the average size needed on the jobs you do.

Once you have typical costs from the electrician and furnace man, add markup to cover overhead, tearing out the old furnace, hauling it away, floor patch, and maybe grille patching if the holes for the old grilles are too large for the new modern registers. And don't forget to include sales commission as part of your markup.

Kitchen cabinets are usually priced per linear foot of cabinet face. Pricing this way saves time and probably sacrifices little in accuracy. The owner wants to know how much it will cost while you're sitting in the kitchen trying to make the sale. Don't fidget and fumble or beg off with a promise to come back next week with a price. You'll have lost the job by then. If you have a linear foot cost, it's easy to measure the linear feet of cabinet front and multiply by the cost per foot.

To find the linear foot selling price, take 20 feet of wall cabinets of various sizes, including both 12" and 15" high units for over the refrigerator and 30" high units for over the counter. Divide the 20-foot cost by 20 to get the linear foot cost for wall cabinets. Do the same for base cabinets.

Even though cabinet widths vary, you'll be surprised how accurate an average linear foot price will be for most jobs.

For counter tops, use a 20-foot self-edge top with a 4" backsplash. Add a miter or two and a sink cutout. Divide by 20 feet. That's your base cost.

When you have the wall cabinet, base cabinet and counter top price per linear foot, it's a simple matter to add your markup to find the selling price. But be sure to include the cost of removal and disposal of the old cabinets and counter top.

Job or Item Cost	Profit (based on sales price)				
	33-1/3%	40%	50%	60%	63%
$ 50.	$ 75.	$ 85.	$ 100.	$ 125.	$ 135.
100.	150.	165.	200.	250.	270.
200.	300.	335.	400.	500.	540.
300.	450.	500.	600.	750.	810.
400.	600.	665.	800.	1,000.	1,080.
500.	750.	835.	1,000.	1,250.	1,350.
1,000.	1,500.	1,665.	2,000.	2,500.	2,700.
2,000.	3,000.	3,330.	5,000.	5,000.	5,400.
3,000.	4,500.	5,000.	7,500.	7,500.	8,100.
4,000.	6,000.	6,665.	8,000.	10,000.	10,800.
5,000.	7,500.	8,330.	10,000.	12,500.	13,500.
6,000.	9,000.	10,000.	12,000.	15,000.	16,200.
7,000.	10,500.	11,660.	14,000.	17,500.	18,900.
8,000.	12,000.	13,330.	16,000.	20,000.	21,600.
9,000.	13,500.	15,000.	18,000.	22,500.	24,300.
10,000.	15,000.	16,660.	20,000.	25,000.	27,000.
11,000.	16,500.	18,325.	22,000.	27,500.	29,700.
12,000.	18,000.	20,000.	24,000.	30,000.	32,400.
13,000.	19,500.	21,660.	26,000.	32,500.	35,100.
14,000.	21,000.	23,325.	28,000.	35,000.	37,800.
15,000.	22,500.	25,000.	30,000.	37,500.	40,500.
16,000.	24,000.	26,660.	32,000.	40,000.	43,200.
17,000.	25,500.	28,325.	34,000.	42,500.	45,900.
18,000.	27,000.	29,880.	36,000.	45,000.	48,600.
19,000.	28,500.	31,650.	38,000.	46,500.	51,300.
20,000.	30,000.	33,320.	40,000.	50,000.	54,000.
30,000.	45,000.	49,980.	60,000.	75,000.	81,000.
40,000.	60,000.	66,640.	80,000.	100,000.	108,000.
$50,000.	$75,000.	$83,300.	$100,000.	$125,000.	$135,000.
	50%	66-2/3%	100%	150%	170%
	Markup (based on cost)				

Profit vs. markup
Figure 12-1

Your salesman needs only four figures in his price book for each type of cabinet: wall cabinets, base cabinets, counter top, and a total of all three. The basic cabinet types are:

- Good quality stock hardwood prefinished cabinets.

- Formica or laminated plastic face cabinets.

- European style with carved fronts.

Setting the Selling Price
There's a distinction between markup and percentage of profit on sales. Merchants figure their profit as a percentage of the selling price. You should do the same. The following example will show the distinction between markup and profit margin.

Let's say a range costs you $350.00. You want to make a gross profit of 50%. Adding 50% to the cost would mean adding $175.00. Your selling price would be $525. That's a 50% markup. But a merchant would say that's only a 33% profit on the sales price. To make 50%, you have to mark up the range by 100%, or $350. Divide the $350 markup by the $700 selling price and you see that our gross profit is 50%.

Merchants work from the selling price because the cost of doing business is based on the sales, not on the cost of the goods.

Failure to appreciate the difference between markup and percentage of profit on sales has cost many remodelers and contractors lots of money. Figure 12-1 is a table comparing profit percentages and markup. Notice that a 50% markup is a 33%

profit, a 67% markup is a 40% profit, and so on. Use this table to find at a glance the correct selling price to reach the profit margin you want.

Earlier I recommended setting prices at 1.7 times your hard costs. That's a 70% markup and about a 42% gross profit. Hard costs are 58% of the job, and overhead, supervision, profit and selling expense are 42%. To convert markup to percentage of profit, divide the profit by the selling price.

The next chapter begins our detailed explanation of how to sell each type of home improvement work. All of the remaining chapters include pricing tips and suggestions.

Chapter 13

Selling Room Additions

You can't sell a room addition until you know exactly what your client has in mind. Room addition sales begin with a problem: The baby's too big for the crib. Dad needs space for his hobby. Mother-in-law snores so loud that no one can share a room with her. Understanding the problem is the first step. Unfortunately, your clients may not be able to or willing to identify the problem precisely. But putting your finger on the problem and showing how to solve it is the only way to get the sale.

Listen carefully to what your prospects describe and what they assume comes with the job. Then try to figure out what they left unsaid. The only way to discover all this is to go over every detail carefully, discuss every point, and then write into the contract what's to be done and what's not to be done.

Room addition sales are big ticket sales — over $50,000 in affluent neighborhoods. Many room additions cost more than the owner originally paid for the house. Finding out exactly what the prospects want will be well worth your time.

There are plenty of reasons to add a room. Generally it's cheaper to add space than to sell the house and buy one that's larger. Adding space may not require new financing, where buying a new home almost certainly will. Adding a room doesn't create the turmoil that moving does. The kids can stay in the same school and the adults don't have to leave familiar surroundings and their friends and neighbors.

Planning for Space

Once you've qualified the prospect, begin thinking about using space wisely and getting the most extra space at the lowest cost. In some cases, just finding any expansion space may be difficult. Can we add to the side, rear, or front of the house? Lot lines and setback requirements determine how much space is available. Most zoning ordinances won't let you build closer than 5 feet to any property line or within 50 feet of the centerline of the street. The building department can supply exact requirements for your prospect's lot.

It's always cheaper to convert an existing porch or attached garage, or build a rumpus room in the basement. That saves building a whole new foundation and roof. Another alternative is adding a room under a dormer in the attic. You'll be surprised how many families will switch their thinking once you explain the cost advantages. When that happens, you're almost sure to get the job. You came up with the best way to add space at the lowest cost.

Next, think how the space will be used:

- For a mother-in-law or elderly parent?
- For a recreation or family room?
- For a child's bedroom?
- For a dining room?
- For a living room?
- For a library, den, or rumpus room?
- For rental income?
- For more kitchen space?

Once you've found the need, break the answer down further. If the space is to be used by a mother-in-law or parents, will a powder room be needed? Will they make some of their own meals? If so, a kitchenette would be useful. Will zoning permit that? Will they want a separate entrance so they can come and go at will without disturbing anyone?

In many communities special regulations apply when adding both a bathroom and a kitchen. Installation of both is considered to be creating another living unit. Then an additional fire exit may be required. Usually there will be no problem with zoning if you just raise a dormer and add a powder room. This is considered an integral part of the house. But adding a kitchen for the use of in-laws, although still in the family, will be considered creating an apartment. This will require a second entrance and may put you in violation of zoning regulations. Check on this first.

For a recreation room, your client will probably want a built-in bar, either with or without plumbing. In a family room, consider built-in storage space or walk-in closets. In a child's bedroom, include lighting and cross ventilation. When adding a dining room, consider using a snack bar as a natural divider between the kitchen and the dining room. Will the floor be even between the dining room and the kitchen? In a library or den, give special emphasis to bookshelves, built-in curio cabinets, and shelving for the stereo, TV and home computer.

Supplying Materials

If the owner is willing and able (or has friends or relatives who are), suggest that he save money by doing the painting, drywall, or even the floor tile himself. In some cases the owner may also be qualified to do the electrical or plumbing work. Whatever the trade, suggest to the owner that he do it himself and save the labor cost and the overhead. This will give him a substantial savings.

Doesn't that cut your profit on the job? Maybe a little. But it may be the only way to do the job within the loan available. If you don't suggest it, the total cost may be prohibitive. Letting clients create some sweat equity is often the only way to sell the addition. Anyhow, doing only a shell addition (just the concrete, rough carpentry, and exterior finish) can reduce your headaches.

Go one step further. Suggest that you supply the material so the loan covers all material cost. The financing of the materials for most homeowners is extremely important. From your standpoint, the advantage is that you make a profit on the materials. Your price, of course, will be higher than the local lumberyard might charge. But many homeowners are willing to pay for you to arrange the financing.

If the cost of materials is a stumbling block, remove that block. Include supplied but owner-installed materials in the contract price. That way they are covered by the loan. Write into the contract, for example, that you'll supply 3/8" drywall to cover the 12' by 18' family room walls and ceiling, and also supply tape, nails, and joint compound. Installation will be by the owner. The contract might call for you to "supply vinyl asbestos tile in the owner's choice of stock colors for a price not to exceed 90 cents per square foot, including the necessary mastic and base molding. Installation by owner."

It's a fundamental rule in the remodeling business that the fewer trades involved, the better the profit potential. If you can sell a shell room addition instead of a completed room, do it. Adding trades just increases the chance that something will go wrong. And mistakes generally reduce your profit dollar for dollar — even if a sub was at fault. Follow the KISS rule: "Keep it simple, stupid." Sell just a shell addition whenever the opportunity presents itself.

When writing up a shell or semi-shell job, be specific. Describe the materials you will supply. This is so the bank, savings and loan, or FHA can't accuse you of making an illegal kickback. Supplying materials for installation by the owner is legal. But it can be interpreted as a payoff if the contract is not specific on this subject.

Submitting the Plans

You'll always need a written plan for the addition. It's required to get a building permit. That can be a problem in some communities. Some building departments require a plan signed by a licensed architect. In other communities a plan drawn by the contractor is acceptable.

In either case, never leave a plan with your prospects until they have signed the contract or paid for the plan. Keep the plan in your possession. Tell them you can't leave it because . . . some change has to be made back at the office . . . you have to discuss it with your partner . . . you have to improve on it. If you leave the plan with your prospects, every remodeler in the county will be bidding it by dawn tomorrow. You did the work, spent

Survey of Pitfalls — Room Additions

Check the following points before pricing any room addition job.

1)   Does an existing septic tank, drainfield, catch basin, power line, water line, gas line or TV cable obstruct the site? If so, who can move it and at what cost?

2)   Is there an electric riser from the service to the power lines in the way? Can it be relocated and at what cost?

3)   When adding a room above a basement, will the addition have to be built over an existing basement exterior exit? If so, can the exit be relocated without violating the building code? Can the opening be closed? At what cost?

4)   Will there be enough headroom above basement exit stairs if an addition is built over the stairs?

5)   Can the basement exit be extended outside the new addition? If so, at what cost?

6)   Will a cellar door have to be relocated?

7)   Will the addition block off a window, leaving no natural light in a kitchen or a dining room? Would a new window on a different wall restore light and ventilation?

8)   Can a trencher or Bobcat get into the rear or side yard?

9)   Will the foundation have to be excavated by hand?

10)   Can a concrete truck reach all points where concrete will be needed? If not, will pumping be required? Will wheelbarrows be needed?

11)   Will the sidewalk have to be removed and replaced?

12)   Is the present pattern or type of siding on the existing building available at reasonable cost? If not, what are the chances of a fairly good match? If the present siding is prefinished aluminum or prefinished hardboard, does the contract call for the best match possible but make no guarantee of an exact match? Does the owner understand that siding color can vary from batch to batch and that there is no guarantee of a perfect match? Does the owner know that weather ages colors and even an exact match will vary after one sample is exposed to weather for several years?

13)   Will a semi-hip or gable room addition obscure an upper-story window?

14)   Will it be possible to match the existing copper, galvanized or aluminum rain gutter?

15)   Will you have to remove and replace shrubs or trees?

16)   Will the building code require additional exits?

17)   Does a local ordinance prohibit heavy equipment such as ready-mix trucks and lumber trucks from crossing the public sidewalk? If so, have you added the cost of wheeling dirt and debris out, and materials like concrete, lumber and millwork into the site?

18)   Does the customer want a powder room in the addition? If so, can you tie into an existing soil stack or will a new stack be needed?

19)   Does your customer want a new vanity or other decorative item that may be hard to locate? Do they have strong preconceived ideas of what they want? Are they looking for something advertised in *House & Garden* or some other magazine? Have you considered giving them an allowance in the contract so they can buy some item on their own?

20)   Have you included enough extra circuits for the new electrical outlets? Does the contract include the words, "Contractor assumes no responsibility for the existing electrical system or for code violations in that system or for bringing the existing electrical system up to current code requirements"?

Room addition pitfalls
Figure 13-1

your time, came up with the ideas. You've earned the right to a decision on the plan as drawn.

Of course, if the prospects paid for the plan, it's their plan. They can do anything they want with it. And, of course, once the contract is signed, title to the plan passes to the homeowner.

Some home improvement contractors make it company policy to charge a fee for architectural drawings. This discourages shoppers who have no intention of buying. But the fee is credited against the job when the contract is signed. From the prospect's perspective, it's like getting a plan for nothing.

If the city requires that plans be signed by an architect, you can't figure the selling price until you have the final plans and know everything the architect has included. Once you have approval of the tentative plan, inform your prospect that the city requires architectural plans.

"We work very closely with an architect who specializes in room additions. His fee will be $450 for this plan — but the full $450 will be credited against the job when you decide to go ahead with the project. I'd appreciate it if you would make out a check for that amount so I can get him started on the plans right away."

You have two options at this point. You can have the check made out either to the architect or to your firm. If it's payable to your firm, write up a contract for a deposit for architectural plans.

Handling it this way has three advantages. First, you don't have the cost of drawing plans. Second, the customer is getting comfortable with the idea of signing a contract with your firm. The initial step has been taken. The final contract to do the work is that much easier. Third, tire kickers who have no intention of doing the work now, or are only trying to get ideas, or who plan to do the work themselves, will drop out now before you waste more time. You have brought the matter to the decision point — pay for the plans or let me go on my way!

Selling Increased Value

Many prospects will ask how much value the room addition will add to the house. Anticipate this question. Bring it out into the open. Use it as a selling tool.

"You know, Mr. Homeowner, that your home will be worth more. The value of the improvement will increase right along with the value of the rest of the house. I've had mortgage appraisers in this area tell me that houses with more livable space command a premium in this neighborhood. And, of course, your equity and mortgage value will also be higher. When it comes time to sell, your home with this addition will sell more easily and get a better price. In the meantime, you've had the use of the new bedroom and game room. Can I use the kitchen table to write up the order?"

Avoiding the Pitfalls

Every remodeling job has potential traps. Find them before the contract is signed. The survey questions that follow (Figure 13-1) can save you from embarrassing and expensive mistakes when doing room additions. Have your salesmen fill out one of these survey forms on every room addition job. Put a copy of this survey form in your price book.

Find the problems before they become expensive mistakes.

Chapter 14
Selling Awnings, Canopies and Carports

It's easy to sell awnings, canopies, patio covers and carports when your prospects understand the benefits. Your enthusiastic and knowledgeable description of the benefits should clinch the sale in most cases. Let's look at these benefits, starting with awnings.

Aluminum and fiberglass awnings have two major benefits. Emphasize both. First, awnings add to the beauty of a home. They make the home look more spacious, giving an extra dimension of depth. Second, they're functional protection against weather all during the year. They keep drapes, furniture and carpets from fading in direct sunlight. They keep the house cooler in the summer by intercepting the sun's rays — reducing the electricity needed for air conditioning. In winter they keep snow and ice from accumulating at the window and keep chilling winds away, reducing heat loss.

And here's the clincher. Modern awnings never need painting or maintenance. Aluminum has a lifetime baked enamel finish. Fiberglass awnings have color all the way through the material. The color lasts as long as the material itself. Aluminum and fiberglass don't rot or rust, and are just about impervious to normal wear and tear.

The prospects for an awning job probably know these benefits already, or they wouldn't have agreed to talk with you. But reinforce their thinking by ticking off the benefits.

If your prospect is tuned-in on cost savings, emphasize these facts. Any room with west-facing windows will be 8 to 15 degrees cooler on hot summer afternoons if the windows are shaded by awnings. That's the conclusion of tests made by the American Society of Heating, Refrigerating and Air-Conditioning Engineers (ASHRAE). The test was based on a 400-square foot room with two windows protected by aluminum awnings. In the test, a 110-volt, 3/4 horsepower air conditioning unit was able to handle the cooling load. Without the awnings, a 220-volt, one horsepower unit would be required. Awnings reduce both the cost of equipment required for cooling and the amount of electricity needed to operate that equipment.

According to a test made by the Bureau of Standards, awnings cut winter heating bills by reducing drafts from cold winter winds. This, of course, cuts fuel bills.

You can probably think of other benefits of awnings. There are others, such as added resale value, that I haven't mentioned. But the benefits listed here already should close most sales.

Canopies

Sell canopies the same way you sell awnings. The technique is similar because the products are similar. Canopies are like awnings, the difference being that canopies protect doorways. Awnings protect windows.

Start with the proposition that canopies are an

attractive addition to the exterior of a home. Then start listing the benefits. In hot weather, they protect the door from the blistering effects of the sun. In cold weather, they protect the doorway from winter winds, snow, sleet and blizzards. Canopies cut down on drafts. They keep accumulations of snow away from the door. During a rain storm, they protect the door, of course. But they also provide shelter while you're searching for the door key and opening the door.

Needless to say, door canopies protect carpets and floors by keeping snow, slush and rain away from the entryway. A canopy protects the home in all seasons of the year.

How to Measure Awnings and Canopies

Awnings and canopies have three dimensions: width, drop, and projection. Since awnings and canopies are sold by the square foot, you need to know how to compute the total footage from these three dimensions. Use Figure 14-1 to make the computations. Add the drop and the projection together. Use the combined figure to find square footage in the chart.

Awnings— They are usually mounted on the wood window frames. Measure the frame from edge to edge to determine the width. To determine the drop, measure from beneath the drip cap to at least the meeting rail (preferably to 2'' below the meeting rail). Make the projection 4'' less than the drop, unless the drop is 28'' or less. Then make the projection and the drop the same. For example, if the drop is 26'', the projection is also 26''.

Door canopies— The width and depth of the porch or stoop determines the size of the canopy. But the projection of the canopy must be 4'' more than the width of the storm door. To determine the drop, figure one-half of the projection. For example, if the projection is 38'', the drop should be 19''. The drop is important because it determines the slope of the canopy. It must slope enough to provide good drainage.

Patio Covers

When you're selling a patio cover, sell the benefits of the patio. A patio adds a new dimension to the home, increasing the living space and enjoyment. The patio becomes extra space for outdoor living, a place of relaxation, a place to have porch swings, hammocks, leisure chairs, a picnic area. A patio cover next to a swimming pool offers shelter from the sun's direct rays. It creates a place to lounge next to the pool, a place to chat, or relax after a swim.

A shaded patio is a wonderful place to relax with family or friends. But there are other benefits that may be even more important. A cover shades your home from the direct rays of the sun, making your home cooler in the summer and cutting air conditioning costs. In winter it provides shelter from icy blasts and snow, reducing heat loss and your fuel bill.

The patio cover provides shelter during a rain storm. And when it's only drizzling, anyone on the patio will still be protected from moisture.

A patio cover both increases the value of your home and improves its appearance. Of course, aluminum and fiberglass patio covers need no maintenance. That's a real benefit. They never have to be painted.

Carports

The benefits of a carport are obvious. But in selling, it's always important to stress the benefits. Don't assume your buyers already know how beneficial their new carport will be.

A freestanding or attached carport in aluminum or fiberglass will keep the car cooler in the heat of summer. The car won't be like an oven when you get in it at midday, with the steering wheel too hot to touch. And there are few things worse for a car's paint job than baking in the sun. In winter the carport will protect the car from snow and sleet. If you can locate the carport correctly, it will keep ice from accumulating on the windshield. That could put an end to scraping and brushing windows during storms. It also protects you when trying to get a key in the car lock during winter's icy blizzards.

Get the Prospect Involved

It's good sales technique to keep your prospects involved and active during the sales presentation. An excellent way to do this is to have the homeowner help take measurements while you're discussing the benefits. You can't quote a price until measurements are taken, and measurements go faster if you have someone to help hold the tape, hold curtains or shades out of the way, move furniture, hold your pad, or write down figures as you do the measuring.

A homeowner involved with your measurements has taken the first steps toward assenting to the sale. And that's the tone you want to project. You are assuming the sale and want the homeowners to do the same.

Drop plus projection	36"	40"	44"	48"	52"	56"	60"	64"	Width 68"	72"	76"	80"	84"	88"	92"	96"	100"	104"
36"	12	13	14	15	16	17	18	19	20	21	22	23	24	25	26	27	28	29
40"	13	14	15	16	18	19	20	21	22	23	24	25	27	28	29	30	31	32
44"	15	16	17	18	19	21	22	23	24	25	27	28	29	30	31	33	34	35
48"	16	17	19	20	21	23	24	25	26	28	29	30	31	33	34	35	37	38
52"	17	18	20	21	23	24	25	27	28	29	30	32	33	34	36	37	38	40
56"	18	20	21	23	24	25	27	28	30	31	32	34	35	37	38	39	41	42
60"	20	21	23	24	26	27	29	30	32	33	35	36	38	39	41	42	44	45
64"	22	23	25	26	28	29	31	32	34	35	37	39	42	42	43	45	47	48
68"	23	25	26	28	30	31	33	35	36	38	40	41	43	45	46	48	50	51
72"	25	27	28	30	32	34	35	37	39	41	42	44	46	48	49	51	53	55
76"	27	28	30	32	35	36	38	39	41	43	45	47	49	50	52	54	56	58
80"	29	31	33	35	36	38	40	42	44	46	48	50	51	53	55	57	59	61
84"	31	33	35	37	39	41	43	45	47	49	51	53	55	57	59	61	63	65
88"	33	35	37	39	41	43	45	47	49	51	54	56	58	60	62	64	66	68
92"	34	37	39	41	43	45	47	50	52	54	56	58	60	63	65	67	69	71
96"	37	39	41	43	46	48	50	52	55	57	59	62	64	66	68	71	73	75
100"	38	41	43	45	48	50	52	55	57	59	62	64	67	69	71	74	76	78
104"	40	42	45	47	50	52	55	57	59	62	64	67	69	72	74	77	79	81
108"	42	45	47	50	52	55	57	60	63	65	68	70	73	75	78	80	83	86
112"	43	46	49	51	54	56	59	62	64	67	79	72	75	77	80	82	85	88
116"	45	47	50	53	55	58	61	63	66	69	71	74	76	79	82	84	87	90
120"	46	49	51	54	57	60	62	65	68	70	73	76	78	81	84	86	89	92
124"	47	50	53	56	58	61	64	67	69	72	75	77	80	83	86	88	91	94

Note: Add drop and projection. Find the total in the left-hand column, then move across the page to correct width. The number in that column is square feet of awning area.

Awning and canopy measuring chart
Figure 14-1

Drop plus projection	Width																	
	108"	112"	116"	120"	124"	128"	132"	136"	140"	144"	148"	152"	156"	160"	164"	168"	172"	176"
36"	30	31	32	33	34	35	37	38	39	40	41	42	43	44	45	46	47	48
40"	33	34	35	37	38	39	40	41	42	43	44	46	47	48	49	50	51	52
44"	36	37	39	40	41	42	43	45	46	47	48	49	51	52	53	54	55	57
48"	39	40	42	43	44	46	47	48	49	51	52	53	55	56	57	58	60	61
52"	41	42	44	45	46	48	49	50	52	53	54	56	57	58	60	61	62	63
56"	44	45	46	48	49	51	52	53	55	56	58	59	60	62	63	65	66	67
60"	47	48	50	51	53	54	55	57	58	60	61	63	64	66	68	69	70	72
64"	50	51	53	54	56	57	59	61	62	64	65	67	68	70	71	73	75	76
68"	53	55	56	58	60	61	63	65	67	68	70	72	73	75	77	78	80	82
72"	57	58	60	62	64	65	67	69	71	72	74	76	78	79	81	83	85	86
76"	60	62	63	65	67	69	71	73	74	76	78	80	82	84	85	87	89	91
80"	63	65	67	68	70	72	74	76	78	80	82	83	85	87	89	91	93	95
84"	67	69	71	73	75	77	79	81	83	85	87	89	91	93	95	97	99	101
88"	70	72	74	76	78	81	83	85	87	89	91	93	95	97	99	101	103	106
92"	73	75	78	81	82	84	86	88	91	93	95	97	99	101	104	106	109	110
96"	78	80	82	84	87	89	91	94	96	98	100	103	105	107	109	112	114	116
100"	81	83	85	88	90	93	95	97	100	102	104	107	109	111	114	116	118	121
104"	84	86	89	91	94	96	99	101	103	105	108	111	113	116	118	120	123	125
108"	88	91	93	96	99	101	103	106	109	111	114	116	119	121	124	127	129	132
112"	90	93	95	98	101	103	106	108	111	114	116	119	121	124	127	129	132	134
116"	92	95	98	100	103	105	108	111	113	116	119	121	124	127	129	132	135	137
120"	94	97	100	103	105	108	110	113	116	118	121	124	127	129	132	135	137	140
124"	96	99	102	105	107	110	113	115	118	121	124	126	129	132	135	137	140	143

Note: Add drop and projection. Find the total in the left-hand column, then move across the page to correct width. The number in that column is square feet of awning area.

Awning and canopy measuring chart
Figure 14-1 (continued)

Before beginning the measurements, take out your color samples and hand them to the lady of the house. Say, "I'll appreciate it if you could select the colors you prefer while your husband and I are taking measurements." This way you've involved her in the sale. I always leave the husband out of the color selection process. The woman picks out the color and style 99% of the time. You may want to add, "Why not pick out two choices in case your husband doesn't like your first choice."

Demonstration
The demonstration plays a big part in selling awnings. Fiberglass awnings are a natural for demonstrations. Take a small piece of fiberglass

and try to scratch it with a key. "See, this fiberglass doesn't scratch, the colors go all the way through the material." Take a piece of fiberglass and stand on it.

"You see, I weigh 170 pounds. My weight has no effect on this piece. Pound for pound, fiberglass is stronger than steel. It can stand the heaviest snow loads in winter. All the new boats and yachts you see in the harbor have fiberglass hulls. Fiberglass is sturdy, won't rot, doesn't need repairs and is almost impervious to damage.

"Fiberglass is probably the greatest structural material invented by man since the invention of steel. It's taking over the roofing market and I wouldn't be surprised to see the day when they make beams out of fiberglass instead of steel. So the awnings our company will manufacture for you, which are custom designed to fit your actual windows in the style and color you prefer, will be made out of this amazing material and will last a lifetime.

"By the way, the frame of the awnings will be aluminum which is anodized, so it won't pit or get discolored. Our awnings are installed by our own workmen, who are bonded, and covered by worker's compensation and public liability insurance. We offer an easy monthly payment plan down at First National Bank. Do you bank there? No? Well, I can take an application for you and the monthly payments will only be $26.50 for 60 months. Would you prefer a smaller payment or a shorter term? I can arrange it. Just tell me what you prefer. O.K. Let's use the kitchen table and I'll write up the order. Our foreman will recheck the measurements in a couple of days just before we put your order into production."

Does that sales pitch sound like a winner? It should. I've used it successfully many times.

Chapter 15
Selling Bathroom Remodeling

Bathroom remodeling is big ticket work. When your prospects want the bathroom remodeled, they want more than three new plumbing fixtures. If that was all they wanted, they would just call a plumber. They want something that will reflect favorably on their taste and preferences. They want more than the purely functional, conventional 5' x 7' bathroom intended only for washing and bathing. They want more than a utilitarian, nondescript, hotel-like bathroom.

The look of the master bathroom is the second or third most important feature that women consider when buying a new home. The kitchen is probably first, followed by the bath and then space for furniture in the dining area, bedrooms and living room. A woman assumes that the bath will be functional. That goes without saying. But she also wants it to be a showplace she can be proud of.

As a salesman, you should make one point very clearly when closing on a bathroom job. Impress both the husband and wife with this point: When you get finished with the bath, it will be beautiful. They'll be proud to show it to friends and neighbors. You're going to provide a luxurious, stylish bathroom that is both functional and spacious. They'll use it with pride for many years. And when it comes time to sell, the remodeled bath will attract buyers and recover the purchase price plus about 50% more.

Start selling a bathroom job by qualifying your prospects — both as to ability to pay and their needs. Answers to the following questions will provide all the information you need:

1) Is this bathroom intended primarily as a powder room for use by guests?

2) Is this the master bathroom used primarily by a husband and wife? If so, is it also a dressing area for them?

3) Is this a family bathroom used primarily by two or more children?

Next, study the floor plan. It's hard to do much on a grand scale if space is limited to 4' by 5'. Can space be added to the present area? Can an adjacent pantry or walk-in closet be added to the bath area? Can some part of an adjoining bedroom or porch be absorbed into the bath area? Can you cantilever a bathroom addition over an exterior wall? Can space be "borrowed" from an attached garage? If you can find a few extra feet, consider dividing the bath into two areas with a partition separating the water closet and shower area from the grooming and wash basin area.

If more space isn't available, judicious use of mirrors can create the illusion of space. And there's always a little more space available. Just remove the wallboard between two studs and install an exposed linen shelf in the wall cavity.

Deciding on the Fixtures

After the room size has been set, the selection of fixtures becomes the next important item. The choice between white and colored fixtures is a decision the homemaker will usually make. I recommend white fixtures. Here's why. If you get burgundy, blue or some other color, you're stuck with that color scheme in the bathroom for life. Here's my pitch:

"I bet you're like my wife and want a change of scenery every once in a while. Nobody wants the same colors in a room forever. If you *may* want a change of color some day, white is your best choice. Everything goes with white fixtures. You can change your accessories whenever the mood strikes you. Your choice of color for guest towels, Kleenex holder, curtains, bath mat, and wallpaper aren't limited by the color of the fixtures. With white fixtures you still can use plenty of color. But you're free to change at any time."

This pitch works 99% of the time. It is true, as far as the statements go. But there are other good reasons to avoid color fixtures. It saves time with the customer while she decides on the color she wants. It saves time on callbacks when the fixtures don't exactly match the sample or don't exactly match each other. It prevents delays when your supplier is out of that particular shade of lavender tub. It prevents disappointments when the manufacturer has discontinued slow-selling lavender fixtures entirely.

True, the color surcharge yields a few dollars in extra profit. But forget it. Those dollars aren't worth the trouble.

Picking the Sink

The old wall-hung lavatory that had chrome legs and side towel bars is now a thing of the past. Don't even think about it. Even vanities with his and her bowls are taking a back seat to sleek contemporary pedestal sinks that bear little resemblance to the familiar pedestal sink that we used to see in barber shops. These new pedestal sinks come in a variety of colors and shapes. They have only one functional drawback. There's no storage space under the sink. In bathrooms that have room for a linen closet or even a big (48" or 72" wide) medicine cabinet, contemporary pedestal sinks are a good choice. They add a contemporary accent to the remodeled bathroom.

After you've settled on either a sink or a vanity,

pick out the style. Color brochures are essential here. Do you want a white vanity with gold trim or a natural finish fruitwood vanity? A cultured marble sink? A shell styled bowl? A bowl with a Grecian pattern? Some other pattern? A plain white or colored bowl?

Then select the counter top. Laminated plastic such as Formica with a 4" backsplash is the standard. You can do better in this bathroom. Cultured marble? Ceramic tile? What color?

Next comes the question of faucets, handles and spouts. The choice is between a single-lever faucet and separate hot and cold faucets. More than enough styles and price ranges are available to please every taste, whim and pocketbook. Give your prospects the widest possible variety to select from. Some will want brass and hardwood, others may prefer porcelain and brass with dainty flowers, another may even fall in love with a brass swan head and neck with upright wings, or perhaps brass with cut crystal handles.

Handle and spout selection may be the primary reason why one contractor is selected over another to do the job. I know. I've seen it happen. The fact that you can supply a particular piece of hardware may guarantee that you do the work.

If your buyer can't decide on the hardware, don't let the sale get hung up on that point. Write a fitting allowance into the contract:

At a later date Buyer will select sink and shower fittings consisting of valves, handles, spouts and shower head. Contractor will install these fittings and has included an allowance of $350 in the contract price to pay for these fittings. If the cost exceeds $350, Buyer will pay to Contractor the excess. If the cost is less than $350, Contractor will credit Buyer for the difference.

Selecting an Elegant Tub

Now start talking about the tub. There are two ways of looking at a tub. First, it could be just a functional part of the bathroom. But it can also be a reflection of the owner's lifestyle. If you can find space, suggest a whirlpool or soaking tub rather than a simple 5' tub. If space isn't available, at least recommend a tub with a hydromassage unit, double contour backrests, slip resistant bottom, grab bar, angled arm rests, beveled head rest or built-in lumbar support system.

Be aware of new trends in fixtures. Suggesting these modern fixtures to prospects identifies you as a bathroom designer and puts you a step ahead of other contractors who have never installed anything but a 5' white tub. Suggest contemporary fixtures. Have sales literature ready to show your prospects. Most plumbing supply houses have stacks of color flyers that promote the lines they carry. Your prospects may not be interested. But for those who are, you're ready.

But be aware that some of these modern fixtures come with installation problems. Whirlpool and soaking tubs require steps up the side of the tub. Usually these steps are done in ceramic tile. Sunken tubs aren't practical when remodeling a second story bathroom. Ask your plumbing sub for help in anticipating problems like this.

Here are some of my favorite tubs. One of these will be perfect for almost any situation. I try to offer at least one of these on every bathroom job.

1) Vintage tub by Kohler

2) Infinity whirlpool tub by Kohler

3) Continental tub by Eljer

4) Tranquility whirlpool tub by Owens Corning Fiberglass

5) Lexington whirlpool tub by American Standard (fits 5' tub area)

6) Greek tub by Kohler. (A 48" by 22" deep fiberglass reinforced acrylic tub designed for limited space. Deep enough for tall bathers.)

Usually your prospect will want a shower over the tub. That makes some kind of an enclosure or shower curtain essential around the tub. But it's a shame to enclose one of these elegant tubs. Instead, if there's room, suggest a separate shower stall in a corner. Install ceramic tile up two walls, lay a receptor on the floor, and enclose the other two sides with glass panels. If you have 36" along two walls at a corner, you have room for a shower stall.

Fiberglass shower stalls are also available. Some of the better units are both attractive and durable. But be sure the unit you select will fit through the doorway. Some larger units have to be installed before the walls are enclosed. Don't wait till the new stall is jammed in the doorway to discover this.

If there's no room for a separate shower stall, suggest a tub enclosure with obscure glass or a frosted design. Mirrored glass is also available. A mirrored glass enclosure with bronze anodized aluminum trim gives a feeling of depth and opulence that your prospects will appreciate.

Selecting the tub material also deserves some thought. Tubs come in cast iron, steel and fiberglass. If the style selected is available in all three, ask, "Do you want the tub in cast iron, steel or fiberglass? Cast iron costs a little more, but has its advantages. Cast iron tubs keep the water warm longer and muffle the sound of running water better. The finish is more durable because the tub doesn't flex when used."

Tub color should be no problem. It will be the same as the water closet and the sink.

Remember, you're selling a feeling of luxury, not just a cosmetic fixture change. It's excitement and anticipation that close the sale. You're creating a room of beauty that your competitors can't match. There's no way to compare what you propose with what others may offer. It would be like comparing fine wine with grape juice.

The Water Closet

The next fixture to discuss is the toilet. Without some other suggestion, you'll sell a standard grade close-coupled water closet. Instead, offer a low profile, quiet flush model that complements the other fixtures. Most remodeling contractors supply only low cost, commodity grade toilets. Give your prospects a wider choice. Explain the advantages of contemporary fixtures. You're up-to-date on fixture style and features and can recommend the water closet that will best complement the bathroom your prospects have in mind. You'll quote prices on any fixture, of course. But ask Mr. and Mrs. Homeowner to consider one of the attractive, contemporary toilets now available.

Watch a few points when selling a new toilet. Is the old floor so rotten that it will have to be replaced or built up? This would mean adding a collar to the soil stack. If the toilet is very old, you may need to rough in a new arm to the soil stack so the fixture can reach it. Is the present piping lead? It's harder to extend lead pipe than more modern cast iron pipe. Is there a fixture wall valve on the water supply line under the toilet? Modern codes require it. If not, include it in the job and charge for it.

Make it clear that your company does only first class work. A first class job requires a wall stop valve under the toilet. If the toilet backs up, the valve lets you shut off the water. This will be another plus in your favor when the prospects evaluate competitive bids. You're bidding a quality job. Others may not be doing the same.

The Bidet

The bidet (pronounced be-DAY) is a fourth bathroom fixture. You won't see it often, but I've sold some, usually where the bathroom area was large. In parts of Europe it's considered primitive to have a bathroom without one.

Evaluate your prospect before trying to make this sale. If they've never heard of a bidet, any sales pitch is a waste of time. But if they've travelled a great deal in Europe, are immigrants, or have friends that use a bidet, they know exactly what you're selling. Usually, if you sell one in this country, it's sold primarily on snob appeal. They've seen it in a magazine, or they've seen one in someone else's plush bathroom and don't want to be outdone. If you're selling in that kind of market, give it a try.

Bathroom Finishes

The next item to consider is the wall finish. Does your owner want tile only in the tub area? Or is tile to go on other walls? How high on the walls? How about the ceiling? Keep asking questions, getting answers. Every time you ask a question, the owners recognize that a decision is needed. Every decision is one step closer to getting a signature on the dotted line. Time spent making decisions reinforces the assumption that you'll get the job.

When the question of wallpaper or paint comes up, consider leaving that work to your prospects. There's very little wall area in a bathroom to paint or paper. You can't charge enough for that work to make the aggravation worthwhile. A contractor who builds a spec house paints and papers any way he wants. But helping Mr. and Mrs. American Homeowner select a few square feet of wallpaper or a pint of paint is a lost cause. The first attempt will seldom be exactly what they had in mind.

You can waste hours getting a paint shade just right. Suppose you agree to paint the wall the same color as the tie Mr. Homeowner hands you. Time passes, the painter you hire can't satisfy the owner on the color. In the can, the paint looked O.K. But once it dried on the wall, it was all wrong. The painter wants to get paid anyway, insisting that the owner is a nut. No one can satisfy him. The painter quits. But that doesn't end your problem. You want to collect for the job. You offer to settle with a credit for the unpainted wall. That credit has to come out of your profit, of course. Hiring a different painter would prolong the job, delay collection, and still may not satisfy Mr. Homeowner.

Even if the second painter does satisfy the owners, they're mad now and feel you're trying to skip out without finishing. They want a discount for aggravation suffered. The only way out now may be to give a cash allowance so they can hire their own painter. You end up paying for the paint job two or three times.

Here's a sales pitch that will make hiring a painter more palatable to the homeowners:

"You know, Mrs. Homeowner, we're carpenters and general contractors. We sub out the painting and, of course, have to add our markup to the cost. You can save our overhead and profit by hiring your own painter. Work with that painter directly. I can recommend several painters in this area who are highly respected."

Deciding on Flooring

Sheet goods are the popular choice in a bathroom. But maybe your prospects prefer vinyl tile. Do they want ceramic mosaics? Do they want quarry tile or maybe even marble? But remember that ceramic tile and marble are slippery when wet.

Carpet makes a good bathroom floor. But carpet can't be laid over a deteriorated floor. Either put Masonite underlayment over the existing floor, or strip off the flooring to expose the original underlayment.

Let your prospects select the carpet on their own. Handle this with an allowance in the contract. The area will be small, so the cost of installation will probably be the installer's minimum charge. This minimum, when added to the carpet price, will seem exorbitant to the owners. If so, let the owners take care of it.

Consider a loose-laid carpet in the bathroom. That way it can be removed easily for drying if it gets saturated. The owner can probably fit the carpet himself and save quite a bit of money. Unless you're laying other carpet in the house, leave the carpeting to others.

Lighting and Heating

Good lighting is essential in a stylish bathroom. A single fixture on the ceiling or over the medicine cabinet is fine in a warehouse. But it isn't enough in an elegant bathroom. Luminous ceilings with either pebbled or ornamental lighting panels provide good illumination and show off the bathroom to good advantage. But fluorescent lighting is harsh and uncomplimentary. It makes facial features seem sharp, making both Mr. and Mrs. Homeowner look older than they are, or at least, than they want to look. Consider combining fluorescent area lighting with incandescent task lighting in front of the medicine cabinet.

Provide a theatrical-style lighting strip over or on both sides of the mirror. That provides good but flattering light when Mrs. Homeowner is putting on her makeup. Offer several choices in lighting strips. And be sure each style selected will harmonize with the general decor of the room.

I suggest that you carry a lighting fixture catalog in your sales kit. Let your prospects select the fixtures they want. Write the name and model number of each into the contract. But be sure the contract says, "subject to availability" so conditions beyond your control don't delay completion. I sometimes write a second choice into the contract to protect myself.

Always consider ventilation when remodeling a bathroom. Many old houses have a small double hung window over the tub area. High moisture has probably caused the window to deteriorate badly. Replace the window with obscure glass block. Then install an exhaust fan to improve ventilation. This makes a window curtain unnecessary, provides better ventilation, gives light without loss of privacy and gets rid of the rotting wood window. If your prospect insists on a window over the tub, replace the window and provide a Formica sill that can tolerate constant moisture.

Always include an exhaust fan in bathrooms that don't have a window. The fan will reduce condensation, humidity and odor problems. Many combination fans are available. Some include fan, light and heat lamp in one compact unit. If the fan doesn't incorporate a heating unit, consider an electric wall heater. But don't forget to charge for the electrical requirements: a separate circuit, a switch and a run from the GFCI switch to the appliance.

Old gravity heat systems had larger ducts and grilles than modern forced air systems need. If a forced air system has replaced gravity heat in the house you're working in, consider installing a contemporary, smaller grille in the remodeled bathroom. And be sure that the grille opening is reduced before ceramic tile or other wall finish is applied. It's easy to overlook something like this, but the owner expects you to anticipate such problems. Just point out in your sales pitch that, of course, the grille will be replaced with a modern unit.

Here's a list of the items your client should consider in a bathroom job. Each has a cost that should be listed in your price book.

1) *Carpentry*
   a) Remove existing wall.
   b) Frame new wall.
   c) Install new door and frame.
   d) Replace a window.
   e) Install suspended ceiling for luminous panels.
   f) Install medicine cabinet and mirrors.
   g) Lay new floor underlayment.
   h) Build linen closet or shelves.
   i) Set vanity cabinet.

2) *Plumbing*
   a) Lavatories
   b) Water closet
   c) Tub
   d) Shower head, stall
   e) Bidet
   f) Change supply, drain or vent piping, and shut-off valves.

3) *Finishes*
   a) Ceramic tile - wall, bath, shower, floor
   b) Flooring - vinyl, carpet, tile, sheet goods.

4) *Electrical*
   a) New circuits run to panel
   b) New switches
   c) New fixtures — light, fan, heat
   d) New wall outlets
   e) New ground fault interrupter
   f) Bring wiring up to code

5) *Miscellaneous*
   a) Medicine cabinets
   b) Towel bars, hooks, accessories
   c) Debris removal
   d) Building permit
   e) Glass block

Consider the Pitfalls

Use the survey questions in Figure 15-1 to help you avoid the costly traps in bathroom remodeling.

As I pointed out at the beginning of this chapter, the bathroom remodeling business is a fashion and glamor business. Stay up with trends and styles. Subscribe to a shelter magazine that shows current trends in bath remodeling. Be a bath remodeling expert. That expertise will pay off on every bath job you sell. Your confidence when talking with a prospect will inspire confidence in your counsel. That's going to bring in a lot of profitable business.

Survey of Pitfalls — Bathroom Remodeling

Before pricing the remodeling of a bathroom, make a survey of the problems that might be encountered.

Your survey should ask these questions:

1) Is the present plumbing lead?

2) Is the toilet the old-fashioned wall-hung type with a flush elbow? If so, a new close-coupled toilet can't be installed in the same location. Be sure to charge for roughing in at the new location and new floor underlayment.

3) Will the new toilet location be within 5 feet of the soil stack?

4) Do the current fixtures have shut-off valves?

5) Will heat ducts, radiators or electric lines have to be relocated?

6) Will a riser have to be installed for the shower head?

7) Will removal of the tub cause damage to the walls?

8) Do the present walls have a plastic or tile finish that will have to be removed? Removing any tile or wallboard may make it necessary to replace all tile or wallboard on that wall.

9) Do the present electrical outlets meet current code requirements? If not, they may have to be brought up to code.

10) Is the present ceiling fixture operated by a pull chain? Charge to install new wiring to a wall switch.

11) If the linoleum or tile floor is badly rotted, assume the underlayment is spongy and charge for replacement.

Survey of pitfalls in bathroom remodeling
Figure 15-1

Chapter 16

Selling Ceilings

Work done on ceilings is usually part of a larger remodeling job. Once in awhile, however, you'll get a lead for just ceiling work. There are four general types of ceiling sales: conversions, fire repairs, other repairs, and new construction. We'll cover them one at a time.

Conversions

A pure ceiling conversion lead can usually be upgraded to include more work. Try to expand the job to include windows, a ceiling fan or perhaps even a completely remodeled kitchen.

Dome Ceilings and Ceiling Fans

Dome ceilings are popular ceiling conversions, especially in condos with suspended ceilings. To create an illuminated dome ceiling, first remove the existing suspended ceiling. Then install a curved suspended ceiling with luminous panels around the perimeter of the room. The panels can be prismatic white, mist, or pebbled, whatever your supplier stocks. Next, finish off the existing ceiling with white Marlite. Be sure to include fluorescent fixtures and the wall switch. Sell a dimmer switch if you use incandescent lighting.

Dome ceilings are perfect for kitchens because they allow more light and make it possible to install a ceiling fan. Before air conditioning became common, many commercial buildings had ceiling fans.

Today, the high cost of energy is making ceiling paddle fans practical again. They do a good job of dispersing hot air that accumulates at the ceiling during meal preparation, thus making the kitchen more comfortable. And they save energy by reducing air conditioning requirements. There are many days when it's not hot enough to run an air conditioner but it's still too hot for comfort in the kitchen. A paddle fan keeps the kitchen comfortable without the expense of cooling the entire house.

When you're installing a ceiling fan, it's important to pick the right size. For rooms up to 9' by 12', use a 36'' diameter fan. This is large enough for small kitchens, bedrooms or utility rooms. Install a 48'' fan for living or family rooms up to 12' by 15'. Recommend a 56'' fan for rooms larger than 12' by 15'. An undersized fan won't do the job.

Ceiling fans are available with wood, metal or lucite blades. Discuss the different options with your prospect. Metal blades move more air than wooden blades. They're even more effective with the ends curved upwards. Four blades move more air than three blades. Some fans come with a built-in light fixture. Be sure the fan you recommend has a switch to regulate the fan speed. That makes it even more energy efficient.

An illuminated dome ceiling with a paddle fan adds a touch or charm and luxury to any kitchen. When your customer's friends and neighbors see it, you'll probably get calls for similar jobs.

It should be fairly easy to convert a kitchen ceiling lead into a complete kitchen remodeling job. Consider new cabinets, counter tops, sink, flooring, windows and an electrical upgrade. It works the other way around, too. If you have a kitchen remodeling lead, try to include a ceiling conversion in the job.

Sell just one luminous dome ceiling in a neighborhood. Word of mouth will keep you busy with dome ceiling jobs in that neighborhood for quite a while.

Beam Ceilings

Another common ceiling conversion is installation of a beam ceiling. Ceiling beams are easy to sell because they're an inexpensive way to change the decor of a room. Many homeowners associate a beam ceiling with wealth. Ceiling beams add a feeling of stability in a room.

Beams are usually installed in a living room or den. You can install ready-made ceiling beams or have your carpenters build them on the job. Consider the new styrofoam beams. They look so real that they'll fool everyone but the owner who pays the bill and the tradesman who lifts them into place.

Fire Repairs

In fire repair jobs, the ceiling is probably water-soaked and smoke stained. If the ceiling is plaster, it's probably badly cracked and buckled in places. A drywall ceiling will have many nail pops. Before the fire the nails were invisible. After the fire, many nails will have popped up above the surface. Those that haven't popped will be highly visible. Smoke seems to find each nail and discolor the head.

Selling fire repair work should be more than just restoring the room to its original condition. This is the time to suggest that homeowners upgrade or modernize their home. It's a real opportunity for them to make the changes that they've dreamed about. Those dreams can now come true. A fire can be a blessing in disguise. The house is already torn up from the fire, and the repair work has to be done. It will cost a lot less to upgrade now, while your men and equipment are already on the job. You can help them finance the cost of the job that goes beyond the insurance settlement.

Ask the homeowners what improvements they have in mind. You'll be surprised how much additional work you can pick up. It might lead to a complete kitchen or bath remodeling, room enlargement, or new aluminum siding or trim.

Other Ceiling Repairs

Every type of ceiling is subject to damage. Plaster can crack and fall, ceiling tiles can drop off as the adhesive ages. Water from an overflowing tub above or a leaky roof can stain and damage any ceiling.

The key to selling ceiling repairs is working out the financing, if the job is large enough. Today, most home improvement lenders have a minimum loan amount. The same is true for some home improvement contractors. On a minimum sale, the paperwork and collection efforts can eat up all the profit. Yet I have seen many ceiling leads turn into quite large jobs. It's common with a ceiling lead to find that the kitchen or bath also needs repairs. A ceiling repair lead is a good lead if you see the opportunities.

Plaster Ceilings

Replastering a deteriorated plaster ceiling may not be a good choice. When a prospect asks for a bid on replastering a cracked ceiling, explain that breaking out the old ceiling, shoveling up the debris and hauling it away can be a major task. In cold weather, plaster dries very slowly without sufficient heat. That can make replastering a lengthy task. And after it's replastered, the homeowner will have to paint it. There are better ways to go.

Of course, you could install drywall over the old plaster ceiling. But there will be a minimum charge, even for a small room. The drywall taper will have to make several trips to complete the job. And the owner is still faced with a painting job. In most communities, the building code requires 5/8" drywall for ceilings. Again, drywall may not be the best choice.

Suspended Ceilings

Modern suspended ceilings have many advantages. First, they're very attractive. Second, you can drop the ceiling from nine feet (the common ceiling height in older homes) to eight feet (the standard for modern homes). This gives the homeowner less space to heat and cool, so he'll save on energy costs. Third, the suspended ceiling never needs painting. If it's stained by a water leak, the homeowner can just dry off the panel or replace it by dropping a new panel into place.

This is the easiest ceiling to sell and the most practical for the average homeowner. But there's one problem to consider before you bring it up. Take a quick look at the windows. In many old homes the windows go up almost to the ceiling. Then there's no room for dropping the ceiling unless, of course, you can sell the homeowner on the idea of changing his windows.

There's a lot to sell in modern windows. They snap out for convenience, have less heat loss in the winter, and save on air conditioning in the summer. The dropped ceiling is a natural lead into this type of sale. Adding in the cost of the windows might make the sale large enough to finance. The homeowner gets a new modern ceiling, new windows and perhaps new storm windows and screens. You can do it all at the same time for one small monthly payment.

Acoustical Tile

If you can't drop the ceiling, sell acoustical tile over the present ceiling. If the existing ceiling is in very bad condition, plan on laying 1" by 2" furring strips over the plaster and under the new tile. Here are the benefits you're selling: The homeowner gets a modern look, the ceiling doesn't need to be painted and the finish ceiling absorbs stray noise. You can install the tiles with nails, staples or clips. Be sure to charge for furring.

Luminous Ceilings

If the bathroom or kitchen ceiling is damaged, sell a luminous ceiling. It's an easy way to modernize the bath or kitchen. There are two things to consider when selling a luminous ceiling. Since it's a dropped ceiling, first check the height of the windows. Second, consider the electrical requirements. Many old houses have string-operated light fixtures. In this case you'll have to install a wall switch in addition to the fluorescent light fixtures and luminous panels.

This is often a good time to upgrade the entire electrical system in the kitchen. The electrician will be there to install the new ceiling lights. Suggest that now's the time to install the additional outlets that every old kitchen needs. That saves the cost of another trip by an electrician later. This suggestion will usually increase the value of your sale, especially when it can be added to the loan for just a few dollars more per month.

New Construction

Most ceiling jobs are part of a room addition, attic conversion or perhaps a recreation room in the basement. When installing a new ceiling, don't take anything for granted. Don't assume that a plain drywall or plaster ceiling will do. Suggest alternatives to upgrade the sale. If the owner wants a plaster ceiling, try to upgrade to a swirl ceiling. Where it's appropriate, suggest installing beams, a suspended ceiling with luminous panels, acoustical tile, ceramic tile in a bathroom, or a dome ceiling in the kitchen. It doesn't cost you one red cent to make the suggestion. And every upgrade increases your profit. Remember the old adage: nothing ventured, nothing gained.

Chapter 17

Selling Concrete Work

Since most concrete work is part of a remodeling job, your sales presentation is based on the entire project. The cost of the cement work is part of the total package. The prospect won't shop for bids on the concrete section of the job only.

The sales problem arises when you get a lead for concrete work only. The prospect tells you what he wants to have done. The homeowner can use the Yellow Pages to find any number of concrete contractors and get several competitive bids. To him, concrete work is concrete work. Your interest is to avoid a low-bidding war and still get the job. This is where selling skill comes in.

Sell Your Skill and Reputation
Sell the benefits of doing business with *your* company. Here are some of the benefits you can name. You'll probably be able to add a few of your own.

1) We're a reputable company, in business for ten years now. Our reputation is what separates us from the fly-by-night companies that do shoddy work and then aren't around when you have a complaint. Our reputation is our most valuable asset. We aren't going to risk losing it.

2) We're licensed, bonded and insured. This means our men are covered by Worker's Compensation and liability insurance. You don't have to worry if a man gets injured on the job. We have full insurance. Even though we're very careful, accidents can happen. A man can get hurt by a paving breaker, or a jackhammer, even a pickaxe. These are dangerous tools, even in the hands of an experienced worker. Anything can happen on a construction project. We're also covered by insurance in case there's any damage to your shrubs or other property. We don't expect any problems, but accidents do happen. Since we're fully protected, that's one less problem for *you* to worry about.

3) Our men are skilled professionals and have been with us a long time. They know not to leave any trash on your property. You won't find any banana peels or beer cans laying around. Drinking on the job is definitely out. Our men are orderly and polite. There won't be any cussing. You'd be surprised what you can hear on some jobs.

4) Our finishers are experienced in commercial and residential jobs. Finishing is the key to any good cement work. When the job is done, you won't find any "dishes" in your patio or driveway. A dish is a low spot in the surface where water collects. We'll give you a smooth surface that drains like water off a duck's back. I'm sure that's what you want. We do only first-class work. That's what you want and what we're noted for.

Customer name _____ Phone_____

Address_____ City, Zip_____

Work ordered	**Size**
Apron _____	_____
Slab _____	_____
Driveway _____	_____
Parkway _____	_____
Patio _____	_____
Sidewalk _____	_____
Stoop, stairs _____	_____
Curb _____	_____
Piers _____	_____
Concrete breakout _____	_____
Other _____	_____

Specifications

Thickness _____	Plat of survey furnished _____
Bag mix _____	Rear line setback _____
Color _____	Side line setback _____
Finish_____	Setback from house to apron _____
Wood dividers _____	Other instructions _____
Drain tile _____	_____
Wire mesh _____	_____
Rods _____	_____
Retaining wall needed _____	_____
Fill needed_____	_____

Salesman _____   Owner _____

Date _____   Owner _____

Concrete work order
Figure 17-1

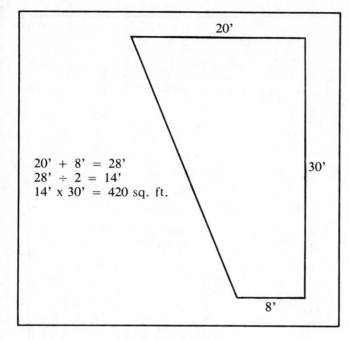

20' + 8' = 28'
28' ÷ 2 = 14'
14' x 30' = 420 sq. ft.

Figuring square feet
Figure 17-2

5)   When the job is done, we'll pick up all the form material and haul away the dirt and debris. If you'd prefer us to leave the dirt because you have use for it, no problem. Would you like us to spread the dirt behind the garage? Or in that low spot in the yard? Of course, we'll also haul away the broken concrete. You probably don't want *that* around.

6)   We'll leave the forms on until the concrete is properly set. Some companies strip the job right away because they need the forms on another job. We have plenty of forms. Rest assured that your concrete will be cured properly.

7)   The foreman on the job will check the weather conditions for you. He'll tell you if the concrete has to be watered for proper setting, and for how long.

8)   This job calls for a six-bag mix. Let me explain what that is. Most contractors won't explain it because they don't want you to know. Concrete isn't all the same. It's sold by the *mix*. A *five-bag mix* means five bags of Portland cement for each cubic yard of concrete. A *six-bag mix* means six bags of cement for each cubic yard. The more ce-

ment in the mix, the stronger the concrete. We never use less than a five-bag mix. I suggest that you have us use a six-bag mix. It's only a few dollars more, but you'll have a job that will last and last. Let me figure up the difference in cost for you.

(This sales pitch does two things at once. You've upgraded the sale *and* led into a strong closing statement.)

9)   We'll give you a waiver of lien when the job is finished, showing that all the labor and material is paid for.

10)   We have a good financing plan. We've been a dealer with the National Savings and Loan for eight years. We can do the work for no money down and finance it under the FHA for about $25.00 a month. I've figured these payments on a 60-month loan. That's what most homeowners want. If you'd like a shorter term or prefer a smaller payment, I'll work it out. I can schedule the job for the week after next. Your first payment won't be due until two months after we finish the work. Why don't we step into the kitchen? I'll just use the kitchen table to write up the order. The paperwork will take only a few minutes.

These are the benefits you have to sell. Use them to take yourself out of the "reverse auction" and convert the lead into a sale.

The Work Order
Figure 17-1 is the work order I use for concrete jobs. You can also use it as a checklist for bidding concrete work. Fill it out as you're figuring the job, then have the customer sign it. This defines exactly what work will be performed (and excludes everything not specifically covered). Attach the work order to the contract, which includes this statement: "All work to be done under this contract is indicated on the signed concrete work order dated _____ which is hereby made a part of this contract."

Figuring Square Feet and Cubic Yards
There's an easy way to figure the square feet in an irregularly-shaped driveway or patio slab. Say you're going to put in a driveway to a garage 30 feet from the street. The garage is 20 feet wide. But because of the shape of the lot, the driveway has to narrow to 8 feet where it meets the street. See

Area (square feet)	Thickness of slabs						
	3"	3½"	4"	4½"	5"	5½"	6"
10	.09	.11	.13	.14	.15	.17	.19
20	.19	.22	.25	.28	.31	.34	.37
30	.28	.33	.37	.42	.46	.51	.56
40	.37	.43	.50	.56	.62	.68	.74
50	.46	.54	.62	.70	.77	.85	.93
60	.56	.65	.74	.83	.95	1.02	1.11
70	.65	.76	.87	.97	1.08	1.19	1.30
80	.74	.87	1.00	1.11	1.24	1.36	1.48
90	.84	.97	1.11	1.25	1.39	1.53	1.67
100	.93	1.08	1.24	1.39	1.55	1.70	1.85
200	1.85	2.16	2.47	2.78	3.09	3.40	3.70
300	2.78	3.24	3.70	4.17	4.63	5.10	5.56
400	3.70	4.32	4.94	5.56	6.17	6.79	7.41
500	4.63	5.40	6.17	7.00	7.72	8.49	9.26
600	5.56	6.48	7.41	8.33	9.26	10.19	11.11

Estimating cubic yards of concrete in slabs
Figure 17-3

Survey of Pitfalls — Concrete Work

1) Will the excavators be able to move their equipment into the rear yard or other location where digging is to be done?

2) Will trenching have to be done by hand?

3) Will dirt have to be wheeled out to the truck in the street?

4) Can the ready-mix truck get into the rear yard or will the concrete have to be hand-wheeled?

5) Can a bobcat be used?

6) Is there a local ordinance against heavy equipment crossing city sidewalks?

7) Will you have problems with culverts, swales or utility lines? What about underground lines?

8) Will you have to work around a septic system, catch basin or well?

9) Will you need barricades?

Survey of pitfalls
Figure 17-4

Figure 17-2. To find out how many square feet of concrete you'll need, add the width of the two ends of the driveway together, then divide by two. Multiply that answer by the length of the driveway. In our example, the driveway is 420 square feet.

Figure 17-3 will help you estimate the cubic yards of concrete needed for slabs. Once you know the square footage and the thickness of the slab, just read the cubic yardage on the chart.

Watch for the Pitfalls

When pricing concrete work, as with most remodeling, make a careful survey of job conditions before bidding. Any problems you miss will reduce or eliminate your profit, or worse. Use the questions in Figure 17-4 to help you evaluate the problems you'll face.

Chapter 18

Selling Doors

There was a time when remodeling contractors passed up leads for a door replacement. The job was considered too small, better suited for the neighborhood carpenter. But today you'll see ads in local newspapers promoting the advantages of replacing exterior doors. They're selling security, energy savings and prestige. Steel entry doors, hand-carved wood doors, storm doors and garage doors can be a very profitable part of your home improvement business.

The installation of interior doors, on the other hand, is usually just a part of an interior remodeling job. But it shouldn't be routine. It's easy just to replace existing doors with whatever your lumber yard has on sale. Many salesmen simply note the style of the existing doors and recommend the same style for the new doors. This is the easiest way to do it. But it's neither the most profitable nor the best way to offer a distinctive service that sets your work apart from what every other remodeler is offering.

Look for opportunities to upgrade the doors. Sell a louvered door or bi-passing closet doors. Offer a choice that makes a difference.

Selling Exterior Doors

With all the choices available, selling doors is a big topic. To make it manageable, we'll divide it into two general areas, exterior and interior doors.

Entry Doors

When remodeling a home exterior or adding a room, you'll often include a new entry door. Now's the time to upgrade the job by suggesting an entry with style. Offer something different from the standard flush door that your competitor is pushing. Suggest a prestigious entry, both to increase customer satisfaction and to give you a competitive edge. Your customers may reject the suggestion, of course, and select the plainest, cheapest door in the catalog. But they may fall in love with one particular door — and only you are offering it. That door may clinch the sale.

Emphasize that the entry provides the *first impression* of the home — both for guests and for prospective buyers when it comes time to sell. The front entry is the focal point. It sets the tone of the home. The elegance of the entry reflects the craftsmanship of the remodeler and taste of the owners. Explain that you'll design an entry that enhances the beauty of the home and matches the present architectural style.

Carry photos of various styles of entries in your sales kit. Have attractive brochures from several door manufacturers. They're a great sales tool. The brochures show the variety of doors available and provide a lot of useful information. At the end of the book you'll find the names and addresses of many manufacturers. Write to them for brochures.

Clip pictures from the magazines featuring home improvement ideas. Use the brochures and pictures to illustrate your ideas.

Learn about architectural styles— To be effective in designing and selling entry upgrades, you must be familiar with architectural styles. There's a front entry appropriate for each. The first step in selling a door is to identify the architectural style of that house. Is it Early American, Southern plantation, New England salt box, Midwest farmhouse, Spanish hacienda or one of the numerous other styles found in this country? A door that's perfect for a Spanish hacienda will look out of place on a colonial home. Decide what type of entry will blend with the decor of the house. Design an entire entry to carry out the motif. The door is the focal point of the entry. But you're selling more than just a door.

For a colonial home, recommend side lights, fluted pilasters with a sunburst top shelf, or perhaps a pediment with urn to complete the decor. Don't just sell the door, sell the entire package. Anyone can sell a door. Sell the package, the complete ensemble, or *surround,* as it's called in the trade. Suggest a cross buck door with diamond lites or nine square lites. How about a polished brass kickplate and a door knocker and handle, along with the surround? If space permits, sell a double door to make the entry even more impressive.

Be like the waiter who sells the entire meal, instead of just taking an order for the entree. The entree is the door; the entire meal includes the door surround.

For a Southern manor style, suggest a six-panel door or a carved colonial panel door. Use double doors if it's possible. Add side lights if there's room. Finish it off with fluted pilasters. Help the homeowner visualize a plantation manor house. An impressive entry like this will be a source of pride for many years.

A sprawling ranch home calls for a carved double door with a heavy knocker.

A Dutch colonial home can be upgraded with Colonial panel doors with one or two side lights. A Dutch door would also be appropriate for this style of home.

A solid oak or mahogany carved door with an emblem or crest is fitting for a Mediterranean or Spanish style home. For a hacienda styled after the stately mansions of old Spain, suggest a door with high-relief metal facing in brass, bronze, copper or pewter, or perhaps an arched door.

Georgian style homes adapt readily to the same treatment as colonial or Early American homes. An English manor house might call for a colonial carved panel door with a leaded glass panel and one or two side lights of leaded glass.

A room addition on a contemporary house might call for an atrium door, where a massive metal-clad relief door would be out of place. A polished chrome kick plate and knocker would be out of place on a colonial house, but appropriate in a modern contemporary home. There's a carved, insulated door with a transom, leaded or etched glass, side lights, pilasters, or pediments to fit any architectural style. The choice is endless. Don't settle for the stereotype flush door with three staggered lites. Have product literature on the styles that are available in your area.

Present the door as a focal point in a complete package that includes the surround, transom, and side lights. That's creative salesmanship. A fine entry creates a satisfied owner who sends referrals your way.

Sell the benefits. People buy benefits. Prestige is a benefit. Energy savings is a benefit. Security is a benefit that has no price limit. Vanity is a benefit. Don't sell just the door. Sell what the door package will do for your prospects.

Atrium or Garden Doors

Many years ago, the open look became popular: French doors opening out onto a lawn. After World War II, the sliding patio door replaced the French door as the standard. The sliding door provides easy entry when open, and a scenic view when closed. But there are disadvantages to common sliding glass doors. They offer easy access to burglars, are seldom well insulated, and need maintenance occasionally.

The atrium door may be a better choice. An atrium or garden door has a wood frame, insulated glass, weatherstripping, a tight threshold, and can take a deadbolt lock. It is more secure and more energy efficient. The atrium door is a door on hinges that also functions as a window wall. The panorama of the outdoors is visible from the comfort of the home. Atrium doors are made so they won't warp or twist.

Atrium doors are available in single door, two-door or three-door units. In a two-door unit, one door is fixed and one swings. In a three-door unit, the center door or either end door swings. This gives you a great deal of design flexibility. Two-door units come in 5'0'' and 6'0'' widths. Three-door units come in 7'6'', 8'0'' and 9'0'' widths.

An entire wall can be converted to atrium doors by combining more than one unit. If necessary, you can fill in with a single door. Atrium doors add a touch of elegance to the home. You can make them a focal point by adding grilles, or transoms, or both. What is richer than an arch transom in leaded glass? A rakehead or trapezoid transom is very distinctive. Squares, rectangles and ellipses are also available, with leaded glass if desired. Full arch transoms come with both eight and twelve lites. Leaded glass can be an option for the doors as well as the transom.

Atrium doors are an excellent choice when converting a garage to living quarters. They're an attractive way to fill in the space previously taken by the overhead door. For a room addition, atrium doors are a practical way to make the addition into a room with a view. They open up a previously dark room to light and scenic views.

Use an atrium door to provide access to a patio, lawn or walk. They make a distinctive entrance and are adaptable to any room of the house. They're elegant, functional, and practical for remodeling existing bedrooms, porches, dining rooms, kitchens and dens.

Use an atrium door to close in a porch, a patio, a sun deck or as a replacement for a sliding glass patio door. Every time you see a sliding glass door in a home, you've found a candidate for an atrium door. You may make an extra sale, and the extra profit that goes along with it.

Use the Energy Tax Credit— The insulated glazed atrium door qualifies for the Energy Tax Credit. By including an atrium door in the remodeling job, you can in effect reduce your customer's cost by up to $300.00. Use this as a selling tool. There's more information on the tax credit in the section on storm doors. When closing a sale on atrium doors, or using atrium doors as a component of a larger remodeling job, stress the benefits:

- They provide natural light and a panoramic view.

- They have a deadbolt lock to increase security.

- Their weatherstripping prevents drafts.

- The insulated glass prevents transmission of cold air.

- They won't frost up.

- Since the door is on hinges, it won't get stuck or slide out of the track.

- You can add a grille to make it even more attractive.

- Insulated atrium doors qualify for the Energy Tax Credit of up to $300.00.

Patio Doors
Wood-framed insulated sliding glass or patio doors are an improvement over metal patio doors for cold climates. The wood frame doesn't conduct cold like a metal frame. The doors come equipped with weatherstripping. They're available in single stationary units, double units and triple units. Screens and security locks are provided by the manufacturer. Key cylinder locks and decorative grilles are optional.

The usual sizes of wood-framed insulated patio doors are:

3'0'' or 4'0'' x 6'8'' single door.
6'0'' or 8'0'' x 6'8'' stationary double door.
5'0'', 6'0'' or 8'0'' x 6'8'' operating double door.
9'0'' or 12'0'' x 6'8'' operating triple or quad door.

In most two-door units, either door can slide. In the triple unit, the center slides and the ends are fixed. In the quads, the two center panels open and the ends are fixed. Patio doors use tempered glass to meet federal requirements. The wood frame can be clad, primed or vinyl sheath.

For those homeowners who want a wide, unobstructed view of the outdoors and easy access, these doors are a sensible choice. They are excellent for converting a garage into a room. Use them to open up a bedroom, dining room, den or living room to the outdoors. But their use isn't confined to remodeling existing rooms. They are also very adaptable for closing in porches, sun rooms, decks and patios. You can plan a room addition with an entire wall serving as a picture window by combining two or more units.

Aluminum-frame sliding glass doors— are practical in warm climates where freezing temperatures and the buildup of ice and snow aren't a problem. They provide the homeowner with a view of the outdoors, as well as direct access to it.

Modern aluminum-frame sliding doors have been improved to provide thermal protection. They have thermal glass with weatherstripping to reduce air infiltration. Grilles are available. The sizes are approximately the same as wood-frame patio doors. They are excellent for use in new room additions, or in remodeling existing rooms to convert solid wall space to a window wall. Sliding glass doors are very adaptable. Combine units to enclose a porch, sun room or deck.

French doors— are hinged and usually have either five or ten lites. They're common in homes built before the 1950's. French doors were usually installed overlooking landscaped gardens. This type of door is traditional with the French chateau style, but any house with a mansard roof is a candidate for French doors. If the owner prefers, they can be installed in pairs with one door fixed and only one door operable. You can use French doors for both remodeling and new room additions. In fact, you can substitute French doors wherever a patio or atrium unit makes sense.

The final decision is up to the homeowners. They're going to pay the bill. Present the choices and explain the features of each type. Discuss the architectural style of the home and suggest which type of door would be most appropriate for that style. Don't insist on a certain type of door. You might blow the sale. Tell them it's their choice. Just present the options that are available and the advantages and disadvantages of each. That way they can make an informed decision.

Utility Doors

Kitchen doors and rear or side entry doors have little prestige value. You'll seldom get involved in the sale of this type of door except as a component of a remodeling job. The owner usually won't express a preference. He just wants a functional door.

But stress during the sale that the door will be solid core. Rear, side and kitchen doors are most attractive for burglars. So it's important to use a solid door. This isn't the place to try to save money with a hollow-core door. Here's an excellent opportunity to suggest a steel insulated door. Read the section on steel insulated doors later in this chapter. Include deadbolt locks in the specs. If you're selling a utility door with glass lites, suggest that thermal glass is a good choice. Remind the customer of the Energy Tax Credit of up to $300.00.

Basement doors should also be solid core, with a deadbolt lock. In high crime areas, suggest installing a cross bar on the inside of the basement door. A steel insulated door is the most secure. Suggesting this protection is both providing a service to the homeowner and increasing your profit on the sale. You're selling benefits to the homeowner.

A cellar door, also known as a bulkhead door, is a door that covers the exterior stairway to the basement. It's different from the basement door, which opens from the stairs into the basement wall. You won't find cellar doors in all parts of the country. But where they are used, they provide a convenient access to storage space in the basement.

I know of only one company that manufactures steel basement door covers, the side wall and the stringers. For brochures and information write to Bilco, Department I.C., New Haven, CT 06505. Their steel cellar doors are available in eight sizes.

Unless you're selling a cellar door as a replacement, remember to charge for the excavation, the poured concrete wing walls, the concrete floor, the opening of the basement wall and the installation of the basement door. Also charge for the carpenter-built wood treads installed in the steel stringers. The cellar door comes primed only. Be sure to specify this in your contract. Make the finish painting the responsibility of the owner.

Interior Doors

The sale of interior doors in a remodeling contract is always part of a larger sale. Use your knowledge of interior doors to give you an edge over competitors who are bidding on the same job. Offer suggestions to the homeowner that change and improve the job. This takes it out of the bidding or auction category. You increase the benefit to the owner, as well as increasing your profit.

The variety of interior doors seems almost endless. You can sell solid or hollow-core doors in flush or panel styles. There are louvered and mirrored doors, bi-pass or bi-fold, and accordion doors in vinyl, wood grain or laminates. Consider pocket doors and cafe or bar doors where appropriate. You may even be able to sell a steel closet vault door to security-conscious prospects.

Here's how to use your knowledge of interior doors to upgrade and close the sale:

"Did the other builder tell you what kind of a door he was going to use? Oh, he just mentioned a door. Well, let me explain something. A lot of builders use hollow-core doors for jobs like this.

We only use solid-core doors. I could punch a hole through a hollow-core door with my fist. We use solid doors because they're stronger, they swing smoother and they provide privacy. Sound travels right through a hollow-core door. It's like a drum.''

Follow through by describing the wide range of doors available. Show the homeowner the brochures and pictures you've collected. Suggest pocket doors where space is at a premium. Ask if they've thought of cafe or bar doors between the kitchen and dining room. These are excellent when you're entertaining and live in somewhat cramped quarters. The person working in the kitchen doesn't always want the guests as an audience, but doesn't want to cut off the air circulation. Look at the doors in the house now. Suggest staying with the same general style unless the owner indicates he'd like something different.

Closet Doors

When you're selling closet doors, the first step is to determine the type of door: hinged, sliding, bi-fold or accordion. Each is appropriate in certain situations.

For the front hall guest closet, suggest a louvered door with a colonial panel. It will give the entrance hall a look of elegance.

For walk-in bedroom closets with only one door, recommend a louvered door that allows ventilation. We all know about the problems with moths, how expensive clothes are today, how important ventilation is. The wood louvered door with a raised panel is not only very rich looking, but has the extra function of ventilation. The same benefits also apply to a louvered bi-pass or bi-fold door. Sell the benefits.

When looking over the job, see if there's a full-length dressing mirror in the bedroom, If not, close the sale by suggesting a mirrored closet door. This gives the wife a dressing mirror. You're thinking not only of a functional door, but an added benefit for her. Both bi-pass and bi-fold closet doors come with mirror panels.

Suggest to the homeowners that they use mirrored doors in the master bedroom and louvered doors in the other bedrooms. If they don't want louvered doors, you can still offer a choice of raised panel, colonial doors or the contemporary flush doors.

When they're not limited to a single hinged door, homeowners have a wide choice of closet doors. Ask if they want full height closet doors that go up to the ceiling. This gives easy access to the top shelves and an unobstructed view of the contents. Then discuss the cost of framing above the doors if only 6'8'' height is needed.

Bi-pass doors— These are common in bedroom closets. They don't take up any floor space, since they don't swing. They're available louvered and mirrored. The usual objection is that they block off one side of the closet.

Bi-fold doors— These are often the most practical for wardrobe closets. Since they open fully, all of the contents of the closet are easily accessible. Mirrored bi-fold doors serve a double function. With both of the doors open, someone standing between them can see both a full front *and* rear view. Women especially appreciate this when they're dressing. A mirrored bi-fold door is both functional and attractive.

Louvered bi-fold doors are an excellent choice, not only for clothes closets and linen closets, but for work areas like laundry rooms and utility closets. They're good for dens and passageways, and are often used for space dividers.

Folding or accordion doors— Like the bi-fold, accordion doors allow full access to a closet. Recommend them for closets where the swing of the hinge door is a problem. When two hinged doors are hung back-to-back, one door will bang into the other, constantly nicking paint and eventually ruining the surface. The solution is to replace one of the hinged doors with a folding door. Folding or accordion doors are also a good way to divide a multipurpose room.

Modern accordion doors are sturdy and are available in either laminated wood or vinyl. The vinyl comes in a wide range of colors and textures, including a wood grain look. There's bound to be one that will please your buyer.

Pocket doors— Install pocket doors between two rooms when one is to be closed off from time to time. They are appropriate when privacy isn't an issue, since they usually don't have a lock. Pocket doors are ideal when space is limited and a hinged door would be awkward to open or would bump into the furniture.

Steel security doors— For security-conscious homeowners, suggest a steel security door that converts a closet into a vault for storing valuables.

Carry brochures in your sales kit to show the variety of closet door systems available. Offering the perfect door to fit that homeowner's needs can wrap up the sale.

Insulated Steel Doors

Replacing wood entry doors with steel doors is now big business. Security is the watchword in selling this type of door. Many people are very concerned with the safety of their homes, possessions and their lives. The market for these doors isn't limited to the more prosperous neighborhoods. You can sell them in any neighborhood where there's been a burglary in the last six months. That's most communities in the U.S. today. In other words, all homeowners are prospects.

Steel doors have deadbolt locks for extra security. They have 3/4'' recessed hinges that can't be reached from the outside. They are available in many styles, so you can recommend one that will make the home more attractive as well as more secure.

There are other benefits to sell besides security and beauty. Steel doors won't split, shrink or swell like wood doors. And since the doors are insulated, they save energy. The doors have a polyurethane core with insulation factors of R14 to R15. That prevents sweating or frost buildup on the inside of the door. They come with magnetic weatherstripping on the top and striker sides of the door, and compression weatherstripping on the hinged side. The bottom of the doors have a vinyl weatherstrip. Together, these provide a weathertight seal. An adjustable threshold keeps dust from getting under the door. The door itself is clad with 24-gauge electrogalvanized steel and carries a 1½ hour fire rating.

Steel doors close tight like a refrigerator door. That prevents drafts and saves energy by lowering fuel costs. They form a tight seal against dust, rain, heat and cold. An insulated steel door doesn't sound hollow, like the old steel doors.

You can promote these doors for the replacement market. But don't forget to sell them when doing a front elevation job or a room addition with an exterior entry.

Steel doors make good replacements for sliding glass patio doors. Many homeowners with sliding glass doors are worried about the burglary problem. Sliding glass doors are an invitation for burglars. Offer to replace such doors with attractive steel security doors. The active door swings in.

The stationary door creates additional wall space for furniture. The homeowner gets the same security in the patio door that he has in the entry door. The doors look like wood, and the glass is insulated and tempered.

Storm Doors

Storm doors have changed dramatically in the last ten years. The cumbersome wood storm door is gone for good. The wide range of attractive, effective storm doors available today makes your job a lot easier.

If you do business in colder climates, there will be many opportunities to sell storm doors. The first is, of course, a straight lead for a door. But a good builder-salesman can create additional business by selling storm doors as part of other remodeling jobs. When you're selling siding, windows, kitchen or bath remodeling, a porch enclosure, room addition, or even an attic conversion, suggest a new storm door.

Sell Energy Conservation and Comfort

The main purpose of a storm door is energy conservation. It prevents heat from escaping and cold air from entering the house. But there are other benefits as well. The storm door stops snow from piling up around the entry door. Water doesn't seep in. It keeps frost off the entry door window. It prevents drafts.

In the summer, the storm door goes on working for the homeowner. When the air conditioning is on, it helps keep the cool air in the house. If there's no air conditioning, a screen insert will help cool and ventilate the house. It works all year long. It also helps reduce the amount of outside noise that enters the house.

An anodized aluminum storm door never needs painting. It stays clean and new-looking for years. The glass is marine glazed. That means there are no air leaks and it has a permanent seal.

The Energy Tax Credit

Don't forget one of your major selling points — the Energy Tax Act of 1978. Storm doors are such an important energy saver that the government will give the homeowner a tax reduction of up to $300 for installing them. The requirements are simple. The home must be in the U.S. It must be the taxpayer's principal residence. It must have been substantially completed before April 20, 1977. The energy-saving device (the storm door) must be new, with a life expectancy of at least three years.

Here's the formula for figuring the tax credit. The maximum accumulated credit for energy conservation items is 15% of $2,000.00, or $300.00, for each principal residence. This includes the installation cost as well as the cost of the door itself.

The government has given you extraordinary help in selling storm doors. Take advantage of it. Carry a copy of IRS Form 5695, the application for a residential energy credit. Show it to the homeowners. Tell them you'll make sure they get a copy. When the door is installed, deliver the form in person. Tell them you thought it was important enough to bring yourself instead of having the office mail it. Use this opportunity to ask for referrals. Remember, referrals are usually the easiest leads to sell.

The Sales Pitch

There are times when you'll find it hard to close a sale on a remodeling job. Just lowering the price may not be enough. In fact, lowering the price may be counterproductive. The customer may feel that you weren't being honest with him in the first place. This is when many successful salesmen offer a free gift to close the sale. A storm door makes a perfect free gift. Here's your pitch:

"Our company is a one-price house. We offer the lowest price we can manage the first time. But at the moment we're overstocked on storm doors. The boss told me Monday that I could include one of these beautiful storm doors at no cost on sales that close by this coming Saturday."

Or use the same pitch, but charge some nominal amount for the door. Explain that your price doesn't even cover the cost of the door, much less the installation. You can even figure the cost of the door into the job ahead of time if you plan to use this pitch. You're selling the door at the same time you're using it to clinch the sale.

On a straight sale of a storm door, you have to be knowledgeable about its features. You're competing with cheap storm doors the homeowner can pick up from any discount house and install himself. Sell the quality features of your door that make it worth the extra cost. For example:

"Our storm doors are custom-made, not like those you get from mail order or discount houses. Those are the kind that blow off in the wind. You want a good door that will last and won't get torn off in the first breeze that comes along. You need a door that's tight enough to keep heat from leaking from your home. In short, an energy saver. Our doors come with a piano hinge, not like the mail-order doors with only two hinges. A piano hinge goes the whole length of the door. We use a commercial heavy-duty hydraulic door closer that will close your door tight, not one of those flimsy closers that you see on those junky screen doors. This door has an astragal. That's a vinyl sweep on the bottom of the door that prevents the snow and rain from blowing under the door. And it has a key lock for security.

"We have all these different models to choose from. They're made from virgin aluminum, not recycled. Here are samples of each. See, I can twist this piece of recycled aluminum. If you're paying for a good door, you deserve good quality. Our aluminum is rigid and doesn't twist. The door comes complete with a fully weatherstripped "Z" bar installed on the jamb. The door is 1⅛" thick. Look at this heavy double kick plate. It won't get kicked out like the ones on the cheap doors. All the corners are butted for extra strength. We use rivet construction, not screws. That makes it stronger. When your door is installed it will close with a whisper, not with a slam. That's a tight energy-saving fit that will save you money for years.

"The aluminum is fully anodized. It won't pit or scar, so it will stay new-looking for years. You can choose the satin finish or the bright. The glass insert is double strength and marine glazed. That's a vinyl wraparound glazing. It's called marine glazing because it's as watertight as the glazing used in the portholes on boats. And a porthole in a boat had better not leak. In the summer, replace the glass with this sturdy aluminum screen. We don't use fiberglass because it rips so easily.

"We recommend a high kick plate. Before the days of air conditioning, people wanted as much air as they could get, so the doors were made with upper and lower sash and screens. But nowadays, with air conditioning, the upper screen is enough. Without the lower sash, you don't have the kids smearing up the glass with their hands, or your dog's paw marks. The high kick plates come in five styles: cross buck, provincial, classic, Dutch, or regency. The cross buck is the most popular, but the provincial would look real nice on your house. We can install a mail slot in it if you want. Do you want the stainless steel facing or one of these popular colors?"

Show the homeowners your brochures and get

them involved in picking out the style and color of door. You've closed the sale.

Financing Storm Doors
A storm door sale by itself is usually a cash sale. It's very difficult to finance any sale under several thousand dollars. When you add the door to a sale of storm windows, siding, awnings or remodeling, it brings the price into the financeable range. This helps you make the sale, and the additional monthly payment for the door will seem negligible to the homeowner.

To make a cash sale more attractive to the homeowner who needs financing, you can ask for a deposit of just half the price now. The balance is due on completion. This stretches the payment over a longer period. It will take several weeks for

the door to be measured, manufactured and shipped. During the busy fall season, it can take up to four months to get delivery. Keep in touch with your supplier so you know how long the waiting period is. Let the customers know how long they'll have to wait for these custom doors. If you don't level with them, complaints from angry customers will make your life miserable. They may even cancel the sale.

If you sell the benefits, including the tax credit, and help the homeowner with financing, selling storm doors can be relatively easy way to add to your profit picture.

Look for the list of door manufacturers at the end of the book. Write to them for brochures. Keep the brochures in your sales kit and use them to close more of your door leads.

Chapter 19

Selling Attic Conversions

One of the least expensive ways to add living space is an attic conversion. Raising the roof with a dormer can create enough space under the roof to make the attic into a room. Figure 19-1 shows a typical shed dormer.

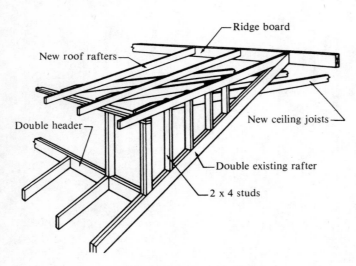

Typical shed dormer
Figure 19-1

An attic conversion lead is a good lead. A dormer is usually a big ticket item, with few subs. Remember the axiom in the remodeling business:

The fewer the subs, the better the profit. You'll usually make the best profit from a straight carpentry job like an attic conversion.

Most people have a specific reason for considering a dormer. They may need an additional bedroom or an apartment for in-laws, or want an apartment for rental income. They already know the benefits. What you have to sell is skill and experience. What you have to watch out for is the hidden problems lurking in that old attic.

If he's adding the space for in-laws or family members, the homeowner will often ask you to build a shell that he can finish himself. You only have to raise the roof, install the cheeks and face of the dormer and put in the wall studs and a subfloor. *Always* include a subfloor. Your men need a safe place to work. You just can't afford to have someone crashing through the ceiling below.

When the prospect wants an apartment he can rent, he'll usually ask for more than a shell. He wants an interior that's finished, with complete plumbing, heating and electrical systems. This can mean a good profit. But before calling on the lead, check the applicable building regulations and zoning ordinances. Don't waste your time on a pipe dream. Some communities prohibit dormer apartments. In some cities you need a plan drawn by a licensed architect to get a building permit. But you may be able to turn this to your advantage. Have the lead sign a contract with you to obtain the architect's drawings. The fee is payable now. When the final contract is signed, you'll credit the architect's fee against the contract price. This closes the sale for you.

Watch Out for the Pitfalls
When you're selling a dormer, be wary of the possible pitfalls. Take the time to check out the conditions you'll face. You don't want any surprises once you're on the job. Here are some of the things to look for:

1) Measure the headroom under the ridge board, the highest point on the roof. Is there enough headroom at that point? Stand in the center of the attic and raise your hand as high as you can. If you can't touch the ridge board, a new shed dormer roof will provide adequate headroom for living space below. If you *can* touch the ridge board, you'll have to build a new roof to replace the existing one. In effect, you'll be building an additional story with roof and walls.

2) Are the present ceiling joists adequate to carry the floor load? Check the building code requirements for attics used as sleeping quarters. If they're not adequate, what will it take to bring them up to code?

3) Next check the stairway. Is it wide enough? Does it meet code requirements for access to living areas? Will you need two stairways to pass the fire code? If so, where will you put the second one? You may have to add a handrail on the existing stairwell. Don't forget that stairs need adequate light. Will you need to install a light fixture and feed?

4) Now think about the plumbing. Just about every dormer addition will need a bathroom or powder room. Can you lay out the bathroom so the toilet is within five feet of the present soil stack? If not, plan to extend the plumbing stacks as needed. If the owner is doing his own plumbing or having his own sub do it, point out the problem.

5) The present chimney may have to be extended if a new roof is built. Include this item when pricing the job.

6) Consider the heating situation. If the house has warm air ducts accessible from the attic, it isn't too difficult for the heating man to run an exten-sion. But he'll probably need to put in a booster fan in the duct. Otherwise, the dormer won't get enough heat. Sometimes it will be cheaper to install a gas wall furnace. There's a wide selection of heating units available now. Recommend the same type of heating system as in the rest of the house, if possible.

If you're not confident of your ability to figure Btu's and recommend the best type of heating, just say, "I'll have our heating engineer check out what's needed. Let's set a time when I can come back with him." You won't be able to close the sale in one "sit." But it will impress the customer. You're a professional, bringing in your heating engineer to do the job right.

Here's an important tip: Do *not* have the heating man meet you in front of the house in his "Joe's Plumbing" truck. Pick him up in your car, and walk in together. You don't want the lead to start thinking that he can get the heating cheaper if he calls several heating companies direct. Then some other heating company gets the lead and tries to swing in their own carpenter for the job. You could lose out all around. You may be able to guess how I learned this lesson.

If you're just building a shell, you avoid all of the heating problems. If there's major heating work in a finished addition, you may or may not want to include it in the contract. Leaving it out may be best.

"Mr. Homeowner, I know you want to save as much money on this job as you can. We're carpentry contractors, so we have to sub out the heating. I'm going to suggest that you sub it out yourself to save money. If *we* handle it, we have to charge for the insurance, plus the overhead. Now I know that for most people it's difficult to lay out the money. But we can include the cost of the heating in the loan without any problem. You save quite a bit. And I'll supply you with the names of some very reliable heating men."

This way, you have one less sub to contend with. You won't be called for service when a problem arises. You've shed all responsibility for heating and cooling. Everyone wants to make a profit, but the wise man skips it when it can only lead to aggravation.

You could also ask the owner if he or his friends want to do the heating. Let your buyer take responsibility for getting it done. Point out all the money he can save on labor by doing it himself.

The third choice is to charge enough to cover the extra trouble and include the work in your contract. You may be able to sell an air conditioner, too.

7) Figure the electrical requirements. How many outlets and circuits are needed? The electrical section of your price book should offer some help here. If the dormer room is going to be rented out, be sure to include a new meter box and circuit breakers.

8) Are new windows needed? If the contract is for a finished room, be sure to charge for window, frame, sash, trim and flashing. If the present attic windows are barn sash, figure replacement with double hung, casement or awning windows for improved livability.

9) If you'll be working on the third or fourth floor, will you need a debris chute or scaffolding? Will you charge an extra handling fee for hauling materials up?

10) Frequently the owners will say they just need a couple of bedrooms for the in-laws, and a bath and a small kitchen. *This is a pitfall.* In most communities, this will be considered an apartment, no matter who lives in it. You'll have to comply with building and zoning regulations for multiple housing units. This almost always means two exits for fire regulations.

11) Is the attic cluttered with boxes, old furniture and a lifetime of discarded items? It will cost you money if your carpenters are continually having to move it out of the way to get on with their work. Charge for the extra labor, or get a commitment from the owners that the attic will be cleaned out before your men start work. Put this statement in the contract: "The attic is to be cleared of all items so the workmen have a clear space to work."

12) Is part of the attic currently finished? Will this have to be torn out when the dormer is raised? Charge for wrecking the unwanted partitions and debris removal. Check to see if any existing electrical wiring or plumbing will have to be removed, relocated or brought up to code.

13) If you're selling a shell, roughing in the plumbing for a future powder room is O.K. But if the owners ask you to rough in for a future kitchen, stop, look and listen! That future kitchen might make your job illegal. Save headaches by clearing it with the building department first.

Sell Some Add-ons
Here's a natural when selling a dormer job. Sell aluminum siding on the eaves, fascia, and soffit. Sell aluminum trim on the windows and exterior door. Point out that with aluminum siding, the owner will never have to climb a ladder to paint again. He eliminates the risk of getting hurt and saves the cost of repainting every few years. He'll save money by getting the siding now, when your men are on the job. Then sell aluminum gutters and downspouts that are prefinished and never need painting.

Sell aluminum storm windows and screens as part of the package. Add a storm door for the entrance. You can probably think of one or two more extras.

Writing the Contract
When you write the contract, it's just as important to state what you are *not* doing as what you are doing. Say that there is no plumbing, electrical, heating, painting, tile work, or finish flooring in the contract, if that's the case.

Sometimes the family just needs an extra bedroom. They want you to build one room and leave the rest of the attic alone. Then be sure to specify in the contract the size of room to be built. Add the words "No work is to be performed in the balance of the attic by the contractor." List the specific work that you will do and exclude what you won't do.

Make Sure Your Price is Complete
If you're just building a dormer shell, you probably won't forget any important items. But if you're doing a finished room or apartment, overlooking something is easy. The cost of anything you forget comes out of your profit. Figure 19-2 is a checklist to use any time you're pricing a dormer job.

Attic Conversion Checklist

Carpentry
- ☐ Raise dormer or new roof _____
- ☐ Roofing for dormer _____
- ☐ Reinforce floor joints _____
- ☐ Install subfloor _____
- ☐ Wall studs or partitions _____
- ☐ Install windows _____
- ☐ Install door and frames _____
- ☐ Widen or install stairs and handrails _____
- ☐ Insulation _____
- ☐ Install and tape drywall _____
- ☐ Door and window trim _____
- ☐ Siding for fascia and soffit _____
- ☐ Gutters and downspouts _____
- ☐ Extend chimney _____
- ☐ Other _____

Electrical
- ☐ Install service entrance and breakers _____
- ☐ Outlets and circuits _____
- ☐ Light in stairwell _____
- ☐ Exhaust fans in kitchen and bath _____
- ☐ Other _____

Plumbing and heating
- ☐ Bathroom fixtures _____
- ☐ Extend soil stack _____
- ☐ Kitchen sink and appliances _____
- ☐ Extend present warm air ducts _____
- ☐ Install booster fan _____
- ☐ Install new heater _____
- ☐ Other _____

Finish
- ☐ Kitchen cabinets and soffit _____
- ☐ Closet shelves and poles _____
- ☐ Medicine chest and vanity in bath _____
- ☐ Tile in bath, kitchen _____
- ☐ Finish flooring _____
- ☐ Painting and decorating _____
- ☐ Other _____

Miscellaneous
- ☐ Architect's fees _____
- ☐ Building permit _____
- ☐ Bond and license fees _____
- ☐ Rubbish removal _____
- ☐ Other _____

Attic conversion checklist
Figure 19-2

Chapter 20

Selling New Facades

Once in a while you'll get a lead for installing a new facade on a house. You'll probably be talking to owners of a house in an older neighborhood where houses are increasing in value. They probably paid a good price for the home and want to update its appearance. Other homes on the street have been remodeled or have new facades and your current prospects want the same treatment. To make this sale, you must show the owners how modern and up-to-date the house will look after the remodeling. They'll be proud of the home's new look. The neighbors will admire it. The home's value will increase. You have to paint a picture of the modernized home in the owners' minds.

Painting an oral picture can be difficult. Most people don't get as excited about an oral description as they would over a big color picture torn from a magazine. Today most people buy ready-to-wear clothes. Few start out at the tailor with a description of what they need. One reason is the cost of the clothes, of course. But the most important reason is that they can't visualize a finished suit or dress from a swatch of cloth.

The same holds true when buying a home. Instead of having a custom home built, most home buyers troop through model after model, looking for a house that meets their needs.

When selling a new facade, we run smack into the same problem of visualization. The owners can't visualize what the final product will look like.

If you can't help them *see* how their house will be transformed, you'll never get a signature on the contract.

Use Pictures to Sell New Facades

As the salesman, you can see the new facade in your mind's eye. How do you plant that picture in the mind of the buyer? You need a tool to do this. Remember the old proverb, "One picture is worth a thousand words." You've found your tool.

Collect a pile of pictures to use when making the sales pitch. Find pictures of every conceivable kind of elevation. You need pictures of contemporary homes, colonial homes, split-level ranches, plantation manor houses, and more. To do a really good job, take pictures of Cape Cod houses, New England salt boxes, raised ranches, Georgians, Tudors, chateaus, bungalows and Spanish styles.

You want examples of every type of window, every kind of siding. Collect pictures of houses with picture windows, bay and bow windows, casements and sliders. Present examples of patio or atrium doors, balconies, concrete stoops, canopies and wrought iron trim. Bring out pictures of houses with cedar shakes or diagonal cedar siding, redwood, sawtooth, board and batten, aluminum or vinyl siding, hardboard and stucco board, brick veneer and stucco finishes.

You can't have too many pictures. When your prospects start to explain what they want, select the exact picture that illustrates and expands on the treatment they are describing. That's the way to clinch the sale when selling a facade.

Calling on a prospect without an album of pictures is like going into a boxing ring with one arm tied behind your back.

There are several ways to get the pictures you need. One is to take them yourself. Drive around town with your camera and take snaps of the best front elevations you can find. Concentrate on the styles that are popular in your part of the country. Present these to the buyers, explaining that they are typical elevations. Their home could look like this after the renovations.

Second, get whatever pictures siding and window manufacturers have available. They can supply you with pictures and brochures showing elevation changes using their products.

Third, keep your ideas and your photo album up-to-date with clippings from home improvement magazines. These pictures are easy to get and will quickly round out your collection.

Fourth, and possibly most important, take "before and after" pictures of the jobs you do. Consider using a professional photographer for the highest quality photographs. Before putting them in your album, label each with the address of the home. These pictures are a very effective sales tool. Point out to the prospects that you can make changes like the ones illustrated, which will blend into the present architectural style while improving the visual appeal of the home. Use the "after" pictures to show how your staff of experts will transform the house into the neighborhood showplace.

Go through your entire album with the prospects. Explain and dramatize each transformed facade. Point out how the cantilever of the angle bay window or the board and batten siding gave it a new look. Take plenty of time to discuss the features in each set of photos. Help the prospects to picture similar improvements in their home. As the buyers are impressed by what you've done, they'll start to visualize their house renovated into a showplace. And you're on your way to a signed contract.

Find Out the Owners' Preferences

Take time to listen to the homeowners' responses to the pictures. It's important to learn what features they like. Then build on their preferences as you describe the transformation of their home:

"First we'll remove the front porch. Then we'll patch up the front wall where the porch was fastened to the house. Next, we'll take out those old-fashioned high windows and install a triple picture window for you. The center glass will be fixed but the two sides will open. I'd recommend double hung windows for the sides, like you have in the rest of your house. But these will be the modern kind that snap out. You just press the window and you can take it out and carry it to the kitchen or the basement. You won't have to lean out the window to wash it. Or we could install casement windows, if you prefer. That's the kind that swings out from hinges on the side. You might like awning, or Miami windows, as we call them. These open outward by pushing the bottom of the window out. They're nice to have when there's a gentle rain. You can leave the window open without the rain getting in. Both the casement and awning windows come with built-in screens.

"Which type of window do you like best? I think the double hung windows are the most practical for our climate. Of course, we can install storm windows at the same time. I suggest that you have a storm door put in, too. Now's the best time to do it, while you're having the rest of the work done. They'll only cost a few dollars more in the monthly payment. And you'll get the whole job done at one time.

"To make the window really look effective, we'll build a canopy over the window and clear across the house and over the new concrete front stoop. This sets off the new windows, like the eyebrow over your eye. It dresses up the whole house. We'll install wrought iron rails on the stoop. You have your choice of these colors for the insulated aluminum siding on the balance of the front. Also, we'll cover the soffit and fascia with aluminum siding. You'll never have to paint them again. No more climbing up on dangerous ladders to reach those high places. By the way, we can also cover the window trim, including the bedroom and attic windows upstairs, and the front door casing with aluminum. We'll put in new aluminum gutters.

"While we're at it, I suggest replacing your old-fashioned front door with a modern steel insulating door in the design of your choice. The three staggered lites are the most popular, but some people like a triangle. I'll show you some pictures so you can pick the one you like best. These doors are 1¾" thick, with a deadbolt lock. They're so heavy that we use three hinges on them. With so many people worried about security these days, you'll be comforted to know that your house has the most burglar-proof front door available. Of course, these doors are beautiful. They look like wood, but they cut down the possibility of burglary. Which style of door would you like to have? I'll show you brochures so you can pick a pattern that fits the new facade.

"You'll also need a new light. We can install a coach light that blends right in. While the electrician is here, do you want him to install an outside outlet? They're sure convenient for Christmas decorations or electric lawn mowers. Now just give me a minute or two and I'll figure up the cost and the monthly payment for you."

Of course there are endless variations. Perhaps a bay window with a seat instead of the picture window. Then the canopy would cover only the new front stoop, not the window. Some facades lend themselves to wrought iron corner trellises on the stoop. Your customers might prefer hardboard siding or stucco board instead of aluminum siding. Even with wood siding, the soffit, fascia, and window and door trim can be covered with aluminum.

The important thing is to paint a picture of a modern-looking home with the features the owners want. Point out step-by-step how you'll transform their house into a showplace. Sell the benefits of convenience and energy savings as well as appearance.

Pricing the Job
In pricing a front elevation remodeling job, be sure to include all the charges. Don't forget permits and removal of debris. If you're removing a porch or stoop, you'll have to patch the wall. If you replace windows, include the inside window trim and plastering or drywall if needed.

If the house has a gable roof, there won't be any gutters in the front of the house to replace. If you install a wood canopy over the stoop, charge for gutters and downspout for the canopy. If it's a hip roof and the present gutters are galvanized, you can't attach aluminum to them. So either sell a

complete gutter job or just replace the galvanized gutter to the front elevation if necessary.

Front elevation work takes a number of trades. Figure 20-1 is a checklist of trades commonly involved in remodeling a facade. Before pricing the job, check off the items and trades you'll need for this particular job. Refer to your price book for each item. You don't want to miss any item when totaling the selling price. Facade remodeling can be profitable work if you price it right.

Checklist for Facade Remodeling

1) Canopy

2) Carpentry

3) Concrete work

4) Electrical

5) Gutters and downspouts

6) Masonry

7) Millwork (windows)

8) Permits

9) Plaster patching

10) Rubbish removal

11) Storm windows and doors, screens

12) Wrought iron

Checklist for facade remodeling
Figure 20-1

Chapter 21

Selling Fences

When you get a fence lead, the prospects probably have a pretty good idea of whether they want a chain link or wood fence. If they want wood, there are several popular styles to choose from. The most popular are the basketweave and the stockade fences. You might get an occasional lead for a split rail fence from people who have horses or live in a rural setting. There won't be many requests for picket fences.

Carry pictures of the different styles of wood fences available — redwood basketweave, board and batten styles, cedar picket, rustic stockade, cedar round rail, and the alternating vertical or horizontal panel or louvered fences which are popular in shielding swimming pools. A plain board fence is often the answer when the owners are looking for privacy.

Have pictures of chain link fencing as well as a list of options available, like vinyl coated wire. Aluminum and wrought iron ornamental fences are also available. Sell the benefits of metal fences. They don't need maintenance, and the aluminum fence will never have to be painted. Present them as an option if a wood fence doesn't fill the bill.

Be sure to put the addresses on photos of fences you installed. Take "before and after" pictures that show what an improvement an attractive fence can make.

In planning and selling a fence, there are two factors to consider: the terrain of the property and the desires of the owner. The terrain dictates how the fence will be designed. You can install a basketweave or stockade fence in a straight line on level ground. On sloping ground the fence has to be stepped up the hill. On gently rolling ground, install a fence that twists and follows the contours of the land.

First, find out why the owners want a fence. Are they looking for privacy? Do they have small children they want to keep in the backyard? Is the fence to confine a pet on the property? Design a fence that meets their needs and stress the benefits of that fence. Explain how easily it can be financed, so the homeowners can enjoy those benefits with no money down and only a small monthly payment.

Check the Property Survey

It's very important to have the owner show you the survey stakes on the property. Also ask for a copy of the survey. If the owner doesn't have survey stakes and tells you the property line is "about here," then it's prudent to insert the following clause into the contract:

The Owner of the property on which the fence is to be located accepts full responsibility for location of the fence and holds the Contractor free and harmless from any liability for location of the fence.

Date _____

Customer name _____ Telephone _____

Address _____

City, State _____ Zip _____

Survey of Property

Show *all* driveways, sidewalks, alleys. Show all points of entry and obstacles in relation to fence. Indicate north side of property.

Overall width in feet →

← *Overall length in feet* →

Check one:

☐ *Contractor removes old fence.*
☐ *Customer removes old fence.*
☐ *No existing fence to remove.*

New fence:

☐ *Chain link (gauge _____)*
☐ *Wood (style _____)*
     (kind of wood _____)

Total length _____ *Height* _____
No. of gates _____ *Height* _____ *Width* _____
No. of posts _____
No. of concrete breaks _____

Special Instructions
(If installation address is different from home address, specify here.)

Owner _____

Salesman _____ *Owner* _____

Fence sketch sheet
Figure 21-1

To be even safer, insist that the owners have the property resurveyed and the stakes flagged. This is the best way to avoid trouble. It also prevents the owner from using this ploy: "I'm not going to pay you for the fence. You didn't install it on *my* property."

Check the Building Code

Before selling a fence, know what the building code and zoning ordinances require and prohibit. Check for the following:

1) What is the height limit on solid fences in residential areas? Can a "cross topper" extend above that height?

2) What is the height limit on chain link fences in residential areas? Can you install barbed wire strands on top of a chain link fence in residential areas?

3) Is it legal to fence in parkways?

4) Do you need a permit to erect a fence? If there is a permit charge for erecting a fence, be sure to charge the customer.

5) How close can the fence be to the property line? How far does it have to be set back from the street?

Check the Fence Line for Obstructions

Find out if there are any trees or other obstructions on the fence line. If there are, discuss it with the owner. Does he want the tree or obstruction removed, or will the fence butt up against it? If it's to be removed, it's best to have the customer sub this out himself. This avoids problems for you. If you include it in your bid, it makes your price seem that much higher. And the sub might want to be paid before you can collect.

Here's the best way to handle the problem:

"Why don't you arrange to have a tree man take down the tree? It'll be cheaper that way. If we do it, we have to charge more than the tree man because we'll have to cover the insurance and our overhead. I can recommend a good tree man. You'll save money by taking care of it yourself. I'm sure you want to save money. And if you like, we can include the cost of tree removal in the loan. This way you don't have to lay out the money now, even if you make the arrangements yourself."

Who can say no to that?

The Fence Sketch Sheet

Figure 21-1 is a sketch sheet for fence orders. Fill it out completely. Note the style and size of the fence and any obstructions. Specify the gauge for chain link fences or the kind of wood for wood fences. Indicate the type, size and number of gates. Have the owners sign the sketch sheet. Insert the following statement in the contract:

The attached signed fence sketch dated _____ is hereby made a part of this contract.

Be sure to specify in the contract who is to remove the old fence, if there is one. Don't forget to charge for removal and hauling.

Chapter 22
Selling Flooring and Tile Work

It isn't simple to sell flooring today. There are too many choices. The hardest part of the sale will probably be selecting the color, texture or finish, presenting all the alternatives and describing the advantages and disadvantages of each.

I'm not saying that you have to know everything about tile or vinyl or carpet or hardwood flooring to make a sale. But you do need to know the key facts that make a difference to your client. You can't sell what you can't explain. You can't describe benefits if you don't know what those benefits are. This chapter summarizes the key points a salesman must know about modern flooring and suggests some selling points that have worked for me many times.

Clay Flooring

Clay tile has been used in homes for centuries. I have seen a mosaic tile pavement in an excavation in Caesarea, an ancient seaport in Israel. The tile is as beautiful today, both in color and design, as it was when it was laid. The mosaic tile floor in the Dormition church on the shores of Lake Galilee, where Christ is said to have multiplied two fish and two loaves of bread to feed thousands, is still there and is still in almost perfect shape. I've seen it.

A clay tile floor will last longer than you *or* the house. It doesn't corrode, rust, deteriorate or rot. There's just about no such thing as wear and tear on a clay tile floor. In fact, clay pieces are ar-

chaeologists' keys to the study of ancient history. What a story you have to tell when selling tile!

Selling Clay Tile Floors

Today, factories in America, Mexico, Italy, and Japan produce many kinds of clay tile. The most common are quarry and ceramic tiles, pavers and bricks. They're available glazed or unglazed, in many shapes, sizes and colors. They're frostproof, impervious to water damage, resist alkali and grease stains, withstand abrasion, and tolerate powerful cleaning solutions.

Clay tile is an excellent choice when appearance is the primary consideration. And it's practical, because cleaning is a breeze. Even frequent mopping with strong detergents won't damage it. This makes tile floors a natural for entries and kitchens. But don't limit your selling effort to those obvious uses. Tile can be used to advantage in any room, including bathrooms, dining rooms, dens, balconies, terraces — even on kitchen counter tops and vanities.

Since glazed tile tends to get slippery when it's wet, I usually recommend unglazed tile for heavy traffic areas.

Your sales kit should have brochures showing tile used in attractive room settings. There's a list of flooring manufacturers at the end of the book. Write to them for brochures and selling information.

Wood Flooring

Wood flooring also has a long and proud history. Some polished hardwood plank floors in Japan have been in regular use for over a thousand years. And they are still as attractive as the day the wood was laid! Today, mills produce a large variety of patterns that can please every taste and pocketbook. Parquet (laminated blocks of hardwood strips) and strip patterns come in a variety of woods.

Your job is to recommend flooring that complements the architectural style of the house. For some architectural styles, wood flooring is the first choice.

Residential flooring is usually made from the following woods:

Oak, either red or white, is used in block, parquet, plank and strip flooring. This is the most common hardwood flooring.

Maple, from the sugar or rock maple, is recommended for heavy traffic areas, because it's very hard and strong. A maple floor can be a true work of art and is among the most desirable and durable of all floors.

Pecan, a member of the hickory family, is the hardest of hardwoods. Its heartwood is darker than other hardwoods.

Birch, both yellow and sweet, is occasionally made into flooring. It has a reddish-brown color with a slight difference in shade according to the species.

Ash, cherry, hickory and *teak* are hardwoods sometimes chosen for their attractive grain and color.

Walnut, a moderate reddish-brown, is a beautiful hardwood.

Softwoods, like fir and pine, are not as durable as the hardwoods. Fir flooring is mostly used for porches. Fir and pine are not resistant enough to impact or heavy wear to be commonly used for interior flooring.

To combine the beauty of wood with easy care and resistance to wear, recommend acrylic impregnated hardwood or hardwood that has a vinyl wear surface.

Selling Wood Floors

Your prime prospect for a real wood floor is someone who appreciates Early American or colonial furniture and has some in their home. These people are drawn to a historical period when wood was the first choice in flooring. Look at your prospects' living room furniture. If you see colonial or Early American furniture, mention how attractive it is and how much you admire that style. Early American flooring is hardwood strip flooring. Your clients may want flooring coordinated with their choice of furniture.

If the house or furnishings are colonial style, recommend plank floors. Very few remodeling salesmen know much about plank floors. Demonstrate your knowledge, and you've eliminated the competition. You've convinced the homeowner that you're an expert. People like to deal with experts. They want to work with someone who knows his business. Suggesting unusual and appropriate flooring stamps you as a flooring expert. It reinforces the impression that you're a true professional.

Educate yourself about the types of wood flooring available. Be ready to discuss plank floors in oak or maple, with pegs or wrought iron head nails, in random lengths, prefinished or unfinished. Let the customers know that you're familiar with all the options. You can meet their needs exactly.

If your customers are interested in parquet flooring, show them brochures or samples of the various patterns. There are six popular patterns: basketweave, herringbone, Mt. Vernon, Monticello, unit block and teak.

When selling strip flooring, explain the difference between tongue and groove and square cut strips. Discuss the advantages of the different kinds of wood. Know which kinds are appropriate for each style of architecture. Ask if they want a prefinished floor or one that's finished after installation.

To sell a new wood floor, stress the benefits of wood flooring:

• Hardwood flooring like _____ (name the type, such as Mt. Vernon parquet or colonial oak plank) is beautiful and rich-looking, and excellent for high-traffic areas.

• The flooring reflects the architectural style of the home.

• Modern wood floors require very little maintenance.

• Hardwood flooring will last a lifetime.

• Everyone who visits the home will notice and admire the beautiful floor.

Stressing the benefits and showing a unique type of flooring makes your bid unique. Other bids are meaningless, because they don't include what your clients really want. You can charge a fair price and earn a legitimate profit. And you're more likely to get referrals, the lifeblood of the remodeling business, from a job that is different and especially attractive.

When selling wood floors that aren't prefinished, be sure to include sanding and sealing in the price of installation.

Resilient Flooring

Asphalt, rubber, vinyl and vinyl asbestos tile and sheet goods are all called resilient flooring. All of these surfaces are pleasing to the eye, easy to maintain, durable and safe.

Every home needs flooring that will take heavy use in the kitchen work center and around the kitchen or dining room table. Hallways and stairways are other high traffic areas. Homeowners need flooring that won't be damaged by spills or detergents used in mopping. It's also important that the flooring can endure the spiked heels that seem to be back in fashion, and heavy furniture. Resilient flooring meets these requirements. It also has a good comfort rating. Some kinds are available with a no-wax finish that keeps its shine for many years.

Resilient flooring is appropriate *only* for interior use with ordinary household traffic, and over surfaces that are not transmitting water vapor.

At one time, asphalt-asbestos tile was the most popular surface for kitchens and bathrooms. Today, vinyl sheet goods are more popular than tile. That's good news for home improvement contractors. It's harder to lay sheet goods than tile. Most homeowners would be well advised to leave the laying of resilient sheet flooring to experts.

When your client decides on resilient flooring, don't insist on selecting a pattern and color right away. Instead, estimate the approximate cost per square yard, and write this amount into the contract as an allowance. Let the customer select the flooring from the dealer you recommend or any dealer of the customer's choice. This relieves you of the chore of pattern selection, while guaranteeing that your cost doesn't exceed your estimate. If the owner chooses a more expensive pattern, the owner pays the difference. Be sure your contract makes this clear.

There's one unusual type of tile that makes a good upgrade. Natural wood tile covered with a tough transparent vinyl combines the advantages of vinyl with the beauty of natural wood. Styles available include all the woods commonly used for floors. For a brochure, write to the Natural Vinyl Floor Company. The address is listed with addresses of other flooring manufacturers at the back of this book.

Ceramic Wall Tile

The most common sizes for ceramic wall tile are 4¼'' x 4¼'' or 6'' x 6''. Mosaic tiles can also be used on walls, counter tops and floors.

Many ceramic tile jobs are very small — sometime only about 25 square feet around the tub. Your tile sub may have a minimum charge for small jobs. Sometimes you can add a tile counter or backsplash for little or no additional charge. Use this point to upgrade the sale by suggesting that your clients can save money by having the counter top or other work done now.

Ceramic tile costs more than wallboard or plastic coated hardboard. Why would anyone pay extra for ceramic tile wall? Because they're buying the benefits. Here are some benefits to stress when selling wall tile:

- Tile is sanitary and noncombustible.
- Tile never needs painting.
- Tile is easy to clean.
- Tile doesn't corrode, stain, char or deteriorate. The colors stay bright.

Point out the benefits. Use brochures showing typical installations, patterns and color samples. Have samples and pictures in your sales kit. Tile manufacturers offer free brochures that show beautiful installations. They're excellent sales tools.

How to Measure for Wall Tile

Here's a handy rule of thumb when you're estimating quantities for pricing ceramic wall tile. Just add the linear measure of all walls and multiply by the height of the wall or wainscot. For example, a 5' by 7' bathroom has 24 linear feet of wall. (Add 5 plus 5 plus 7 plus 7.) If you're installing a tile wainscot 5 feet high, multiply 24' by 5'. Figure 120 square feet of tile area and price it on that basis. Don't deduct for openings. This will provide a margin for waste, breakage and trimming.

Selling Flooring and Tile

Either tile work or resilient flooring will be needed in almost every major remodeling job you have.

But your company advertising should bring in some leads for replacement flooring or tile work alone. There are two keys to converting these leads to sales: making the homeowner's decision less difficult, and offering affordable payment terms.

Help the Homeowners with the Choices

When a floor or tile replacement is part of a remodeling job, the homeowners often don't have a clear idea of what they want. It's up to you to make suggestions. The first step is to find out what they like. Listen to what they say and note their responses to the brochures you show them. Narrow down the choices to a general category. If they're picturing shining hardwood floors, don't waste time showing tile samples.

When remodeling kitchens or dens, many homeowners will respond favorably to a suggestion of brick decorative facing. This isn't real brick. But it looks and lasts like real brick! Brick facing comes in both plain brick and used or antique brick patterns. Stone patterns in the same material are available. Brick facing is both fireproof and insulated and needs only an occasional wipe down to stay new clean and bright. The material is permanent and strong. Your knowledge of brick facing, called on when appropriate, should increase your percentage of closes.

When selling "extras" like brick facing, quote the additional cost in dollars per month. Stress how little these quality extras will increase the monthly payment. Remember, people buy major benefits with minor monthly payments.

As I said, there are a lot of choices when selling floor cover. But making choices is good for sales. If you know the key choices, you can present them to the homeowners as either/or questions. "Do you like the walnut or the oak parquet?" If they make a choice, they've come part way toward saying "yes" to the sale. Then you can proceed with the sales presentation. Describe in detail what you're going to do. Stress the benefits as you go along. Suggest a monthly payment and ask if they can handle that without any problem. If they answer "yes" to that question, you're ready to close. The next step? Easy! "Can we use the kitchen table to write up the order?"

Don't Beat a Dead Horse

Remember, when a prospect says "I have to think it over," or "I'll just discuss it with my mother-in-law," you blew the sale. Once in a while you'll hear "I have to talk to my lawyer." This is also a put-off. But you can counter it. "Fine, I'm glad to know that you're a careful person. We like to have everything clearly understood in advance. Set up an appointment with your lawyer and let us know so we can be there. We can answer his questions and explain any facts that he may need to know. Okay?"

If the answer is "yes," you have a sale. But if the answer is "no," the excuse was just a brush-off. One of two things has happened. Either they're "brain-pickers," not sincere buyers, or they're stalling to get other bids. Maybe you didn't qualify them correctly, or you did a poor selling job. Give it one last shot. Ask if they have any more questions. "Now is the time for me to answer them. I can only answer your questions while I'm here." If you can get them to ask more questions, the deal might still be alive. If they're noncommittal or vague, don't waste any more time. Go to a live lead instead. Life is too short. Use it profitably.

Watch for the Pitfalls

Remember that flooring and tile work done in the context of a remodeling project will always cost more than flooring and tile work in new construction. The quantities are smaller, tear out is the starting point for every job, more surface prep is needed, working conditions include delay and obstruction by the occupants, and the client is likely to be both more critical and demanding of your work. Price the job accordingly.

It's a mistake to quote a new construction cost for tile in a remodeling project. You call your favorite tile sub. "Hey, Bill, what's my cost for ceramic wall tile, oatmeal pattern?" He gives you a square foot cost. You use it. Now you're in trouble. Here's why. You sell the job at his price, plus your usual markup. He starts the job. Then you get Bill's phone call explaining that the charge has gone up a couple of hundred dollars because plaster is crumbling over the tub. The whole wall needs a new brown coat and scratch coat before Bill can lay any tile. Now take that news back to your client!

Never assume that any job will be simple and straightforward. Look for the problems that *will* crop up. Plan for them, and include them in your price for the job. Exclude everything else from your contract. Figure 22-1 lists the survey questions for flooring and tile sales.

Survey of Pitfalls — Flooring and Tile

Here are some of the things to look for when pricing a replacement flooring job:

1)   What is the old floor surface? Will you have to tear out and dispose of an old wood, tile or resilient floor? If so, include it in your price.

2)   What's the condition of the concrete subfloor? Is it so cracked or uneven that you'll have to put down a latex skim coat? Charge for it.

3)   Has the wood subfloor in the bathroom rotted out from too much water? Check around the tub and toilet. If you have to lay a new subfloor, let the owner know that you have to do it and include it in the price. Check for the same problem in the kitchen or pantry.

When possible, don't specify the type or thickness of the underlayment. Leave it up to the tile sub. In the contract, use the words "with the necessary underlayment" after specifying the flooring to be used.

4)   How many square feet are there in the bathroom? Does the sub have a minimum charge for small jobs? Don't throw away your profit by forgetting to charge the minimum.

When you're selling new tile on walls or counter tops, watch for these potential problems:

1)   Check the condition of the wall behind the old tile. If the plaster is in bad shape, you'll have to include a new plaster wall. You might be able to substitute greenboard drywall if the owner will go for it. Either way, it's a small area, so remember that the plasterer has a minimum charge.

Whenever you sell a tile wall replacement, sell a new wall behind it. At least figure it into your selling price. You can't afford not to.

2)   Don't forget the cost of the debris removal. It can be substantial when you're replacing old tile.

3)   When selling a bathroom wall tile job, assume that the accessories will be damaged. Sell a new set of accessories with the job.

4)   The old base will have to be removed. Include and charge for a new wall base. It can be vinyl, ceramic or wood, depending on the type of flooring and wall material.

5)   In an old bathroom, beware of plumbing problems. An old toilet may be fragile. It can crack when moved to install tile or flooring. If the porcelain has age lines, sell a new toilet along with the tile job. Use this sales pitch:

"Mrs. Homeowner, you're going to have a nice new tile floor in the bathroom. It would be a shame to reinstall that old toilet. Look how green the pipe is from the tank to the toilet. Since we're going to have to take it out anyway to put down the floor, putting that old thing back again is a real waste of your money. Now you can get a new toilet in for just the materials cost. The labor for putting a new one in is the same as for putting back the old one. Also, when it finally *has* to be replaced, and it looks like it's had its day, they're going to have to tear up your new floor to do it.

"Why don't I figure in a new toilet? That way you'll have a complete new bathroom. I can add it into the monthly payments for you. It'll only be a few dollars more per month."

Quote a realistic figure for the length of the loan, of course. "For that small amount," you continue, "it would be a real shame not to do it."

6)   If you're replacing an old-fashioned toilet, the new one might not fit the riser of the soil stack. Include a charge for relocating the riser.

Survey of pitfalls
Figure 22-1

Chapter 23

Selling Garages

Selling detached garages is a profitable part of the home improvement business. The beauty of the garage business is that you need few subs. You'll just need carpenters, a cement sub, an electrical sub and a door company. Remember the rule: the less subs, the more profit.

Garages can be good business. I know a builder who started out doing garages and made enough money to buy several lumberyards.

One part of the garage business is selling replacement garage doors. Replacing swinging wood or jamb hinge wood doors with modern steel sectional doors can be profitable work too.

Let's concentrate on detached garages first. Then we'll move on to door replacements.

How to Sell New Garages

Every garage salesman worth his salt knows exactly what the code and zoning ordinances will permit. Know what the building code requires and what setback is needed before making any sales calls. Most garage sales can be made on the first call if you know what can be built and where. Of course, some of the leads will turn out to be shoppers, just out to get bids. But a good garage salesman will always try to close on the first call. You can't close if you have to call back after checking the code.

From the outside, a garage just looks like a garage. But building codes can make a big difference to a garage builder. In most communities, studs can be 24'' o.c. But a few insist on 16'' o.c. double wall construction rather than single wall construction. Minimum sizes for rafters, cross ties and headers and the minimum thickness for the slab depend on the code in force. Can you use a floating slab, or do you need grade beams, reverse retaining walls and water ledges? To talk intelligently with your prospect and price out the job accurately, have the code at your fingertips.

Qualify the Leads

Begin the sales pitch by qualifying the lead: Do you have a van? Do you intend to buy one? Is your car a compact? A midsize car? A big American car?

You have to know the size of the vehicles to sell the right-size garage. If you sell a standard-size garage with 7'6'' wall studs and a 6'6'' high door and it won't accommodate his car, you've got collection problems that won't quit. And perhaps you deserve them.

Both the height of the door and the length of the garage can be critical. Almost all garages built today are 20' deep. But that's not enough for some cars. When in doubt, measure the prospect's car. Then price and sell a garage 22' deep if necessary.

Remember that the depth of the wall studs decreases the usable depth of the garage. The depth of the overhead door and its track reduce the depth of the garage. Most people can only tell you that they want a one-car or two-car garage. It's up to you to make sure that the garage is large enough to meet their needs.

Next, find out how much room they need for work benches and storage. Do they want to keep the mower and the snow blower and all the garden tools and the kids' bikes in the garage? Is the husband a handyman with a collection of woodworking tools?

Here's the formula for figuring the amount of usable space. The standard overhead double door is 16' wide. This is wide enough for two cars. Figure a 1' offset on the wall farthest from the service door. Add 16' for the overhead door to get a total width of 17'. That's the minimum *interior* width. If you sell the customer a 20' wide garage, he'll have 3' x 20' for storage space along the side of the garage where the service door is located. This, plus any space at the end of the garage, is enough for the average family. If the handyman wants a large work bench, sell an extra 2' in width if the lot size and zoning will allow it. Side space is more accessible than end space because you don't have to go around the cars to use it.

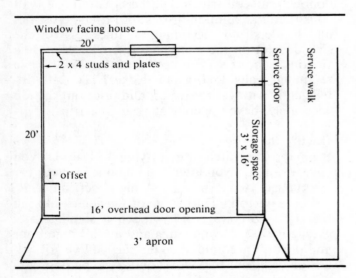

Typical garage layout
Figure 23-1

Use a Sketch and Specifications Sheet

Customers are grateful when you explain why you're laying out their garage in a particular way. To help them picture it better, make a sketch of the layout, showing the work bench, service door, window, light, switch, and storage space, if any.

Figure 23-1 is a typical garage sketch. In our example, we've placed the service door 16' from the front of the garage so the hardboard siding can be used full length. This benefit is a selling point. It lets the prospects know that you're knowledgeable and thinking of the best way to do the job for them.

At about this point in the discussion, take the garage specifications sheet out of your kit. Figure 23-2 is the spec sheet I use.

Now Fill in the Details

When the spec sheet is on the table, it's time to make the rest of the decisions. What kind of roof, siding and door do they want?

The roof— Once the size of the garage has been determined, the next question is whether they want a hip or gable roof. They'll usually ask which is the cheaper. The answer is a hip roof. On a hip roof the weight of the roof is carried on all four walls. A gable roof's weight is carried on only two walls. Suggest a hip roof unless they have a gable roof on the house and want to match it.

Your prospects will often say, "Why is a hip roof cheaper? It seems to me a gable roof should be cheaper." Here's the answer as my lead carpenter once explained it to me. There's more labor in a gable roof. When the carpenters build a gable roof, they set up their scaffolding inside the garage to put up the rafters and the ridge. Then they have to dismantle and reset the scaffolding outside for each gable end, which means three setups. That takes time. For a hip roof, our men set up a scaffold inside the garage. A helper hands up the rafters, the sheathing and finally the roofing. It's one operation so it takes less time and costs less. This wouldn't be true in a large building. But it's cheaper in a 20' garage.

The siding— The next decision is usually whether to use aluminum or hardboard siding. Your pitch might go like this:

"Yes, aluminum siding costs more. A garage with aluminum siding usually costs about 20% more than one with hardboard. Well, when we use aluminum siding, we have to build the garage with a double wall. First our men have to install sheathing. Then the aluminum siding with the insulated backerboard goes over that. So you're getting an extra wall but need twice the labor. Yes, we have it in several stock colors. Will it dent? Well, I couldn't dent it with my fist. But a baseball or bat could make a dent. You know best if this can hap-

Garage Specifications

Concrete specifications:

Floor size: _____ Apron size: _____

Mesh: yes ☐ no ☐ Conduit stub for electric: _____

Driveway: _____ Patio: _____ Sidewalk: _____

Retaining walls: _____ Footings: _____

Hauling of dirt: yes ☐ no ☐ Hauling of debris: yes ☐ no ☐

Remove present garage floor: yes ☐ no ☐

Contractor not responsible for condition of existing concrete floor.

Carpentry specifications:

Garage size: width _____ length _____ wall height _____

Extensions: _____

____ x ____ rafters _____ O.C. with ____ x ____ hip and ridge

2x4 studs _____ O.C. 2x6 cross ties (#_____)

1x4 notched sway braces (#_____) 2x12 overhead door headers (#_____)

Roof style: hip _____ gable _____ other _____

Style of gable ends: front _____ rear _____

Shingles: type _____ color _____ Roof vents: _____

Windows: aluminum jalousie _____ aluminum slider _____ other _____

Service door: _____ Overhead door: _____

Siding: type _____ color _____ insulation _____

Wreck and haul away present garage: yes ☐ no ☐

Note: We use all kiln-dried lumber and construct 8'' boxed eaves on all sides.

Electrical specifications:

Reconnect existing service: _____ Install underground standard: _____

Number of switches: _____ outlets: _____ fixtures: _____

Automatic door operator: yes ☐ no ☐ Number of transmitters: _____

Other electrical work: _____

_____

The above specifications are hereby made a part of and incorporated in the contract dated this day _____ month _____, 198___.

Owner _____ Salesman _____

Owner _____

Garage specifications sheet
Figure 23-2

pen in your neighborhood. We can also cover your eaves with aluminum so you'll never have to paint them. This way the only paint the garage will need is on the doors. They're easy to paint with a roller.

"I'll tell you frankly that most of our customers don't spend that extra 20% for aluminum. They take textured prefinished hardboard siding. Boise Cascade guarantees it for 5 and 25 years. I'll show you a copy of their written guarantee. It comes in the most popular stock colors. For example, we often use clay, avocado green and cobble brown. There are also stucco and sawtooth patterns. This makes a very good looking garage that doesn't need painting. We can also cover the eaves and fascia with siding material. Just a minute. I'll run get my sample board out of the car so you can pick the one you like."

When your prospects have a home with a stucco exterior, sell a garage with siding that matches the house. Tell them that you'll use stucco board with a texture similar to the texture on their home. A home is a big investment. Don't make it an eyesore by putting up a garage that sticks out like a sore thumb. Stress that the garage that *you* build will be esthetically and architecturally sound — it and the house will appear a unified whole. *You* don't just throw up a structure without a thought of whether or not it conforms in appearance to the rest of the property. You build so that it fits. The property is increased by a lot more than the cost of the garage. Stress this benefit.

Suggesting stucco finish hardboard should clinch the sale. No other salesman has suggested stucco board. They offered only the standard hardboard or aluminum. By suggesting stucco board, you've tilted the playing field in your favor. The job is going to the builder offering the best value, not the lowest price. You're doing the homeowners a real favor. A stucco garage will enhance the value of their home, not detract from it.

Notice the siding on the house before you push the doorbell. If the house has drop siding, vinyl, lap cedar, redwood or shakes, sell a garage with matching siding. That pushes your prospects' buying button. They'll be gratified that you had enough interest to check out the siding. You're thinking of their benefit, not just selling a garage.

The overhead door— Next come the questions and answers about overhead doors. Experience has taught me that it's best to describe the different doors before asking for a decision.

"Mr. and Mrs. Prospect, garage doors come in three styles. We recommend only sectional overhead doors. We don't use the old fashioned tilt-up doors. They're heavy and hard to handle. They won't open when snow piles up against the door or when a car parks close to the door.

"Fiberglass doors let light into the garage while preserving privacy and keeping wind and weather out. A lot of home auto mechanics use them to improve interior lighting. They're built on an aluminum frame so there are no maintenance problems and no painting — ever. The only disadvantage is that the aluminum frame conducts the cold more than wood. Most people want to keep their garages as warm as possible.

"If this garage were on an alley, I'd recommend a steel door. Vandals or kids can't damage steel garage doors. But they're easy to operate. Anyone can open the door with two fingers because it's so well-balanced. It comes factory primed and complete with an astragal. That's the vinyl molding under the door. It keeps rain or snow from blowing into the garage and cushions the door when it closes. You don't need a door operator with a steel door because it's so perfectly balanced. We can install an operator if you wish, but I recommend that you spend the money only if your wife drives into the garage at night. With an automatic opener, she can open the garage door from the safety of the car. The garage light will come on when the door opens.

"Except for the safety factor, there's no need for an automatic opener for a steel door. But the steel door has the same disadvantage as fiberglass. It's colder in the winter, since steel conducts the cold.

"Your third choice is a wood door. The modern styles are mostly flush, which look clean and uncluttered. They're also easier to paint. The flush door comes primed, with a key lock and astragal. We have a choice of designs, so you can customize your door. That makes the garage more attractive, which is important since this garage is on the front of the house. Since wood doors are heavy, we recommend that you have an operator installed with the door. When we install the automatic opener, you get transmitters for two cars and a button at the service door. That way you can open the door from inside the garage. Our flush and panel doors all use commercial grade torsion springs. You've probably noticed in gas stations that the spring is over the door, not on the sides. That's a torsion spring. It's the best and carries the heaviest loads. These doors need it since they're so heavy.

"We service all three types of doors. A phone call to our service department will bring someone right out. The overhead door is the only mechanical device on your garage. But it needs to work right.

"Which door do you think best fits your needs?"

The Close
You've been asking qualifying questions about the size of the garage, the type of roof, siding and overhead door. Each question gets a response, which helps carry the prospect along to the final signature. Now that you have all the information on your spec sheet, it's just a matter of summing up the details. For example:

"Let me just review the facts now so I can figure the cost of the garage. We'll build the garage according to code, of course. That puts it 3' from the alley so you can have a 3' apron. It will be 2½' from the north lot line to comply with the zoning ordinance. We'll pour a monolithic 10 x 20 grade beam around the perimeter according to code, with 4" of fill and 4" of five-bag Portland cement mix over wire mesh. Monolithic means it's all poured at one time. We use wire mesh like they do in street paving so you get a sturdy floor that should be virtually free from cracks. The floor will be pitched slightly from the rear to the front so it drains completely when you wash it out or when the snow melts from under the fenders of your car in the winter. We'll install a water ledge under the bottom plates so they won't rot out from any moisture in the garage.

"The studs will be 16" on center, like house construction. The code says we can build on 24" centers but we think it's better to go with the same type of framing as in house construction. We double the corners and the top plates. The header, the wood beam over the overhead door, is a double 2 x 12 clear across the garage. The siding is prefinished hardboard, like we discussed, with a 5 and 25 year guarantee from Boise Cascade. We'll install it over a waterproof vapor barrier and insulation. We use metal corners and rustproof nails.

"We'll install a solid core service door which is 1¾" thick. It weighs nearly 100 pounds. That discourages burglars. We'll install three hinges on the door to carry the weight. Notice that most of the doors on your house have only two hinges. That was considered O.K. when your house was built. But quality construction today is three hinges

on a solid core door. We use a solid core door because almost anyone can kick in a hollow core door. You don't want to have the expense of replacing a door that's been punctured, either by accident or by vandals.

"We'll use a seal lock aluminum threshold under the door to make a tight seal against rain, snow and cold. The door has a regular house-style lock. We'll box the eaves around the garage. This way no bees or wasps can nest in the eaves. You know what a problem that can be.

"For roofing, we use #240 fiberglass shingles in standard colors. I've got sample shingle colors in my car. One will be very close to the color of your house roof. We'll install a Boston ridge. That's what we call the small shingles that cover the ridge and the corner angles of the roof. That way there are no exposed nails to become rusty and cause the roof to leak.

"For the window, you can choose from two standard styles. The first is a jalousie aluminum picture window. It's attractive and never needs painting. Or you can have an aluminum slider window. I'd recommend a slider if you plan to work in the garage very much. It's nice to have the extra ventilation when you need it. Which one do you like?

"Oh! You want a barn style window instead. That's fine. It will cost a little more, of course. But it's no problem. Let's do it this way. I'll write a $50 allowance into the contract. Any time before we start work, select the exact window you want down at Jensen's Lumberyard. We have an account there. I'll have Jensen's send the window out and will charge you exactly what they charge me for the window. I get a 10% contractor's discount at Jensen's, and I'll pass that on to you. If it comes to less than $50, you'll get a credit. If it's more, you'll have to pay the difference. We call that an allowance and we do it all the time.

"I'll have to charge a little more for labor too. There's no trim on an aluminum window, of course. But you'll want exterior trim on the barn window to finish it off nicely. And, of course, you realize you'll have to paint the window and trim.

"By the way, I forgot to mention that in each corner there will be a sway brace for rigidity, six sway braces in all, each notched into the studs. There will also be three cross ties, 2 x 6's trussed to the roof. Throw a piece of 4' x 8' plywood up there over the sway braces and you have an extra 32 square feet of storage space. You can probably use a little more storage space. Right? I might even be able to get the Boss to throw in a couple of sheets of plywood at no charge if you can give me an answer on this today.

"We also install a roof vent for each car. It's required by the city fire code. It helps prevent spontaneous combustion from gasoline in the summer when it gets real hot This is especially important if you keep a power mower or snowblower in the garage. Yes, it does make the garage colder in the winter. But most people just cover the vents in the winter."

Your summary covered every part of the job. You've been truthful, pointing out the good points and the bad points. The customer knows that his steel door and the roof vents will make the garage colder. He has his eyes open. He knows you've been honest with him. And he recognizes that you're a knowledgeable professional.

But the most important point is that you've set a standard for every other bid and bidder on this job. After your sales pitch, would your prospect buy:

- A door *without* commercial grade torsion springs?

- A slab *without* reinforcing mesh?

- A slab that *won't* drain properly?

- A garage floor *without* a water ledge?

- Studs *more than* 16" on center?

- Framing *without* double corners and top plates?

- Siding *without* a guarantee?

- A hollow core door with *only two* hinges?

- An open soffit *that attracts bees and wasps*?

- Anything *but* a Boston ridge on the shingles?

- From a builder who *won't* install a barn window or something else the owner wants?

- A garage *without* sway braces and cross ties?

All the time you're describing the job, the prospects are wondering if the other builders they talked to plan to include these features. Some may

have. But if the other salesmen didn't emphasize these points, the job is yours, even at a higher price. Next, figure the price, and estimate the monthly payment. And of course tell them that under the FHA you can build their garage for no money down, and that the first payment won't be due for about 60 days. If that's satisfactory, quote the total price. What are your next words? "I'll just use the kitchen table to write up the order, if that's O.K. with you." Have the owners sign the specification sheet and attach it to the contract.

Your job is done. Nice work. You've earned the commission. But be sure they get the plywood as promised. And come back when the work's finished to get referrals to neighbors who need a good home improvement contractor.

Selling Replacement Garage Doors

The first step, as always, is qualifying the prospect. Ask these questions: Is your car a subcompact, a midsize, or a large car? Do you expect to put a van or pickup truck in the garage? Do you have carrier racks on the roof of your car or van? Does your car fit easily into the garage now, or is it a tight fit?

Know the answers to these questions to avoid costly mistakes.

If the prospect has a van, truck or carrier racks, sell a 7' or 8' high door. Be sure the walls are high enough to allow room for the tracks and header above the door. The standard garage door height is 6'6". If this customer needs a 7' or 8' high door, framing a new opening will be a major cost item.

Note that zoning regulations in some cities limit the height of garage doors in residential neighborhoods to 8'. This prevents garaging commercial trucks in residential areas. Before you sell any garage door, check the zoning requirements.

If the prospect's car is currently a tight fit, measure the depth of the garage. It may be only 18' deep. *Beware of a garage only 18' deep.* You're only selling a garage door. But problems lurk in 18' garages. Here's why:

In most old 18' garages the original doors were probably strap hinged. Those doors were hung on the front of the jamb. At some time they were replaced with tilt-up doors. Jamb hinge tilt-up doors fit inside the jamb. Like strap hinged doors, they didn't take up any space inside the garage. When you install a new sectional overhead door, both the tracks and the door itself are inside the garage, behind the stud wall. That reduces interior space by 4". Subtract another 1¼" for the thickness of the door and track. This loss of 5¼" can be just enough to keep the car from fitting into the garage. It just barely fit with the tilt-up door. Now it won't close at all! The customer phones. He's as mad as a wet hen. "Hey, why doesn't my car fit into the garage now? What did you do? Look at all the money you charged and now my garage is useless."

When you get a lead with an 18' deep garage, sell a "nose job" as part of the door replacement. That's an extension on the front of the garage, usually the width of the eaves. This gives extra space for the track and the door so the door will close with the car inside.

Be sure to check the header. Is it high enough for the tracks? When in doubt, tell your door man to install low-headroom hardware.

What if you forget all this advice and install a door where there's not enough room. The garage wasn't measured or the prospect wasn't properly qualified. Sometimes there's still a way to solve the problem. Use a router to cut out about 2'' of the studs where the front bumper hits the wall. Make cuts so the bumper just fits into the wall. Then install a ledger to brace the studs that have been cut. If you need only another two inches, this should do the job.

On every shallow garage job I write some protective wording into the contract:

Contractor is installing an overhead garage door only and is not responsible for garage interior height, width or depth measurements when the installation is complete. Nor does the Contractor guarantee that any particular vehicle will fit in the garage once the new overhead door is installed.

Selling Replacement Doors
Almost all sales for garage doors will be replacement doors. As a rule, the customer only knows that he needs a new door. He hasn't considered what the choices are. After you've measured the old door to get the correct size and to see if the opening will have to be reframed, discuss the alternatives.

Follow the basic sales pitch about the three types of garage doors that I described earlier. Explain the advantages and disadvantages of each type of door. Earn the prospect's trust by being honest about the drawbacks of each type. Since you're concentrating on the door in this sale, not the entire garage, there's time to discuss some additional features you might not bother with when selling the entire garage. Here are some of the advantages to stress:

Advantages of steel doors— Besides being vandal-resistant and easy to operate, steel doors are rugged. They'll last longer than the house itself and will take hard use that would wear out other doors. The steel panels are bonderized and factory primed with corrosion-resistant paint, so they resist rust. They're welded, so there are no bolts, screws or rivets to come loose. The hinges are factory oiled, making for smooth, quiet operation. Each door has a handle key lock and comes complete with astragal or bottom weatherstrip to seal out wind, dust and snow. When snow piles up in the alley, it won't rot the bottom panels of a steel door. And snow won't interfere with opening of the door. It opens straight up without tilting out.

Advantages of wood doors— Both the regular and the insulated wood doors come either flush (which is the contemporary style) or with panels to match the architecture of more traditional homes. Flush doors are easier to paint. A roller does it in minutes. They come from the factory with a coat of primer already applied. I've sold a lot of wood doors on homes with front driveways because it's easy to match the architecture of the house. We can customize the door by adding moulding, special panels or decorative hardware. Since the wood door is heavy, we use commercial-grade torsion springs. This makes it easier to open.

I always recommend installing an electric door operator with a wood door. Wood doors are heavy. Hauling one of those things up every time you drive home isn't something everyone wants to do. And you don't have to. A door opener offers many benefits, aside from the lifting job. One benefit is the safety feature. You just drive up to the garage, activate the door with the transmitter provided, and drive straight in. You never have to leave the safety of your car. There's no fumbling around in the dark for keys or keyhole, or struggling with an obstinate lock, all the while being a prime target for a mugger. There's no getting soaked when you come home during a rainstorm — you just drive straight into the house, so to speak. And when the door opens, a light goes on automatically in the garage, so you know there are no intruders waiting for you, and there's no tripping over things as you stumble around in the dark. These are benefits no one will deny. Point them out to the customer.

Another benefit is that wood doors, especially the insulated ones, help keep the garage warmer. Wood is a better insulator than steel or fiberglass.

**Survey of Pitfalls —
Garages and Garage Doors**

1) If you're replacing a tilt-up door with a sectional door, you'll have to reframe the door opening. Charge for it.

2) If the old doors were on strap hinges, the center post will have to be removed and a new header or dropped header installed. Add this to your price.

3) If the old door was on interior roll-away tracks, the opening will have to be reframed. Again, this means extra charges.

4) Notice the condition of the concrete floor at the lip of the door. Is it badly cracked so the new door won't make a tight fit? Most owners ignore the floor condition. But they'll complain when the new door doesn't fit tight against a cracked and subsiding concrete floor. They seem to think that a new door is going to work miracles. Be blunt. Point out that the new door can't possibly fit tight against the slab. If the owner wants a new concrete floor, you'll be happy to figure the cost and install it.

If the owner seems a little hesitant to make the deal because of the cost of the floor, here's your pitch: "Of course we can finance the new floor and the overhead door in one package at First Federal Savings. Your monthly payment will only be about $18 per month, with no money down. Why don't we figure it out and see exactly what the monthly payment will be?" You've upgraded the sale even before the close.

If the owner doesn't want to pay for a new floor, write this into the contract:

Contractor isn't responsible for the cracked concrete floor. The new door won't make a tight fit due to the floor condition.

The astragal will help a great deal, but it won't solve the problem. Don't get into the clutches of a wiseacre who tells you that there's light coming under the door and he won't pay for the door until it's tight.

5) Specify whether or not you're going to haul the old door away. In your sales pitch, ask the question, "Do you want us to haul away the old door, or shall we leave it in the alley?" Include the cost of hauling the door in your price book. Then, if the owner doesn't want it hauled, lower the price as a sales inducement.

6) When you sell an automatic door opener, make sure there's electrical power for the operator. Note that some cities prohibit plugging the opener into a receptacle. It must be wired to the electrical circuit. Turn on the garage light to make sure that it's working. It's a common trap: Your customer orders a door with an operator. The installer gets through with the job and discovers that there's no power or not enough amperage to operate the door. The owner blames your installer, claiming it's *his* fault that the door won't work.

Be safe. Test the electrical system while making the sale. If the wiring is very old or in bad condition, write this into the contract:

Contractor will connect the door operator to an electrical receptacle furnished by Owner. Receptacle shall be approved, and carry sufficient amperage. Contractor is not responsible for any wiring or electrical fixtures now located in the garage.

For the door opener, be sure to specify whether you'll supply one or two transmitters. Usually a one-car garage needs only one transmitter. Sometimes the owner of two-car garage wants only one transmitter if one side of the garage is intended for storage.

**Survey of pitfalls
Figure 23-3**

Wood doors are available with a key handle lock and an astragal, or bottom weatherstrip, to keep out snow, rain and dust.

Have some brochures in your sales kit that show the various treatments available for wood doors. Show some of the many patterns available. You'll probably upgrade the sale by explaining the benefit of having the garage conform to the architecture of the house.

Advantages of fiberglass doors— Fiberglass doors are opaque and let the light filter in. They're good for handymen who like a lot of light in the garage. They come in several colors. Since the color is actually part of the material, they never need painting and are easy to clean. The most popular colors are white, beige, green, brown and gold. Different manufacturers have different colors available.

Fiberglass garage doors offer complete privacy and good protection from the weather, as do steel and wood doors. The fiberglass sections are ribbed to make them shatter resistant, and are built on an aluminum frame. They come complete with a handle key lock and an astragal, or bottom weatherstrip, that both keeps out rain, snow and dust, and cushions the door as it closes.

Selling garages and replacement garage doors can be a profitable part of your business *if* you plan the job carefully and avoid the pitfalls. Use the survey questions in Figure 23-3 to help you plan and price the job correctly.

Chapter 24

Selling Gutters and Downspouts

When you get a lead for gutters, it might seem at first blush that there's no real selling involved. Gutters are gutters. So measure the job, work up the bid, and hope — hope that you're the lowest bidder, get the job, and manage to squeeze out a profit.

But if you've followed my thinking so far in this manual, you know there's a better way: persuasive selling based on solid information and emphasis on benefits to the customer. *Sell* the job. Don't just take orders. That spells profits.

The Sales Pitch
After the icebreaker and warmup, use a pitch like this:

"Mr. and Mrs. Homeowner, I know how disgusted you must be with the gutters up there now. It's a shame that they've rusted out and have to be replaced. I'll be happy to measure your job. We use seamless aluminum gutters that don't leak or wear out. They're prefinished, like your stove and refrigerator, so they never need painting. Because they're seamless, they're leakproof, just like an aluminum pot or pan. An aluminum pan lasts forever, even when heated and cooled many times. Your new seamless aluminum gutters will take the same punishment.

"Most people order white gutters. White would look good on your house. But we can supply several other stock colors. Would you like white or a color?

"We don't bring out lengths of gutters from the shop and then try to fit them together. That leaves lots of seams. And it's the seams that leak in gutters. Instead, we have gutter fabricating equipment mounted in a truck that comes right to your home. We make high-quality custom gutters right here for you. The crew loads big rolls of aluminum stock in the machine — in the color of your choice. They just push a button and the gutter comes out the exact length to fit your house. In fact, our men have to block off about 60 feet of the street to accommodate the longest lengths that the machine can make. It's just like squeezing a tube of toothpaste and watching a ribbon of paste come out. But instead of toothpaste, you've got a full length of high-quality aluminum gutter. It's really a marvelous invention.

"I hope you're home the day our men do the job so you can see the equipment at work. It's quite a sight to see your custom-made gutter rolling out the back of that truck, exactly as long as the wall it will protect. And remember: no seams — no leaks.

"We pitch the gutters approximately one inch in every 16 feet so they drain properly to the downspouts. We use only aluminum nails. We'd save a few dollars by using ordinary galvanized steel nails. But galvanized nails on aluminum gutter cause oxidation. It doesn't make sense to use the best aluminum and then ruin it with galvanized nails. But a lot of companies do it. We install a ball strainer in every drop outlet so leaves won't clog your downspouts.

"We only use spikes and ferrules, not the old-fashioned wire hangers. Of course, we'll flash the gutter to the roof so the rain goes from the roof directly into the gutter. That way rain won't drip between the gutter and the fascia board.

"We'll miter the ends and all inside and outside corners. After the gutters are hung, we'll seal all joints with a special gutter compound.

"While we're doing the job, we can install a leaf guard over the gutters for a very small fee. This way you'd never have to clean out the gutters. It's certainly worth the cost of the guard. I'll quote a linear foot price for leaf guard and you can tell us how much to install. As a minimum, I'd recommend it on the east side of the house where the trees are.

"Our gutters are permanently finished in the color of your choice. They're the modern 5" box style, with 3" corrugated square downspouts. The downspouts can drain to splash blocks. The building code here doesn't require draining to a storm drain like it does over in Centerville.

"Of course our men are gutter experts. They're fully insured with workers' compensation, liability and scaffolding insurance. You don't have to worry about getting sued if someone is hurt on the job. In seven years we've never had a serious accident. But an accident can happen to anyone — and at any time.

"Finally, we'll haul away the old gutters and leave your property clean. Your trash service won't take the old rusted gutters unless they're cut up into 3' lengths and tied into small bundles. I doubt that you want to do that. We have a trash truck that will pick them up and take them to the dump.

"It'll take only a few minutes for me to measure your house. Then I can give you the exact cost. I'll also figure the monthly payments if you prefer to handle it that way. On a job this size you can pay it off over 24 months or 12 months. You decide which is best. We work closely with First National Savings and can handle the paperwork for you. Your first payment will be due two months after we finish the job. There's no down payment if you want their monthly payment plan. Of course, if you want to make a down payment, it will make the monthly payments smaller.

"Why don't you look over the color samples and decide what color you like while I do the measur-

ing."

Upgrade the Sale

I've described a good basic sales pitch for gutters. But don't stop there. Every sales pitch should include upgrades as an option. When measuring is finished, discuss any defects you noticed.

"I think some of those fascia boards may be rotten. Notice that area over there that's shaded by the tree? If it needs replacing, we can do it at the same time we put the gutters up. I wouldn't recommend putting new gutters up over rotten fascia. Of course, it's hard to tell the condition of the wood from the ground. When the men start stripping off the old gutter, I'll ask them to check for rotten fascia. If you want, we'll replace any we find. I'll quote a price per linear foot for replacing fascia. One labor saver, if we do replace any fascia boards, is for you to paint them while they're still on the ground. Why wait till they're nailed up on the roof and you've got to go balancing up on a ladder? We'll wait till you've got them painted, *then* we'll put them up. Is that O.K? I don't send anybody up on a ladder to work if there's a way around it.

"By the way, this is a good time to consider covering the fascia with aluminum. We can do it at the same time. Then you'll never have to climb up and paint the fascia again. Aluminum facing protects the wood so it won't rot and may never need replacing again. I'll quote a price for covering your fascia with aluminum. It will add only a few dollars a month to your payment on First National's 24-month plan. If you end up having to replace the fascia once the new guttering is up, then you'll have to pay for it all to be taken down, and put up again. I'm sure you'd like to avoid that additional expense."

My experience is that most homeowners take the aluminum fascia cover when it's offered on these terms.

Before you came, your prospects were thinking only of gutter replacement. But a lot of homeowners know the advantages of aluminum or vinyl siding. Many have considered getting it "some day." Now that you have their interest, take one more step to increase the sale. Suggest aluminum siding to cover the soffits, frieze and rake boards. You may be able to turn a lowly gutter lead into a major sale. Stress these benefits:

Date _____

Customer name _____ Phone _____

Address _____

City, state, ZIP_____

☐ **Aluminum gutter**   ☐**Galvanized gutter**

Show location of gutters and downspout on above sketch. Indicate direction of flow from each downspout. Draw in any additions, porches, or bays. Show amount of clearance on each side of the house.

Gutter specifications:

Length of gutter installed: _____ Color: _____

Type of roof: gable _____ hip _____ gambrel _____ other _____

Condition of existing fascia: good _____ fair _____ poor _____

Height from grade level to eave:_____

Downspout specifications:

Number of downspouts: _____ Number of elbows: _____

Roof overhang (measured from fascia to building): _____

Downspouts drain onto: splash block_____ ground _____ other _____

Miscellaneous:

Remove and haul away existing gutters: metal _____ wood _____

Replace existing fascia: _____

Minimum job: _____ feet

Special instructions:_____

_____

Owner _____ Salesman _____

Owner _____

Gutter and downspout sketch sheet
Figure 24-1

• The homeowner will never have to hire a painter again.

• The homeowner won't risk injury by climbing up a ladder to repaint.

• In the long run, money saved on painting pays for aluminum or vinyl siding. It's essentially cost free.

• Siding protects the wood, reducing rot or eliminating it entirely.

• Modern aluminum gutters make the house more attractive.

• New siding will increase the value of the house.

Writing Up the Order

If you've followed my guide for the sales pitch and upgrading the sale, writing up the order should follow routinely. You've built up to the close by asking for decisions throughout the sale. The prospects have participated by choosing a color, discussing the monthly payments, and responding to your suggestions for upgrades.

You've demonstrated that you're concerned about their job and knowledgeable about aluminum gutters. You've asked about rotten fascia boards and suggested replacement now and protection for the future. You know the local code requirement for drainage and will be sure their job complies.

In general, you've shown more knowledge about gutters and explained the job better than anyone else they've talked to. If they get a lower bid from another contractor, the homeowner probably doubts that contractor's competence and thoroughness. His lower price is now suspect. The prospects have every reason to believe that you'll provide a quality job. You've made a quality presentation, answering all questions and emphasizing all the benefits.

Getting the order should be a natural. Write it up on a gutter and downspout sketch sheet like the one in Figure 24-1. Go over each item with the customers as you fill it in. This ensures that the homeowners understand exactly what's included and excluded. There shouldn't be any surprises when the crew goes out to do the job. Make the sketch sheet part of the contract. Include in the contract the words: "Work to be done is identified on the attached signed gutter and downspout sketch dated _____."

Price the Job Correctly

Beware of minimum charges on small jobs. Some gutter and downspout subs won't send a crew out for less than half a day's work. Note the minimum in your price book.

Add height charges if the job is more than 24' off the ground. If it's over 30', add a scaffolding charge. Check with your sub to find out the amount to add.

It's important to note on the sketch sheet the minimum clearance on all sides of the building. It's harder (and therefore more expensive) to remove and install gutters with less than 8' of clearance. In some cases, the crew will have to work off the roof if there's not room to prop the ladders safely against the building. If there's any doubt, get a quote from the sub before pricing the job.

Follow these three steps to turn a gutter lead into a profitable job: First, sell a quality job at a quality price. Don't play the "low bidder" game. Then evaluate the job carefully so there are no costly surprises during installation. Finally, upgrade the sale with fascia, aluminum fascia cover and siding. Follow these three rules and you're on the way to a steady source of profitable business.

Chapter 25

Selling Kitchen Remodeling

A kitchen remodeling lead is my favorite sales call. When a woman tells you she wants her out-of-date kitchen remodeled, you know you have a serious buyer who's ready to spend money.

The very best kitchen remodeling prospects live in an older home in a neighborhood that's holding its value. The owners are in their 40's or 50's, know what they want and can borrow enough to do it right.

Young marrieds and the college set tend to be a different story. They've just bought an older home and plan to modernize it. They've read all the kitchen planning books and home magazines. They want professional help with the design but don't want to pay for it — and certainly have no intention of having you do the actual work. Once they come up with a good plan, they'll either do the work themselves or hire a few tradesmen to save money. Why have you been invited into their home? Easy. They plan to pick your brain for kitchen remodeling ideas.

Spot dedicated do-it-yourselfers by the condition of the house. You'll probably see a half-completed construction project that gets a little work each weekend. This is a red flag. Admire the work in progress or compliment Mr. Homeowner on something that looks like a completed do-it-yourself project. You'll be surprised at how anxious the homeowners are to show off their handiwork.

Spend a minimum of time with do-it-yourselfers. There are exceptions, of course. But I've sold very few remodeled kitchens to Mr. and Mrs. Handyman.

Learn the Rules of Good Kitchen Planning
Kitchens come in all sizes and shapes. There's no such thing as a routine kitchen do-over. You'll work with everything from a large farm-size kitchen in an old house to a compact galley kitchen in a 1950's home. Every kitchen is unique. Each demands a distinct plan to make it both attractive and efficient. The homeowners are ready to modernize their old-fashioned kitchen. It's up to you to design the kitchen of their dreams. If you come up with the perfect plan, they'll sign the contract.

As I said, the best kitchen leads originate in older residential areas. An older home needs a complete remodel, not just new counter tops or some modern flooring. In homes over 50 years old, there's often a pantry, bedroom or bathroom just off the kitchen. Some will have an attic or basement stairway or a laundry room leading from the kitchen. Kitchen remodeling in these homes will require structural changes to bring the entire kitchen and dining area up-to-date.

That leads to the main sales point when selling new kitchens. Kitchen design has changed dramatically in the last 40 or 50 years. Most of these changes do one important thing. They make life easier and more convenient for the owners. Every modern kitchen includes labor-saving appliances, easy-care surfaces and a floor plan that minimizes time spent preparing food, serving the meal and cleaning up after meals.

Of course, there's no reason why a functional, efficient kitchen can't be attractive, too. The kitchen should be a pleasant place for meal preparation as well as for family members to meet, relax over a snack, and chat. But think first about creating the ideal space for food storage, meal preparation, eating, and meal cleanup. That's the payoff from your remodeled kitchen.

All kitchen planning begins with a good basic floor plan. There are four possible choices. Let's cover these first.

The U-shaped Kitchen
The U-shaped kitchen in Figure 25-1 has an efficient triangle work pattern. There are three major work centers: the sink, the range and oven, and the refrigerator. These three areas form a triangle in a U-shaped kitchen. The sink is the apex of the triangle, since all work flows to or from the sink.

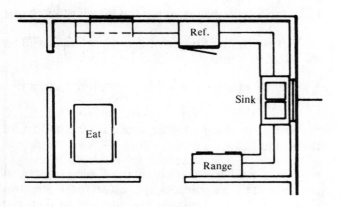

U-shaped kitchen
Figure 25-1

The refrigerator is on one leg of the triangle, and the stove is on the other. The distance between the three points of the triangle is just enough to allow adequate counter and cabinet space for food preparation and storage. Each side of the triangle should be between 4' and 7' long. The total of the three sides shouldn't exceed 21'. Make the triangle as tight as possible. The housewife will benefit by saving steps between the work centers.

Make a sketch of the proposed layout, highlighting the triangle with a colored marker. Explain why you're laying out the kitchen this way. Describe how much easier cooking and cleanup will be in this kitchen. Also point out that this plan provides counter tops next to each work center so there's plenty of room for food preparation.

The L-shaped Kitchen
Figure 25-2 shows an L-shaped kitchen. A plan like this allows space for a small kitchen table at the edge of the work triangle. Notice that the table in a U-shaped kitchen has to be remote from the work triangle. But like the U-shaped kitchen, the L-shaped kitchen has an efficient work triangle.

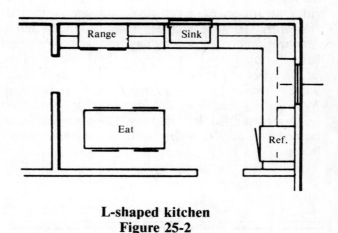

L-shaped kitchen
Figure 25-2

The Straight Wall Kitchen
Straight wall kitchens like the one in Figure 25-3 are still built in smaller apartments today. They're O.K. for a family of two or three if the space is fairly compact. But many older homes have straight wall kitchens with the stove, sink and

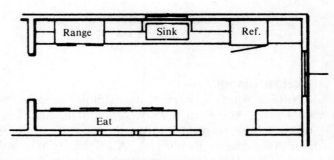

Straight wall kitchen
Figure 25-3

refrigerator spread over 15 feet along one wall. Obviously, that's not considered good planning today.

A straight wall layout is more efficient if the refrigerator is placed near the kitchen door. This makes it easy to put perishables away as soon as the shopper enters the kitchen. Position the sink in the middle and the stove at the other end. Provide counter tops between each work center for convenience.

The Corridor Kitchen

Galley or corridor kitchens are compact working areas best suited for childless couples or those that do very little entertaining. Figure 25-4 shows a corridor arrangement. Even though space is limited, the work triangle makes it an efficient meal-preparation center. There may be space for a small eating nook as well. For a more thorough coverage of the types of kitchens and ideas for each, and the work involved, see *Manual of Professional Remodeling* and *Spec Builder's Guide*, published by Craftsman Book Company. Both manuals may be ordered on the order form in the back of this book.

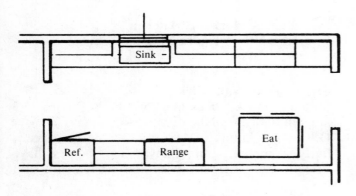

Corridor kitchen
Figure 25-4

Kitchen Islands

Create a dramatic kitchen by placing the range on an island. See Figure 25-5. Of course, an island doesn't have to hold a range. It could be used for counter space or even a sink. A kitchen island with a bar sink is an excellent suggestion for a family that entertains a lot. But the vogue for several years has been an island range with cooking grill. Be sure

the kitchen island has enough clearance all around. Allow at least a 36'' clearance.

If the island will house the range, as in Figure 25-5, sell a vented range hood to suck up cooking fumes. But get a bid from your sheet metal sub before pricing this hood. This is high-cost custom work. Charge for venting and either gas piping or electrical wiring to the range and wiring to the hood. If there isn't space in the ceiling above to run ducting from the hood, a ductless hood will work. Better still, recommend one of those ranges (Jennaire, for example) that have an exhaust fan built right into the top surface of the range. That avoids the whole problem of a hood, and eliminates the need to bring in another sub. Tell the homeowner you can include the price of the new range in the loan.

If a sink will go in the island, don't forget to charge for supply and waste piping to the island. This can be a big item if pipe has to be run under a concrete slab.

If the kitchen isn't big enough for an island, suggest a peninsula to separate the work area from the eating area.

Kitchen Design Tips

Here are a few tips on laying out efficient kitchens:

• Put the range and oven on the exterior wall so the exhaust venting is as short as possible.

• Manufacturers discourage installing ranges in a corner.

• Try to provide counter space on both sides of the range.

• Put a wall oven at the end of the counter, if possible. This guarantees space for food preparation adjacent to the oven and a place to dish out the meals.

• Refrigerators should be at the end of the counter nearest the kitchen entry door, if possible. This way, anyone coming home from grocery shopping can store the perishables away immediately.

• Standard refrigerator door hinges are on the right side. Plan on the refrigerator door opening from the left to the right. Nothing is more frustrating than a refrigerator door that's on backwards and gets in the way every time it's opened.

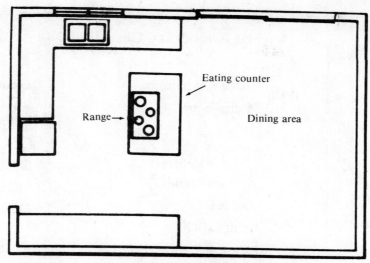

A typical kitchen island
Figure 25-5

• Don't place the refrigerator right next to the oven or range. Refrigerators need a certain amount of air space on all sides to operate efficiently, and they cost enough to run without an oven heating them up. You need at least four feet of uninterrupted counter space between the range and refrigerator.

The Twelve Parts of a Kitchen

You may find it convenient to think of kitchen jobs as having 12 parts: appliances, cabinets and counter tops, ceilings, electrical, flooring, heating and cooling, doors, plumbing, structural changes, wall cover, ventilation, and windows. Of course, not every job includes all 12 parts. But you should think of each of these 12 components when remodeling any kitchen. On the following pages I'll cover each part in detail.

Figure 25-6 is a condensed outline of the discussion that follows. Use it as a checklist when preparing to sell a remodeled kitchen.

Appliances

As a remodeling contractor you're in a different position than a housing tract developer. Spec builders can install whatever brand of appliances they want. But don't try that in someone's home! Your homeowner clients have brand preferences. And, of course, they have strong feelings about style and color. Do they want that side-by-side refrigerator-freezer with an icemaker in avocado green, wheat yellow or eggshell white? Choices on major appliances are nearly endless. You can waste a lot of time if you get involved in the decision-

making process.

I recommend very strongly that you stay out of the appliance business. Major kitchen appliances are advertised heavily. Your prospects have been planning to remodel their kitchen for some time. They've been watching sale prices for the models they want and know what store is offering what price. If you charge the regular retail price, they'll feel overcharged. You can't make a decent profit under these circumstances.

And there's another reason to avoid furnishing appliances. If you sell an appliance, it's your fault when it stops working. No home improvement contractor wants to be called at all hours of the day or night to handle service complaints on dishwashers, refrigerators, garbage disposers or trash compactors. Just telling your clients that it's not your problem and they have to go to the manufacturer for service leaves a bad impression. If your clients picked out the appliance and had it delivered, they know that keeping it running is strictly between them and the manufacturer or dealer.

The best solution is to create an allowance for appliances in the contract. Your owners can finance the appliances as part of the remodeling cost, but you've taken yourself out of the decision-making process. Write a clause like this into the contract:

The contract price includes an allowance of $_____ for the purchase of the following appliances by Owner: _____

_____

_____

Kitchen Remodeling Checklist

Appliances
☐ Dishwasher
☐ Disposer
☐ Microwave oven
☐ Oven
☐ Range
☐ Refrigerator
☐ Trash compactor
☐ Washer/dryer
☐ Other _____

Cabinets
☐ Material and style
☐ Convenience features
☐ Counter tops
☐ Soffits
☐ Backsplash
☐ Utility cabinet
☐ Remove old cabinets and debris
☐ Other _____

Ceilings
☐ Repair or replaster existing ceiling
☐ Acoustic tiles
☐ Suspended ceiling
☐ Dome ceiling
☐ Dropped ceiling
☐ Other _____

Doors
☐ Interior, door and trim
☐ Exterior, door and trim
☐ Locks
☐ Close up transoms
☐ Storm door
☐ Other _____

Electrical
☐ Circuits needed
☐ Outlets
☐ Wall switch
☐ Appliance wiring
☐ Ceiling fixture
☐ Ground fault receptacles
☐ Wiring for exhaust fans
☐ Other _____

Flooring
☐ Underlayment
☐ Resilient tile
☐ Sheet goods
☐ Ceramic or clay tile
☐ Carpet
☐ Remove old floor and debris
☐ Other _____

Heating and Cooling
☐ Relocate ducts
☐ Relocate baseboard radiator
☐ Install paddle fan
☐ Install smaller registers
☐ Other _____

Plumbing
☐ Sink relocation
☐ Bar sink in island or peninsula
☐ Reventing
☐ Move stack
☐ Installation of appliances
☐ Gas line relocation
☐ Other _____

Structural changes
☐ Partitions moved
☐ Cantilever addition
☐ Doorways relocated
☐ Other _____

Wall repairs and covering
☐ Plaster/drywall repair
☐ Prepare wall for paint or paper
☐ Ceramic tile
☐ Paneling
☐ Other _____

Ventilation
☐ Range hood
☐ Ceiling exhaust fan
☐ Wall exhaust fan
☐ Ductless exhaust
☐ Other _____

Windows
☐ Windows replaced
☐ Windows relocated
☐ Storm windows
☐ Other _____

Kitchen remodeling checklist
Figure 25-6

If the cost of appliances exceeds the amount stated above, Owner will bear the additional cost. If the cost of appliances is less than the amount stated, Contractor will issue a credit for the difference. Contractor will install these appliances and install the required gas piping, water lines, drain, vent and waste lines and electric outlets as needed for the appliances. Once these appliances are installed, Contractor is not responsible for appliance service or maintenance.

Cabinets and Counter Tops
Kitchen cabinets come in many styles and finishes. What you recommend depends on what's appropriate in the kitchen, what's currently available, and your client's budget and taste. Layout of the cabinets is your job. Start with a good plan, probably either U-shaped, L-shaped or island, as we discussed earlier.

Cabinets have changed even more than appliances in the last 30 years. Utilitarian cabinets sold in the 1950's are very different from modern cabinets. Today homeowners can select metal cabinets that are attractive as well as sturdy and functional. They're available with finishes in popular colors as well as traditional white. Finishes can match the refrigerator and oven.

Stock wood cabinets are factory-made like pieces of furniture. They come in many styles and woods. Oak, fruitwood, and maple are the most popular. Doors can be flush, raised panel, planked or flat panel.

Discriminating upscale buyers who have definite ideas on how they want their cabinets finished may prefer custom-made units. Other buyers may want laminated cabinet faces of Formica or Melamine. Plastic-faced cabinets are both durable and, with wipe-clean interiors, easy to maintain.

Kitchen cabinets today aren't just boxes with shelves. Options include lazy susans for corners, cutlery trays, pot lid baskets, vegetable baskets, cutting boards and butcher blocks, to mention a few. Offer these options to your prospects.

But don't forget one important thing in this maze of choices. The old cabinets have to go somewhere. Charge for hauling them to the dump.

Planning for cabinets begins with a good storage plan. In many older homes there will be plenty of floor and wall space. The kitchen is big by contemporary standards. There are already plenty of cabinets and drawers. The problem is that the cabinets are not arranged in a convenient work triangle. In newer homes the problem may be a simple lack of space. It may be hard to find enough wall space for cabinets. Solving that problem can make structural changes necessary.

Here are the accepted standards when planning cabinets. Begin with 12 square feet of *wall* cabinet (height of the cabinet face times the face width). Then add six square feet of *wall* cabinet for each person living in the home. If it's a three bedroom home, count two residents for the master bedroom and at least one resident for each of the two other bedrooms. Your calculation for wall cabinets in a three bedroom house would look like this: The basic 12 S.F. plus 24 S.F. (4 times 6 S.F.) is 36 S.F.

For example, you get 36½ square feet of wall cabinet from the following arrangement:

- One 36" wide by 18" high cabinet over the refrigerator (4½ S.F.)

- Three 36" wide by 30" high wall cabinets (22½ S.F.)

- One 36" wide by 18" high cabinet over the range hood (4½ S.F.)

- One 24" wide by 30" high corner wall cabinet (5 S.F.)

That's enough wall cabinet space for a family of four or even five. Planning for base cabinets takes care of itself if there's a base cabinet under all wall cabinets (except under the appliance cabinets).

If placement of a window makes it difficult to provide enough wall cabinet space, make up the difference with an extra base cabinet in the kitchen or a utility cabinet by the back door.

Most wall cabinets are 30 inches high and are mounted 24 to 30 inches above the counter. If the counter top is 36 inches above the floor, the top of the wall cabinet will be 7'6" to 8' above the floor. In a kitchen with a 7'6" ceiling, reduce the space between the counter top and the bottom of the wall cabinet to 24". If the ceiling height is over 8", consider an illuminated suspended ceiling, or frame a soffit down to 7'6" over the cabinets. To give the room an extra nice touch, sell a soffit about 2 inches wider than the cabinets. It will make the cabinets look recessed.

Suggest a shelf for cookbooks, racks for cooking equipment and utensils, and dedicated shelves for small appliances such as waffle irons, toasters, toaster-ovens, blenders, mixers, food processors, juicers, yogurt makers or coffee makers. Ceiling racks for pots and pans, as they have in restaurants, have become popular of late. Suggest you put one in. Show them color pictures cut from home improvement magazines. Collect a portfolio of pictures that may appeal to your clients so you can present a picture for every suggestion you make.

Utility cabinets— Don't overlook utility or broom cabinets when planning kitchen remodeling. Every housekeeper needs a tall cabinet for brooms and mops. But put the utility cabinet outside the food preparation triangle — near the back door is best.

Counter tops— Offer a choice of counter tops in laminates or ceramic tile in either a self-edged top or a roll-formed style and a 4'' backsplash. Suggest that a built-in bread board or chopping block is extremely useful and will preserve the counter top. Sell a ceramic counter top if this kitchen is intended to be a cut above average, especially if you suspect the owner is shopping for bids. Switch the sale to ceramics, so you are designing a different job. The close might go like this:

"I'd like you to consider something other than a laminated counter top. Recently my wife got a phone call while she was cooking. Without thinking, she put the hot skillet she had in her hand down on the counter top. It got scorched pretty badly. With the scratches from knife cuts and wear and tear, we just had to replace it. This time we installed ceramic tile. It's more attractive, richer-looking and the most durable counter you can buy. As you know, ceramic tile doesn't burn or stain and resists water. There's a rainbow of colors to choose from. A tile counter top will last almost forever. It's worth the little extra it costs. Which do you think you would prefer?"

Yet another choice for counter tops is stainless steel. It has the same advantages as ceramic tile.

Remember, when you're planning the kitchen out, that there should be no less than 4 feet and no more than 6 feet of counter between the refrigerator and the sink. Leave at least 3 feet but no more than 4 feet between the sink and the range.

Ceilings
Many older homes have 9' ceilings. The plaster is probably cracked. If the kitchen has been remodeled before, it probably has acoustical tile stapled to sleeper strips that are nailed to the ceiling. To modernize the ceiling you have the following choices. What you do depends on the owner's taste and pocketbook:

1) Replaster the ceiling.

2) Install acoustic tile over the old ceiling.

3) Install a grid-lock suspended ceiling.

4) Install a grid-lock suspended dome ceiling.

5) Build a dropped ceiling.

Before pricing out a dropped, suspended, or dome ceiling, make sure there's enough space between the top of the windows and the ceiling. This isn't a problem if the owner is going to have the old windows replaced. But if he's not, point out that old-fashioned windows can really spoil the effect of the brand new, modern kitchen you're putting in. And installing new tight-fitting removable sash windows will save on heating and air conditioning costs. Remember to charge for the electrical outlets and switch for either the recessed light fixture or for the luminous panels in a suspended or dome ceiling.

Doors
If there's a pantry or another room leading off the kitchen, sell replacement interior doors. The old panel doors will look out of place in the modern kitchen. Sell flush doors with new passage locks and modern ranch or colonial trim, depending on the owner's preferences. Neglect this little step when modernizing a kitchen and you've blown the job. The entire kitchen has to be coordinated. If the door is in a non-bearing wall, consider replacing it with a pocket sliding door. That keeps the door out of the way when it's not needed.

Replace the old-fashioned back door with a modern door that has a deadbolt lock and metal threshold. Replace the wide paint-encrusted trim with modern trim that matches the trim on the new interior doors. If there's a transom over the door, close it in. And sell a storm door if the kitchen door leads directly to the exterior.

Electrical
Most building codes have minimums for electrical work in the kitchen: at least one wall switch, a ceiling outlet, three standard receptacles and two

ground fault receptacles for appliances. Ground fault receptacles need a special circuit.

A circuit is needed for each eight outlets in a room. When you're calculating outlets on each circuit, be sure include both the existing outlets and the new outlets.

Remember, these are minimums. A better quality job will have more wiring. Use this checklist to be sure you've thought of every outlet needed:

1) Outlet for clock in soffit

2) Outlet for light in soffit over kitchen sink

3) Receptacle over counter top for coffee maker, mixer, waffle iron and other small appliances. The customer might want more than one.

4) Wiring for dishwasher

5) Wiring and switch for disposer

6) Wiring for electric stove

7) Wiring for microwave oven

8) Wiring for trash compactor

9) Wiring for hood fan, ceiling or wall exhaust fan

10) Wiring for washing machine and dryer

11) Wiring and fixtures for lights in luminous ceilings

12) Ground fault circuit for the refrigerator

Flooring

In old kitchens, you'll usually find either worn linoleum or brittle asphalt tile. Don't forget to charge for removal of the old surface and laying Masonite over the old subfloor, or a skim coat over a concrete floor.

Flooring choices include vinyl or vinyl-asbestos tile, sheet vinyl, ceramic or clay tile, or carpeting. In most cases, the choice will narrow quickly to either resilient tile or sheet goods. But always start selling the best quality flooring. Don't assume that your prospects will reject the more expensive flooring.

You'll probably make the best profit on a resilient tile floor. Your own crew can install it.

Other types of flooring are usually laid by specialists. That reduces your profit. If the owner wants carpet, put it in as an allowance in the contract. The cost of carpeting varies so enormously, and there are so many styles and colors available, that if you get involved, you'll also be involved when the customer decides it doesn't look exactly the way he thought it would. Take my advice — stay out of it.

Heating and Cooling

Before you finish planning the kitchen, check to see what heat ducts, cold air returns or baseboard radiation units will be obstructed. If you can't plan around these obstacles, charge for relocating them or for reducing the size of the registers to the smaller style used with modern forced-air heating and cooling. And remember to add the cost of wall cutting and patching for the new ducts. The heating section in your price book should cover these costs.

To cool the kitchen and save energy, suggest a ceiling paddle fan. These are now very much in style for home use. During meal preparation the kitchen will sometimes be warmer than any room in the house. The rest of the house won't be hot enough to run the air conditioner. If the kitchen ceiling is high enough, a fan may provide just enough cooling power — and at a very low energy cost.

Plumbing

Nearly all kitchen remodeling includes plumbing. Replacing the kitchen cabinets almost always requires plumbing. And, of course, installing a new porcelain or stainless steel two bowl sink with a mixer valve faucet and vegetable spray is probably the most common kitchen remodeling item.

This is a good place to try an experimental close. Ask questions that lead the buyers into making decisions. "Do you want a single bowl or a double bowl sink? Do you want a porcelain or stainless steel sink? Do you want a single lever faucet with vegetable spray or an antique faucet with fancy knobs?" The prospects have to make a choice. Each time they choose, they're one step closer to signing the contract.

Check out the existing plumbing before selling any kitchen fixture that requires a supply or waste line. The plumbing in old houses seldom meets modern code requirements. Here are some of the things to look for:

1)   Look under the sink to see if the present piping is lead, galvanized or copper. If you find lead piping, extra work is needed to convert to copper or extend the lead pipe.

2)   Is there a shutoff valve under the sink? The code now requires it.

3)   Does the sink trap appear to be within five feet of the stack?

4)   Turn on a faucet to see how the sink drains. Slow drainage or the presence of sewer gas may indicate that the drain line isn't properly vented. Any modernizing of the existing supply, drain, vent or waste system will mean opening up the wall and repairing the damage after plumbing is completed. Don't forget to charge for that. It could mean several hundred dollars in extra expense.

5)   Check to see if the faucet chatters when you turn it on. If it does, it may be that the plumbing isn't properly vented behind the wall. Walk outside and look for a stack coming through the roof about where the kitchen sink is. If there's no stack poking through the roof, chances are that a new vent will be required.

Anything can go wrong in a kitchen job — and something will unless you use a good checklist when planning the job. The checklist I've included in this chapter is the place to start. It's saved me thousands of dollars over the years. Run over the checklist on every job. Improve on it if you can. But use some checklist on every sale to avoid unpleasant surprises.

You're the expert remodeler. Protect yourself. Spend an extra five minutes thinking about the existing plumbing. It's discouraging to sell a job and think you have a nice profit, only to have the plumber discover that the plumbing isn't up to code. Your plumber has to do the job by the code and he'll always send you a bill for extra work. Collecting the extra amount from the owner under those circumstance will never be easy.

Structural Changes
Structural changes are often needed in older homes. For example, there's no reason to have a bedroom or bathroom opening on the kitchen. Close up the doorway and open a new passage to a hallway.

Older homes had pantries directly off the kitchen. Today, we're happy to use that space for storage. But the pantry concept is obsolete. The homemaker will usually want you to remove the pantry door and install one wall to create a nook for a small desk, laundry equipment or maybe the refrigerator-freezer. If the pantry backs up to a bedroom, consider partitioning the pantry, using half for additional kitchen area or a nook, and half for new closet space in the bedroom.

Occasionally the owners will want to increase the size of the kitchen. If there's an adjacent porch, laundry room or pantry, include that space in the remodeled kitchen. Removing the porch wall will increase kitchen space enough to add extra cabinets and a breakfast bar or breakfast nook. Removing the partition wall between the kitchen and an existing breakfast room gives a lot more flexibility in planning the new kitchen. If there's a small bedroom off the kitchen that's no longer needed, consider removing that wall to add extra kitchen space.

If there isn't any usable space to incorporate into the kitchen, add a bay window or a cantilever section. Even a 2' or 3' cantilever can create enough space for a kitchen table and give the impression of roominess. Transform a small, cramped kitchen into an attractive and spacious room and you've got the contract.

Ventilation
Mechanical ventilation to remove cooking fumes is important in every kitchen. Today many ranges come with a built-in exhaust system. These are functional. But adding a range hood can beautify the existing kitchen while serving an important purpose.

When laying out the kitchen changes, it's best to put the range on an outside wall. This way the exhaust duct of the range hood can be vented with a short run. Short venting helps the fan operate more efficiently and reduces installation costs.

Consider three types of ventilation. Range hoods are the most popular. They come in a number of stock colors and add a nice finishing touch to the kitchen. Hoods come as ducted or ductless. Ducted units need a duct run from the top of the hood to the roof or an exterior wall. If that's impossible, use a ductless hood. Ductless hoods have charcoal filters that remove much of the smoke and odor before exhausting the air back into the room. Ductless hoods cost less to buy and install and don't exhaust heated or cooled air to the exterior. That can takes some of the load off the heating or cooling system. The disadvantage is that they don't do as good a job in removing smoke and odors.

If neither a ducted or a ductless hood is desirable, install a ceiling or wall fan with a wall switch.

Wall Repairs and Cover

In many old kitchens you'll find wainscot of wood, plastic tile or even linoleum. The plaster under this old-fashioned wainscot is sure to be in bad shape. It will either have cracks and nail holes or will pull off in large chunks where the linoleum or tile adhesive was thickest. Either way, the plaster is ruined. Charge for either a plaster repair job or new drywall.

The trend today is to the clean look, with walls simply painted or papered. Some people still want ceramic tile wainscot because it's easy to keep clean. But the wall above will always be either painted or papered.

Be sure to remember debris removal when pricing the job. The old plaster will have to be removed from the premises. And remember that most plasterers have a minimum charge. If the area is small, specify drywall. Your carpenter can handle that by himself.

Window Changes

Opening up a dark, gloomy kitchen with a modern window is the single biggest favor you can do for Mr. and Mrs. Homeowner. Many old houses have only a single narrow sash window in the kitchen. The window is probably tall and narrow and reaches nearly to the ceiling. The trim is wide and encrusted with paint. The sash balance cords have been repaired many times. The sash may be painted shut or frozen in place by broken sash pulleys.

Modernize the kitchen by replacing the window with modern units in sizes proportionate to the room. If the new window isn't as tall as the old window, close up the balance of the old opening on the interior and the exterior and add new trim. The window to use depends on climate. In cold climates, wood windows are more energy efficient and, with the modern snap-out hardware, easy to clean. In milder climates, metal casement, awning or sliding windows may be a better choice.

Most homemakers want a window over the kitchen sink unless the view would be objectionable. Find out what the owners want. Just remember that sink placement may be dictated by window placement. Suggest the latest style — a planter picture window over the sink. These are very popular

in the expensive, architect-designed homes that you see in magazines. Point out that you can give the homeowner just this kind of look for just a few dollars more a month.

If you're installing new windows, suggest a Formica or ceramic tile window sill. They're durable and easy to clean and never have to be painted or varnished. They're perfect for people who like to have a couple of potted plants over the sink.

If the room will be divided into a kitchen and a breakfast nook, suggest a triple picture window by the breakfast table. The large window gives the nook a feeling of spaciousness. This openness appeals to many people. Sell the window with a color picture from a magazine showing a breakfast nook opening onto a garden.

The Sales Presentation

This chapter wouldn't be complete without a sample sales presentation. Here's how I would sell a remodeled kitchen to a middle-aged couple living in an older house. They've lived there for years. The wife is fed up with the old-fashioned, inconvenient kitchen. It has double hung windows that stick, linoleum on the floor, a string pull on the ceiling light fixture, an old fashioned pantry and a bedroom leading off the kitchen.

Mrs. Homeowner tells you she wants cabinets and a new sink. But you realize that she's visualizing a complete new kitchen. Find out what she really wants by asking questions.

"Have you considered using the pantry space? We could recess the refrigerator in that space, then block off the back of the old pantry to add closet space in the bedroom behind the pantry.

"I'd advise replacing those old-fashioned windows. We can replace them with the new style that you can snap out to clean from inside the house. We could also shorten the windows and make them a bit wider so they're more in proportion with the new kitchen. New windows will be more energy efficient and can lower your heating and air conditioning costs.

"Would you like your ceiling lowered to eight feet? We can install a beautiful suspended ceiling, with recessed lights. This saves money because you've got less space to heat and cool. And it gives the kitchen a totally modern look.

"What kind of cabinets and sink do you like? Would you prefer a stainless steel sink with nickel finish and a lever faucet, or the more traditional porcelain sink? They now come in a variety of colors. What stock color would you like?''

Dramatize the Sales Pitch
When discussing the layout, use a little showmanship. Dramatize the benefits of the new kitchen. Most people feel friendly to a showman; that's why they stand up and applaud a performer. A builder-salesman who can put a little drama into his presentation will win the customer's esteem.

Walk around the kitchen as you paint a word picture of the family enjoying their new kitchen. Walk over and point to the space near the kitchen door where the refrigerator will be. Speak directly to the wife.

"When you come home from shopping, you can put the perishables in the refrigerator right away, without having to move them two or three times. It'll save a lot of steps. This is the food preparation area. The sink will be here, in the middle, with the refrigerator to the left and cabinets here for food storage. This kitchen will be as efficient as an assembly line. The food flows from the refrigerator to the sink, where you'll wash it, then to the counter top to the right here where it's prepared for cooking. Then on to the stove. Dishes go in a cabinet here to the right of the sink, where they're handy for dishing out the food when it comes off the range. The pots and pans will be in this cabinet next to the range and oven.

"When it comes time to clean up the kitchen, you can scrape the dishes into the disposer, then put them directly into dishwasher, here to the right of the sink. It's one step away. When they're clean, you'll unload them right into the cabinets directly above the dishwasher.''

Improvise as you go along. Ask questions and use the answers as a guide for suggesting features the homemaker wants. If she does a lot of cooking, there may not be enough cabinet space for all her pots and pans. Suggest a decorative rack on the ceiling where her pans will be handy.

The layout depends, of course, on placement of the kitchen entry door, windows, and the shape of the room. But the guiding principle should be the most efficient assembly of the 12 components discussed in this chapter. Sometimes existing windows or doors make a U-shaped or L-shaped plan impossible. Then you've got to improvise as best you can. But keep the fundamentals of good kitchen planning in mind. Create a work triangle that

is no more than 22 feet and no less than 13 feet long. Include enough cabinet space. Then explain why preparing and serving and clean-up will be a breeze in this beautiful new kitchen.

Sum Up the Benefits to Close the Sale
When summing up the work you're going to do, explain to the homemaker that this kitchen is designed especially for her. If she has a large family, it's designed as a family kitchen, an efficient and attractive space to prepare large meals. If you're talking to a young working couple that plans to spend a minimum of time in the kitchen, picture the new kitchen as a breeze to maintain. It's functional, yet will be as pretty as a picture in a magazine.

Stress that the kitchen will reflect the personality of the homemaker. It'll be warm, restful and pleasant. A joy to cook in, and a relaxing place for the family to eat. It'll be a pleasant place for a coffee klatch or even a game of cards.

Finally, stress the special benefits you've built into this kitchen. For example, the job might include:

• An efficient triangle work pattern that means fewer steps. Food preparation and cooking are streamlined operations.

• A traffic pattern that keeps family members passing through the kitchen out of the way of the cook.

• Special cabinets designed for storage of food, dishes, pots and pans, small appliances, and even cookbooks.

• Modern features like a cutlery tray, pot lid basket, vegetable basket, cutting board and butcher block.

• A desk to make planning and telephoning more convenient, and a place for a television set.

• All of the surfaces are easy to clean, so it takes a minimum of effort to keep the kitchen sparkling.

• The large utility closet keeps the mop and broom handy.

Selling benefits is the best way to get a profitable contract. When you've stressed all the benefits, lead into the close:

"This kitchen was designed just for you. When you add some plants and the curtains, I know you're going to be proud of it. I'll just figure up the cost and see what the monthly payments will come to. I'll use your kitchen table if you don't mind. It won't take long. While I'm doing that, why don't you select your cabinet hardware from this catalog."

Chapter 26

Selling Painting and Paper Hanging

Here's the best way to sell painting and paper hanging: Don't do it. Include painting in your contract and you've got trouble. The problems aren't worth the aggravation. Complaints about painting slow up collections, tie up cash, and eat up more profit than any other part of the job.

Here's a frequent scenario:

You make what looks like a profitable sale. The owner wants the painting and decorating included in the contract. You agree on a price and sign the contract. Everything looks rosy. The remodeling work goes without a hitch. You pay the subs and suppliers as the job progresses. You sub out the painting, of course, to a competent pro. The painter arrives and goes to work. The next day you get a disturbing phone call from the owner. The colors aren't right. You call the painter. He insists that the owner is color-blind. The owner approved the sample swatches he painted on the wall. But when the paint dried, the owner didn't like it. The painter did his best. He throws up his hands and dumps the problem in your lap.

You decide that cooler heads will prevail. You're going to visit the job yourself and settle the problem! When you arrive, both owners are there. They want the room repainted, gratis of course. They won't pay for repainting because your painter didn't match the sample. They want a different painter, one who can match the color of the drapes, furniture or a scarf. Reasoning gets you nowhere. It's irrelevant that matching a scarf and the wall may be impossible. They don't see how paint from two different buckets that carry identical product numbers can be anything but exactly the same color. You explain that paint is like roofing or floor tile. No two lots will be exactly alike.

After nearly an hour of pleading, you still can't get them to sign a completion ticket. They won't pay and don't care that you've already paid the subs and suppliers. They won't go for the holdback you propose. Not a cent until it's done right!

Now, you're stuck. You need the money. The painter won't go back. He thinks your clients are nuts. He needs to work for them like he needs a hole in the head. Anyway, he's already started one of his own jobs and won't pull off until it's completed. So you can just wait. But you know that waiting is only going to make matters worse. And it's going to be hard to find another painter to do the job. Down at the paint supply store, your first painter has been telling other painters about your nutty clients.

You know that the only way off the hook is either to pay for a second paint job or give the owners a credit so they can hire their own painter. You also know that negotiating a painting credit won't be easy. The owners have all the leverage. They can get just about anything they please.

For a day or two you consider withholding pay-

Ceiling height / Room size (in feet)	8'	9'	10'	11'	12'	Single rolls needed for ceiling
	Number of single rolls needed					
8 x 10	9	10	11	12	13	3
10 x 10	10	11	13	14	15	4
10 x 12	11	12	14	15	16	4
8 x 14	12	14	15	16	18	5
12 x 12	12	14	15	16	18	5
12 x 14	13	15	16	18	19	6
12 x 16	14	16	17	19	21	6
12 x 18	15	17	19	20	22	7
12 x 20	16	18	20	22	24	8
14 x 14	14	16	17	19	21	7
14 x 16	15	17	19	20	22	7
14 x 18	16	18	20	22	24	8
14 x 20	17	19	21	23	25	9
14 x 22	18	20	22	24	27	10
16 x 16	16	18	20	22	24	8
16 x 18	17	19	21	23	25	9
16 x 20	18	20	22	24	27	10
16 x 22	19	21	23	26	28	11
16 x 24	20	22	25	27	30	12
18 x 18	18	20	22	24	27	11
18 x 20	19	21	23	26	28	12
18 x 22	20	22	25	27	30	12
18 x 24	21	23	26	28	31	14

Note: Deduct one single roll for each two window or door openings.

Wallpaper chart
Figure 26-1

ment to the painting sub. But all thought of this evaporates when the sub notifies the owners that he's going to lien the property and file suit against both you and the owners if he's not paid by Friday. Next, the homeowners' attorney advises his clients not to sign the completion ticket unless a contractor's statement and the proper waivers are furnished.

End of scenario. But if you think this has been a fairy tale, you haven't been in the home improvement business very long. Exactly this type of thing happens all too often when you deal in aesthetics. Most people recognize quality construction when they see it. But selecting colors is purely a matter of taste and style. That's dangerous territory for most home improvement contractors.

How to Avoid the Painting

Maybe you'll take my advice and keep painting out of your contract. I hope so. If you do, here's the best way to handle it:

"Mr. and Mrs. Homeowner, our strongest suit is carpentry contracting. If we do the painting, we sub it out to a union painter. And we have to mark up the sub's bill to cover supervision and our overhead, plus the cost of public liability,

Worker's Comp and scaffolding insurance. What I'd suggest is that you save this cost by doing the painting yourself, or by hiring your own painter. Either way you'll save money. We can even include the painting money in the loan, if you like, so you won't have to lay out any extra cash.''

If the owners go for it, write this clause in the contract:

The contract price includes an allowance of $_____ for painting. Contractor will furnish neither labor nor materials needed for painting and is not responsible for the quality of paint, color or application. Owner will hire a paint contractor to do all painting required under this contract. Owner agrees that the lender may make payment of this allowance directly to the paint contractor.

The Benefits of Avoiding the Painting

This time I'm going to list the benefits for *you,* not the benefits you'll sell to the prospect. These are some of the ways you can save time and money by making a painting allowance in the contract:

- You won't spend time in color selection.

- You'll avoid disputes with the customer.

- You won't have to pay twice for the paint job.

- Collection won't be delayed.

- You won't be sued when the paint job isn't right.

- You won't have a dissatisfied customer knocking your company.

There's an old axiom that sums it up: The best you can get by doing the painting is the worst of it.

If You Can't Avoid the Painting

Occasionally you'll have a customer who won't agree to handle the painting part of the job. He wants to sign one contract to cover the entire job. This leaves you with two options: refuse the job, or take on the decorating and try to make the best of it.

If you take it on, either sub it out to the best painter you know or get your most reliable employee to do it. Any painting you handle yourself should be done at a good markup. Set a minimum cost for small jobs. Price surface preparation on a time and material basis. Set square foot prices for walls, ceiling, doors, windows, siding and trim. *Paint Contractor's Manual,* by this publisher, can help you out here.

If you're willing to tackle the painting, you're also going to end up doing some papering. Your price book should include figures for removing old wallpaper and hanging new paper. But don't get into picking patterns. Include an allowance for the cost of paper in the contract. You can either specify a dollar amount per roll or a lump sum for the paper. Use the chart in Figure 26-1 to figure the number of rolls needed. Make the owner responsible for any cost over the contract amount.

With good planning and a little luck, you'll do no worse than break even on the painting and decorating work.

Chapter 27

Selling Roofing and Siding

Roofing can be a profitable part of any remodeling business. True, there isn't much snob appeal in a new roof. It's not the type of thing your clients will want to show off to their friends. And few people buy a new roof just to modernize the look of their home. In fact, it's hard to sell a new roof at all as long as the old one keeps the rain out. But a deteriorated roof has a way of becoming the owner's top priority when it's raining.

To get an idea of the size of the roofing business, look up the listing for roofing contractors in the Yellow Pages of your phone book. If your phone book is like mine, there will be many more pages of roofing contractors than there are listings for grocery stores or gas stations. Yet you know how keen competition is for the food dollar. And there's a gas station at almost every important intersection. But ads for roofing contractors far outnumber either of these industries. What does this tell us? It tells us that competition for the roofing dollar is intense.

Intense competition usually means that the business is overcrowded. That's usually because it's an easy business to get into. Knowing that, we can assume that a good share of the competitors are incompetents. But don't let heavy competition from cutthroat incompetents discourage you. I'll stand by my opening statement: roofing can be a profitable part of your remodeling business. Many remodelers have done very well with roofing. How

did they do it in a business overcrowded with competitors? They used expert selling methods. And that, as you might guess, is what I'm going to explain in this chapter.

With so many roofers listed in the Yellow Pages, every prospect for roofing probably gets a dozen bids to replace his roof. Most roofing contractors will come out to the house, measure, compute the number of squares, and write a price down on the back of a business card. If only the wife is home, the roofer will ask her to pass the card along to her husband. That ends the sales call — and all selling effort by this contractor.

The contractor leaves hoping he's the low bidder. He made no effort to upgrade the sale. He just put his figure into a low-bid auction. You know by now that there's a better way to do it.

How to Sell Roofing

Here's the right way to handle roofing leads. Use the same basic formula I've recommended from the beginning. First, make sure that all parties will be home so a decision can be made on the spot. After the icebreaker and warmup, find out if financing is needed and, if so, if it's financeable. Most homeowners focus on the estimate and will ignore the financing unless you bring it up. All roofers who did no more than leave a price and their business card are left out when you offer to finance the job for no money down and with small monthly payments.

There's another way to distinguish your proposal. Find out how many times the house has been re-roofed. In many communities the building code prohibits putting more than two layers of shingles on a roof. If the house has been re-roofed already, you have to do a tear-off before new roofing goes on. Even if the code permits more than two roof layers, don't sell a new roof job without a tear-off if there are already three layers of shingles on the roof. Removing the old roof and hauling it to the dump adds plenty to the cost of the job.

When the owner is vague about how many times the house has been roofed, check for yourself. Determine the layers by counting the number of shingle courses that are a different color.

If it's necessary to remove the existing roofing, explain why. Let the homeowners know that your price includes removing and hauling away the old shingles. That saves unpleasant surprises later when the low bidder's men get on the roof, find out there's a removal job, and boost the price of the job. Your price is firm, includes all costs, and is for a job that complies with the code. You've destroyed the credibility of the low bidder without saying a bad word about him.

Sell a Complete Job

Take time to discuss the job. Where are the leaks? How bad are they? Ask to see the leaks in the attic. While there, check for deteriorated roof boards. Figure out how many square feet of boards have to be replaced. Explain that putting new shingles over rotted boards is a waste of time and money. Make it clear that you'll do the job right or not at all. The low bidder with the business card didn't say that.

Next, investigate the roof vents. If you don't see good venting that complies with the standards given in the next column, explain the importance of venting: Moisture from cooking, washing and the shower condenses into droplets of water on the underside of the roof in cold weather. If this moisture isn't removed by air circulation, there's trouble. Constant moisture in the attic encourages decay of the rafters and sheathing. Eventually, the roof surface will collapse into the attic.

Explain that standards for venting have changed in the last 20 years. Tighter, well-insulated homes need more attic ventilation to prevent moisture damage. Here's the information the low bidder didn't offer:

• For a gable roof with vents in the gable ends, you need one square foot of screened vent for each 150 square feet of ceiling.

• For a gable roof with vents at the soffit and the gable ends, allow one square foot of screened soffit vent and one square foot of screened gable vent for each 450 square feet of ceiling.

• For a hip roof with vents at the soffit, allow one square foot of screened soffit vent and one square foot of globe-type vent or ridge vent screen for each 450 square feet of ceiling.

• For a flat or low pitch roof, allow one square foot of screened soffit vent for each 125 square feet of ceiling.

These are the generally accepted standards. For more information, see Chapter 16 of the book *Wood-Frame House Construction*. An order form at the back of this book explains how to get a copy.

The most economical time to improve venting is when your workmen are on the roof. It's a small investment that can save thousands of dollars in repairs later. Offer to replace all decayed sheathing and rafters before laying the new shingles. Emphasize that having the work done *now* will save the homeowner a considerable amount of money. This is a benefit you can stress that doesn't cost you a dime. It just upgrades the job.

Emphasize the Quality of Your Work

Explain that you never use anything lighter than 240-pound fiberglass shingles and recommend heavier textured shingles for many jobs. Better quality shingles add very little to the cost of the job, but look a lot better and will last longer.

Explain that you always finish the job with a Boston ridge. If that doesn't mean anything to them, make a little sketch of a Boston ridge. See Figure 27-1. Better yet, point out a neighbor's roof with a ridge roll. Compare the Boston ridge and the ridge roll. Show them that exposed nails in a ridge roll rust out and eventually cause leaks. Explain how the Boston ridge covers all the nails so they won't rust. Your prospects don't know what the other bidders planned to do at the ridge and hips. But they're going to get a Boston ridge on their roof after you show them the difference. As always, demonstrating something is far better than just describing it.

Now's the time to pull out your sample board and ask for that first decision: the color. Show them the available colors. Explain that the trend is away from dark, heat-absorbing colors that were once popular. True, dark colors absorb more heat and keep the house warmer in the winter. But air-conditioned houses should have light shingles to reflect the sun's rays. Today's frosted colors are a compromise. They help keep the house comfortable in both summer and winter.

"What color do you like?" is a question that follows naturally. It leads to a definite answer by the homeowners. When they choose a color, they've come a long way toward saying "yes" to the sale.

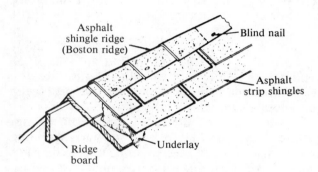

**Boston ridge
Figure 27-1**

Stress the Benefits
After you've asked all the questions, defined the scope of the job, and elicited a color preference, it's time to recap the job. Stress the benefits. It might go something like this:

"First, we're going to strip off the old roof and haul away the debris. This ensures that the nails will penetrate to the wood. Your new shingles won't blow off because they're securely nailed down.

"Second, we'll check the roof boards for soundness and replace any rotted boards. You'll know that the sheathing and rafters are sound.

"Third, we'll install roofing felt over the roof boards. This extra layer prevents leaks. (Omit this, of course, if it's not needed. If the code requires 30-pound felt, stress its weight.)

"Fourth, we'll replace the rotted soffit and fascia boards. That will save you money because you won't have to hire someone to do it later. It

always costs less to finish all the work at once rather than come back several times.

"Fifth, we'll install roof vents to improve air circulation and reduce the chance of more decay.

"Sixth, our experienced workmen will fill in missing shingles on the old roof. That guarantees a smooth surface for the new shingles. Some roofers don't go this extra step. We do and always have. Then we'll look for raised or buckled shingles which indicate loose nails or warped roof boards. Our workmen will drive down any loose nails and renail any warped roof boards.

"Finally, they'll install fiberglass shingles. The fiberglass shingles cost us a little more, but the difference in quality in our opinion is like the difference between a Rolls Royce and a Ford.

"The shingles we use are rated Class A fire-resistant by Underwriter's Laboratory. No one even wants to think about the possibility of his house burning. But many house fires are set from outside, by fireworks, sparks from chimneys or fireplaces, or even airborne debris from a nearby fire. The Underwriter's Laboratory classifies shingles by their resistance to fire outside the house. The Class A means that a 12" by 12" by 3" burning wood brand ignited on the roof and fanned by a wind of 12 miles per hour will burn out harmlessly without damaging the deck below. This is a very important benefit. And it doesn't cost one cent more in labor to apply Class A shingles than cheaper grades of shingles.

"Another benefit of our Class A shingles is that they're made with a fiberglass mat. They don't rot. Class C shingles have an organic felt mat, like a piece of cardboard. Class C shingles cost less initially. But they're more expensive in the long run because they have to be replaced much sooner.

"Fiberglass shingles are strong and weather-resistant. Pound for pound, fiberglass is stronger than steel. Most modern boats have hulls of fiberglass. The hull has to be sturdy and waterproof, just like your shingles. You probably know that some car bodies are made of fiberglass. It's virtually indestructible. The shingles we use are heavy and thick. A 240-pound shingle means that the shingles covering an area of one hundred square feet weigh 240 pounds. The original roll roofing on this house probably weighed only 90 pounds. No wonder it leaked! Some old hexagon shingles weighed only 135 pounds.

"Our heavy shingles come with a spot of roofing cement under each tab. The heat of the sun melts the cement, sealing it to the shingle below. That keeps the shingles tight so they don't blow off in the wind.

"I've explained that we'll use a Boston ridge so there are no exposed nails to rust and cause leaks. And while our workmen are on your roof, they'll check all flashing, chimney, valleys and the vent flashing. They'll reseal the valleys, vents, flashing and the chimney with plastic roof cement. We want to eliminate all possibility of roof leaks.

"We even consider the nails important. We only use galvanized nails, long enough to go through the layers of roofing and penetrate into the roof boards at least 3/4".

"Our roofers are fully covered by Worker's Compensation, liability and scaffolding insurance. I'm sure, Mr. and Mrs. Homeowner, that you want to be protected from responsibility if there's an accident on the job. Our policy provides full coverage. We're grateful that we've never had an accident. But an accident can happen at any time. That's why we protect you with comprehensive insurance coverage.

"We can do the work for no money down, with payments of $40 a month for 60 months under the F.H.A. program at Federal Savings & Loan. Is it O.K. to use the kitchen table to write up the order?"

How to Measure for Roofing

Of course, you can't quote the exact price until you know the area to be covered. If you're on the roof, make a little sketch of the roof and measure the length and width of each area. List all the important measurements on your drawing. The most important dimension is the rafter length. You can't measure that length directly when on the ground. When you get back to the ground, calculate the roof area by multiplying widths by lengths.

If you're not on the roof, you have to calculate the area by measuring the lengths of the walls and estimating the pitch of the roof. The steeper the pitch, the greater the roof area and the more shingles required.

To calculate the roof area from the ground, measure the width of the building. Add the overhang on both ends. Multiply this total by the length of the building, including the overhangs. For example, if the house is 26' wide and the soffits are 2', you would add 26' plus 2' plus 2' for a total of 30'. If the house if 40' long including soffit width, multiply 40' times 30' to get 1,200 square feet. To this figure, add 10% for gable roofs, 15% for hip roofs, and 20% for hip roofs with dormers

or valleys. If the roof is very steep, you'll need to increase these percentages.

To convert square feet to *squares* of 100 square feet, divide by 100. A 1,500 square foot roof needs 15 squares, plus an allowance for waste and cutting.

The Asphalt Roofing Manufacturer's Association, at 1800 Massachusetts Avenue, N.W., Suite 702, Washington, D.C. 20035, phone (202) 659-3934, offers several manuals and sales tools that can help you sell asphalt shingles for residences.

How to Sell Siding

In the remodeling business, roofing and siding go together like ham and eggs. A roofing lead can often be upgraded to include siding on the entire house, or at least aluminum covering for the soffit and fascia.

After the icebreaker and warmup, determine if the job can be financed. Then find out what type of siding the owners are thinking about and why they want siding. This is your clue to what benefits need emphasis for this prospect.

If you suggest alternate types of siding, remember the cardinal rule in selling: Keep the final choice between one of only two items. It's either this or that. Offering too many choices invites a request for more time to think it over.

Keep the choices in siding to a minimum. If you start pitching four or five types of siding, most customers won't be able to decide. Find out at the beginning what type is siding is most likely to make the sale. Here's how:

"What kind of siding are you thinking about for your home? Have you considered vinyl? What do you think about aluminum (or hardboard or plywood) siding?"

The answers will tell you what kind of siding to pitch (and will probably indicate what other bids the prospects have).

Make Your Bid Unique

If the homeowners seem very knowledgeable, the odds are that they have several estimates already. If so, it does no harm at all to ask, "By the way, how many bids do you have already?" You have nothing to lose. Maybe they intend to buy from the contractor who makes the biggest arithmetic mistake in his bid. To some buyers, only price matters. But sometimes you can plant a seed of healthy skepticism in the mind of your prospect — without knocking your competition directly. Just say something like this:

"I'd like to suggest a few points you should consider about aluminum siding. Our siding is tested for impact. If you hit it with your hand, there won't be a dent. The backerboard on our siding gives it extra resistance to impact. But a baseball hit will damage any siding, of course.

"Our siding is tested for resistance to abrasion by blowing sand over it at high speed. It's also tested for resistance to sulfur and salt. That can be a problem in this part of the country, you know.

"Then it goes from a deep freeze to a hot oven to test its response to extreme temperature changes. Our backerboard, by the way, is an insulator. It's made of styrofoam, just like the insulation in a picnic cooler.

"By the way, some salesmen will insist that aluminum siding is an insulator because the aluminum reflects the sun's rays. I won't tell you that because it's pure bunk. My wife has been cooking with aluminum pots and pans for over 50 years. Aluminum makes excellent cookware because it's such a good conductor of heat. And so is aluminum siding. Without extra insulation, aluminum siding does very little to keep your house warm in winter or cool in summer."

If your competition has pitched aluminum as an insulator, that destroys them. They're revealed as people who would say anything to make a sale. The homeowners will remember this even if they get other bids after yours. And the casual statement about a baseball denting aluminum siding establishes your credibility.

Stress the Benefits
To sell aluminum siding, stress these benefits:

• Aluminum siding ends the cost and bother of painting. Even trim around the doors and windows can be covered, so nothing needs to be painted.

• Over the years, the savings on painting will virtually pay for the siding.

• New aluminum siding will protect the old wood from deteriorating, saving the cost of future repairs.

• Aluminum siding always looks clean and neat. It won't peel, blister or flake.

• The factory backs up aluminum siding with a guarantee. They do this because it's been thoroughly tested.

• You can do the job for no money down and only so many dollars per month at Federal Savings, where you have been a dealer for many years. The first payment won't be due until 60 days after the work is finished. "Can I use the kitchen table to write up the order now?"

Selling Steel or Vinyl Siding
No matter what type of siding you're selling, the technique is the same. Qualify the prospects and stress the benefits. Make up your own list of the benefits for each type of siding. For example, vinyl siding has most of the same benefits as aluminum. T-LOK brand vinyl siding has a 50-year transferable warranty which the homeowner can pass along to the buyer if he sells the house. This is a terrific selling tool. The manufacturer of T-LOK siding will supply sample boards, brochures, color charts and copies of their warranty. The manufacturer is Mastic Corporation. The address is at the end of this book.

Selling Stucco
Stucco is a cement product. In the West and some parts of the South it's the most popular siding material. The original cost is high, but it lasts a long time and usually doesn't need painting because the color is an integral part of the material. You won't have to redo many stucco siding jobs.

I've made my living selling home improvements in the Chicago area for nearly 50 years and have had only two stucco jobs in my lifetime. The first was a fire job. The second came when a homeowner saw us doing the stucco work on the fire job. He was happy to see a stucco job in progress. He had been looking for someone in Chicago that knew how to do stucco exteriors. These were easy sales.

If you're working in a area where there are a lot of stucco homes, sell new stucco siding to replace wood. Stress the benefits of stucco. Explain that your tradesmen are experienced in this type of work. Sell the beauty and quality of stucco. It's fireproof, and the owner will have a pleasing facade for many years with a minimum of maintenance.

Selling Hardboard Siding
Prefinished hardboard siding is a good choice to upgrade the appearance of an older home. Your

lumber dealer will have access to literature from Boise Cascade, Masonite and other manufacturers. You can also write to the manufacturers listed at the end of the book. Get samples of their complete line. Ask for brochures, sample boards, and copies of their warranties. The usual warranty is 5 and 25 years — 5 years on the finish and 25 years on the material. These sales aids can be very persuasive when calling on leads. In fact, it's hard to close without color and material samples for siding.

Hardboard siding comes primed as well as factory-finished in many colors and styles. The homeowner can choose from rough-sawn or textured panels or lap siding, in natural wood grain or vinyl-faced. They're all attractive and durable. Some are rated Class 1 for fire-resistance by U.L.

Again, stress the benefits to make the sale: no painting, a 5/25 year factory warranty, durability of the surface, protection of the wood underneath, and convenient financing. The siding will virtually pay for itself in savings on painting and repair. Some benefits are available in hardboard alone:

• Hardboard blends perfectly with rustic styles and natural settings.

• There's a wide selection of styles, colors and textures — something to satisfy nearly any taste and pocketbook.

• Hardboard siding helps keep the home warmer in cold weather. Quote specific figures for R-values of the brand you're selling.

• The U.L. label guarantees its quality and safety.

• Although the siding has the beauty of wood, it doesn't have knots or splits, won't warp, and resists cracking and chipping.

Stucco texture hardboard is a unique product. It has the look and feel of real stucco at a fraction of the price. I've sold stucco board when my competitors probably didn't even know that it existed. The homeowners were grateful that I could match the stucco exterior without going to the expense of bringing a stucco crew to the job. Consider it whenever selling siding.

Miscellaneous Sidings
Most of your siding business will be aluminum, vinyl or hardboard. But there are homeowners that don't like any of them. Selling siding is like selling

ice cream — you've got to offer a lot of flavors because there's such a wide variety of tastes. And there's also a seemingly endless variety of architectural styles. You've got to be aware of them to sell to the owners who don't want the run-of-the-mill look for their house.

Suppose you get a lead in a wooded area. It might be appropriate to suggest wood shakes. That just could remove you from the bidding race and set up a profitable order.

Plywood siding comes primed, ready to paint or stain, in fir, southern pine or western red cedar. You can offer board and batten styles, or grooved and textured.

Shingle siding is available in western red cedar shingles or shakes, and shingle or shake panels. There are even aluminum shake-pattern panels, recommended for mansards.

Wood siding includes fir, spruce or pine drop siding, beveled or rough-sawn redwood or cedar, and spruce shiplap, just to name a few. There's barnboard siding, rough-sawn with vertical grooves, or a reverse board and batten effect for a rustic look. Wood siding can be applied in horizontal, vertical or diagonal patterns.

Get samples of all these sidings from your lumberyard and carry them in the trunk of your car. Also carry brochures from the siding manufacturers and pictures from home magazines to illustrate the latest styles. Of course you'll carry before and after pictures of all the siding jobs you've done. You may be surprised at the extra sales you can generate by being knowledgeable about wood siding.

Selling the Add-ons
I've talked about how important it is to change the job so the homeowners can't do a straight price comparison between your bid and the others they've collected. In a siding job, there are several naturals for adding onto and changing the job:

• Suggest that the job wouldn't be complete without covering the soffit and fascia, or the frieze boards. It only costs a few dollars a month more, and they'll never have to be painted again. No more hiring painters or scrambling up ladders to do it yourself.

• How about new aluminum gutters while our men are here to do the job? It'll cost less than doing it later, and the seamless gutters don't rust, leak or corrode, and never need painting. Doing it later will cost far more.

• Recommend aluminum covers for the window trim and door casing. Stress the benefits of doing the entire job at once, not piecemeal, where the cost of builders going back and forth, onto and off jobs, taking off materials and putting them back on, can cost the homeowner double.

• What better time to install aluminum storm windows? They'll enhance the beauty of the new siding while saving energy costs. Of course, only a few dollars more a month.

• Consider offering a free storm door as a premium to close the siding sale, especially for the homeowner who's collecting bids. Of course, this offer is only good *this* week.

Measuring for Siding
In selling any siding, of course, you'll have to compute how many squares are needed. Figure the walls full. Don't deduct for doors or windows. This will compensate for the waste and the extra corners the house might have. Figuring full will cover most contingencies.

Chapter 28

Selling Windows

Many remodeling jobs include new windows. Updating a facade, raising a dormer or adding a room are just a few. Selling replacement windows takes knowledge. You have to be familiar with all types of windows and storm windows to make an effective window sales presentation.

Window Types

Most windows are made from either wood, aluminum or steel. Each has advantages and disadvantages. Familiarize yourself with the characteristics and benefits of each.

Wood windows are the most popular and practical in cold climates. They don't accumulate condensation like metal windows. Puddles don't form on the sill of a wood window. Also, wood is a better insulator than metal. That makes steel and aluminum windows energy-expensive in cold climates.

Aluminum windows are very popular in the sun belt. They don't corrode, rust or need painting. Marine glazing means they never have to be puttied. And they don't rot like a wood window can.

Residential steel windows were once popular, but are seldom used today. They don't rust or need painting, but they're puttied rather than marine glazed.

Once the type of window has been chosen, the next choice to be made is the style. Recommend a window style that conforms to the architecture of the house. If the customer has definite ideas about the kind of window he wants, don't argue. You don't have to live in the house. The customer does. And he's paying the bill. So let him talk you out of the style *you* would have chosen.

Here are brief descriptions of the window styles commonly used in remodeling.

Awning Windows

Awning windows open horizontally from either a top or bottom hinge. Top-hinged windows open to the outside. Screen and storm windows must be installed on the interior. Bottom-hinged windows open to the inside. They're generally set low in a wall.

Bay Windows

There are three basic styles of bay windows — the angle bay, the bow bay, and the box bay. The angle bay usually extends out from the house at a 30-degree or 45-degree angle. The bow bay is bowed the width of the opening. The box bay extends out at a 90-degree angle, giving a square box effect.

Most bay windows, regardless of style, have a fixed center window and opening windows on the sides. The side windows may be double hung, casement or awning units. They can have single or multiple lites.

Basement or Utility Windows

This is sometimes called a hopper window. It's

usually hinged at the bottom and opens inward at the top.

Casement Windows

Casement windows are hinged on the side and usually open outward with a push bar or a crank. Since they open outward, screens and storm windows have to be installed on the inside. They're popular in warm climates because the entire window opens completely to allow 100% ventilation.

Decorative Windows

Full circle, octagonal or half circle windows come with either single or double glazing. They're available in decorative glass, such as petals, with the perimeter glass in colors. Octagonal windows can have a single lite or a nine-lite grille. Half circle windows have a four-lite grille. Full circle windows have a choice of wagon wheel or nine-lite grilles.

Double Hung Windows

Double hung windows have one sash mounted above the other. Each sash can slide up and down. They can be used in single, double, triple or quad installations. Double hung windows are often used to flank a picture window. Each sash can be a single pane or divided into two or more lites. A window with one pane to each sash is called one over one. If each pane is divided horizontally, it's called two over two. Double hung windows with six or nine lites per sash are common.

Modern double hung windows have removable or tilt-in sash. That makes them easy to clean from inside the house. Always stress this benefit.

Jalousie Windows

Jalousie windows have horizontal glass slats about 4" wide that pivot horizontally and in unison with a crank. Insect and burglar screens can be installed on the inside. These are often recommended for porch enclosures or garages that aren't heated in winter or cooled in summer. They're available in clear or obscured glass.

Picture Windows

Picture windows have fixed glass. They're usually installed with operable windows on either side. This gives the double advantage of an unobstructed view and adequate ventilation.

Sliding Windows

These windows have at least one sash that slides horizontally. This is usually the least expensive window. Horizontal sliders made from aluminum are common in warmer climates where air leaks are less important. Wood or wood clad sliding windows cost about the same as comparable double hung windows, and are as energy efficient.

Skylights or Roof Windows

The American Indian tepee, with its hole in the top to admit light and let smoke escape, was the forerunner of the modern skylight or roof window. Before electric lighting became common, many larger buildings such as train stations and libraries had ceilings of glass to let in natural daylight. Modern buildings have skylights for the same reason. They increase natural light, and some can be opened to vent excess heat or fumes. Some units are made with tempered, insulated glass and screens. They're still a good way to provide continual sunshine for plants and to admit light while preserving privacy. A skylight is an excellent suggestion for an interior bathroom.

Check the Building Codes

Find out what your local building code requires for windows. Many building codes set maximums and minimums for glazed window space in residential and commercial construction. Maximums are established for air conditioned residential and commercial buildings to reduce the amount of cooling needed. The code may also require a minimum amount of operable windows in residences. Frequently the operable window space must be at least a certain percentage of the floor area in a room. As a rule of thumb, plan to install windows totaling 10% of the floor area. This is intended to protect the safety and health of the occupants.

Special Considerations

Once you've met code requirements, begin planning the job. First, see if there are any special problems. If any member of the family is handicapped or in a wheelchair, suggest casements that open with a crank at the bottom of the window. It's a formidable task to open a double hung window from a wheelchair. Carefully consider both the placement and the type of windows to be installed.

When selling an awning or casement window that projects to the outside, be aware of the hazard an open window creates. Check to see if there's a sidewalk or passageway under the window. If so, suggest another type of window. It's easy for someone to walk into an open window protruding into a walkway. Children are especially vulnerable. A kid running and playing in a yard where there's a projecting window is sure to knock himself silly on it.

Here are some other important considerations:

• Try to position the windows so they take advantage of the prevailing breeze. But avoid exposures open to an icy winter wind.

• Don't use metal windows where exposure includes salt air, corrosive elements or sulphur, or where frost buildup will result in condensation.

• In cold climates, the lifetime energy costs of the window will exceed the purchase price by far. Metal and glass are good conductors of heat and cold. Advise the homeowner to use double glazing and wood windows, rather than metal. Offer practical alternatives.

Your clients have certain expectations for any window, even if those expectations are not expressed. They expect the windows to be air- and watertight, to withstand high winds without breaking, and to prevent condensation and frost buildup. During the sales presentation, bring out these unspoken expectations as benefits. Add any other benefits you can think of: ease of operation for the disabled, a sunny kitchen during breakfast from the eastern exposure, or a minimum of window area on the northern exposure to protect from cold winter winds. Stress the benefits — always the benefits. That's what people buy.

Window Glass
Although the invention of glass has been attributed to the Phoenicians way back when, it seems not to have been till some time later, in Ancient Rome, that anyone thought of using it for windows. Today, we have several types of glazing available for residential windows:

1) Single strength glass, 3/32" thick
2) Double strength glass, 1/8" thick
3) Obscure glass for bathrooms
4) Insulated glass
5) Leaded glass
6) Tempered glass

Federal safety regulations require tempered glass in atrium doors, patio doors, storm doors or any doors with large areas of glass. Glass inserts such as a small lookout square or diamond are exempt.

Acrylic glazing can be substituted for tempered glass.

When writing a contract, be sure to specify the type of glass for each window. For example, the contract might contain this statement: "All windows to be single strength glass, except the bathroom to be obscure and the picture window to have insulated fixed glass."

How To Measure Windows
The simplest way to measure a window is by the glass size. Most windows are sold by the glass size. Measure the width of the glass first, then the height of the glass in one sash only. Typical sizes will be 24" x 24", 24" x 26" and so forth. This is the method used for double hung windows. The construction foreman or the carpenter sub can translate this into the actual size of the window needed. Casement windows and awning windows are measured the same way. Always specify the width of glass first, then the height.

For a bay window, measure from the rough opening and use the word "approximate" in your contract and in your discussion with the owners. For example, state that you'll install a bow bay window approximately 8' by 5'.

Writing the Contract Specifications
Specify all the pertinent information in the contract. For example:

Windows are to be wood, double hung, 24" x 24" double strength glass, removable sash, trimmed both sides with Formica sill on the interior and wood apron. No storms or screens included.

Contractor will install a header, frame an opening which meets code requirements and install a box bay vinyl-covered wood window in the west wall of the living room as follows: The window size will be approximately 8 feet wide by 5 feet high. The center lite will have insulated glass. Side panels will have one over one double hung windows with insulated glass. Contractor will install window trim on both sides of the window and a window seat on the interior. The top of the window will be covered with 240-lb. thick butt fiberglass shingles in a color to match the existing shingles as closely as is reasonably possible. Two decorative brackets will be installed on the exterior under the window unit. This window will replace the present double hung mullion window. Contractor will remove and dispose of the existing window and patch drywall as needed. Contractor will do no painting of the window or anywhere patching is needed.

If there is any chance that the wall might be concealing electric lines, water pipe, gas pipe, T.V. cable, or heating duct, include the following paragraph:

Contractor is not responsible for concealed heat ducts, pipes or conduit in the existing wall. Cost to the Owner for rerouting any of these lines will be the actual cost to the Contractor plus 25% for overhead and markup.

The contract should specify not only the style of the window, its location and size, but how it is to be finished off, both in the interior and exterior.

Complete specifications eliminate misunderstandings that can cause collection problems.

Selling Replacement Windows

The replacement window business was born about 20 years ago to meet a clear need. Most older homes have double hung windows that are ploughed for ropes and sash balance weights. Age and weather have taken their toll on the window frame and sash. The ropes have broken, the weights aren't working. The wood sash has deteriorated and the glass is loose in the frame. The weatherstripping is either absent or so worn that it's useless. The sash looks old-fashioned and is encrusted with many coats of paint.

Windows in older homes with single glazed wood sash or steel sash are big energy wasters. There's no practical way to bring the window up to current standards. It has to be replaced with a modern window that will:

1) Conserve energy by minimizing air infiltration and reducing heat loss through conduction.

2) Prevent condensation and frost buildup on the window and sill.

3) Fit tight so water and dirt don't enter and the window doesn't rattle.

4) Reduce the amount of exterior noise entering the house.

5) Operate easily, with no sticking or swelling.

6) Provide a long service life with no maintenance.

7) Be easy to clean from inside the house.

There are plenty of windows on the market that meet this description. But the biggest problem is that stock windows seldom fit exactly in the old opening. That's why replacement windows have become so popular. They're custom made to fit exactly into the old opening with little or no carpentry. That saves you far more than the extra cost of manufacturing a special window.

The Energy Tax Credit

The U.S. Congress, recognizing that the windows in older homes are often great wasters of energy, enacted the Residential Energy Tax Credit in November, 1978. It provides a tax credit of up to $300 for installation of qualifying energy-conserving components, including storm or thermal windows. Take advantage of this extraordinary sales tool.

Here's how to qualify for the tax credit:

• The home must be located in the United States.

• The home must be the principal residence of the taxpayer.

• The home must have been substantially completed before April 20, 1977.

• The taxpayer must be the first one to use the energy-conserving component.

• The item must be expected to last for at least three years.

The maximum *accumulated* credit for energy conservation items cannot be more than 15% of $2000.00, or a total of $300.00, for each principal residence.

In other words, if you sell $2,000 worth of thermal replacement windows to a qualified taxpaying customer, they get a tax credit of $300.00. The tax credit is based on the cost of installation as well as the cost of the windows themselves. Bring the tax credit to the attention of every lead. It's a powerful tool, and it comes out of Uncle Sam's pocket, not yours.

Carry a copy of IRS Form 5695, Residential Energy Credit. Show it to your prospects and point out that thermal windows qualify. Promise the customers that you'll provide a copy of Form 5695 when the windows are installed. Deliver the form personally. Tell them that you wanted to be sure that they received it. That's why you didn't have the office mail it out. Then use this sales call to get referrals. A recommendation like this is priceless. It's the best lead you'll ever have.

Features of Replacement Windows

Replacement windows are manufactured in both vinyl and aluminum, with thermal or regular glass. They're available in all the common styles and in various finishes and colors. Most replacement windows have the following features:

Marine glazing— to eliminate the need for putty. Marine glazing provides a permanent seal against the elements, preventing water seepage and air transmission.

Insulated glass or thermal barrier— to cut down on heat loss through conduction. In the summer, it keeps cooled air in and hot air out. Thermal glass makes storm windows obsolete.

Tilt in or snap out sash— that can be either removed from inside the house or tilted in for cleaning. That's a feature designed to win the heart of the window washer in any family.

Weatherstripping— to prevent passage of heated or cooled air to the exterior. It also keeps out dirt and dust and makes operation of the window smoother and quieter.

Vinyl and aluminum frames— which are virtually maintenance-free. They never need painting and clean easily with soap and water. The finish won't chip, flake, peel, crack or chalk. The frame can't rot, corrode or rust.

P.V.C. vinyl frames are resistant to cement, mortar, lime, salt air, corrosion, industrial pollution and impact.

Easy operation— a feature in all modern windows. The windows won't get stuck due to shrinking or swelling. There are no ropes or chains to break. They never get painted shut because they never need painting.

There's lots to sell about replacement windows. These improvements translate into benefits that will usually be worth more than the cost. And don't stop there. Replacement windows come in styles to match any taste or type of architecture.

Add-on Sales

It should be easy to upgrade the sale once you've sold a replacement window. This is the time to suggest that you cap the frame with aluminum so neither the frame nor the trim will ever need painting. The new windows and the frame cap create a unit that enhances the beauty, and the resale value, you should stress, of the home.

And note that adding replacement windows is an excellent way to upgrade most kitchen and bathroom projects. Suggest modern replacement windows. Emphasize the fact that they're energy savers and that a tax credit may be available.

If you suspect that the lead is getting several quotes, change the job scope by including replacement windows. Most general contractors know very little about replacement windows. They don't know the advantages and aren't aware of the tax credit. They usually suggest standard wood sash windows.

If the lead is just for remodeling the kitchen, you might only sell a replacement window for that room. But on an older home with deteriorating windows, come back and sell a complete window replacement job when the kitchen loan is paid off. Or perhaps you can sell the entire job now by suggesting that it be added to the loan, especially if you're getting financing for the homeowners. But try to sell at least four replacement windows at a time. That's the minimum number that can be replaced economically at one time.

Ask a replacement window supplier to furnish you with a demonstration unit and some brochures. Practice using the demonstrator until you're familiar with it. Stamp your company name on the brochures. Learn all the features and be ready to emphasize the benefits of the window. Become an expert on the energy tax credit and financing. Selling replacement windows should be a snap. They're a good product. Start every sales call with the icebreaker, warmup and qualification. Emphasize the benefits and sales should be almost automatic.

Selling Storm Windows

Storm windows are another good way to cut energy costs. In this country, the energy used to light, cool and heat homes and public buildings amounts to approximately 33% of all energy used. In homes and public buildings, about 15% of all energy used for heating and cooling is wasted by air leakage and the conduction of cold through windows and doors. That's why Congress passed the Residential

Energy Tax Credit. For complete information on the credit, refer back to the Tax Credit section earlier in this chapter. Storm windows also qualify for this credit. That's a real windfall for everyone selling home improvement services. The customer needs and wants storm windows. You meet that need and offer them a tax break as well. What a sales pitch!

I suggest that you avoid leaving a copy of IRS Form 5695 with the customer. There's always the possibility the customer will cancel within the three day limit. Once you've educated him and given him a copy of the form, there's nothing to stop him from going to a competitor who undercuts your price. Avoid this by delivering the tax form *after* the windows are installed. You kept a promise to supply the form *and* you were interested enough to deliver it personally. Be sure to get some referrals while you're there. Prospective clients are the essential raw material needed to make home improvement sales.

The Benefits of Storm Windows
Storm window sales are good business. The day when everyone hired the neighborhood handyman to put up and take down wood storm windows is gone. Even the newer aluminum storms installed 20 years ago need replacing. The mill finish aluminum has probably become so badly pitted that the window won't operate.

Modern homeowners want easy-to-operate, energy-saving storm windows permanently installed. They probably know the advantages of storm windows. But you're competing with the low-priced storm windows they see advertised in the daily paper. Your job is to emphasize the benefits of your high-quality windows.

Explain that in storm windows, as with every kind of merchandise, manufacturers often "build down" to meet a price. When price is the object, quality suffers. Heavily advertised windows are made to sell at a given price, not meet generally-accepted quality standards. They're made from mill finish aluminum which will pit and become inoperative in time. In fact, you make a good living replacing those cheap storms with quality storm windows.

Quality storm windows have the following features:

Anodized or acrylic finish— They won't pit, corrode or rust. The anodized finish can be either satin or bright. Acrylic units come in several colors. They're rich-looking and easy to clean. They resist the ravages of winter weather. It's easy to select an attractive unit that will complement the exterior of any home.

Ease of operation— They go up and down with fingertip action. They tilt into the house for easy cleaning.

Superior construction— The corners are mitered, not butted, as in the cheap storms. They have hollow tube sill construction.

Security— The windows lock into position when partially open. A burglar can't push the sash open. This is especially important on summer nights when the windows are left open a little for ventilation.

Marine glazing— The windows never have to be puttied and won't leak. It's called marine glazing because it's as watertight as the glazing on ship portholes. To demonstrate the quality of the glass and glazing, hit the glass in a demonstration unit with the palm of your hand. This is a very effective bit of showmanship. Of course, practice a little before doing this in a customer's home. I've never had one break. But don't get carried away on how hard you hit it.

Tight interlock— To demonstrate how tight the interlock is between the top and bottom sash, place a dollar bill between them. Have the customers try to pull it through. It can't be done. To make this demonstration very dramatic, tell the customers they can have the bill if they can pull it through. No fair tearing it, of course! I've used a $5.00 or $10.00 bill without any fear of losing it. That shows real confidence in your product.

Weatherstripping— Show the customer how weatherstripping is fastened to the sash. Weatherstripping makes a tight seal and prevents the passage of air. Some window manufacturers use a brand named Schligal. If your window uses the Schligal brand, point it out. Explain that this is the trademark of the maker of the best weatherstripping available. A person only wants to buy windows once in a lifetime. It pays to buy the best, because they last a lifetime. On a monthly payment basis, it costs so little more to buy quality.

Aluminum or fiberglass screens— Some factories offer either aluminum or fiberglass screen wire. It's your customer's choice. Aluminum screen is sturdy, taut and doesn't bulge or sag. It resists tearing and won't rust, corrode or rot.

Fiberglass screens usually cost less than aluminum. The big selling feature is that a small hole can be closed up if the threads aren't torn. Have the homeowner poke a pencil through the fiberglass without tearing the wire. Then rub the screen between the palms of your hands. The hole disappears! It's a terrific demonstration. But be careful not to break the threads.

Virgin aluminum— Some companies make storm windows with frames of virgin aluminum. Have your window company give you a sample of their frame. Then get a piece of frame made from recycled aluminum. Show the homeowner that it's easy to bend recycled aluminum. Virgin aluminum has the strength to resist bending. This emphasizes the inherent quality in your windows and makes them worth the few dollars a month more than other highly advertised windows. They'll stand the test of time and weather, as well as the settling, shrinking and swelling that a house goes through during season changes.

Your windows are made from virgin aluminum and have mitered corners. They won't come apart at the seams. If your prospects don't know what mitered corners are, show them the miters on some door trim. They'll feel good that their house has quality corners on the trim. Sometimes a sale comes from just pointing out the obvious.

Use All Your Selling Tools
It's said that nothing worth having comes easy in this world. This is certainly true when selling windows, or any other component of the home improvement business. But selling is easier when you're knowledgeable and motivated. Selling storm windows requires both knowledge and motivation, mixed with a healthy measure of persistence.

Keep your remodeling salesman's tool kit in tip-top shape. Keep each sample case clean. Remove finger marks after each demonstration. Wipe the dust off before bringing the cases into the customers' house. The sash should work with ease. The insect screening should not be torn or warped. This seems so elementary. But it's easy to forget how shopworn or shoddy a sample probably looks to your prospects. You've had the demonstration unit so long and made so many sales with it that you don't even notice the nicks and scratches. But your prospects will. Don't try to sell with any demonstration unit that's in less than mint condition.

After the icebreaker, warmup, and qualification, the demonstration is probably the most important part of selling storm windows. Practice the demonstration until you have it down cold. Do it over and over until it becomes second nature. Then practice your explanations. The demonstration with the dollar bill locked into the interlock proves that the storm windows are airtight. Bending the recycled aluminum proves that your window is stronger and can withstand settling of the house. The marine glazing prevents water seepage. Striking the glass with your palm shows that the glass will withstand impact from strong winds. These demonstrations speak volumes about the benefits.

People buy benefits. Stress these benefits to sell storm windows:

• Storm windows are energy-savers. They keep expensive heated and air-conditioned air in the house, and prevent cold drafts.

• The government recognizes the energy savings with the Energy Tax Credit — up to $300.

• Storm windows are watertight, and eliminate condensation and frost buildup.

• They reduce the amount of outside noise that enters the house.

• These storm windows are practically maintenance-free. You don't have to remove the windows or the screens seasonally, and they don't need to be reputtied like the old windows.

• The windows can be washed from inside the house. It's safer and easier.

• These good-looking windows will add to the beauty and resale value of the home.

• And finally, you can finance the windows with no money down and only a small monthly payment. The FHA loan is government insured, and the interest is tax deductible.

How to Measure for Storm Windows
Storm windows are sold by the *united inch*. There

are three formulas for finding the united inches for each window:

1)   Opening width plus opening height.

Example: Opening width is 28'' and opening height is 82''.

> 28''   opening width
> +82''   opening width
> ──────────────
> 110   united inches

2)   Opening perimeter divided by two.

Example: Opening width is 30'' and opening height is 90''. So the total opening width of the perimeter is 60'' (30'' x 2), and the total opening height of the perimeter is 180'' (90'' x 2).

> 60''   perimeter width
> +180''   perimeter height
> ──────────────
> 240'' ÷ 2 = 120 united inches

3)   Convert glass size to opening size.

This is the formula most commonly used by storm window salespeople. If the window's stuck shut, it may be hard to measure from the outside. Using formula 3, you can measure from inside.

Measure the glass size of one sash. Add 4'' to the width of the glass.

Double the height of the glass size if there are two sashes, then add 7'' to the combined glass height. Add the total width and height to get the united inches.

Example: Each lite of glass is 24'' x 24''.
24'' width plus 4'' = 28'' total width
24'' height doubled is 48''. The combined height is 7'' more or 55''.

> 28''   total width
> +55''   total height
> ──────────────
> 83''   united inches

Now It's Up to You

If you've followed my narrative to this point, you know most of what it took me 40 years to learn in home improvement sales. Any eager young salesman worth his salt will probably insist on learning many of these lessons the hard way — making some of the same mistakes I've made — before coming to the conclusions I've outlined in this book. There's nothing wrong with that. Anyone who follows exactly every word of advice in this book is missing most of the challenge in remodeling sales — adapting, learning, improvising and improving every day.

But I'm convinced that just a fraction of the advice I've given in this book makes your purchase price and the time you've spent reading these pages well worthwhile. If just one sentence in this book prevents an expensive mistake, you're money ahead.

I've covered all the major and minor topics in remodeling: organizing a sales crew, getting leads, making the sale, financing, insurance work, permits, contracts and pricing. We've covered every kind of sale, from reroofing to room additions. If nothing else, this book must have given you a better understanding of a remodeling salesman's job. You shouldn't ever have a question about what you're supposed to do next.

But one of the most important things you must have gotten from this manual is confidence — confidence that you know your trade, that you can handle any situation that's likely to come along, and confidence that there's a clear path to financial success and personal satisfaction in remodeling sales. If I've helped develop your confidence, if I've shown the way for you to succeed, if I've given you the tools to do the job, then my effort in writing this book has been rewarded.

Now the rest is up to you. Good selling!

Manufacturers and Suppliers

Door Manufacturers

Benchmark
General Products Co., Inc.
P.O. Box 7387
Hamilton's Crossing
Fredericksburg, VA 22404

Castlegate Industries, Inc.
Sub. of United States Gypsum
101 S. Wacker Drive
Chicago, IL 60606

Columbia Door Division
Simpson Timber Co.
3201 N.W. Lower River Road
Vancouver, WA 98660

Contractors Wardrobe
25555 Avenue Stanford
Valencia, CA 91355

Elegant Entries
45 Water Street
Worchester, MA 01604

International Doors
Simpson Timber Co.
900 Fourth Avenue
Seattle, WA 98164

Maywood, Inc.
P.O. Box 30550
Amarillo, TX 79120

Midwest Door
3620 Ohio Avenue
St. Charles, IL 60174

Moulding Products, Inc.
P.O. Box 150798
Irving, TX 75015

Nord Company
P.O. Box 1187
Everett, WA 98206

Overhead Door Corporation
One Oaks Plaza
6750 LBJ Freeway
Dallas, TX 75240

Panelfold, Inc.
10700 Northwest 36th Avenue
Miami, FL 33167

Peachtree Doors
Box 5700
Norcross, GA 30091

Pella Wood Folding Doors
Rolscreen Company
Pella, IA 50219

Perma-Door
American Standard Co.
9017 Blue Ash Road
Cincinnati, OH 45242

Pinecrest Co.
2118 Blaidell Avenue
Minneapolis, MN 55404

Regency Door & Hardware, Inc.
6720 N.E. 4th Court
Miami, FL 33138

Stanley Door Systems
1225 E. Maple Road
Troy, MI 48084

Sun-Dor-Co
P.O. Box 13
Wichita, KS 67201

Woodfold-Marco Mfg. Inc.
Box 346
Forest Grove, OR 97116

Flooring Manufacturers

Ceramic Tile

American Olean Tile Co.
P.O. Box 271
1000 Cannon Avenue
Lansdale, PA 19446

Dal-Tile Corp.
P.O. Box 17130
Dallas, TX 75217

Florida Tile
Sikes Corp.
Lakeland, FL 33802

Franciscan Ceramics, Inc.
2901 Los Feliz Blvd.
Los Angeles, CA 90039

Gail International Corp.
14791 Myford Road
Tustin, CA 92680

IMPO Glaztile
Diastone U.S.A. Corp.
P.O. Box 207
2852 West 167th St.
Markham, IL 60426

Marazzi USA, Inc.
55 Clay and Sceyene Road
Sunnyvale, TX 75182

Villeroy & Bosh (U.S.A.), Inc.
Interstate 80 at New Maple Ave.
Pine Brook, NJ 07058

Resilient Flooring

Armstrong World Industries, Inc.
P. O. Box 3001
Lancaster, PA 17604

Azrock Floor Products
P. O. Box 34030
San Antonio, TX 78265

Burke Flooring Products
2250 So. 10th St.
San Jose, CA 95112

Kentile Floors
979 Third Ave.
New York, NY 10022

Natural Vinyl Floor Co., Inc.
4401 Mars Hill Road
P.O. Box 1302
Florence, AL 35631

Wood Flooring

Bangkok Industries, Inc.
Gillingham & Worth St.
Philadelphia, PA 19124

Bruce Hardwood Floors
16803 Dallas Parkway
Dallas, TX 75248

Color Tile Factory Sales
P. O. Box 2475
Fort Worth, TX 76113

Harris-Tarkett Inc.
P.O. Box 300
Johnson City, TN 37605

Hartco Flooring
P.O. Box 1001
Oneida, TN 37841

Kentucky Wood Floors
4200 Reservoir Ave.
Louisville, KY 40213

Memphis Hardwood Flooring Co.
P. O. Box 7253
Memphis, TN 38107

Robbins Hardwood Flooring
3626 Round Bottom Road
Cincinnati, OH 45244

Siding Manufacturers

Boise Cascade
Timber and Wood Prod. Group
St. Louis Park, MN 55426

Masonite Corporation
29 N. Wacker Drive
Chicago, IL 60606

Mastic Corporation
A Subsidiary of Bethlehem Steel
131 S. Taylor Street
South Bend, IN 46624

Index

A B C D E F G H I J K L M N O P Q R S T U V W X Y Z

Acceptance clause 138
Accountants 119, 143
Acoustical tile 164, 212
Acrylic
  finish 233
  glazing 230
Actual cash value (ACV) 103, 108
Additions, selling 147-150
Add-on sales 232
Adjusters, insurance 43-44, 95, 97,
  99-101, 136
Adjustment form 95, 97-98, 106
Advertising 19-21, 126
Agreement and completion clause
  138
Air conditioning 151-152
Allowance, buyer's 134, 149, 157,
  159, 190, 197, 209, 213, 220
Aluminum
  awnings 151-155
  carport 152
  door and window trim 227
  door frames 172-173, 196

fascia cover 180, 203, 226
fence 185
gutters 183, 202-203, 205, 226
nails 202
patio cover 152
screen 176, 234
siding 180, 183-184, 196,
  224-225
storm door 176
threshold 197
windows 41, 197, 228-229,
  232-233
American Society of Heating,
  Refrigerating and Air-
  Conditioning Engineers
  (ASHRAE) 151
American Standard plumbing
  supplies 46
Anodized aluminum 155, 175-176,
  233
Anti-Coercion Statement 74, 87
Apartment addition 148, 178, 180
Appliance wiring 212-213
Appliances 207, 209-211, 213
Approximate dimensions 132, 134
APR 59-60
Architects 131, 150, 178-179
Architectural styles 171, 182, 189
Articles of agreement 71

Asphalt
  flooring 190, 213
  shingles 224
Asphalt Roofing Manufacturer's
  Association 224
Assignment clause 138
Assignment form 95, 97-98
Assumption close 91
Astragal 37, 176, 196, 201
Attic
  apartment 136
  conversion 164, 175, 178-181
  dormers 178-181
  stairway 206
  ventilation 222
  windows 180
Attorney 71-72, 97, 106, 116, 136,
  138, 141, 219
Authorization form 106
Authorized dealer 12
Automatic door opener 196, 200
Awnings 41, 151-155

B

Backsplash 93, 144, 157, 210, 212

Bag mix (concrete) 46, 144, 167
Bank, relationship with 51, 57, 60
Bar
  doors 173-174
  sink 208, 210
Barbed wire 187
Barricades 169
Base cabinets 144-145, 211
Baseboard radiation units 213
Basement
  conversion 147, 149
  doors 173
  exit 149
  rumpus room 40, 47
  stairway 206
  wall 173
  windows 228
Bathroom
  addition 156
  remodeling 156-161
  wall tile 192
Beam ceilings 163
Bedroom
  additions 147-148, 178
  closet doors 174
  "Before and after" pictures 183,
    185, 226
Benefits, selling 29, 40, 47

Bidding, how to 92, 101, 143, 165,
  168, 202, 205, 221
Bilco steel cellar doors 173
"Board up" contractor 100
B.O.C.A. 128
Body language 27, 33
Boise Cascade siding 196-197, 226
Boston ridge 197, 222-224
Brand names 134
Brick
  decorative facing 191
  tile 188
  veneering 182
Brochures
  contractor's 12, 19
  manufacturer's 170-171, 174,
    183, 188, 201, 226, 232
Broker notification form 114
Btu's 144, 179
Building
  code 94, 128-129, 131-132, 149,
    179, 187, 193, 212, 222, 229
  inspector 94, 129
  permits 128-132, 138, 144, 148,
    160, 178
Bureau of Standards 151
Business
  cards 15, 126, 221
  owner 12
  problems 116

Buyer's allowance 134, 149, 157, 159, 190, 197, 209, 213, 220

Cabinet
  face 144
  hardware 217
  space 207, 216
Cabinets
  pricing 144-145
  selling 211-212, 215-216
Call sheet 12, 14
Calls
  sales 27-35
  telephone 23
Cancel, right to 57-58
Cancellation clause 138
Canopies 151-154
Canvassers 10-12
Canvassing
  house-to-house 10-15
  telephone 15, 17-18
Carpentry 19, 131, 135, 160, 184, 231
Carpeting 135, 159, 213
Carports 151-152
Cash
  bond 131
  buyers 25, 74
  contracts 136
  jobs 87
  sales 136, 177
Casualty adjusters 44
Ceiling
  beams 163
  exhaust fan 210
  fixtures 161, 210
  joists 37, 179
  leads 163
  lights 164
  outlet 164
  paddle fan 213
  racks 211-212
  repairs 163
  tile 163
Ceilings, selling 162-164
Cement
  pricing 144
  selling 165-169
Ceramic
  counter top 212
  tile 159, 188, 190, 212, 215
Certificate of Insurance 119
Change of ownership clause 137
Change order form 139-140
Checklists
  attic conversion 181
  concrete work 169
  electrical 213
  facade remodeling 184
  kitchen remodeling 209
  plumbing 214
Chimney 179, 224
Circulars 15
Claims adjusters 44, 97, 113
Claims, insurance 95, 97, 114, 136, 138
Clauses, contract
  acceptance 138
  agreement and completion 138
  appliance allowance 209, 211
  assignment 138
  cancellation 138
  change of ownership 137
  code violations 132
  completion 136-137
  concrete work 134
  contractor's notice 137
  default and collection 138
  extra charges 139
  fence location 185
  finance 135
  fitting allowance 157
  garage concrete and electric 200
  garage measurements 199
  governing laws 137
  insurance 137
  miscellaneous 139
  no side agreements 138
  painting allowance 220
  payment 136

permit 138
site problems 139
title 137
warranty 139
window specs 230
Clay tile 188, 210, 213
Closes
  assumption 91
  either-or 91
  kitchen table 88
  price conscious 92
  story 91
  summary 92
  take it away 93
  team sales 89
  T.O.'s 88-89
Closing costs 64, 69, 135
Closing the sale 36-37, 44, 88-94
Code, building 94, 128-129, 131-132, 149, 179, 187, 193, 212, 222, 229
Collateral 62, 69
Collections 113, 132, 135, 138
Color
  fixtures 157
  samples 134, 155, 190, 203, 226
  stock 134
Co-makers 72
Commissions
  canvasser's 10, 12, 17
  salesmen's 118-119, 121
Compensating deposits 72, 83
Compensation, salesmen's 116-119, 121-122
Completion clauses 136
Completion form 108, 114
Completion, satisfaction and authorization form 108
Concrete
  apron 57
  contractors 16
  floor 57, 173, 200, 213
  forms 167
  slab 144, 209
  stoop 182-183
  subfloor 192
Concrete work order 166
Concrete work, selling 165-169
Consolidation of debts 69, 71
Contents claim 103
Contract clauses 132, 134-139, 157, 185, 199, 200, 209, 220, 230
Contract price 74, 134-135, 139, 143, 148, 157, 179
Contractor's notice 137
Contractor's verified statement 62, 64, 74, 104, 138
Contracts 51, 131-141
Conventional mortgage loans 63-69
Co-ops, financing 62, 63, 83
Copper
  gutters 149
  piping 214
Corridor kitchen 208
Co-signer 57, 137, 139
Crane plumbing 46
Credit applications 51-56, 65-66, 76-77
Credit sales 51-87
Credit union financing 62, 83
Cubic yards, estimating 168

Dealership, home improvement 51, 60, 93, 116, 167
Debris removal 180, 184, 192, 215
Deductible, insurance 101, 106
Default and collection clause 138
Demonstrations 41-42, 154, 234
Direct lenders 62-63
Direct payouts 64
Dome ceilings 162-164
Door
  canopies 152
  leads 177
  manufacturers 173, 236
  operator 196, 200
Doors
  atrium 230
  cellar 149, 173
  closet 91, 174, 175

entry 91, 170, 175
exterior 142, 170-173
French 171-173
garage 193, 196-197, 198-201
interior 142, 173-175
patio 172, 175, 182
screen 176
steel 175
storm 175-177
Dormer
  additions 147, 178-181
  apartments 178
  benefits 40
  checklist 181
  room 180
  shell 180
Downspouts 202-203
Drainage 152, 205, 214
Dropped ceiling 46, 164, 210-212
Drywall
  ceiling 163
  repair 210
  taper 163
Ducts 160, 179, 213

Easy payments 57, 60, 93
Eaves, boxed 29, 196-197
Either-or close 91, 191
Electric
  door opener 43, 90, 199
  lines 161, 231
  riser 149
  wall heater 160
Electrical
  finishing by owner 135
  fixtures 134
  permit 131
  requirements 160, 180, 184, 210, 212-213
  upgrade 163
Elevations 182-183
Eljer plumbing fixtures 158
Employee credit unions 62, 63
Employees 10-15, 116-127
Energy
  conservation 175-176
  efficiency 171, 215, 229
  savers 175, 184, 232, 234
  wasters 231
Energy Tax Credit 172, 173, 175-176, 231-234
Enthusiasm, need for 27-30
Entrances, remodeling 151-152, 170-171, 175
Equal Credit Opportunity Act 74, 82
Equity analysis chart 71
Escrow 74, 135
Estimate take-off form 109-112
Estimating 142, 190
Excavation 134, 173
Exhaust fan 43, 160, 207, 209
Exterior remodeling 151, 182-184
Extra charges 139, 144

Facade remodeling 182-184
Family room 18, 147-148, 162
Fans 160, 213-214
Farm Bureau loans 62-63
Farm co-ops 62
Fascia, covering 10, 12, 17, 43, 180, 183, 196, 203, 224, 226
Federal
  Housing Administration (FHA) 51
  Regulation Z 141
  Reserve 74
  safety regulations 230
Fence sketch sheet 187
Fences, selling 185-187
FHA loans 51-53, 57, 74, 76-77, 86
Fiberglass
  awnings, canopies & carports 151-155
  garage doors 196, 201
  mat 223

patio covers 152
screens 234
shingles 197, 222-223, 230
shower stalls & tubs 158
F.I.C.A. 119
Finance
  charge 60
  clauses 135
  companies 57, 83
Financial Publishing Company 69
Financing 51-88
Finish flooring 180, 188-189
Fire
  code 179, 198
  exit 148
  policy 136
  rating 175
  repairs 162-163
Fire insurance repairs 100-106
Fitting allowance 157
Fixtures
  allowance for 134
  bathroom 157-159
  color 157
Flintkote shingles 46
Floor
  area 229
  condition 200
  finishing 135
  replacement 191
  sanding 135
  space 174, 211
  surface 192
  underlayment 160-161
Flooring
  manufacturers 190, 236
  pitfalls 191
  selling 188-192
Flooring materials
  ceramic 159
  clay 188
  hardwood 189-190
  marble 159
  resilient 190
  softwood 189
  tile 159, 188, 190-192
  wood 189
Fluorescent fixtures 159-160, 162-164
Forced air heat systems 160
Formica 145, 157, 160, 211, 215, 230
Foundation 40, 47, 147
Front elevation 182-184
Fuel costs, saving 93, 151-152, 175
F.U.T.A. 119

Gable
  ends 194, 222
  roof 184, 194, 222, 224
  room addition 149, 178-181
Galley kitchen 206-207
Galvanized
  gutters 149, 204
  nails 202-203, 224
  piping 214
Game room 150
Garage
  door 37, 170, 196, 198-199
  floor 198
  layout 194
  light 196, 200
  sketch 194
  specifications sheet 194-195
Gas
  line 149, 210
  piping 207, 231
  wall furnace 179
Gates 187
Gerber plumbing supplies 46
GFCI switch 160
Glass
  block window 43, 160
  insert 176, 230
  panels 158
  size 230, 235
Glazing 176, 230, 233
Good Faith Estimate 74, 85
Governing laws clause 137
Gravity heat systems 160
Grid-lock suspended ceiling 212
Grilles 144, 160, 172-173, 229
Gross profit 145-146
Gutter sketch sheet 204

Gutters and downspouts, selling 184, 202-205

Hanging wallpaper 220
Hardboard siding 182, 184, 194, 196, 224, 226
Hardwood flooring 188-189, 191
Hauling 135, 142, 144, 163, 167, 200
Heat
  ducts 161, 213, 231
  loss 151-152, 164, 231-232
Heating
  bills 151
  problems 179
  sub 144, 179
  system 179
Heating and cooling 210, 213
Height charges 205
HIP application 51, 54-55
Hiring 10, 116-125
Home improvement dealer 116
Home improvement loans 51-87
Homeowners insurance 108, 136
Hooks 90-91, 101

I.C.B.O. 128
Icebreakers 33-34, 35
Important notice form 97, 100, 113
Incentive compensation 116
Independent adjusters 99
Inspector, building 94, 129, 131, 132
Installment contract 56, 136
Insulation 197, 225
Insulation factors 175
Insurance
  adjusters 19, 43-44, 95, 97-99, 101, 103
  brokers 95, 103
  claims 101, 136
  clauses 137
  leads 99-101
  policy requirements 95
  referrals 99-101
  repair work 95-115
  telephone directory 99
  terminology 97, 99
Insurance information form 106, 108
Interest rates 51, 57, 59-61, 69
IRS Form 5695 176, 231, 233

Jennaire ranges 208
Jones Legal Forms 136

Key locks 172, 176, 196, 201
KISS rule 148
Kitchen
  appliances 93
  cabinets 144, 207, 211-212
  ceiling 213
  design 206-208, 216
  doors 173, 207, 209, 216
  fixtures 213
  islands 208
  leads 206
  planning 206-209, 216
  sink 93, 213-214
Kitchen remodeling 206-217
Kitchen remodeling checklist 210, 212
Kitchen table close 31-32, 88
Kohler plumbing fixtures 158

L

L-shaped kitchen 207, 211, 216
Laundry rooms 174, 206, 214
Lavatory 157, 160
Lawyer, when to consult 63, 71, 116, 136
Lead form 12-13
Leads, obtaining 10-21, 43-44, 99-101, 125-126
Ledger form 119, 120
Liability insurance 119, 165, 203, 224
License fees 131
Licensed adjuster 97
Lien, waiver of 74, 103, 105
Light fixtures 92, 160, 162, 164, 179
Loan applications
  FHA 52-53, 76-77
  HIP 54-55
  mortgage 65-66
  retail instalment 56
  VA 76-77
Loans 51-88
Loss
  check or draft 103, 106
  schedule 95, 101
  settlement 103

M

Mailing lists 19, 99-101
Manual of Professional Remodeling 208
Manufacturers
  door 173, 236
  flooring 190, 236
  siding 236
Markup 143-146, 191, 220, 231
Masonite 159, 213, 226
Material
  cost 143, 192
  samples 155, 226
  shortages 137
Measuring
  awnings and canopies 152-154
  garage depth 198
  roofing 222, 224
  siding 227
  square feet 167
  storm windows 234
  wall tile 190
  windows 230
Mechanic's lien 137
Melamine 211
Method of compensation, salesmen 116-122
MGIC (Mortgage Guarantee Insurance Co.) 73-74
Minimum charges 192, 205
Miscellaneous clause 139
Monthly payment charts
  conventional 70
  FHA 86
Monthly payments, easy 25, 60, 69, 71, 177
Mortgage
  applications 64-66, 74, 76-77
  bankers 57, 63, 74
  brokers 127
  financing 63-74
  lender 64, 69, 71, 106, 108, 11
  payment analysis 72
Mortgage Guarantee Insurance Company (MGIC) 73-74

N

Name brands 46
National Housing Act 137
National Underwriter Co. 99
Newspaper advertising 21
No side agreements clause 138
Notice of cancellation 137
Notice to Borrowers 74, 83
Notification to mortgage holder 108, 113

O

Obstructions
  fence line 187
  flooring 191
  heating and cooling 213
  site problems 139
Occupancy form 74, 81
Open-end mortgages 63-64
Opening, storm window 235
Overhead expense 143-144, 146
Overhead doors 193, 196-197, 198-199
Owens Corning Fiberglass fixtures 158
Owner's labor 135

P

Paint Contractor's Manual 220
Painting
  allowance 220
  avoiding 135, 159, 218-220
  pricing 220
Paper hanging 218-220
Par system 118-119, 121
Patio covers 151-152
Payment clause 136
Payment procedure 103
Payouts, direct 64, 74
Payroll 116, 119
Permit
  book 129-130
  clause 138
  cost 129, 131
Permits 128-131, 138, 148, 187
Phone canvassing 15, 17-18
Pitches 33, 36-51, 101, 113-114, 126, 157, 176, 202
Pitfalls
  attic conversions 179
  bathroom remodeling 161
  concrete work 168-169
  flooring 192
  garage 200
  legal 131-132
  tile 192
Plan check fee 131, 138
Plaster
  ceilings 163-164, 212
  patching 184
  walls 191-192, 215
Pledges 73-74
Plumbing 157-159, 161, 192
Power of Attorney 106
Premiums 19, 90-91, 101
Prepayment privileges 60
Price
  book 129, 143-146, 150
  list, insurance 100-102
Pricing 142-146
Profit 118-119, 121-122, 143-146
Proof of loss 95, 136
Promissory note 57
Property improvement loan 51
Public adjusters 99
Public Liability Insurance 48, 50, 119, 137, 155, 219

Q

Qualifying the leads 8-9, 22-25, 147, 193

R

R-values 226
Rate book 60-61, 69
Rebate for prepayment 60
Recasting the loan 69
Referrals 18, 42-44, 124
Regulation Z 59, 141
Rescission (right to cancel) 57-58, 106-107

Residential Energy Tax Chart 172, 175-176, 231-232, 234
Retail installment contract 51
Retail Installment Sales Act 137
Retail price book 143-146
Right of redemption 72
Roofing, selling 221-224
Room addition pitfalls 149
Room additions, selling 147-150
Rule of 78 60
Rule of the three C's 62-64, 69

S

Sales
  calls 26-35
  commissions 118-119, 121-122
  force 116-127
  kit 15, 43, 126, 143, 160, 170, 234
  knowledge 36-50
  literature 15
  manual 43
  meetings 126-127
  pitches 33, 36-51, 101, 113-114, 126, 157, 176, 202
  team 89-90
  techniques 31-35
  tools 15, 27, 39, 43, 43, 126, 170, 234
Salesmen, hiring 116-127
Savings and loan associations 51, 57, 60, 62-64, 69, 72-74
Scaffolding insurance 48, 50, 119, 203, 220, 223
Schligal 233
Security locks 172
Selling tools 43, 101, 150, 172, 225
Setback requirements 147, 187, 193
Shell addition 148, 178-180
Shingles 40, 197, 222-224, 230
Shower
  area 156
  door 43
  fittings 157
  head 157, 160-161
  stall 158, 160
Siding
  aluminum 194, 196-197, 224-225
  hardboard 194, 196-197, 225-226
  plywood 226
  shingle 226
  steel 225
  stucco 225
  vinyl 225
  wood 226
Sink
  location 207, 209
  relocation 210
  selection 157
  shutoff valve 214
  trap 214
Site problem clause 139
Sketch and specification sheet, garage 194
Sketch sheets
  fence 186-187
  garage 194
  gutter and downspout 205
Skylights 229
Soffit, covering for 17, 43, 180, 183-184, 203
Soil stack 149, 158, 161, 179-192
Southern Building Code Congress 128
Spec Builder's Guide 208
Specifications 32, 72, 91, 135, 194, 23
Specifications sheet, garage 195
Square foot prices, painting 220
Staff adjusters 9
Stainless steel
  counter top 212
  facing 176
  sink 213, 215
Stairs 131, 149, 173, 179
State Unemployment Insurance 119
Steel
  closet vault doors 173
  entry doors 170
  garage doors 196
  insulated doors 173, 183

sectional doors 193, 199
security doors 174-175
  tubs 158
Stock colors 134, 202, 216
Stock mortgage application 64
Story close 91
Straight wall kitchen 207
Structural changes 210-211, 214
Stuart-Hooper Company 136
Stucco 40, 182, 196, 226
Stucco board siding 182, 184, 196, 226
Subcontract costs 143
Subfloor 178, 192, 210
Summary close 92-93
Supervision 119, 139, 143, 146, 219
Supplemental financing 64, 69, 83
Survey of pitfalls
  bathroom remodeling 161
  concrete work 168
  flooring and tile 192
  garage 200
  room additions 149
Suspended ceiling 160, 162, 164, 210, 212, 215
Sworn statement, contractor's 137

T

Take-off form 108-112
Tax Credit, Energy 172, 176-177, 231-233
Taxes 62, 71, 119, 129, 143
Team sales 89
Telephone canvassers 19
Testimonials 43-44, 92, 99
Third-party selling 42-43
Tile
  ceiling 164, 212
  counter tops 212
  floor 159, 188, 190-192
  roof 40
  wall 159, 190-192
Title clause 137
Title company 71-74
T-LOK vinyl siding 225
T.O.'s 88-89
Traffic patterns 29, 41, 216
Triangle work pattern 207, 216
Trust deed 51, 63

U

U.L. label 226
U-shaped kitchen 207, 211, 216
Underlayment 159, 161, 192, 210
Uniform Building Code 128
Uniform Commercial Code 137
United inch 234-235
Utility
  cabinet 210-212
  closets 174, 206
  doors 173
  grade lumber 46
  lines 169
  rooms 162
  services 137

V

VA loan 64, 71, 74-79
Ventilation
  bathroom 160
  closet 174
  kitchen 214-215
  roof 222
  storm doors 175
  windows 234-235
Verification of Deposit 74, 78
Verification of Employment 74, 79
Verification of Terms and Payment Experience 74, 84

Vinyl
  flooring 148, 159, 190, 213
  frames 232
  sheet goods 190
  siding 182, 203, 205, 225

W

Waivers of Lien 24, 30, 62, 64, 74, 103, 114, 167
Wall
  cabinets 37, 144, 145, 211
  cavity 156
  cover 209
  fan 210, 215
  finish 159-160
  outlets 160
  paneling 134
  repairs 210, 215
  studs 178, 193
  switch 161, 164, 210, 212
Wallpaper 157-159, 219
Warmup 34-35
Warranty 138, 139, 226
Warranty deed 71
Warren's Forms of Agreement 136
Water
  closet 135, 156, 158, 160
  damage 44, 188
  leak 163
  ledge 144, 193, 197
  line 149, 158
  pipe 230
Window
  glass 97, 230
  seat 230
  size 230
  trim 183, 184, 227
Windows
  awning 180, 228
  basement 228-229
  bay 184, 228, 230
  casement 91, 180, 183, 215, 228-230
  decorative 229
  double hung 160, 180, 183, 215, 228-231
  jalousie 197, 229
  picture 229
  skylights 229
  sliding 229
  storm 93, 232-235
Wiring 131-132, 160-161, 200, 207, 213
Wood
  beam 197
  canopy 184
  doors 175, 196, 199, 201
  fence 185-187
  flooring 189-192
  sash 231-232
  shakes 226
  siding 184, 226
  windows 215, 228, 230
Wood-Frame House Construction 222
Work order 168
Worker's Compensation Insurance 48, 50, 119, 137, 155, 165, 203, 220, 224
Wrought iron
  fence 185
  nail heads 189
  rails 183
  trellis 184
  trim 182

Y

Yellow pages 19, 44, 99-100, 165, 221

Z

Zoning 94, 127, 138, 147-148, 178-180, 187, 193

OTHER PRACTICAL REFERENCES

Painter's Handbook

Loaded with "how-to" information you'll use every day to get professional results on any job: The best way to prepare a surface for painting or repainting. Selecting and using the right materials and tools (including airless spray). Tips for repainting kitchens, bathrooms, cabinets, eaves and porches. How to match and blend colors. Why coatings fail and what to do about it. Thirty profitable specialties that could be your gravy train in the painting business. Every professional painter needs this practical handbook. **320 pages, 8½ x 11, $21.25**

Remodeler's Handbook

The complete manual of home improvement contracting: Planning the job, estimating costs, doing the work, running your company and making profits. Pages of sample forms, contracts, documents, clear illustrations and examples. Chapters on evaluating the work, rehabilitation, kitchens, bathrooms, adding living area, re-flooring, re-siding, re-roofing, replacing windows and doors, installing new wall and ceiling cover, repainting, upgrading insulation, combating moisture damage, estimating, selling your services, and bookkeeping for remodelers. **416 pages, 8½ x 11, $18.50**

Wood-Frame House Construction

From the layout of the outer walls, excavation and formwork, to finish carpentry, and painting, every step of construction is covered in detail with clear illustrations and explanations. Everything the builder needs to know about framing, roofing, siding, insulation and vapor barrier, interior finishing, floor coverings, and stairs. . . complete step by step "how to" information on what goes into building a frame house. **240 pages, 8½ x 11, $11.25. Revised edition**

Rough Carpentry

All rough carpentry is covered in detail: sills, girders, columns, joists, sheathing, ceiling, roof and wall framing, roof trusses, dormers, bay windows, furring and grounds, stairs and insulation. Many of the 24 chapters explain practical code approved methods for saving lumber and time without sacrificing quality. Chapters on columns, headers, rafters, joists and girders show how to use simple engineering principles to select the right lumber dimension for whatever species and grade you are using. **288 pages, 8½ x 11, $16.00**

Building Cost Manual

Square foot costs for residential, commercial, industrial, and farm buildings. In a few minutes you work up a reliable budget estimate based on the actual materials and design features, area, shape, wall height, number of floors and support requirements. Most important, you include all the important variables that can make any building unique from a cost standpoint. **240 pages, 8½ x 11, $14.00. Revised annually**

Building Layout

Shows how to use a transit to locate the building on the lot correctly, plan proper grades with minimum excavation, find utility lines and easements, establish correct elevations, lay out accurate foundations and set correct floor heights. Explains planning sewer connections, leveling a foundation out of level, using a story pole and batterboards, working on steep sites, and minimizing excavation costs. **240 pages, 5½ x 8½, $11.75**

National Construction Estimator

Current building costs in dollars and cents for residential, commercial and industrial construction. Prices for every commonly used building material, and the proper labor cost associated with installation of the material. Everything figured out to give you the "in place" cost in seconds. Many time-saving rules of thumb, waste and coverage factors and estimating tables are included. **528 pages, 8½ x 11, $18.50. Revised annually.**

Manual of Professional Remodeling

This is the practical manual of professional remodeling written by an experienced and successful remodeling contractor. Shows how to evaluate a job and avoid 30-minute jobs that take all day, what to fix and what to leave alone, and what to watch for in dealing with subcontractors. Includes chapters on calculating space requirements, repairing structural defects, remodeling kitchens, baths, walls and ceilings, doors and windows, floors, roofs, installing fireplaces and chimneys (including built-ins), skylights, and exterior siding. Includes blank forms, checklists, sample contracts, and proposals you can copy and use. **400 pages, 8½ x 11, $18.75**

Contractor's Guide to the Building Code

Explains in plain English exactly what the Uniform Building Code requires and shows how to design and construct residential and light commercial buildings that will pass inspection the first time. Suggests how to work with the inspector to minimize construction costs, what common building short cuts are likely to be cited, and where exceptions are granted. **312 pages, 5½ x 8½, $16.25**

Contractor's Year-Round Tax Guide

How to set up and run your construction business to minimize taxes: corporate tax strategy and how to use it to your advantage, and what you should be aware of in contracts with others. Covers tax shelters for builders, write-offs and investments that will reduce your taxes, accounting methods that are best for contractors, and what the I.R.S. allows and what it often questions. **192 pages, 8½ x 11, $16.50**

Residential Electrical Design

Explains what every builder needs to know about designing electrical systems for residential construction. Shows how to draw up an electrical plan from the blueprints, including the service entrance, grounding, lighting requirements for kitchen, bedroom and bath and how to lay them out. Explains how to plan electrical heating systems and what equipment you'll need, how to plan outdoor lighting, and much more. If you are a builder who ever has to plan an electrical system, you should have this book. **194 pages, 8½ x 11, $11.50**

Basic Plumbing with Illustrations

The journeyman's and apprentice's guide to installing plumbing, piping and fixtures in residential and light commercial buildings: how to select the right materials, lay out the job and do professional quality plumbing work. Explains the use of essential tools and materials, how to make repairs, maintain plumbing systems, install fixtures and add to existing systems. **320 pages, 8½ x 11, $17.50**

Spec Builder's Guide

Explains how to plan and build a home, control your construction costs, and then sell the house at a price that earns a decent return on the time and money you've invested. Includes professional tips to ensure success as a spec builder: how government statistics help you judge the housing market, cutting costs at every opportunity without sacrificing quality, and taking advantage of construction cycles. Every chapter includes checklists, diagrams, charts, figures, and estimating tables. **448 pages, 8½ x 11, $24.00**

Paint Contractor's Manual

How to start and run a profitable paint contracting company: getting set up and organized to handle volume work, avoiding the mistakes most painters make, getting top production from your crews and the most value from your advertising dollar. Shows how to estimate all prep and painting. Loaded with manhour estimates, sample forms, contracts, charts, tables and examples you can use. **224 pages, 8½ x 11, $19.25**

Stair Builders Handbook

If you know the floor to floor rise, this handbook will give you everything else: the number and dimension of treads and risers, the total run, the correct well hole opening, the angle of incline, the quantity of materials and settings for your framing square for over 3,500 code approved rise and run combinations—several for every 1/8 inch interval from a 3 foot to a 12 foot floor to floor rise. **416 pages, 8½ x 5½, $13.75**

Carpentry for Residential Construction

How to do professional quality carpentry work in homes and apartments. Illustrated instructions show you everything from setting batter boards to framing floors and walls, installing floor, wall and roof sheathing, and applying roofing. Covers finish carpentry, also: How to install each type of cornice, frieze, lookout, ledger, fascia and soffit; how to hang windows and doors; how to install siding, drywall and trim. Each job description includes the tools and materials needed, the estimated manhours required, and a step-by-step guide to each part of the task. **400 pages, 5½ x 8½, $19.75**

Carpentry in Commercial Construction

Covers forming, framing, exteriors, interior finish and cabinet installation in commercial buildings: designing and building concrete forms, selecting lumber dimensions, grades and species for the design load, what you should know when installing materials selected for their fire rating or sound transmission characteristics, and how to plan and organize the job to improve production. Loaded with illustrations, tables, charts and diagrams. **272 pages, 5½ x 8½, $19.00**

Roof Framing

Frame any type of roof in common use today, even if you've never framed a roof before. Shows how to use a pocket calculator to figure any common, hip, valley, and jack rafter length in seconds. Over 400 illustrations take you through every measurement and every cut on each type of roof: gable, hip, Dutch, Tudor, gambrel, shed, gazebo and more. **480 pages, 5½ x 8½, $22.00**

Video: Roof Framing 1

A complete step-by step training video on the basics of roof cutting by Marshall Gross, the author of the book **Roof Framing**. Shows and explains calculating rise, run, and pitch, and laying out and cutting common rafters. **90 minutes, VHS, $80.00**

Video: Roof Framing 2

A complete training video on the more advanced techniques of roof framing by Marshall Gross, the author of **Roof Framing**, shows and explains layout and framing an irregular roof, and making tie-ins to an existing roof. **90 minutes, VHS, $80.00**

Builder's Office Manual Revised

Explains how to create routine ways of doing all the things that must be done in every construction office — in the minimum time, at the lowest cost, and with the least supervision possible: Organizing the office space, establishing effective procedures and forms, setting priorities and goals, finding and keeping an effective staff, getting the most from your record-keeping system (whether manual or computerized). Loaded with practical tips, charts and sample forms for your use. **192 pages, 8½ x 11, $15.50**